User-Interface
Screen Design

User-Interface Screen Design

Wilbert O. Galitz

A Wiley–QED Publication

John Wiley & Sons, Inc.

New York • Chichester • Brisbane • Toronto • Singapore

Library of Congress Cataloging-in-Publication Data

Galitz, Wilbert O.
    User-interface screen design / Wilbert O. Galitz.
    Includes bibliographical references and index.
    ISBN 0-471-56156-8
    1. User interfaces (Computer systems) 2. Information display systems—
Formatting. I. Title.
    QA76.9.U83G35 1992
    004'.01'9—dc20   91-43963
                                                         CIP

Printed in the United States of America

10 9 8 7 6 5 4 3 2

Again, to Sharon, who so ably handles all the many other things that must be done with a business so that this book could be written.

Contents

Introduction

Today the most common communication bridge between a person and a computer system is a visual display terminal. The medium of this communication is a cathode ray tube upon which data and information are electronically inscribed. What information or data is placed on a display tube, how it is structured, and where it is located make up what is called screen design.

A well-designed screen can increase human processing speed, reduce human errors, and speed computer processing time. A poorly designed screen has the opposite effect: It will decrease human processing speed, encourage mistakes, and complicate machine operations. A well-designed screen, then, will increase human productivity; a poorly designed screen will reduce it.

Screen format design—or screen design as it is commonly called—is the topic of this handbook. In some quarters, screen design is perceived as encompassing the programming steps necessary to provide a finished product to a user. It should be recognized that a discussion of this design activity is beyond the scope of this book. This document will only be concerned with how a screen looks and behaves for a user. It is directed toward developing a screen product that is easily used and visually clear. Simple programming concepts introduced are only those necessary to accomplish this objective.

AN HISTORICAL REVIEW

During its first 20 years, the data processing industry paid little attention to the human/computer interface in system design. The focus instead was on efficient use of central processing units and storage media. The high cost of technology and the fact that computers were used by relatively few specialists sublimated the interface between humans and computers. Systems were, in effect, designed from the "inside out."

As computing power increased and computing costs decreased, computers touched more work lives. Computer usage by several users became usage by several hundred users, and, thus, personnel costs became a dominant factor in total systems costs. In the early 1980s the ratio of office workers to display terminals was on the order of 10 to 1. That is, for every 10 white-collar workers there was only one display terminal available in offices across the country. With the increasing popularity of the personal computer, this ratio has dropped dramatically, now being close to 2:1.

Economics thus forced a refocusing of system design emphasis onto the user. It became more widely recognized that the ease and effectiveness of human interaction with computers depended on how well the interface reflects people's needs. Thus, the system design emphasis shifted to "outside in." Effective screen design from a user's perspective assumed increasing importance.

Historically, screen design responsibility has fallen on programmers and systems analysts—those charged with designing and building computer systems. The design process, unfortunately, has developed with few guidelines. Technical considerations have received the most attention, and the human factors involved have not been well understood or have been neglected entirely. As a result, screen design has tended to be unsystematic and inconsistent, and has failed to adequately reflect human perceptual and processing capabilities. As a result, many screens in today's office systems are difficult to use and lack visual clarity.

At best, a poorly designed screen can exact a toll in human productivity, as illustrated in Figure 1.1.

Based on an actual system requiring processing of 4.8 million screens per year, an analysis established that if poor clarity forced screen users to spend 1 extra second per screen, almost 1 additional person-year would be required to process all screens. A 20-second degradation in screen processing time would cost an additional 14 person-years.

At its worst, a poorly designed screen can create an impression that understanding it will require more time than one can afford to commit, or that it is too complex to understand at all. Those who have the luxury of doing so (managers and professionals) may refuse to use it, and the objectives of the system for which it was designed will never be achieved.

The benefits of a well-designed screen are coming under much closer experimental scrutiny. Dunsmore (1982) attempted to improve screen clarity and readability by making screens less crowded. Separate items, which had

Figure 1.1   Impact of inefficient screen design on processing time.

Additional Seconds Required per Screen in Seconds	Additional Person-Years Required to Process 4.8 Million Screens per Year
1	.7
5	3.6
10	7.1
20	14.2

been combined on the same display line to conserve space, were placed on separate lines instead. The result: Screen users were about 20 percent more productive with the less-crowded version. Keister and Gallaway (1983) reformatted a series of screens following many of the same concepts to be described in this handbook. The result: Screen users of the modified screens completed transactions in 25 percent less time and with 25 percent fewer errors than those who used the original screens.

Tullis (1981) has reported how reformatting inquiry screens following good design principles reduced decision-making time by about 40 percent, resulting in a savings of 79 person-years in the affected system. In a second study comparing 500 screens (Tullis, 1983), it was found that the time to extract information from displays of airline or lodging information was 128 percent faster for the best format than for the worst. Other recent studies have also shown that the proper formatting of information on screens does have a significant positive effect on performance (Mann and Schnetzler, 1986; Pulat and Nwanko, 1987).

Screen design may also be contributing to the visual fatigue reported by some system users. Dainoff et al., (1981) have estimated that as many as 45 percent of all users may be victims of a CRT-induced visual fatigue. Matthews et al., (1989) report that in a study requiring extended CRT viewing, 60 percent of subjects reported eye-focusing problems and 40 percent reported pain in the eye area.

In relation to screen design, studies of people's eye movements in using screens have uncovered instances where visual movements between screen and source documents exceed several thousand for one work day. At this number of movements, a significant difference in the brightness level between display screen and source document can fatigue the muscle of the eye. This has led to attempts to brighten the display screen or lower the illumination to try to achieve the proper balance. But what about the design of the screen? Several thousand eye movements a day may reflect poor screen design rather than an unsatisfactory environment or terminal. The symptoms of a problem rather than the cause are perhaps being addressed in some cases.

What can be done, then, to improve the screen design process? Plenty. While screen design is not yet a precise science, the body of knowledge derived from experimental studies is growing. And a wealth of information derived from printed material research (e.g., books and newspapers) and the graphics arts discipline is available to provide guidance until more research questions are answered. This material simply awaits conscientious application to the screen design process.

HANDBOOK OBJECTIVES

The purpose of this handbook is to assist a designer in developing an effective screen interface between a program and its users. It is intended as a ready reference source for all screen design. Its specific objectives are to enable the reader to:

- describe the considerations that must be applied to the screen design process,
- describe a series of design rules that can be applied to the several categories of screens, and
- perform the design steps necessary to develop and lay out effective screens.

HANDBOOK SCOPE

The materials in this handbook, although far from exhaustive, represent an attempt to identify, collect, and/or deduce, and ultimately document a useful set of guidelines for screen design. This handbook is the most complete and thorough reference source available to the screen designer today. The guidelines have been culled from a variety of sources:

- known human factors and psychological principles,
- analysis of the results of experimental studies in the behavioral disciplines,
- available guideline documents for people/machine interfaces,
- informal studies conducted by the author, and
- the author's experience.

Although the validity of some guidelines cannot be absolutely guaranteed, as a whole they will provide a solid foundation for most screen design activities, at least until experimental evidence is available to prove, disprove, or modify them.

These guidelines will not answer every design problem that may be encountered. Application-specific requirements and guideline incompatibilities will never free the designer from performing design tradeoffs. It is hoped, however, that these guidelines will promote "wiser" decisions than have been possible in the past.

Types of Screens

Screens can be developed for a wide variety of purposes and in a wide variety of styles. Unfortunately, no consistent naming conventions exist in current documentation, various names being affixed to screens whose purpose seems similar. For this handbook, screen types will be catalogued as described below. This categorization is based on differences in screen functions that cause fundamental differences in screen structure and layout.

Data entry screens. Data entry screens are designed to collect information quickly and accurately. Commonly called data collection screens, they usually contain a number of captioned fields into which data is keyed. Data entry screens are sometimes referred to as fixed form or form fill-in screens.

All data entry screens are not alike. Whether or not data keying is being performed from a specially designed (or dedicated) source document to be used with the screen will cause fundamental differences in screen design.

- *With a Dedicated Source Document*—When keying is performed from a dedicated source document, the document will be the visual focus of the user's attention. Keying aids will be built into the document itself, and the design of the screen will be interwoven with the design of the document.
- *Without a Dedicated Source Document*—When there is no dedicated document from which keying is performed, the primary visual focus of the user will be the screen itself. Screen clarity as an end in itself will assume a much more important role in the design process.

Both kinds of data entry screens are discussed in this handbook.

Inquiry screens. Inquiry screens are used for displaying the contents of computer files. Data on these screens does not change, and they are designed for ease of information location and visual clarity.

Multipurpose screens. Multipurpose screens are combination screens achieving more than one objective. They may be used to enter data into the system, review what is there, and possibly change what is displayed. As such, they combine the characteristics of the data entry and inquiry screens.

Question and answer screens. A question and answer screen consists of alternating communications between the computer and the user. Each communication is short and contains one idea at a time. Communications may contain captions or be free-form (without captions).

Menu screens. The primary purpose of a menu screen is to permit a user to select one or more alternatives from a variety of alternatives. As such, it combines the characteristics of both data collection and inquiry screens.

These screens may be designed for use on a monochromatic (one-color) alphanumeric terminal, a color alphanumeric terminal, or a graphics terminal. Three separate chapters will be devoted to color and graphics and the unique considerations they present.

OVERVIEW

Chapter 2 sets the stage for the screen design guidelines by looking at the user, discussing why people have trouble with computer systems and their typical responses to poor design. It explains the differences between discretionary and nondiscretionary system use and then sets forth four commandments for designing for users. The chapter concludes with a review of critical human considerations in screen design. Chapter 3 addresses the dialogue between people and computers. It defines the concept of ease of use and the kinds of dialogues available, and presents directions and guidelines for achieving an effective people/computer interface. Chapter 4 focuses on actual screen design. It discusses a test for good design, visually pleasing composition, objective measures of a well-designed screen, the structure of words and messages, and how to use the various monochromatic display features.

Following Chapter 4 emphasis shifts to specific types of screens. Chapter 5 treats data collection or data entry screens; Chapter 6, inquiry screens; and Chapter 7, multipurpose screens. Chapters 8 and 9 deal with question and answer screens and menu screens respectively.

As graphic screens are becoming so widespread, graphical interfaces, including the concepts of direct manipulation and windows, are described in Chapter 10. Chapter 11 surveys the use of icons on screens, and Chapter 12 addresses statistical graphics, including such topics as bar charts and pie charts. Guidelines for the use of color in screen design are presented in Chapter 13.

Also, since effective data entry screen design occasionally involves development of source documents, Chapter 14 presents guidelines for good source document design.

The concluding Chapter 15 provides an illustrated review of the design steps necessary to define, design, and lay out a typical data entry screen.

HOW TO USE THIS HANDBOOK

This handbook provides some general design considerations and guidelines (Chapters 2, 3, 4), guidelines applicable to specific kinds of screens (Chapters 5 through 9), unique situation design guidelines (Chapters 10, 11, 12, 13, 14), and a design steps review (Chapter 15). After an initial reading, the handbook user need only be concerned with the chapters relevant to the kind of screen being designed. Table 1.1 serves as an aid in determining chapter relevancy.

Topic Organization and Illustrations

Each handbook chapter contains important points, concepts, or guidelines organized by topic and presented in a highlighted checklist format. Following each checklist is a narrative that provides further detail on much of the highlighted material. The reader who finds the checklists of satisfactory clarity and scope need not be concerned with the narrative. The reader desiring more information on any topic will find the narrative valuable.

The guidelines also contain many illustrations and examples. These illustrations of screen display will be designated as follows:

```
NUMBER:x_____xxxTIME:x_____

MODEL          YEAR
_____xxx____
_____      ____
_____      ____
```

Table 1.1   Chapter relevancy for various types of screens.

If you are going to design . . .	See chapter . . .
A data entry screen and related source document	2, 3, 4, 5-1, 5-2, 14
A data entry screen to be used without a related source document	2, 3, 4, 5-1, 5-3
An inquiry screen	2, 3, 4, 6
A question and answer screen	2, 3, 4, 8
A menu screen	2, 3, 4, 9
A multipurpose screen	7, plus chapters relevant to the particular kind of screen
A screen using graphics	10, plus chapters relevant to the particular type of screen
A screen using icons	10, 11, plus chapters relevant to the particular type of screen
A screen using statistical graphics	12
A screen using color	13 plus chapters relevant to the particular type of screen

For clarity of interpretation, spaces in a screen example important to a particular guideline are designated by the lower-case letter x.

A FINAL WORD

While this handbook contains much to aid the screen format designer, there may be shortcomings in its organization, content, or clarity. Readers having comments or suggestions concerning screen design, or the design process, are urged to communicate them to the author so they may be incorporated into subsequent editions. It is only by working together that we can provide an efficient and effective product.

The System User

2

The journey into the world of screen design must begin with a discussion of the system user, the most important part of any computer system, whose needs the systems are built to serve. We will start by looking at why people have had trouble with computer systems and the past results of poor design. Then we will explore the nature of the user, including such characteristics as nondiscretionary vs. discretionary use and varying levels of expertise. Finally, we will look at several human considerations that are critical to the screen design guidelines.

WHY PEOPLE HAVE TROUBLE WITH COMPUTER SYSTEMS

Although system design and its behavioral implications have come under intense scrutiny in the past decade, as we have seen, this has not always been the case. Historically, the design of computer systems has been the responsibility of programmers, systems analysts, and system designers, many of whom possess extensive technical knowledge but little behavioral training. Design decisions have thus rested mostly upon the designers' intuition and wealth of specialized knowledge, and, consequently, poorly designed interfaces often go unrecognized.

The intuition of designers or of anyone else, no matter how good or bad they may be at what they do, is error-prone. It is too shallow a foundation on which to base design decisions. Specialized knowledge lulls one into a false sense of security. It enables one to interpret and deal with complex or ambiguous situations on the basis of context cues not visible to users, as well as knowledge of the computer system they do not possess. The result is a perfectly usable system to its designers but one the office worker is unable or unwilling to face up to and master.

9

What makes a system complex in the eyes of its user? Listed below are five contributing factors.

Use of jargon.   Systems often talk in a strange language. Words alien to the office environment or used in different contexts, such as filespec, abend, segment, and boot proliferate. Learning to use a system requires learning a new language.

Non-obvious design.   Complex or novel design elements are not obvious or intuitive, but they must nevertheless be mastered. Operations may have prerequisite conditions that must be satisfied before they can be accomplished, or outcomes may not always be immediate, obvious, or visible. The overall framework of the system may be invisible, with the effect that results cannot always be related to the actions that accomplish them.

Fine distinctions.   Different actions may accomplish the same thing, depending upon when they are performed, or different things may result from the same action. Often these distinctions are minute and difficult to keep track of. Critical distinctions are not made at the appropriate time, or distinctions having no real consequence are made instead, as illustrated by the user who insisted that problems were caused by pressing the ENTER key "in the wrong way" (Carroll, 1984).

Disparity in problem-solving strategies.   People learn best by doing. They have trouble following directions and do not always read instructions before taking an action. Human problem solving can best be characterized as "error-correcting" or "trial-and-error," whereby a tentative solution is formulated based upon the available evidence and then tried. This tentative solution often has a low chance of success, but the results are used to modify one's next attempt and so increase the chances of success. Most computers, however, enforce an "error-preventing" strategy, which assumes that a person will not take an action until a high degree of confidence exists in its success. The result is that people often head down wrong paths or get entangled in situations difficult if not impossible to get out of (Reed, 1982).

Design inconsistency.   The same action may have different names: for example, "save" and "keep," "write" and "list." Or the same result may be described differently: for example, "not legal" and "not valid." The result is that system learning becomes an exercise in rote memorization. Meaningful or conceptual learning becomes very difficult.

RESPONSES TO POOR DESIGN

Unfortunately, people remember the one thing that went wrong, not the many that go right, so problems achieve an abnormal level of importance. Errors are a symptom of problems. The magnitude of errors in a computer-based system has been found to be as high as 46 percent for commands, tasks, or transactions (Barber, 1979; Card et al., 1980; and Ledgard et al., 1980).

Errors, and other problems that befuddle, lead to a variety of psychological to physical user responses. Some psychological responses are listed below (Foley and Wallace, 1974).

Confusion. Detail overwhelms the perceived structure. Meaningful patterns are difficult to ascertain, and the conceptual model or underlying framework cannot be established.

Panic. Panic may be introduced by unexpectedly long delays during times of severe or unusual pressure. The chief causes are unavailable systems and long response times.

Boredom. Boredom results from improper computer pacing (slow response times) and overly simplistic jobs.

Frustration. An inability to easily convey one's intentions to the computer causes frustration, which is heightened if an unexpected response cannot be undone or if what really took place cannot be determined. Inflexible and unforgiving systems are a major source of frustration.

These psychological responses diminish user effectiveness because they are severe blocks to concentration. Thoughts irrelevant to the task at hand are forced to attention and necessary concentration is impossible. The result, in addition to higher error rates, is poor performance, anxiety, and job dissatisfaction. Further, these psychological responses frequently lead to, or are accompanied by, the following physical responses (Eason, 1979; Stewart, 1976).

Abandonment of the system. The system is rejected and other information sources are relied upon. These sources must be available, and the user must have the discretion to perform the rejection. This is a common reaction of managerial and professional personnel. One study (Hiltz, 1984) found the system abandonment rate to be 40 percent.

Incomplete use of the system. Only a portion of the system's capabilities are used, usually those operations that are easiest to perform or that provide the most benefits. Historically, this has been the most common reaction to most systems.

Indirect use of the system. An intermediary is placed between the would-be user and the computer. Again, since this requires high status and discretion, it is another typical response of managers.

Modification of the task. The task is changed to match the capabilities of the system. This is a prevalent reaction when the tools are rigid and the problem is unstructured, as in scientific problem solving.

Compensatory activity.   Additional actions are performed to compensate for system inadequacies. A common example is the manual reformatting of information to match the structure required by the computer. This is a reaction common to workers whose discretion is limited, such as clerical personnel.

Misuse of the system.   The rules are bent to shortcut operational difficulties. This requires significant knowledge of the system and may affect system integrity.

Direct programming.   The system is reprogrammed by its user to meet specific needs. This is a typical response of the sophisticated worker.

THE NATURE OF THE USER

While we would like to think the system user sits idly at his desk anxiously awaiting the arrival of the computer system and the salvation it will afford, the truth is mostly the opposite. The user in today's office is usually overworked, fatigued, and continually interrupted. Documentation tends not to be read and problems are not well understood, and little is known about what information is available to meet one's needs. Moreover, the user's skills have been greatly overestimated by the system designer, who is often isolated psychologically and physically from the user's situation. Unlike the user, the designer is capable of resolving most system problems and ambiguities through application of experience and background and technical knowledge. Yet, often, the designer cannot really believe that anyone is incapable of using the system created.

The user, while being subjected to the everyday pressures of the office, is probably technologically unsophisticated, computer illiterate, and possibly even antagonistic. He wants to spend time using a system, not learning to use it. His objective is simply to get some work done.

In reality, there is not just one kind of system user, but many. From a design perspective, what distinguishes users are discretionary capability and level of expertise.

Nondiscretionary Versus Discretionary Use

Nondiscretionary use.   Users of the earliest computer systems were nondiscretionary. That is, they required the computer to perform a task that, for all practical purposes, could be performed no other way. Characteristics of nondiscretionary use can be summarized as follows:

- the computer is used as part of employment;
- time and effort in learning to use the computer are willingly invested;
- high motivation is often used to overcome low usability characteristics;
- the user may possess a technical background; and
- the job may consist of a single task or function.

The nondiscretionary user must learn to live comfortably with a computer, for there is really no other choice. Examples of nondiscretionary use today include a flight reservations clerk booking seats, an insurance company employee entering data into the computer so a policy can be issued, and a programmer writing and debugging a program. The toll exacted by a poorly designed system in nondiscretionary use is measured primarily by productivity—for example, speed and errors—and poor customer satisfaction with the product of the system.

Discretionary use. In recent years, as computers have become more common in the office, the discretionary user has become exposed to the benefits, and costs, of technology. He is much more self-directed than the nondiscretionary user—not being told how to work but being evaluated on the results of his efforts. For him, it is not means but the results that are most important. In short, this user has never been told how to work in the past and refuses to be told so now. This newer kind of user is the office executive, manager, or other professional, whose computer use is completely discretionary. Common characteristics of the discretionary user are as follows:

- utilization of the system is not necessary;
- job can be performed without the system;
- will not invest extra effort to use the system;
- technical details are of no interest to user;
- does not show high motivation to use the system;
- is easily disenchanted;
- voluntary use must be encouraged;
- is a multifunction knowledge worker;
- is from a heterogeneous culture;
- did not expect to use system;
- career path did not prepare him or her for system use.

Quite simply, this discretionary user often judges a system on the basis of expected effort versus results to be gained. If the benefits are seen to exceed the effort, the system will be used. If the effort is expected to exceed the benefits, it will not be used. Just the perception of a great effort to achieve minimal results is often enough to completely discourage system use, leading to system rejection, a common discretionary reaction.

Today, discretionary users also include the general population who are increasingly being asked to interact with a computer in their everyday lives. Examples of this kind of interaction include library information systems and bank automated teller machines (ATMs). This kind of user, or potential user, exhibits certain characteristics that vary. Citibank (1989) in studying users of ATMs identified five categories. Each group was about equal in size, encompassing about 20 percent of the general population. The groups, and their characteristics, are the following:

- People who understand technology and like it. They will use it under any and all circumstances.
- People who understand technology and like it. But they will only use it if the benefits are clear.
- People who understand technology but do not like it. They will only use it if the benefits are overwhelming.
- People who do not understand anything technical. They might use it if it is very easy.
- People who will never use technology of any kind.

Again, clear and obvious benefits and ease of use dominate these usage categories.

Novice Versus Expert Use

At one time or another, various schemes have been proposed to classify the different and sometimes changing characteristics of people as they become more experienced using a system. Words to describe the new, relatively new, or infrequent user have included *naive, casual, inexperienced,* or *novice.* At the other end of the experience continuum lie terms such as *experienced, full-time,* or *expert.* The words themselves are less important than the behavioral characteristics they imply. Experience to date is uncovering some basic differences in feelings of ease of use based upon proficiency level. What is easy for the new user is not perceived as easy for the "old hand," and vice versa.

For consistency in our discussion, the term "novice" will be used for the new user; the term "expert," for the most proficient.

Novice users have been found to

- depend upon system features that assist recognition memory: menus, prompting information, and instructional and help screens;
- need restricted vocabularies, simple tasks, small numbers of possibilities, and very informative feedback; and
- view practice as an aid to moving up to expert status.

Whereas, experts

- rely upon free recall;
- expect rapid performance;
- need less informative feedback; and
- seek efficiency by bypassing novice memory aids, reducing keystrokes, chunking and summarizing information, and introducing new vocabularies.

In actuality, the user population of most systems is spread out along the continuum anchored by these two extremes. And, equally important, the behavior of any one user at different times may be closer to one extreme or the other.

A person may be very proficient—an expert—in one aspect of a system and ignorant—a novice—in other aspects at the same time (Draper, 1984).

Exactly how experts and novices actually differ from one another in terms of knowledge, problem-solving behavior, and other human characteristics has been the subject of some research in recent years. To summarize some of the findings (Mayer, 1986; Ortega, 1989):

Experts possess the following traits:

- They possess an integrated conceptual model of a system.
- They possess knowledge that is ordered more abstractly and more procedurally.
- They organize information more meaningfully, orient it toward their task.
- They structure information into more categories.
- They are better at making inferences and relating new knowledge to their objectives and goals.
- They pay less attention to low-level details.
- They pay less attention to surface features of a system.

Novices exhibit these characteristics:

- They possess a fragmented conceptual model of a system.
- They organize information less meaningfully, orient it toward surface features of the system.
- They structure information into fewer categories.
- They have difficulty in generating inferences and relating new knowledge to their objectives and goals.
- They pay more attention to low-level details.
- They pay more attention to surface features of the system.

A well-designed system, therefore, must support at the same time novice and expert behavior, as well as all levels of behavior in between.

DESIGNING FOR USERS—THE FOUR COMMANDMENTS

Designing a computer system is never easy. The development path is littered with obstacles and traps, many of them human in nature. Gould (1988) has made these general observations about system design:

- Nobody can get it right the first time.
- Development is full of surprises.
- Developing user-oriented systems requires living in a sea of changes.
- Making contracts to ignore them does not eliminate the need for change.
- Designers need good tools.
- You can have behavioral design targets, just as you have other capacity and performance targets for other parts of the system.

- Even if you have made the best system possible, users—both novices and experienced—will make mistakes using it.

The process can be simplified, however, if four basic commandments are followed by the designer.

I. Understand the users and their tasks.   This is a difficult and undervalued goal but extremely important because of the gap in skills and attitudes between system users and designers. The following profiles are necessary:

- gender
- age
- education
- training
- ethnic background
- cultural heritage
- motivation
- personality
- physical abilities

The job or task must also be understood prior to design. Gould (1988) describes the following methods to gain an understanding of users and their tasks:

- Visit customer locations, particularly if they are unfamiliar to you, to gain an understanding of the work environment.
- Talk with users about their problems, difficulties, wishes, and what works well now. Establish direct contact, avoid relying upon intermediaries.
- Observe users working to see the tasks, difficulties, and problems.
- Videotape users working to illustrate and study problems and difficulties.
- Learn about the work organization where the system will be installed.
- Have users think aloud as they work to uncover details that may not otherwise be solicited.
- Try the job yourself. It may expose difficulties that are not known, or expressed, by users.
- Prepare surveys and questionnaires to obtain a larger sample of user opinions.
- Establish testable behavioral target goals to give management a measure for what progress has been made and what is still required.

It is always helpful to recognize that users are people whose outlook is probably different from your own.

II. Involve the user in design.   Involving the user in design from the beginning provides a direct source to the extensive knowledge she possesses. It also allows the designer to confront the user's resistance to change. People dislike change for a variety of reasons, among them fear of the unknown and lack of identification. Involvement in design removes the unknown and gives the user a stake in the system, or an identification with it. One caution, however: User involvement in design should be based on job or task knowledge, not status or position.

III. Test the system on actual users.   Something that is still not well understood is the human mind. No mathematical formula exists to describe it. While the design guidelines that follow go a long way toward making systems and screens easier to comprehend, factors like ease of learning, the most useful system features, and all possible problems cannot be predicted. So pilot, prototype, and acceptance testing with actual users is a necessity and must be included as part of the design process itself. If it is not built into the design process, the testing must occur in the user's office, often leaving a negative first impression in the user's mind. First impressions harden quickly, causing attitudes that may be difficult to change. The testing process should record any difficulties, errors, or hesitations, and users should be interviewed to uncover what was difficult, what problems existed, what was not understood, and what could have been done differently.

IV. Refine as necessary.   Since testing is an iterative process, system refinement will be ongoing as testing proceeds. A good benchmark for success is the point at which 95 percent of the typical users are performing the tasks without difficulty and without consulting manuals, help facilities, or other users.

HUMAN CONSIDERATIONS IN DESIGN

A human being is a complex organism with a variety of attributes that have an important influence on screen design. Of particular importance are perception, memory, visual acuity, learning, skill, and individual differences.

Perception

Perception is our awareness and understanding of the elements of our environment through physical sensation of our various senses. It is influenced, in part, by achieved experience: We classify stimuli based upon models stored in our memories and in this way achieve understanding. Comparing the accumulated knowledge of the child with that of an adult in interpreting the world is a vivid example of the role of experience in perception. Perception is also influenced by expectancies. Proofreading errors are a perceptual expectancy error; we see not how a word is spelled but how we expect to see it spelled. Context, environment, and surroundings also influence individual perception. For example, two drawn lines of the same length may look the same length or a different length depending upon the angle of adjacent lines or what other people have said about the size of the lines.

The human sensing mechanisms are bombarded by many stimuli, some of which are important and some of which are not. Important stimuli are called *signals*; those that are not important are called *noise*. Signals are more quickly comprehended if they are easily distinguishable from noise in the sensory environment. Noise interferes with the perception of signals to the extent that they are similar to one another. Noise can even mask a critical signal. For example, imagine a hidden word puzzle where meaningful words are buried in a large block matrix of alphabetic characters. The signals, alphabetic characters constituting meaningful words, are masked by the matrix of meaningless letters.

Stimuli may also assume the quality of signals in one situation and that of noise in another. Just as things may be important in one context and unimportant in another. Imagine, for example, walking on a downtown sidewalk in a large city and hearing a train whistle in the distance. Then imagine walking down a train track and hearing the same whistle in the distance. On the sidewalk the train whistle may not even be perceived, but walking down the train track, it will most certainly be heard loud and clear.

Other perceptual characteristics include the following.

Proximity.   The eye and mind see objects as belonging together if they are near each other in space.

Similarity.   The eye and mind see objects as belonging together if they share a common visual property, such as color, size, shape, brightness, or orientation.

Matching patterns.   We respond similarly to the same shape in different sizes. The letters of the alphabet, for example, possess the same meaning, regardless of physical size.

Closure.   Perception is synthetic; it establishes meaningful wholes. If something does not quite close itself, such as a circle, square, triangle, or word, we see it closed anyway.

Balance.   We desire stabilization or equilibrium in our viewing environment. Vertical, horizontal, and right angles are the most visually satisfying and easiest to look at.

The human perceptual mechanism has significant implications in the screen design process.

Memory

Memory is not one of the most developed of human attributes. Short-term memory is highly susceptible to the interference of such distracting tasks as thinking, reciting, or listening, which are constantly erasing and overwriting it. Remembering a telephone number long enough to complete the dialing operation taxes the memory of many people. The short-term memory limit is generally viewed as 7 ± 2 "chunks" of information (Miller, 1956), and knowledge and experience govern the size and complexity of chunks that can be recalled. To illustrate, most native English-speaking people would find recalling seven English words much easier than recalling seven Russian words. Short-term memory is thought to last 15 to 30 seconds. Unlike short-term memory, with its distinct limitations, long-term memory is thought to be unlimited. An important memory consideration, with significant implications for screen design, is the difference in ability to recognize or recall words. The human active vocabulary (words that can be recalled) typically ranges between 2,000 and 3,000 words. Passive vocabulary (words that can be recognized) typically numbers about 100,000. Our powers of recognition are much greater than our powers of recall.

Visual Acuity

The capacity of the eye to resolve details is called visual acuity. It is the phenomenon that results in an object becoming more distinct as we turn our eyes toward it and rapidly loses distinctness as we turn our eyes away—that is, as the visual angle from the point of fixation increases. It has been shown that relative visual acuity is approximately halved at a distance of 2.5 degrees from the point of eye fixation (e.g., Bouma, 1970). Therefore, a 5-degree diameter circle centered around an eye "fixation" character on a display has been recommended as the area "near" that character (Tullis, 1983) or the maximum length for a displayed word (Danchak, 1976).

If one assumes that the average viewing distance of a display screen is 19 inches (475 mm), the size of the area on the screen of optimum visual acuity is 1.67 inches (41.8 mm). Assuming "average" character sizes and character and line spacings, the number of characters on a screen falling within this visual acuity circle is 88, with 15 characters being contained on the widest line, and 7 rows being consumed, as illustrated below.

```
      3213123
    54321212345
   6543211123456
  765432101234567
   6543211123456
    54321212345
      3213123
```

The eye's sensitivity increases for those characters closest to the fixation point (the "0") and decreases for those characters at the extreme edges of the circle (A 50/50 chance exists for getting these characters correctly identified). This may be presumed to be a visual "chunk" of a screen.

Learning

The human ability to learn is important—it clearly differentiates people from machines. A design developed to minimize human learning time can accelerate human performance. Given enough time, of course, people can improve their performance in almost any task. Most people can be taught to walk a tightrope, but a designer should not incorporate a tightrope into his design if a walkway is feasible.

Evidence derived from studies of computer system learning parallels that found in studies of learning in other areas. Users prefer to be active (Carroll, 1984), to explore (Robert, 1986) and to use a trial-and-error approach (Hiltz and Kerr, 1986). There is also evidence that users are very sensitive to even minor changes in the user interface, and that such changes may lead to problems in transferring from one system to another (Karat, 1986). Moreover, just the "perception" of having to learn huge amounts of information is enough to keep some people from using a system (Nielson et al., 1986).

Learning can be enhanced if it

- allows skills acquired in one situation to be used in another somewhat like it (design consistency accomplishes this),
- provides complete and prompt feedback, and
- is phased, that is, it requires a person to know only the information needed at that stage of the learning process.

Skill

The goal of human performance is to perform skillfully. To do so requires linking inputs and outputs into a sequence of action. The essence of skill is performance of actions in the correct time sequence with adequate precision. It is characterized by consistency and economy of effort. Economy of effort is achieved by establishing a work pace that represents optimum efficiency. It is accomplished by increasing mastery of the system through such things as progressive learning of shortcuts, increased speed, and easier access to information or data.

Skills are hierarchical in nature, and many basic skills may be integrated to form increasingly complex ones. Lower-order skills tend to become routine and may drop out of consciousness. Screen design must permit development of more skillful performance.

Individual Differences

A complicating but very advantageous human characteristic is that we all differ—in looks, feelings, motor abilities, intellectual abilities, learning abilities and speeds, and so on. In a keyboard data entry task, for example, the best operators will probably be twice as fast as the poorest and make 10 times fewer errors.

Individual differences complicate design because the design must permit people with widely varying characteristics to satisfactorily and comfortably learn the task or job. In the past this has usually resulted in bringing designs down to the level of lowest abilities or selecting people with the minimum skills necessary to perform a job. But office technology now offers the possibility of tailoring jobs to the specific needs of people with varying and changing learning or skill levels. Screen design must permit this to occur.

System Considerations 3

A computer, the most powerful tool in the array of office equipment, must be an extension of the worker. This means the system and its software must reflect a person's capabilities and respond to his or her specific needs. It should be useful, accomplishing some business objective faster and more efficiently than did the previously used method or tool. It must also be easy to learn, for people want to do, not learn to do. Finally, the system must be easy and fun to use, evoking a sense of pleasure and accomplishment, not tedium and frustration.

The system interface itself should serve as both a connector and a separator: a connector in that it ties the user to the power of the computer, and a separator in that it minimizes the possibility of the participants damaging one another. While the damage the user inflicts upon the computer tends to be physical (a frustrated pounding of the keyboard), the damage caused by the computer is more psychological (a threat to one's self-esteem).

As part of the overall person/computer interface, system design focuses on these three considerations:

- the language by which people express their needs and desires to the computer,
- the display representations that show the state of the system to workers, and
- the more abstract issues that affect a person's understanding of the system's behavior.

Ideally, a system's design should enable a person to develop a conceptual model of the system itself.

CONCEPTUAL OR MENTAL MODELS

A conceptual or mental model of a system is what a person gradually develops in order to understand, explain, and interact with the computer. A well-established mental model of a system enables a person to predict the necessary actions to do things if the necessary action has been forgotten or has not yet been encountered.

A mental model is derived from the system image presented to the user. This system image is shaped by the system's input requirements, its outputs, including screens and messages, and its help facilities. System manuals and training sessions also play a formative role.

The development of a mental model can be aided by the following:

Providing design consistency.   Design consistency greatly reduces the number of concepts to be learned. Inconsistency requires the mastery of multiple models.

Drawing physical analogies.   Replicate the environment that has become familiar and well known. Use words and symbols in their customary ways. Duplicate actions that are already learned, such as changing screens by paging rather than scrolling.

Complying with expectancies and stereotypes.   Avoid new and unfamiliar associations. With color, for example, accepted meanings for red, amber, and green are already well established. Directional movement is strongly associated with the face of the compass so directional orientation should mimic this expectancy.

Providing action-response compatibility.   All system responses should be compatible with the actions that elicit them. Command names, for example, should reflect the actions that will occur. Organization of function key names on menus or help screens should reflect the spatial organization of the keys themselves on the keyboard. Action-response compatibility promotes rapid transfer of information between the user and the system.

Providing necessary and proper feedback.   Feedback shapes human performance. Efficient learning of the mental model will not occur unless feedback is provided concerning the correctness of all actions taken.

SYSTEM USABILITY

Since early days, ease of use has been frequently mentioned as the ultimate design criterion for a system. Although it is a simple expression, it has complicated implications. It has been used to refer to a single operation, task, procedure, or an entire job. One of the earliest to attempt to define ease of use was Miller (1971) who proposed the following criteria to measure it:

1. *The training time required to achieve satisfactory performance* is important because in office systems, brevity equals goodness. Most managerial and professional personnel are too busy to devote much time to training in new technologies. In light of this, and considering high turnover rates, satisfactory performance levels must be achieved as soon as possible. It is critical that people be able to learn to operate a system within the time they allot to the learning process.

2. *Number of errors* refers to the maintenance of a reasonable error rate by competent people measured in units of time or number of operations.

3. *Integration of automated and nonautomated tasks* means that there must be a good fit between automated tasks and tasks the technology does not address. That fit must be achieved quickly and with few errors.

4. *Exasperation responses* are the "Oh damn!" reactions that express user annoyance or frustration. Their frequency may foretell a strong rejection of a tool or technology. The absence of exasperation, however, may not represent acceptance.

5. *Habit formation rate* refers to how quickly people learn to use a facility and how quickly that use becomes more or less automatic, so that they no longer have to think about what they are doing. This variable can be measured by observing a person's speed, lack of hesitation, and apparent ease in working with a device or system.

6. *How many people want to use the system* reflects the attitude of actual or potential users toward a device or system. There are, of course, many reasons for liking or disliking a system, and not all of them are necessarily connected with the device itself or the service it provides. In any case, these attitudes may be a more powerful factor than any other in a given system's acceptance.

7. *Irrelevant supporting actions required to perform a task* are the incidental actions required for, but not directly related to, doing a job. They include translating computer code into English, performing frequent or extensive *log-on* procedures, or going through several operations to find the right page in an instruction manual.

8. *Irrelevant display events* include information items that must be disregarded but that use up part of the capacities an individual could devote to relevant tasks.

9. *Time and frequency for user warm-up* means how long it takes to relearn the necessary skills involved in using infrequently used tools or procedures. It also refers to the number of minutes required for warm-up each time a frequently used tool is used before satisfactory speed and accuracy are achieved.

10. *Decision-making time* is the amount of time required to decide what to do after receiving all the information necessary to analyze a problem and select a suitable action.

11. *Shift or work time* is the length of time a person can work without becoming fatigued.

12. *Failure recovery time* includes the amount of time, the number of operations, and the cost of resources required for the user to recover from failures caused by either operator or system errors.
13. *Technology transition time* means the time necessary, where multiple systems are employed, to achieve a satisfactory performance level after shifting from one tool to another.

Over the years, concern with ease of use has expanded to also encompass effectiveness of human performance. Not only must a system be easy to use, it must also accomplish some meaningful objective. The term used to describe this enlarged focus was usability (Bennett, 1979). A formal definition of usability was then proposed by Shackel (1981) and modified by Bennett (1984).

Shackel (1991) presents a shortened form of this definition where usability is defined as "the capability to be used by humans easily and effectively, where:

easily   = to a specified level of subjective assessment
effectively = to a specified level of human performance."

While he feels the definition is conceptually satisfactory, it lacks specification of what usability is in quantifiable terms. He then suggests the following operational definition:

For a system to be usable the following must be achieved:

Effectiveness

- The required range of tasks must be accomplished at better than some required level of performance (e.g., in terms of speed and errors)
- by some required percentage of the specified target range of users
- within some required proportion of the range of usage environments

Learnability

- within some specified time from commissioning and start of user training
- based upon some specified amount of training and user support
- and within some specified relearning time each time for intermittent users

Flexibility

- with flexibility allowing adaptation to some specified percentage variation in tasks and/or environments beyond those first specified

Attitude

- and within acceptable levels of human cost in terms of tiredness, discomfort, frustration and personal effort
- so that satisfaction causes continued and enhanced usage of the system.

Numerical values for the various criteria should be specified during the design stage of user requirements specification. At this point in the design process various system requirements are specified. Usability requirements should be specified in as much detail as any other aspect of the new system, concludes Shackel.

FRIENDLY SYSTEMS

Another descriptive term commonly used in today's systems literature is *friendly*—a quality that well-designed office systems are supposed to possess. However, the definition of *friendly* (relating to or befitting a friend; showing kindly interest or goodwill; not hostile; inclined to favor; comforting or cheerful) from *Webster's Seventh New Collegiate Dictionary* provides designers with little useful information for developing a friendly system. Much is left to the imagination.

To put the term in a systems context, let us say that any design decision that allows a system to achieve a high score in usability will get a high score in friendliness. But friendliness may mean something more—the harmonious interaction of all the ease-of-use criteria. Achieving this will be slow, as systems implementors gain a better understanding of the role of people in systems, and as they test and then modify those systems.

THE DESIRABLE QUALITIES OF A SYSTEM

The computer, as the office worker's major tool, should, like a friend, be pleasant to be with. It should be seen as possessing a variety of desirable qualities. In recent years, a number of writers and researchers (e.g., Nemeth, 1982) have begun to describe what these desired qualities are. While too abstract to serve as design guidelines themselves, they provide useful criteria toward which design guidelines may be directed. They are discussed in the following paragraphs.

Adaptive.   A system must be adaptable to the physical, emotional, intellectual, and mental traits of the people whom it serves. All office workers should be permitted to interact with a computer in a manner and style that best suit their needs. In essence, the system should be responsive to individual differences in interaction manner, depth, and style.

Transparent.   A system must permit one's attention to be focused entirely on the task or job being performed, without concern for the mechanics of the interface. One's thoughts must be directed to the application, not the communication. Any operations that remind a worker of their presence are distracting.

Comprehensible.   A system should be understandable. A person should know what to look at, what to do, when to do it, why to do it, and how to do it (Treu, 1977). The flow of information, commands, responses, and visual presentations should be in a sensible order that is easy to recollect and place in context (Kaplow and Molnar, 1976).

Natural.   Operations should mimic the office worker's behavior patterns. Dialogues should mimic his thought processes and vocabulary (Foley and Wallace, 1974).

Predictable.   System actions should be expected within the context of other actions that are performed. All expectations should be fulfilled uniformly and completely (Martin, 1973; Treu, 1977).

Responsive.   Every human request should be acknowledged, every system reaction clearly described. Feedback is the critical ingredient in shaping a user's performance.

Self-explanatory.   Steps to complete a process should be obvious and, where not, supported and clarified by the system itself. Reading and digesting long explanations should never be necessary (Eason, 1979).

Forgiving.   A system should be tolerant of the human capacity to make errors, at least up to the point where the task or the integrity of the system is affected. Inflexible, unforgiving systems are a major cause of system dissatisfaction. The fear of making a mistake and not being able to recover from it is a primary contributor to a fear of dealing with computers (Eason, 1979; Hansen, 1976).

Efficient.   Eye and hand movements must not be wasted. Attention should be directed to relevant controls and displays of information. Visual and manual transitions between various system components should proceed easily and freely.

Flexible.   People should be able to structure or change a system to meet their particular needs. Inexperienced people may wish to confront and use only a small portion of a system's capabilities in a specific manner. With experience, they may wish to utilize extended capabilities in some other way. This extension and modification of interaction and control procedures should be permitted at the discretion of the users (Kaplow and Molnar, 1976; Shneiderman, 1980).

Available.   Like any tool, an office system must be available if it is to be effective. Any system unreliability, no matter how good normal system performance is, will create dissatisfaction (Miller and Thomas, 1977).

DIALOGUES

"Dialogue" is the word now commonly used to describe the exchange of information, or communication, between the computer and its user. The dialogue style chosen reflects the forms of communication available and computer and user capabilities.

Forms of Communication

The need for people to communicate with each other has existed since we first walked upon this planet. The lowest and most common level of communication modes we share are movements and gestures. Movements and gestures are language-independent, that is, they permit people who do not speak the same language to deal with one another.

The next level, in terms of universality and complexity, is spoken language. Most people can speak one language, some two or more. A spoken language is a very efficient mode of communication if both parties to the communication understand it.

At the third level of complexity is written language. While most people speak, not all can write. But for those who can, writing is still nowhere near as efficient a means of communication.

In modern times, we have the typewriter, another step upward in complexity. Significantly fewer people type than write, yet a practiced typist can find typing faster and more efficient than handwriting. (The unskilled may not find this the case). Spoken language is still more efficient than typing, regardless of typing skill level.

From the computer's perspective, these four forms of communication are inversely related to its ease of understanding. The easiest and best way for a computer to communicate is through typed input. It can accept a handwritten input but only if the message contains carefully formed letters or symbols. Some computers can be taught to recognize spoken words, but even greater limitations exist in terms of vocabulary size and inflection variation. Computers that can respond to human gestures and movements do not exist, except in a few experimental laboratories. The computer does best, then, with what people do worst, and vice-versa. So the dialogue style chosen reflects a compromise by the user. This does not mean, however, that an effective human-computer interaction is not attainable today. It means that things will move from good today to better tomorrow.

Interaction Styles

An interaction style is the particular technique used for providing an orderly exchange of information between people and computers. Styles include question and answer, menu selection, form fill-in, command language, natural language, and direct manipulation, as described by Chapanis (1984) and Shneiderman (1987).

Question and answer.   The computer asks a series of questions and the user responds to each in turn. Its advantage is minimal training, making it especially useful for the novice or casual user. This approach can become cumbersome for the more frequent system user.

Menu Selection.   A list, or menu, of items or alternatives is presented and the appropriate one selected, either by pointing at it, keying the applicable code, or pressing the proper key. One advantage of a menu is that it structures the decision-making process and reduces learning and keystrokes, making it useful to the novice or casual user. Disadvantages include the necessity to consume screen space to list the alternatives, the danger of too many menus, and the requirement for fast response times. While small numbers of menus and fast response times may not always hinder frequent users, overall, menu dialogues do tend to slow down experts.

Form fill-in.   The computer presents the user with a series of captioned blank fields that the user fills in with the required information. This style requires that the user understand the captions, know the method of entry and the permissible values to be keyed, and be able to respond to and correct errors. Therefore, some knowledge and training is usually necessary. The process is similar to filling out a paper form and it is fairly easy for the system to provide assistance in the event of problems. It is faster than question and answer dialogue because of multiple responses for each computer communication.

Command languages.   The user types a command to which the computer responds. This interaction gives the user a strong feeling of control. Also, complex instructions can be expressed rapidly. Other advantages include minimal screen space requirements and lessened impact of slow response times. To master a command language dialogue typically requires a great deal of memorization and learning, placing it in the domain of the expert user. Its big disadvantage is its training requirements, which are difficult for the novice or casual user to cope with. Error rates for this kind of dialogue tend to be high.

Natural language.   Computer natural languages are sometimes considered synonymous with English prose. Many argue that systems must accept natural language sentences or phrases if they are to move smoothly into the office. The advantage of a natural language is that it is flexible, powerful, and requires no special learning. On the negative side, a natural language interaction provides little context for specifying the next command, frequently requires clarification, and may be slower and more cumbersome than some of the other alternatives.

Natural human communications are characterized by an apparent unruliness. Gould et al. (1976) found that slight variations in instructions for achieving a goal led to large variations in the expressions people used to achieve the goal. There was no particularly strong natural tendency, but the adaptiveness of human linguistic and cognitive systems was apparent. Procedure manuals written by different analysts describing the same activity, or forms they design to collect the same data, are classic examples of this adaptiveness. Chapanis et al. (1977), in a study of communication modes, found numerous errors and irregularities and grammatical rules that were repeatedly violated or ignored in natural language interactions.

If computers are ever to interact with people on human terms, the irregularities and inconsistencies that characterize natural languages must be confronted. Although human communication appears to have no strict standards, it obviously follows some rules because information gets conveyed and quite complex problems get solved.

But perhaps a totally natural language is not necessary. Seeking economy of effort, people tend to be impatient with redundancy (Nickerson, 1969), something that English has in abundance. The objective of any communication is to transmit an idea quickly and accurately. The transmitter's degree of redundancy depends on the recipient's ability to understand. If the communicator limits redundancies, will the message still be effectively conveyed?

The study by Kelly and Chapanis (1977) has a bearing on this question. They required subjects communicating by teletypewriter to use either 300-word, 500-word, or unlimited vocabularies. Subjects who worked with the restricted vocabularies interacted and solved problems as successfully as those who worked with no restrictions. Thus it appears possible, at least for the types of communications studied in this experiment, to develop limited vocabularies for use in human/machine interactions.

Another pertinent study is Gould et al. (1976), which found that subjects who showed a low preference for a restricted-syntax language would readily and sometimes spontaneously use such a language when called upon to communicate.

Schoonard and Boies (1975) tested the ability of typists to type abbreviated words (of one to three characters) in a text-entry process. The typists recognized and typed 93 percent of the abbreviated words, with an error rate no greater than when they were typing unabbreviated words. And the substitution process did not affect the keystroke rate.

The results of these studies and evidence from operating data-processing systems (Galitz, 1979) indicate that well-designed, restricted vocabularies can provide effective language interfaces between users and office systems. But the language must be natural from an application and job-related standpoint.

The search for the ideal language or languages must continue if people and machines are to work in total harmony. The ultimate solution is probably beyond today's technology and will require further refinement and the use of voice and touch. But for now, designs must be developed within the limits of today's technology.

Direct manipulation (iconic).   The newest interaction style is direct manipulation of visual objects representing the world of interest. By pointing at pictures of objects or actions, the user can quickly perform tasks and watch the results immediately. Direct manipulation is believed to be superior to other styles because it is simple, natural, and direct, the keyboard keys being replaced by cursor movement devices (the Mouse, for example). For novice and casual users direct manipulation is appealing. It does have disadvantages, however, in that it is harder to program and requires graphics and a pointing device.

In conclusion, the above interaction styles each have certain advantages and disadvantages for users with differing levels of experience. Are these differences always generalizable, and is interaction style the most critical consideration in ease of use? The evidence indicates no. Whiteside et al. (1985) compared seven different interactive systems possessing three different styles: command language, menu selection, and iconic (direct manipulation). They found that interaction style is not related to user performance or preference, but that careful design is. The care with which an interface is crafted is more important than the style of interface chosen; new interface technology has not solved old usability problems. This, of course, is not to say that interaction style is irrelevant, however. It simply means that poor design can mask any differences that do exist.

CURRENT DIRECTIONS AND GUIDELINES

Design of the human–computer interface still remains more an art than a science. The body of research needed to develop truly effective interfaces is small, and only now is this needed research effort showing signs of awakening. Also, the design issues also have great depth and subtlety. Even seemingly straightforward considerations, such as minimizing the number of keystrokes, may not make a system easier to use. Therefore, we cannot be optimistic that all the answers will be forthcoming in the years ahead.

The office and technology, however, will not wait. We must move forward with what is known today, making decisions as best we can. Toward that goal, what follows is a series of guidelines addressing system design. They reflect not only what we know today but what we think we know today. Many are based on research; others, on the collective thinking of behaviorists working in office automation. The guidelines address only general behavioral considerations when nothing is known about individuals and their functions. Final system design will, of course, require understanding of specific user tasks and goals.

Consistency

A system should look, act, and feel the same throughout.

Design consistency is the common thread that runs throughout these guidelines. It is the cardinal rule of all design activities. Consistency is important because it can reduce requirements for human learning by allowing skills learned in one situation to be transferred to another like it. While any new automated system must impose some learning requirements on its users, it should avoid encumbering productive learning with nonproductive, unnecessary activity.

In addition to increased learning requirements, variety in design has a number of other prerequisites and by-products, including:

- more specialization by system users,
- greater demand for higher skills,
- more preparation time and less production time,

- more frequent changes in procedures,
- more error-tolerant systems (because errors are more likely),
- more kinds of documentation,
- more time to find information in documents,
- more unlearning and learning when systems are changed,
- more demands on supervisors and managers, and
- more things to go wrong.

Inconsistencies in design are caused by differences in people—several designers might each design the same system differently. Inconsistencies also occur when design activities are pressured by time constraints. All too often the solutions in those cases are exceptions that the user must learn to handle.

Users, however, perceive a system as a single entity. To them, it should look, act, and feel similarly throughout. Excess learning requirements become a barrier to their achieving and maintaining high performance and can ultimately influence user acceptance of the system.

Can consistency make a big difference? One study found that user thinking time nearly doubled when the position of screen elements, such as titles and field captions, was varied on a series of menu screens (Teitelbaum and Granda, 1983).

Standards and guidelines.   Design consistency is achieved by developing and applying design standards or guidelines. In the late 1980s the computer industry and other organizations finally awakened to their need, and a flurry of guideline documents have recently been developed and are continuing to appear. Examples of industry-produced guidelines include Apple's *Human Interface Guidelines: The Apple Desktop Interface* (1987), Digital Equipment Corporation's *XUI Style Guide* (1988), IBM's *System Application Architecture Common User Access (SAA-CUA)* (1987, 1989a, 1989b), and Sun Microsystems's *OPEN LOOK Graphical User Interface Application Style Guidelines* (1990). Organizations working on guidelines or standards include the International Standards Organization (ISO) (Brooke et al., 1990; Billingsley, 1991), the American National Standards Institute (ANSI) (Billingsley, 1991), and the Human Factors Society (Billingsley, 1991).

In parallel with the development of these guidelines has been some research looking at both how well guidelines are actually followed and methods to achieve most effective guideline utilization.

Research on guideline utilization has hardly been encouraging. Mosier and Smith (1986) found that only 58 percent of the users of a large interface guidelines document found the information they were looking for, and an additional 36 percent only sometimes found it. deSouza and Bevan (1990) report that designers using a draft of the ISO menu interface standard violated 11 percent of the rules and had difficulties in interpreting 30 percent. Tetlaff and Schwartz (1991) also report difficulties in interpreting guidelines from an interface style guide, although conformance with the guidelines was high. Thovtrup and Nielsen (1991) report designers were only able to achieve a 71 percent compliance with a two-page standard in a laboratory setting. In an evaluation of three real systems, they found that the mandatory rules of the company's screen design standard were violated 32 to 55 percent of the time.

Thovtrup and Nielsen, in analyzing why the rules in the screen design standard were broken, found a very positive designer attitude toward the standard, both in terms of its value and content. Rules were not adhered to, however, for the following reasons:

- An alternative design solution was better than that mandated by the standard.
- Available development tools did not allow compliance with the standard.
- Compliance with the standard was planned, but time was not yet available to implement it.
- The rule that was broken was not known or was overlooked.

Tetzlaff and Schwartz, in analyzing how their guidelines were used, found that designers depended heavily on the pictorial guideline examples, often ignoring the accompanying text.

The implications of these studies for a screen standard design are as follows:

- Include concrete examples of correctly designed screens.
- Provide development tools that support implementation of the screens that follow the standard.
- Provide a rationale for why the particular guidelines should be used. This is especially important if the guideline is a deviation from a previous design practice.
- Provide a rationale describing the conditions under which various design alternatives are appropriate. The examples may illustrate alternatives and the tool kit may produce them, but when these various alternatives are appropriate may be difficult for designers to infer.
- Design the standards document following recognized principles for good document design. Provide good access mechanisms such as a thorough index, a table of contents, glossaries, and checklists.

Two questions often asked are, "Is it too late to develop and implement standards?" and "What will be the impact on systems and screens now being used?" To address these questions, Burns and Watson (1986) reformatted several alphanumeric inquiry screens to improve their comprehensibility and readability. When these reformatted screens were presented to expert system users, decision-making time remained the same but errors were reduced. For novice system users, the reformatted screens brought large improvements in speed and accuracy. Therefore, it appears, changes enhancing screens will benefit novice as well as expert users already familiar with the current screens. It is never too late to change.

Design Tradeoffs

Human requirements must always take precedence over machine processing requirements.

Design guidelines often cover a great deal of territory and occasionally conflict with one another or with machine processing requirements. In such conflicts the designer must weigh alternatives and reach a decision based on accuracy, time, cost, and ease-of-use requirements. The ultimate solution will be a blend of experimental data, good judgment, and the user needs of most importance.

This leads to the second cardinal rule of system development: *Human requirements always take precedence over machine processing requirements.* It might be easier for the designer to write a program or build a device that neglects user ease, but this should not be tolerated.

Log-On

Only one simple action should be necessary to initiate a log-on.

Access to a system must be easy. Like the cover of a book, the log-on process should encourage, not discourage, the desire to go inside. It should be a separate procedure before the operational options are encountered, since having to anticipate additional steps and commands can be distracting and confusing. And it should be nothing more than the depression of a log-on or start key. If more actions are required, the system must lead a person through the necessary steps. A difficult or cumbersome log-on process can discourage a system's use before its benefits can be demonstrated. If for some reason the log-on is delayed, the user should receive an advisory message stating when the system will be ready.

Initiative

Initiative should be commensurate with the capabilities of the system users

- for new and inexperienced people, provide a computer-initiated dialogue;
- for the experienced, permit a human-initiated dialogue.

Initiative is a system characteristic defining who leads the dialogue between the user and the computer. In a *computer-initiated dialogue*, the system leads the dialogue and a person responds to various prompts. These prompts may take the form of questions, directions, menus of alternatives, or forms to fill in. Computer-initiated dialogues are usually preferred by new users of systems because they rely on our powerful passive vocabulary (words that can be recognized and understood) and they are a learning vehicle, implicitly teaching a system model as one works.

Human-initiated dialogue puts the lead in the hands of the system's user. The computer becomes a blackboard waiting to be drawn upon. The user provides free-form instructions from memory—either commands or information—and the system responds accordingly. Human-initiated dialogues are often preferred by experienced system users, since they permit faster and more efficient interaction. A computer-initiated dialogue tends to slow down and disrupt the more experienced user.

Mixed-initiative dialogues have also been designed. An example is the labeled function keys on display terminals. The label itself provides a prompt or memory aid, but the user must remember when it can be used.

Most of the earlier-generation computer systems used human-initiated dialogue, since this was the style designers were most comfortable with. However, because of problems encountered, and because of exposure of computer technology to more nonspecialists, emphasis has shifted in recent years to computer-initiated methods. This new emphasis has brought into focus more clearly the problems of this approach for a person who becomes experienced with a system. So, today we are beginning to see systems that combine both initiative styles. The needs of new and experienced system users can thus be simultaneously satisfied.

A question that has repeatedly been asked is at what point a person is ready to make the transition from computer- to human-initiated dialogue. In a study by Gilfoil (1982) novice system users were given a choice of a menu-driven dialogue (computer-initiated) or a command-driven dialogue (human-initiated). They chose the menu approach to start with and moved to the command approach after 16 to 20 hours of experience. At this point they were found to perform better and to be more satisfied with the command dialogue. A similar study (Chafin and Martin, 1980) found the transition occurring at about 25 to 50 hours.

Of course, these numbers should not be interpreted literally. Many characteristics of the system, task, and user population would substantially influence the results. What is important is the direction these numbers take. They show that it does not take long for new users of a system to start moving from dependent to independent status. To be truly effective, an office system must provide a dual-initiation capability.

Flexibility

A system must be sensitive to the differing needs of its users.

Flexibility is a measure of the system's capability to respond to individual differences in people. A truly flexible system will permit a person to interact with it in a manner commensurate with his knowledge, skills, and experience. One kind of flexibility, which has already been described, is initiation. A system that permits both human- and computer-initiated dialogues is flexible in that regard. Other examples are the display or nondisplay of prompts, permitting defaults and the creation of special vocabularies. An electronic mail system is flexible in that it permits its users to receive their messages in three ways:

- When a message is there, the system sends it (*assertive*).
- The system calls to indicate a message is there, but the message must be asked for (*interrogative*).
- The system never calls; all messages must be asked for (*passive*).

Each person working with such a system can choose the method most comfortable to himself or herself.

Flexibility can have differing levels. At one extreme the user can choose the preferred method and the system will respond accordingly. At the other extreme, the system constantly monitors a person's performance (errors, speed, frequency of use of components, and so on) and modifies itself accordingly. The latter might more appropriately be called an *adaptive system*.

Flexibility is not without dangers. Highly flexible dialogues can confuse inexperienced users, causing them to make more errors. For this reason, such dialogues appear desirable only for experienced or expert users. The novice user should not be exposed to system flexibility at the start, but only as experience is gained. The concept of "progressive disclosure," to be discussed in the *complexity* guideline to follow, is also applicable here.

Another problem with flexibility is that it may not always be used, people preferring to continue doing things in the way they first learned. A variety of factors may account for this, including an unwillingness to invest in additional learning, or, perhaps, new ways may just not be obvious. The former problem may be addressed by making the new ways as easy and safe to learn as possible, the latter by including in training and reference materials not only information about how to do things, but when they are likely to be useful.

Complexity

Complexity should be commensurate with the capabilities of the system users.

Three ways to minimize complexity

- Use progressive disclosure, hiding things until they are needed.
- Make common actions simple at the expense of uncommon actions made harder.
- Provide uniformity and consistency.

Complexity is a measure of the number of alternatives available to the office worker. It is the number of ways something can be done or the number of choices one has at any given point. A highly complex system is difficult to learn. For inexperienced users, complexity frequently degrades performance, especially by increasing error rates. Complex systems are often not fully used, or used ineffectively, because a person may follow known but more cumbersome methods instead of easier but unfamiliar methods. A system lacking complexity may have a different set of faults: It may be tedious to use or may not accomplish much.

Complexity, then, is a two-edged sword. To effectively solve office problems it must exist, but it must not be apparent for the tool to be effectively utilized by the office worker.

There are three specific ways to minimize complexity.

Progressive disclosure.   Introduce system components gradually, only when people see a need to do something they do not know how to do, or when they see they can do something faster or in fewer steps. This is also called the layered, or spiral, approach to learning. Such an approach was taken by Carroll and Carrithers (1984), who called it the "Training-Wheels System." They found that by disabling portions of the system that were not needed and that could lead to errors or confusions, improved system learning efficiency was achieved.

Make common actions simple.   Make common actions within a system easier to accomplish than uncommon actions. Greater overall system efficiency results.

Provide uniformity and consistency.   Inconsistency is a foolish form of complexity. A person has to learn that things that appear different really are not.

Closure

- To provide closure, organize sequences of actions into groups with a beginning, middle, and an end.
- Provide informative feedback at the conclusion of each group of actions.

Closure means to complete, to achieve a satisfactory ending. Closure with its necessary informative feedback provides the user the satisfaction of accomplishment and a sense of relief. It indicates that contingency plans and options are not necessary and the way is clear to move ahead (Shneiderman, 1987).

Power

Dialogue power should be commensurate with the capabilities of the system users.

Power is a measure of the amount of work accomplished by a given instruction to a system. A very powerful instruction can evoke a string of system operations doing many things. This same string of operations can also be evoked by a series of instructions, each directed toward one specific aspect. But each individual instruction is then less powerful because it accomplishes less.

High power is usually associated with high dialogue complexity and reduced system generality. Therefore, while a powerful system can be effectively utilized in the hands of a well-trained person, the untrained may be unable or unwilling to cope. The result is often system rejection. Goodwin (1982) provides an interesting analysis of an electronic mail system whose utility was diminished because of the dialogue power it possessed.

Power, then, is another dialogue property whose effectiveness is directly related to the experience level of people working with a system, and whose optimum level varies along a sliding scale that changes with user needs.

Information Load

Information load should be commensurate with the capabilities of the system user.

Six ways to reduce information load

- Provide graphic rather than alphanumeric displays.
- Format displays to correspond to users' immediate information requirements.
- Use natural languages.
- Move clerical operations into the system.
- Provide less powerful commands.
- Provide less complex dialogues.

Two ways to increase information load

- Permit more powerful commands.
- Permit more complex dialogues.

Information load is a measure of the degree to which a user's memory is being utilized and/or processing resources are absorbed by the design. It is a function of the task being performed, a person's familiarity with the task, and the design of the dialogue itself. Like other dialogue properties, the optimum level can change with a user's experience.

Information loads that are too high or too low can affect performance. High loads strain a person's capabilities and may cause an inability or unwillingness to cope. Low levels create boredom and inattentiveness, fostering errors.

Human memory is a weak link in the human–machine interface and should be supported whenever possible. Information load can be reduced by the actions listed above. As a user becomes more knowledgeable and the information load can be expanded, the direction should be toward greater dialogue power and complexity. These are positive steps toward greater system effectiveness.

Control

General

- The user must control the interaction:
  - —actions should result from explicit user inputs;
  - —actions should be capable of interruption or termination; and
  - —the user should never be interrupted for errors.
- The context maintained must be that of the user.
- The means to achieve goals must be compatible with the user's skills and the desired end result.

Paths

- The capability to go from/to any point or step must exist.
- Input stacking must be possible.
- A home position must always be available.

Options

- Options or actions available at any time must be accessible either on a display or through a help function.
- Only relevant options should be available.

Control is feeling in charge, feeling that the system is responding to your actions. It is achieved when the user, working at his own pace, is responsible for determining what to do, selecting how to do it, entering information into the system, processing that information in conjunction with the system, correcting errors, and later retrieving information from the system. Lack of control is shown by unavailable systems, surprising system actions or responses, tedious and long procedures that cannot be circumvented, difficulties in obtaining necessary information, and an inability to achieve the desired results.

The feeling of control has been found to be an excellent mitigator of the work stress associated with many automated systems (Gardell, 1979; Johansson et al., 1978; Karasek, 1979; Karasek et al., 1981; and Frankenhaeuser, 1979).

General. Control must always be in the hands of the user. Actions must result from explicit human inputs and requests, and should be capable of being interrupted or terminated by the user. User actions should never be interrupted by errors. There should be no delays or paced delays beyond a user's expectancies.

The context maintained must always be the user's perspective. The knowledge carried forward by the system must be that which represents the user's level of understanding. To help the user remember status or context, prior user entries should be available for review as needed. While processing modes are not desirable, if used, a facility should be available to remind the user of which one is current.

The means to accomplish actions should be compatible with the user's skills, either novice, expert, or somewhere in between. Frequent or common actions should be made very easy.

Paths.   Users should, at their option, be able to move from any one point or step in an interaction to any other step or point within the context of the job. In a series of menus, for example, the capability should exist for going from one menu to any other menu in the string. This kind of action is illustrative of a human-initiated dialogue overriding a computer-initiated dialogue.

Stacking of inputs or requests must be possible. Stacking is the process of stringing together a series of discrete requests or commands so that they comprise one input. The system will then perform each action consecutively while the user awaits the result. The order of stacked commands should be the same as if they were discrete commands. Command separators should be standard symbols, preferably a slash (/). No concern with blanks should be required. If the system is unable to complete a series of stacked commands, it should stop and present the next appropriate step or menu. The user should be able to assign a single name to command strings that are frequently used together. This more powerful command should then be recognizable by the system and in the future elicit the discrete actions it refers to.

A home position, such as a primary or main system menu, should always be achievable by a simple user action.

Options.   Options or actions available at any given time must be available on a display or through a help function. All relevant options should be displayed except those that are always available systemwide. Only relevant options should be displayed. Options not currently available to a person should not be provided. If options are designated by codes, these codes must also be provided.

Feedback

A system should acknowledge all actions by

- immediate execution,
- change in state or value,
- correction message,
- confirmation message, and
- IN-PROGRESS message.

Knowledge of results, or *feedback*, is a necessary learning ingredient. It shapes human performance and instills confidence. All requests to the system must be acknowledged in some way. This acknowledgment is normally provided when the system completes the request, and may be implicit—a change in state—or it may be explicit—a message of the kind described above. The screen should not be blank for more than a few moments, as the user may think the system has failed.

If a request requires a longer processing period than is normally associated with the action requested (see the guidelines on response times), the system should acknowledge its receipt and provide an interim IN-PROGRESS message.

Substantial and more informative feedback is most important for the novice or casual system user. Expert users are often content to receive more modest feedback.

Recovery

A system should permit

- commands or actions to be abolished or reversed,
- immediate return to a certain point if difficulties arise.

People should be able to retract an action by issuing what Miller and Thomas (1977) call an *undo* command. Knowing they can withdraw a command reduces much of the distress of new users, who often worry about doing something wrong. The return point could be the previous screen, a recent closure point, or the beginning of some predetermined period, such as back 10 screens or some number of minutes. Reversing or abolishing an action is analogous to using an eraser to eliminate a pencil mark on a piece of paper.

The goal, as Martin (1973) says, is stability—returning easily to the right track when a wrong track has been taken. Recovery should be obvious, automatic, and easy and natural to perform. In short, it should be hard to get into deep water or go too far astray. Easy recovery from an action greatly facilitates learning by trial-and-error and exploration. If an action is not reversible, and its consequences are critical, it should be made difficult to accomplish.

Control Functions

Desirable control functions include:

- page forward
- page backward
- hold/store
- cancel
- end/stop

- retrieve
- help
- resume
- undo/back-up
- print

Interacting with an office system requires that some basic control operations be available at all times. Logical candidates are the following functions, which are ideal for incorporation into function keys.

Page forward and Page backward. PAGE FORWARD and PAGE BACKWARD enable one to move rapidly through a series of display screens.

Hold/store. HOLD/STORE stores something being worked on in a file facility that may later be retrieved.

Cancel. ABORT/CANCEL cancels or erases what the user is working on.

End/stop. END/STOP stops processing immediately; processing may be resumed at that point later.

Retrieve. RETRIEVE brings up from a file facility what has previously been stored.

Help. HELP accesses the HELP facility, to be described.

Resume. RESUME returns to the point where one is working after HELP or END/STOP.

Undo/back-up. UNDO/BACK-UP reverses the action just performed, as previously described.

Print. PRINT provides hard-copy printout of the current display.

Any system application may, of course, require additional control functions based upon its objectives.

Command Languages

Content

- Use words that are familiar, highly suggestive, and discriminating.

Structure

- Use words that are perceptually dissimilar.
- Permit abbreviations but train with full words.

Organization

- Provide a structuring rule.
- Provide customized subsets.
- Permit naming flexibility.

Consistency

- Use a common command discipline throughout all applications.

Defaults

- Within a command, the system should supply missing arguments. Between commands, the system should supply missing commands if a predefined sequence is initiated; supply missing arguments based on previously supplied arguments; supply a missing command based on arguments.

Edits

- Only incorrectly entered command data should be reentered.

Command languages must be logical, consistent, and flexible. A logical and consistent language will expedite the learning process and slow the forgetting that results from language disuse. Flexibility allows users to adapt the command language to themselves instead of the other way around. The following guidelines highlight the more important features of a command language. Engel and Granda (1975) and Watson (1976) also provide detailed discussions.

Content.   Command languages must be familiar and reflect the user's viewpoint, not the system designer's. Users must be able to express their needs with command constructions similar to their own language, thought processes, and natural problem-solving vocabularies. Ledgard et al. (1980) found far better performance after redesigning a commercial text editor so that the commands more closely resembled English phrases. Black and Moran (1982) found words always better than nonwords in free recall.

All too often a command language has been created by the system's designer. Jones (1978) pointed out the discrepancies between designers' assumptions and the realities of the users' language that have made many command languages difficult to use. He concluded the following:

- Designers tend to assume a one-to-one correspondence between newly formed command statements and their meanings. Users see many of the commands as having the same meaning.
- Designers presume nothing is assumed by users except what is expressly stated about a command. Actually, users possess innumerable unstated assumptions that are applied to the interpretation process.
- Designers assume that users' deductions are made from absolutely

unvarying frames of reference. In fact, users often establish meaning based upon immediate context.

Is the user the best creator of a command language for an office automation system? The evidence here is contradictory. Black and Moran (1982) conclude that computer naive people are not good command language designers. They tend to create frequent and general words for commands when the best performance is achieved with infrequent, discriminating words. Furnas et al. (1982) found great diversity in people's descriptions of even the most common objects. The average likelihood of any two people using the same main content word in their description of the same object ranged from 7 to 18 percent. Therefore a common word acceptable to all is difficult to achieve. Similar conclusions have been reached by Barnard et al. (1981) and Carroll (1980).

However, Scapin (1982) found that people performed better with their own command language. Perhaps the best solution is a joint effort between users and designers with the final solution derived from testing and refinement.

Command names should be highly suggestible. A command name is good to the degree that it suggests directly what the command does (PRINT is better than LIST), and that it suggests directly the relationship (whether similar, opposite, or unrelated) of that command to other commands in the system (Rosenberg, 1982). Hammond et al. (1980s) found that the pattern of errors in a dialogue correlates with the extent to which command names are ambiguous about their underlying operations.

Command names should be discriminating. Avoid small and subtle differences such as PRINT versus WRITE. Use specific instead of general words (SUBSTITUTE instead of CHANGE). As described above, both Barnard et al. (1982) and Black and Moran (1982) found that specific words resulted in better performance than general words.

Structure.   Choose command words that are perceptually dissimilar to avoid confusion errors. While command languages must be meaningful and not highly coded, abbreviations and concise notation will support differing user proficiencies, from expert to novice. Advanced vocabularies and short, concise control notations and conventions maximize the performance of expert users. Inability to abbreviate can contribute to user dissatisfaction, since forcing people to enter long words increases keying time, error frequency, and associated time-consuming recovery procedures.

When abbreviations are permitted, however, as discussed in Section 5-1, truncation is the recommended method (Ehrenreich, 1985), and training should always be with the full command word to aid the learning and retaining of command meaning (Barnard and Grudin, 1985).

Organization.   Provide a structuring rule for the population of commands. Scapin (1982) found that providing structure to a family of commands by breaking them into logical groupings was an important factor in aiding learning.

Provide subsets of the command language and features. This is particularly advantageous when the technology is first introduced, since it permits phased learning of system components.

Provide flexibility by permitting users to assign their own names to frequent command sequences. The result, as mentioned earlier, will be a more powerful dialogue.

Consistency.   Consistency in command languages is mandatory if a collection of office systems with which a worker interacts is considered as one system. Table 3.1 illustrates some command words from current systems that are used to accomplish the same purpose. People must be able to learn additional functions by increasing their vocabulary, not by learning separate foreign languages.

Table 3.1   Different command words often having the same meaning.

To begin an interaction:	*To create a hard copy:*
LOGIN	WRITE
LOGON	OUTPUT
HELLO	PRINT
SIGNIN	LIST
SIGNON	DISPLAY

Defaults.   If a person fails to specify a command, the system may prompt him to supply the missing information by listing potential values. This approach is acceptable if the alternatives are limited, but it is less desirable when the list becomes complicated or time consuming. A second alternative is to ask users to supply the missing information from memory, but this is not an optimal approach.

A third option is for the system to supply a default value for the missing information. A *default* is an agreement between the user and the system concerning the normal or usual working environment. Defaults are a powerful aid in achieving a user-oriented language, but they are not without problems. The user may not know or understand the default or may not have a convenient way of changing it. For these reasons, perhaps default usage should be optional.

A *command argument* is an option that qualifies a general command. Figure 3.1 shows two command methods for obtaining a printout of two kinds of insurance transactions—incomplete and complete new business. The first method uses two separate commands, while the second has one command, used with two arguments.

Edits.   A person should never have to reenter an entire command, especially if only one item on a line is incorrect. An appropriate mechanism such as cursor positioning should also exist to help the user by setting up the appropriate spot for reentry.

Figure 3.1   Command argument methods.

```
Command:

        PRINT INCOMPLETE NEW BUSINESS
        (---------Command-----------)

        PRINT COMPLETE NEW BUSINESS
        (---------Command---------)

Command and argument:

    PRINT                   INCOMPLETE NEW BUSINESS

    (command)               (------Arguments------)

    PRINT                   COMPLETE NEW BUSINESS

    (command)               (------Arguments------)
```

Command Language Arguments

Organization

- Few commands with many arguments is a better organization than many commands with a few arguments.

Format

- Keyword argument formats are superior to positional formats.

Organization.   Boies (1974) found that a majority of users in a large time-sharing system used only a few of the many system commands available and frequently employed commands in their simplest and least powerful form. He speculated that this could result from command structures that were difficult for users to recall when needed. Boies subsequently compared the use of a small number of commands and a large number of arguments with the use of many specific commands and few arguments. He found the former more useful. More study is needed to find an optimal command language strategy.

Format.   In a positional command language format, arguments are assigned a relative or absolute position in the argument string. With a keyword format, arguments may be in permutable strings, indicating the argument type and its value. The value of arguments must be remembered in both cases. Positional formats appear to impose greater memory requirements on users, since remembering positions is an additional burden. In an informal study Weinberg (1971) found high error rates in positional format use.

Error Management

Prevention

- Handle common misspellings.
- Permit review of message about to be sent.
- Permit editing of message about to be sent.
- Provide common send mechanism.
- Advise of nonreversible changes.

Detection

- Immediately detect all errors.
- Maintain the item in error.
- Visually highlight the item in error.
- Identify fields requiring missing data.
- Display an error message on the entry screen.
- Position cursor at first error.
- Use auditory signals conservatively.
- Prevent errors from causing the system to go down.

Correction

- Provide constructive error messages.
  - —What error was detected.
  - —Which field was in error.
  - —What corrective action is necessary.
- Initiate clarification dialogue, if necessary.
- Resend only erroneous information back to system.

The magnitude of errors in computer systems is astounding. Shneiderman (1987) describes studies reporting error rates in commands, tasks, or transactions as high as 46 percent. In addition to stranding the user and wasting time, mistakes and errors interrupt planning and cause deep frustrations.

Some experts have argued that there are no "errors" as such; they are simply "iterations" toward a goal. There is much truth to that statement. It is also often said that "to err is human." The corollary to that statement, at least in computer systems, might be, ". . . to forgive, good design."

Whatever we call them, errors will occur. People should be able to correct them as soon as they pop up, as simply and easily as they are made. One objective of this book is to reduce or eliminate errors in computer systems. The focus here is on the mechanics of error prevention, detection, and correction.

Prevention.   Where possible, human misspellings of commands and requests should be accepted by the system. Person-to-person communication does not require perfection. Person-to-computer communication should impose no more rigor. Inappropriate use of shift keys should also be distinguished, where possible, since they are such a large cause of keying errors. Entries made into a system should be reviewable and editable by the person who made them. Human memory is poor and keying errors will occur.

A common *send* mechanism should be provided to transmit an entry to the system. Two or more keys to accomplish the same purpose, especially if their use is mandated by different conditions, can be confusing and more prone to errors. If an action causes a nonreversible change, and the change is critical, the user should be requested to confirm the change. A separate key should be used for this purpose, not the send key.

Detection.   All errors should be immediately detected and communicated to the user through a highlighting display technique (for example, high intensity or contrasting color). This does not mean the user should be interrupted for each error that occurs. It is preferable to wait for a closure point, such as the end of a screen. Identify missing information in fields with question marks (?).

The items in error, and error messages, should be displayed on the entry screen being viewed. If multiple error messages occur, and it is impossible to display all of them at one time, provide an indication that there are additional messages. Say, for example, "+ 2 other errors." Also, provide with a distinct difference the same error message displayed more than once because the first attempt to correct failed.

For ease in correcting, position the cursor in the first field in error when the error message is displayed. Be cautious in using auditory signals to notify of an error. Many users, especially those with status or position, do not want their mistakes advertised.

Correction.   Explicit and constructive error messages should be provided. These messages should describe what error occurred, what field was in error, and how it should be corrected. Corrective actions will be clearer if phrased with words like "must be" or "must have." Shneiderman (1982), in restructuring messages following guidelines such as this, and others to be described in Chapter 4, found improved success rates in fixing errors, lower error rates, and improved user satisfaction.

All error ambiguities should be resolved by having the system query the user. Errors should be corrected with minimal typing. Only erroneous information should be sent back to the system.

Another important error control measure is to have the system identify and store errors. This will allow tracking of common errors so that appropriate prevention programs can be implemented.

Response Time

System responsiveness should match the speed and flow of human thought processes

- if continuity of thinking is required and information must be remembered throughout several responses, response time should be less than two seconds;
- if human task closures exist, high levels of concentration are not necessary and moderate short-term memory requirements are imposed; response times of 2 to 4 seconds are acceptable;
- if major task closures exist, minimal short-term memory requirements are imposed; responses within 4 to 15 seconds are acceptable; and
- when the user is free to do other things and return when convenient response time can be greater than 15 seconds.

Constant delays are preferable to variable delays.

What the ideal system response time is has been the subject of numerous studies. Unfortunately, there still does not exist definitive time or times that are acceptable under all conditions. What is clear is that dissatisfaction with response time is dependent on user expectations. It is also clear that expectations can vary, depending on the task as well as the situation. The ideal condition is one in which a person "perceives" no delays. A response time is too long when one "notices" that the system is taking too long. The following paragraphs summarize some study conclusions, and some tentative findings.

The optimum response time is dependent upon the task.   There is an optimum work pace that depends on the task being performed. Longer or shorter response times than the optimum lead to more errors (Barber and Lucas, 1983). In general, response times should be geared to the user's short-term memory load and to how he has grouped the activities being performed. Intense short-term memory loads necessitate short response times. While completing chunks of work at task closures, users can withstand longer response delays.

The human *now*, or psychological present, is two to three seconds. This is why continuity of thinking requires a response time within this limit. Recent research indicates that for creative tasks, response times in the range of four-tenths to nine-tenths of a second can yield dramatic increases in productivity, even greater in proportion to the increase in response time (Smith, 1983). The probable reason is the elimination of restrictions caused by short-term memory limitations.

As the response-time interval increases beyond 10 to 15 seconds, continuity of thought becomes increasingly difficult to maintain. Doherty (1979) suggests that this happens because the sequence of actions stored in short-term memory beyond that time is badly disrupted and must be reloaded.

The response time guidelines above, then, relate to the general tasks being performed. Their applicability to every situation is not guaranteed.

Satisfaction with response time is a function of expectations.   Expectations are based, in part, on past experiences. These experiences may be derived from working with a computer, or from the world in general, and they vary enormously across individuals and tasks.

Dissatisfaction with response time is a function of one's uncertainty about delay.   The degree of frustration with delay may depend on such psychological factors as a person's uncertainty concerning how long the delay will be, the extent to which the actual delay contradicts those expectations, and what the person thinks is causing the delay. Such uncertainty concerning how long a wait there will be for a computer's response may in some cases be a greater source of frustration than the delay itself (Nickerson, 1969).

People will change work habits to conform to response time.   As response time increases, so does think time (Cotton, 1978; Boies, 1974; and Butler, 1983). People also work more carefully with longer response times (Bergman et al., 1981). In some cases more errors have been found with very short response times. This may not be necessarily bad if the errors are the result of trial-and-error learning that is enhanced by very fast response times.

Constant delays are preferable to variable delays.   Carbonell et al. (1969) point out that it is the variability of delays, not their length, that most frequently distresses people. From a consistency standpoint, a good rule of thumb is that response-time deviations should never exceed half the mean response time. For example, if the mean response time is four seconds, a two-second deviation is permissible. Variations should range from three to five seconds. Shneiderman (1987) suggests, however, that response time variation should not exceed 20 percent. Lower response time variability has been found to yield better performance (Miller, 1977), but small variations may be tolerated (Bergman et al., 1981; Weiss et al., 1982).

More experienced people prefer shorter response times.   People work faster as they gain experience, a fact that leads Shneiderman (1987) to conclude that it may be useful to let people set their own pace of interaction. He also suggests that in the absence of cost or technical feasibility constraints, people will eventually force response time to well under one second.

Very fast or slow response times can lead to symptoms of stress.   There is a point at which a person can be overwhelmed by information presented more quickly than it can be comprehended. There is also some evidence indicating that when a system responds too quickly, there is subconscious pressure on users to also respond quickly, possibly threatening their overall comfort (Elam, 1978), increasing their blood pressure, or causing them to exhibit other signs of anxious behavior (Brod, 1984). Symptoms of job burnout have been reported after substantial reductions in response time (Turner, 1984).

Slow and variable response times have also been shown to lead to a significant build-up of mood disturbances and somatic discomfort over time, culminating in symptoms of work stress, including frustration, impatience, and irritation (Schleifer, 1986).

Specific Response Times

- *Log-on/initialization:* up to 30 seconds, with immediate interim acknowledgment.
- *Error messages:* a brief pause after a closure.
- *Inquiry:* 1 to 15 seconds.
- *Browsing/scrolling:* 1 second or less.
- *Data entry:* within a transaction, 4 to 6 seconds; after completing a transaction, up to 15 seconds.

Acceptable response times for certain office system activities have been put forth. Delays in completing system log-on while the computer reorganizes resources and facilities are not as annoying as long delays during interactions. Therefore, delays of up to 30 seconds for log-on are acceptable, but a fairly quick acknowledgment that log-on is occurring should be given when the process begins.

Interruptions in concentration can be frustrating, so people should be able to finish what they are doing before being told of an error. At task closures, the system should pause briefly to allow a person to change mental modes before having to attend to an error message.

Inquiry response times depend on urgency. They may range from 1 to 15 seconds.

Browsing or scrolling usually involves rapid search for information. Additional information to be searched must maintain the visual searching pace established. A 1-second response time should be expected.

Manual paper shuffling during data entry provides a good closure point. Longer response delays between screens can then be tolerated.

Guidance and Assistance

A system should provide

- on-line documentation that supplements hard copy documentation,
- user-selectable prompting, and
- a HELP facility.

New system users must go through a learning process that involves developing a conceptual or mental model to explain the system's behavior and the task being performed. Documentation, Help displays, and prompting serve as cognitive development tools to aid this process.

While it is desirable that the human-computer interface be so "self-evident" and "intelligent" that people never experience difficulties, this lofty goal will not be achieved in the foreseeable future (Quinn and Russell, 1986). So a great deal of emphasis should be placed on creating good documentation and managing the trouble that does occur. Indeed, a survey by Jereb (1986) found that documentation was the second most important factor influencing the decision to purchase something (quality was first).

Technical information, unlike works of fiction, is seldom read for pleasure. People turn to it only when a question has to be answered. Failure to provide the guidance and assistance needed in learning, answering questions, and problem solving makes it very difficult for the user to recover from trouble on his own and to avoid future trouble by learning from his mistakes. The result is most often more errors and great frustration.

Guidance and assistance is provided through documentation, both hard copy and on-line. Broadly speaking, on-line documentation is every communication provided on-line to help people to do their work effectively. Included are procedure manuals, computer-based training, tutorials, computer-generated messages, and a help facility.

The focus of the next few pages will be on reference information, including prompting and on-line Help. For more information on computer-based training and tutorials, see Charney and Reder (1986) and Dede (1986).

Current problems with documentation.   Wright (1991) feels that poor manuals are usually not the result of stupid and careless writing. Most writers, professional or not, try to communicate their ideas as well as they can. Poor products, however, suggest that being a native speaker of the language is not a sufficient qualification to ensure communicative success. Rather, four other factors contribute to bad design.

First are organizational factors including management decisions concerning who does the writing, product developers, or specialist technical authors. Product developers, by their nature, are more interested in the technical aspects and seldom have time to focus on writing. Another organizational factor is the frequency and nature of the contact between writers and developers. Successful writing requires that frequent contact be maintained between writers and developers. If not, modifications may go undocumented, and functionality may occur that is difficult to explain.

Second is the time scale allocated for the writing process. Successful writing also involves detailed early planning, drafting, testing, and considerable revising. Without adequate time being made available for the writing process, the planning, testing, and revising processes are limited, thereby increasing the potential for a mismatch between the product and its documentation.

Third, there is not yet a clear theoretical rationale about what content should be included in documentation and how this information should be presented. Until this is developed, one cannot be sure that the documentation being developed is the most effective that it can be.

Finally, there are the resources. Adequate resources are needed to include people with different skills in the documentation development process. Required are people good at visual layout, writing, and test and evaluation. Rarely does the same person possess more than one of these skills. Without the proper expertise, documentation will also suffer.

How readers interact with documentation.   Wright (1981, 1988) has suggested that there are three broad stages through which a reader interacts with documentation: finding information that is relevant, understanding what the documentation says, and applying that understanding to the current task in order to solve the problem that prompted them to turn to the documentation.

Finding information is enhanced through use of contents pages and index lists. It is also enhanced if browsing is made easy through clearly visible page headings and subheadings. Pictures and symbols can also be used to draw the reader's attention to particular kinds of information.

Understanding information is achieved through a variety of factors. Included are following good writing principles, many of which will be described in Chapter 4. Understanding can also be maximized through testing and revision of materials as necessary.

Applying information involves reducing the number of inferences that readers must draw. Make all procedures explicit, for example, 1. First, do this . . . , 2. Then, do that . . .

Hard copy versus on-line documentation.   A question frequently asked is whether the system documentation should be hard copy, on-line, or both. Advantages exist for each. On-line documentation is always there and available when needed, can be rapidly accessed, and is difficult to misplace. It is easy to update and guarantees that all users possess the same version. It also does not require workspace for storage.

Its disadvantages include a less familiar format than the traditional manual. It is not as "readable" and is less easy to "browse" in. Less information can be displayed on a "page" at one time. It is not portable and cannot be annotated, written on, or marked in any way. Illustrations may be difficult to include. If the screen is filled with other work, it may require erasing what is being questioned in order to find answers. On-line documentation also requires learning additional commands in order to be effective.

Is on-line documentation or help better than a hard copy manual? The evidence does not always indicate that it is. Several studies have found manuals, or manuals in conjunction with on-line materials, superior to on-line help or documentation alone (Dunsmore, 1980; Watley and Mulford, 1983; and Cohill and Williges, 1985). Shneiderman (1986) reported that people took almost half as long again to use on-line documentation as they did to use the same information in hard-copy form. It appears that the advantages associated with a paper format outweigh those associated with an on-line format.

Is on-line documentation or help better than no hard copy manual? Yes, concluded Cohill and Williges (1985). Task time and errors were reduced when a system version with a help facility was compared to the same system without one.

Is a well-designed help facility better than a poorly designed one? Magers (1983) found that a well-designed one was better. Good writing, task orientation, context sensitivity, and good examples all contribute to a good on-line help.

Does on-line help result in faster problem solving? No, found Czaja et al., (1986) and Elkerton and Williges (1984). Elkerton (1988) suggests that implementation of help or on-line documentation is made difficult by several factors. First, workers tend to be task or goal oriented. Detailed information on how to operate the system to perform a specific task is often lacking, documentation often only referencing commands and functions. Second, people tend to be active learners who learn best by doing rather than by passively reading documentation or training materials. Computer-presented material does not easily keep the user active and involved. Third, current practices in software design consist of iterative design with extensive user testing. Usability problems to be solved through on-line documentation or help cannot be finally resolved until after the user interface is fully implemented. Last, on-line documentation or help is not often viewed as an integral part of interface design. It is often thought of as a remedy for poor design.

In conclusion, the evidence indicates that some kind of on-line help or documentation is necessary. The style, structure, and writing of the materials are crucial to its effectiveness, it should be goal or task oriented, and it should keep the user active. On-line and hard copy documentation should also supplement, not duplicate, each other.

Selective prompting.   Prompting is instructional information. It takes the form of messages or other advice, such as the values to be keyed into a field. Prompting is also the system's way of requesting additional or corrected information, or of guiding users step by step through tasks.

Inexperienced users find prompting a valuable aid in learning a system. Experienced users, however, often find prompting undesirable. It slows them down, then adds "noise" to the screen, and reduces the amount of working information that can be displayed at one time.

Ideally, prompting should be available only as needed. People should be able to selectively or completely turn prompting on or off as needed. As an alternative, two separate sets of screens could be made available, one with prompts, the other without.

Help Facility

The most common form of on-line documentation is the help system. The overall objective of a help facility is to assist people in recalling what to do. Its benefits include improving the usability of a system, providing insurance against design flaws that may develop, and accommodating user differences that may exist (novice vs. expert). Typical methods of invoking help include through a typed command, a help key or pushbutton, or selecting a help option from a multiple-item menu.

Although some studies have found a help system can aid performance (Borenstein, 1985; Magers, 1983), the specific design characteristics that enhance an on-line help are still relatively unknown (Elkerton, 1988; Elkerton and Palmiter, 1991). Elkerton and Palmiter identify three broad areas of help that must be addressed in creating a help: its content, its presentation, and its access mechanisms. Of these, presentation and access are best understood (see Elkerton, 1988; Kearsley, 1988; Wright, 1988). Knowledge about help content, however, is meagre.

Elkerton and Palmiter propose that the content (and structure) of an effective on-line help can be specified using the GOMS model (Card, et al., 1983). Using GOMS, information is provided to the user on GOALS or meaningful tasks, on OPERATORS or actions required to be performed, on METHODS for accomplishing the goals, and where multiple interface methods exist, and on SELECTION RULES for choosing a specific method. Elkerton (1988) presents a set of suggested principles for on-line assistance (which he calls Online Aiding). These principles are reproduced in Table 3-2.

Some general guidelines for help are as follows.

Kind

- Collect data to determine what helps are needed.

Training

- Inform users of availability and purpose of help.

Availability

- Provide availability throughout the dialogue.
- If no help is available for a specific situation, inform the user as such and provide directions to where relevant help may exist.

Structure

- Make as specific as possible.
- Provide a hierarchical framework.
  - — Brief operational definitions and input rules.
  - — Summary explanations in text.
  - — Typical task-oriented examples.

Interaction

- Provide easy accessibility.
- Leave the Help displayed until
  - — the user exits.
  - — the action eliminating the need for help is performed.
- Provide instructions for exiting.
- Return to original position in dialogue when help is completed.

Table 3.2   Suggested design principles for providing on-line advice based on the GOMS model.

Use goals in on-line aiding to do the following:

1.   Describe what can be done in task-oriented terms (interface actions and objects) for improved initial skill learning.

2.   Provide an adjustable level of detail on interface procedures for accommodating the information needs of a wide range of users.

3.   Provide procedurally incomplete advice so that users can actively learn for improved long-term performance and understanding with the interface.

4.   Provide feedback to users that may help in reminding them of appropriate procedures to use particularly when recovering from errors.

5.   Develop modular assistance and instructional dialogues that can be used to describe similar and dissimilar procedural elements of the interface.

Use operators in on-line aiding to do the following:

1.   Describe simple actions, such as pressing specific keys or finding specific objects on the display, that are common to many interface procedures to assist the user in current task performance.

2.   Provide detailed knowledge of interface procedures that inexperienced users can actively learn and that more skilled users can combine with other procedural knowledge to improve long-term performance and understanding of the interface.

3.   Monitor user actions to provide context sensitive help or to actively diagnose user problems.

Use methods in on-line aiding to do the following:

1.   Present step-by-step interface procedures to assist the user with specific problems.

2.   Improve user understanding and acceptance of on-line advice.

3.   Decrease the cognitive load of users who are learning a new interface task by providing an explicit procedure for users to follow.

4.   Provide procedural demonstrations of interface procedures so that users can quickly learn simple operations.

5.   Map sequences of user's actions to a reduced set of interface goals to help provide context-sensitive advice to users.

Use selection rules in on-line aiding to do the following:

1.   Help users select between multiple interface methods.

2.   Provide users with an understanding of representative tasks to increase their knowledge of when to apply specific interface skills.

From Elkerton (1988)

Location

- Minimize obscuring screen content.
- If in a window, position priorities are: right, left, above, and below.

Content

- Minimize the help's length.
- Develop modular dialogues that can be used to describe similar and dissimilar procedural elements of the interface.
- Provide step-by-step interface procedures to assist the user with specific problems.
- Provide procedural demonstrations of interface procedures to aid quick learning of simple operations.
- Provide information to help users select between multiple interface methods.
- Provide users with an understanding of representative tasks to increase their knowledge of when to apply specific skills.

Style

- Provide easy browsing and a distinctive format.
  - Contents screens and indexes.
  - Screen headings and subheadings.
  - Location indicators.
  - Descriptive words in the margin.
  - Visual differentiation of screen components.
  - Emphasized critical information.
- Concise, familiar, action-oriented wording.
- Reference to other materials, when necessary.

Consistency

- Provide a design philosophy consistent with other parts of the system.

Title

- Place the word "Help" in all Help screen titles.

Guidelines for on-line help include:

Kind. Usability problems that exist should be systematically identified through testing and evaluation. Monitoring user actions can be a useful tool in identifying user problems. On-line help can then be developed to address these problems.

Training. Inform users of the availability and purpose of helps. Never assume that it will be obvious.

Availability.   Make help available at all points in the dialogue. It is especially critical that help be available consistently in all similar situations. For example, if one particular system menu has help, assure all menus provide a help. If no help is available for a specific situation, inform the user as such and provide directions to where relevant help may exist, including hard-copy materials.

Structure.   The help response should be as specific as possible, tailored to the task and the user's current position. When accessed, the Help facility should be aware of the kind of difficulties a person is having and respond with relevant information. Only the information necessary to solve the immediate problem or to answer the immediate question should be presented. If the Help facility is unsure of the request, it should work with the user through prompts and questions to resolve the problem.

A help facility should be multilevel, proceeding from very general to successively more detailed and specific explanations to accommodate a wide range of users. The first level should provide brief definitions and rules, simple reminders, and memory joggers sufficient for skilled users. The second level should incorporate more detailed explanations in a textual format. The final, and deepest, level should provide guidance in the form of task-oriented examples.

Interaction.   A help facility should be retrievable simply, quickly, and consistently by either a key action, selection, or command. Leave the Help displayed until the user explicitly exits the Help, or performs the action eliminating the need for help. Instructions for exiting the Help should always be provided. These may take the form of displayed pushbuttons, function keys, or something similar.

Help should not disrupt processing. Easy return to the point of the problem should be permitted. Ideally, the problem or work should be retained on the screen when help is accessed, but this will not always be possible unless the system provides a windowing capability.

One potential danger of the Help facility, as Barnard et al. (1982) found, is that a person's recall of command operations is related to frequency of Help facility access; fewer Help requests were associated with better command recall. The researchers speculate that the availability of Help may become a crutch and lead to less effective retention. People may implement a passive cognitive strategy. A Help facility may influence performance in systematic and subtle ways.

Location.   When a Help is displayed, minimize relevant obscuring screen content. If Help is displayed within a window, position priorities are right, left, above, and below.

Content.   Minimize the Help's length, whenever possible. Carroll, et al., (1986) recommend the development of help text in the form of "minimal manuals." These manuals are explicit and focus on real tasks and activities, and they have been found to be significantly better than traditional help texts (Black et al., 1987; Carroll et al., 1986).

Elkerton (1988) suggests that few Help users want detailed, fact-oriented knowledge such as a hierarchical list showing the syntax of a command. Instead, they want to know the methods to complete a task. Without knowledge of how to do things, users are left to browse through a wealth of information with little understanding of what may be useful. Hence, he recommends, among other things, providing the following features:

- Step-by-step interface procedures to assist the user with specific problems.
- Procedural demonstrations of interface procedures to aid quick learning of simple operations.
- Information to help users select between multiple interface methods.
- Users with an understanding of representative tasks to increase their knowledge of when to apply specific skills.

Wright (1984) recommends that when procedural steps are presented, consecutive numbering will make them easy to follow.

Style.   Provide easy browsing and a distinctive format. Often the exact location of information needed to answer a question cannot be definitely established. Providing information in a format that can be easily skimmed aids the search process and also helps the user become familiar with the information being presented. Techniques that enhance the skimming process are

- contents screens and indexes,
- screen headings and subheadings,
- location indicators,
- descriptive words in the margin,
- visual differentiation of screen components, and
- emphasized critical information.

Wording should also be concise, familiar, and action oriented as described in Chapter 4. Reference to outside material may be included in the Help text, especially if the help information cannot be provided in a concise way.

Consistency.   The help design philosophy should be consistent with the philosophy used in other parts of the system. This includes presentation techniques, style, procedures, and all other aspects.

Title.   For easy identification, place the word "Help" in all Help screen titles.

Considerations in Screen Design

4

A Well-Designed Screen

- reflects the needs and idiosyncrasies of its users
- is developed within the physical constraints imposed by the terminal
- effectively utilizes the capabilities of its software
- achieves the business objectives of the system for which it is designed

---

The considerations integral to screen design are: (1) human, (2) hardware, (3) software, and (4) application.

Human considerations in screen design are the needs and requirements of people. They are oriented toward clarity, meaningfulness, and ease of use. *Hardware and software considerations* reflect the physical constraints of the terminal on which the screen will be used and the characteristics of the controlling program. They provide a framework within which the screen design must occur and define the display techniques available to the designer. *Application considerations* reflect the objectives of the system for which the screen is being designed. They are the data or information building blocks that make up a screen.

A well-designed screen will also be consistent within itself, within related screen formats, and with other screens within the application or organization. If it is used for data entry, it will also be consistent within constraints imposed by related source materials such as worksheets, forms, or manuals.

HUMAN CONSIDERATIONS

Human use of a screen is affected by a variety of design factors that include the format and content of the screen itself, the structure and content of the data or information contained on the screen, the organization of groups of screens, the format and content of related source documents, and the screen keying procedures.

In the following pages some general guidelines concerning the format and content of screens and screen data or information are presented. These broad guidelines are applicable to most kinds of screens. Discussions of source documents, screen groupings, and keying procedures are contained in the chapters detailing rules for specific types of screens, since they are more dependent on screen type. First, however, we will determine what people are looking for in a well-designed screen and present a test that may be applied to a screen to determine how easy it is to use.

Most-Wanted Screen Features

What are people looking for in the design of screens? One organization asked a group of screen users, whose response is summarized as follows:

- an orderly, clean, clutter-free appearance,
- an obvious indication of what is being shown and what should be done with it,
- expected information located where it *should* be,
- a clear indication of what relates to what (headings, field captions, data, instructions, options, and so forth),
- plain, simple English,
- a simple way of finding what is in the system and how to get it out,
- a clear indication of when an action could make a permanent change in the data or system operation.

The desired direction is toward simplicity, clarity, and understandability; these qualities are lacking in many of today's screens.

Screen Format and Content

Clarity, meaningfulness, and ease of use are achieved through the format and content of the screen itself and the information it contains. The format and content of the screen will be determined by where information is placed, how information is structured, and what information is included. The guidelines that follow provide general rules addressing these issues—where, what, and how. Subsequent chapters translate many of these broad guidelines into specific rules for the various types of screens that may be encountered. First, a simple test for good screen design is described.

The Test for a Good Design

Visual clarity is influenced by a number of factors, including information organization, grouping, legibility, and relevancy. Clarity is achieved when display elements are grouped in meaningful and understandable ways, rather than in random and confusing patterns. A simple test for good screen design does exist. A screen that passes this test will have surmounted the first obstacle to effectiveness.

The test. Can all screen elements (field captions, data, title, messages, command field, etc.) be identified without reading the words that make them up? That is, can a component of a screen be identified through cues independent of its content? If this is so, a person's attention can quickly be drawn to the part of the screen that is relevant at that moment. People often look at a screen for a particular reason, perhaps to locate a piece of information such as a customer name, to identify the name of the screen, or to find an instructional or error message. The signal at that moment is that element of interest on the screen. The noise is everything else on the screen. Cues independent of context that differentiate the components of the screen will reduce visual search times and minimize confusion.

Try this test on the front page of your morning newspaper. Where is the headline? A story heading? The weather report? How did you find them? The headline was identified probably by its visually large and bold type size; story headings, again by a type size visually different than other page components; the weather report, probably by its location (bottom right? top left?). Imagine finding the headline on the front page of the newspaper if the same type size and style was used for all components and their positions changed from day to day.

Unfortunately, many of today's screens cannot pass this simple test and are unnecessarily difficult to use. All the tools available to the creator of the newspaper's front page are not yet available to the screen designer. An effective solution can be achieved, however, with the equipment at hand. It simply involves the thoughtful application of the display techniques that exist, consistent locations, and the proper use of "white space."

WHERE TO PLACE INFORMATION ON A SCREEN

- Provide an obvious starting point in the upper left corner of the screen.
- Reserve specific areas of the screen for certain kinds of information, such as commands, error messages, title, and data fields, and maintain these areas consistently on all screens.
- Provide visually pleasing composition, including balance, regularity, symmetry, predictability, economy, sequentiality, unity, proportion, simplicity, and groupings.

Eyeball fixation studies indicate that in looking at displays of information, usually one's eyes move first to the upper left center of the display and then quickly move in a clockwise direction. During and following this movement people are influenced by the symmetrical balance and weight of the titles, graphics, and text of the display. The human perceptual mechanism seeks order and meaning and tries to impose structure when confronted with uncertainty. Whether a screen has meaningful and evident form or is cluttered and unclear is, therefore, immediately discerned. A cluttered or unclear screen requires that some effort be expended in learning and understanding what is presented. The screen user who must deal with the display is forced to spend time to learn and understand. The screen user who has an option concerning whether the screen will or will not be used may reject it at this point if the perceived effort is greater than the perceived gain.

All elements on a screen should be located in a unique and consistent position. The elements of a screen include the following:

- Title
- Screen identifier, or ID
- Screen body, including:
  - Captions
  - Data fields (entry, display, and selection)
  - Section headings
  - Completion aids
  - Prompting messages
- Messages, including:
  - Status, informational, or notification
  - Warning
  - Critical, error, or action
- Command and action techniques
  - Command field
  - Function keys
  - Action/menu bar and pull downs
  - Buttons
  - Icons

The recommended positioning for all but the specific screen body components are described on the pages to follow. The body has considerations unique to the specific kinds of screens and are to be addressed later.

Upper left corner starting point.   Provide an obvious starting point in the upper left corner of the screen. This is near where visual scanning begins and will permit a left-to-right, top-to-bottom reading as is common in Western cultures. Streveler and Wasserman (1984) found that visual targets located in the upper-left quadrant of a screen were found fastest and those located in the lower right took longest to find.

Consistent component locations.   Reserving specific areas of the screen for specific screen elements will aid in memorizing their location. People do tend to have good location memories. Some recommended locations are the following:

Screen title

Upper center, to aid in creating symmetry.

Screen identifier or page number

Upper right-hand corner, a less-frequently used position in most screens. If the screen identifier contains additional reference information (such as date, time, etc.) it may have to be split between the left- and right-hand side for screen balance.

Messages

If a line is allocated, place it at the bottom of the screen just above the command field or function key descriptions. This line will be blank a good portion of the time and will provide a visual break between the command field and/or the function key descriptions. On a 24-line screen, this will normally be line 23. Messages may also be displayed in windows.

Function Key Descriptions and/or Command Field

The bottom line of the screen. The message line serves to break it from the body of the screen. Granda et al. (1982), comparing top and bottom lines of the screen for command field location in a data entry application, found a bottom line location yielded superior performance and a decrease in the number and magnitude of user head movements. The bottom line also maintains sequential top-to-bottom direction flow through the screen.

If both a command field and function key descriptions are included on a screen, display the command field above the function key descriptions.

Action/Menu Bar and Pull Downs

At the top of the screen, just below the title.

Buttons

At the bottom of the screen, below the screen body.

Screen body

The area of the screen between title and message line, usually lines 3 to 22. For captioned data fields the caption should precede the data for reasons to be described shortly. Instructional or prompting information contained within the body of the screen should occur at its logical position in a top-to-bottom progression. Instructions on how to use the screen should precede the data fields or text. Instructions concerning disposition of a completed screen should be at the bottom of the body.

The recommendations found in IBM's SAA CUA are consistent with these recommendations, with one exception. SAA CUA recommends that the Screen ID be located in the upper left corner of the screen. It is the opinion of this writer that this information should not be placed in such a prominent location on a screen.

A formatted screen helps the viewer process information. Guidelines for how to structure and display the screen title, function key descriptions, the command field, and the various kinds of messages follow in this chapter. Similar guidelines for action bars, pull-downs, pushbuttons, and icons are found in Chapters 10 and 11. The layouts of screen bodies are described in the various chapters dealing with these kinds of screens.

Visually Pleasing Composition

A design aesthetic, or visually pleasing composition, is attractive to the eye. It draws attention subliminally, conveying a message clearly and quickly. A lack of visually pleasing composition is disorienting, obscures the intent and meaning, slows one down, and confuses.

The notion of what is artistic has evolved throughout history. Graphic design experts have, through perceptual research, derived a number of principles for what comprises a visually pleasing appearance (Taylor, 1960; Dondis, 1973). These include balance, regularity, symmetry, predictability, economy, sequentiality, unity, proportion simplicity and groupings. Keep in mind that this discussion of visually pleasing composition does not focus on the words on the screen but on the perception of structure created by such concepts as spacing, intensities, and color. It is as if the screen is viewed through "squinted eyes," causing the words themselves to become a blur.

Balance.   Balance, illustrated in Figure 4.1, is a stabilization or equilibrium, a midway center of suspension. The design elements have an equal weight, left to right, top to bottom. The opposite of balance is instability, the design elements seeming ready to topple over. Our discomfort with instability, or imbalance, is reflected every time we straighten a picture hanging askew on the wall.

Dark colors, unusual shapes, and larger objects are "heavier," whereas light colors, regular shapes, and small objects are "lighter." Balance on a screen is accomplished through centering the display itself, maintaining an equal weighting of components on each side of the horizontal and vertical axis, and centering titles and illustrations.

Regularity.   Regularity, illustrated in Figure 4.2, is a uniformity of elements based on some principle or plan. Regularity in screen design is achieved by establishing standard and consistently spaced column and row starting points for display fields. The opposite, irregularity, exists when no such plan or principle is apparent.

Figure 4.1   Balance (vs. instability).

Stabilization or equilibrium. A midway center of suspension.

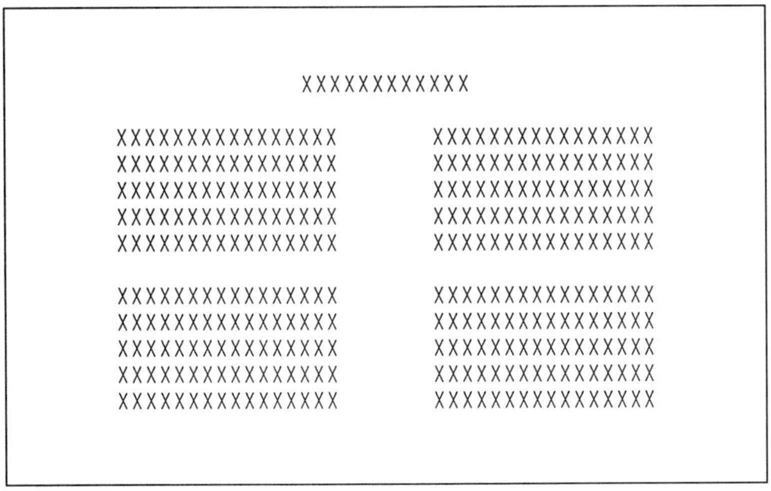

```
                        X X X X X X X X X X X X

        X X X X X X X X X X X X X X          X X X X X X X X X X X X X X
        X X X X X X X X X X X X X X          X X X X X X X X X X X X X X
        X X X X X X X X X X X X X X          X X X X X X X X X X X X X X
        X X X X X X X X X X X X X X          X X X X X X X X X X X X X X
        X X X X X X X X X X X X X X          X X X X X X X X X X X X X X

        X X X X X X X X X X X X X X          X X X X X X X X X X X X X X
        X X X X X X X X X X X X X X          X X X X X X X X X X X X X X
        X X X X X X X X X X X X X X          X X X X X X X X X X X X X X
        X X X X X X X X X X X X X X          X X X X X X X X X X X X X X
        X X X X X X X X X X X X X X          X X X X X X X X X X X X X X
```

BALANCE

```
        X X X X X X X X X X

        X X X X X X X X X X X X X X          X X X X X X X X X X X X X X
        X X X X X X X X X X X X X X          X X X X X X X X X X X X X X
        X X X X X X X X X X X X X X          X X X X X X X X X X X X X X
        X X X X X X X X X X X X X X          X X X X X X X X X X X X X X
        X X X X X X X X X X X X X X          X X X X X X X X X X X X X X
        X X X X X X X X X X X X X X          X X X X X X X X X X X X X X
        X X X X X X X X X X X X X X
        X X X X X X X X X X X X X X
        X X X X X X X X X X X X X X
        X X X X X X X X X X X X X X
        X X X X X X X X X X X X X X
        X X X X X X X X X X X X X X
        X X X X X X X X X X X X X X
        X X X X X X X X X X X X X X
```

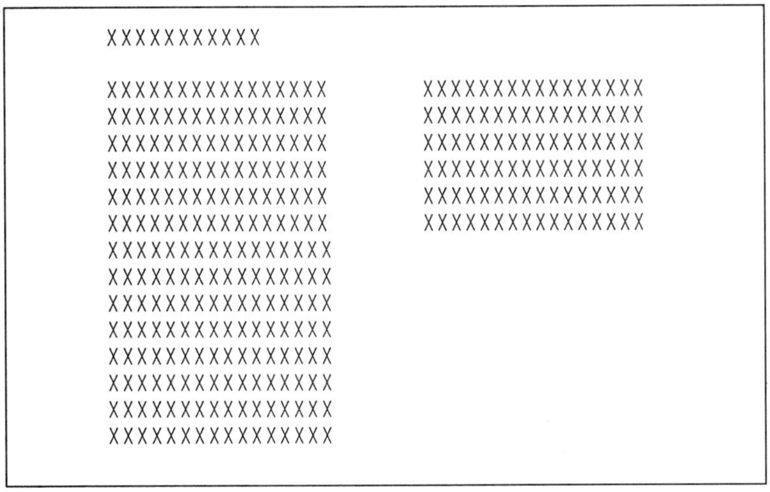

INSTABILITY

Figure 4.2 Regularity (vs. irregularity).

Uniformity of elements based upon some undeviating principle or method.

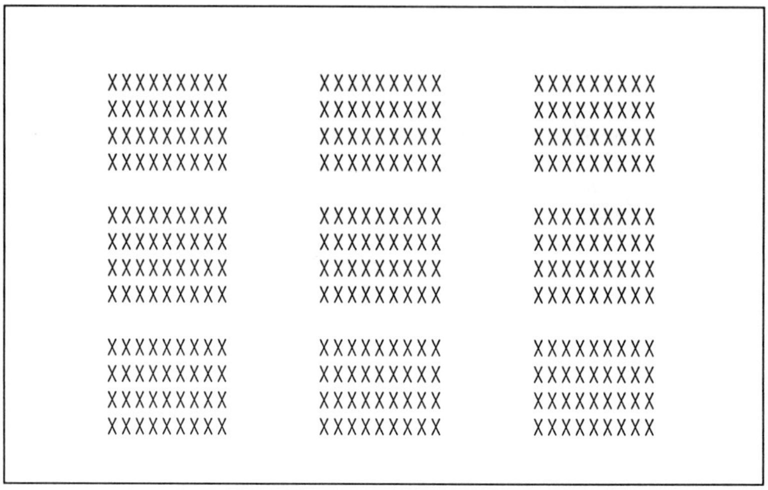

```
XXXXXXXX        XXXXXXXX        XXXXXXXX
XXXXXXXX        XXXXXXXX        XXXXXXXX
XXXXXXXX        XXXXXXXX        XXXXXXXX
XXXXXXXX        XXXXXXXX        XXXXXXXX

XXXXXXXX        XXXXXXXX        XXXXXXXX
XXXXXXXX        XXXXXXXX        XXXXXXXX
XXXXXXXX        XXXXXXXX        XXXXXXXX
XXXXXXXX        XXXXXXXX        XXXXXXXX

XXXXXXXX        XXXXXXXX        XXXXXXXX
XXXXXXXX        XXXXXXXX        XXXXXXXX
XXXXXXXX        XXXXXXXX        XXXXXXXX
XXXXXXXX        XXXXXXXX        XXXXXXXX
```

REGULARITY

```
        XXXXXXXX        XXXXXXXX        XXXXXXXX
        XXXXXXXX        XXXXXXXX        XXXXXXXX
        XXXXXXXX        XXXXXXXX        XXXXXXXX
        XXXXXXXX                        XXXXXXXX
                        XXXXXXXX        XXXXXXXX
XXXXXXXX                XXXXXXXX
XXXXXXXX                XXXXXXXX        XXXXXXXX
XXXXXXXX                XXXXXXXX        XXXXXXXX
                        XXXXXXXX        XXXXXXXX
        XXXXXXXX                        XXXXXXXX
        XXXXXXXX        XXXXXXXX
        XXXXXXXX        XXXXXXXX                XXXXXXXX
        XXXXXXXX        XXXXXXXX                XXXXXXXX
        XXXXXXXX        XXXXXXXX                XXXXXXXX
```

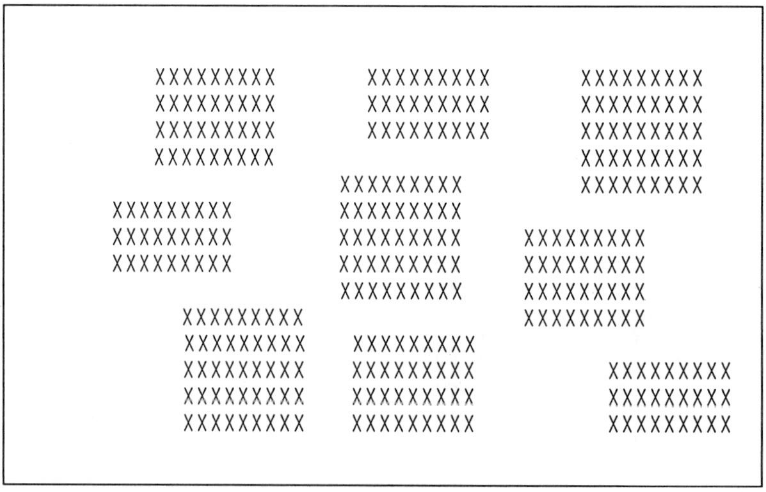

IRREGULARITY

Symmetry.   Symmetry, illustrated in Figure 4.3, is axial duplication: A unit on one side of the center line is exactly replicated on the other side. This exact replication also creates balance, but the difference is that balance can be achieved without symmetry. Symmetry's opposite is asymmetry.

Predictability.   Predictability, illustrated in Figure 4.4, suggests a highly conventional order or plan. Viewing one display enables one to predict how another display will look. Viewing part of a display enables one to predict how the remainder of the display will look. The opposite of predictability—spontaneity—suggests no plan and thus an inability to predict the structure of the remainder of a display or the structure of other displays. In screen design predictability is enhanced through design consistency.

Economy.   Economy, illustrated in Figure 4.5, is the frugal and judicious use of display elements to get the message across as simply as possible. The opposite is intricacy, the use of many elements just because they exist. Intricacy is ornamentation, which often detracts from clarity. Economy in screen design means mobilizing just enough display elements and techniques to communicate the desired message, and no more. The use of color in screens often violates this principle, with displays sometimes taking on the appearance of Christmas trees.

Sequentiality.   Sequentiality, illustrated in Figure 4.6, is a plan of presentation to guide the eye through the screen in a logical, rhythmic order, with the most important information significantly placed. The opposite of sequentiality is randomness, where a flow cannot be detected. The eye tends to move from highly saturated colors to unsaturated colors, from dark to light areas, from big to little objects, and from unusual to usual shapes.

Unity.   Unity, illustrated in Figure 4.7, is coherence, a totality of elements that is visually all one piece. With unity the elements seem to belong together, to dovetail so completely that they are seen as one thing. The opposite of unity is fragmentation, each piece retaining its own character. In screen design similar sizes, shapes, and colors promote unity, as does "white space"—borders at the display boundary.

Proportion.   Displays of greater width than height appear to be more aesthetically pleasing. An old (fifth century B.C.) rule is the Golden Section—the divine division of a line—whereby a length is divided such that the smaller part is to the greater part as the greater part is to the whole. This creates a "golden rectangle" with a ratio of 1:1.618. Several other shapes have also been described as having a mathematical property with aesthetic qualities. These shapes possess height to width ratios ranging from 1:1 to 1:2 (Tufte, 1983).

Figure 4.3 Symmetry (vs. asymmetry).

Axial balance. A unit on one side of the center line is replicated on the other side.

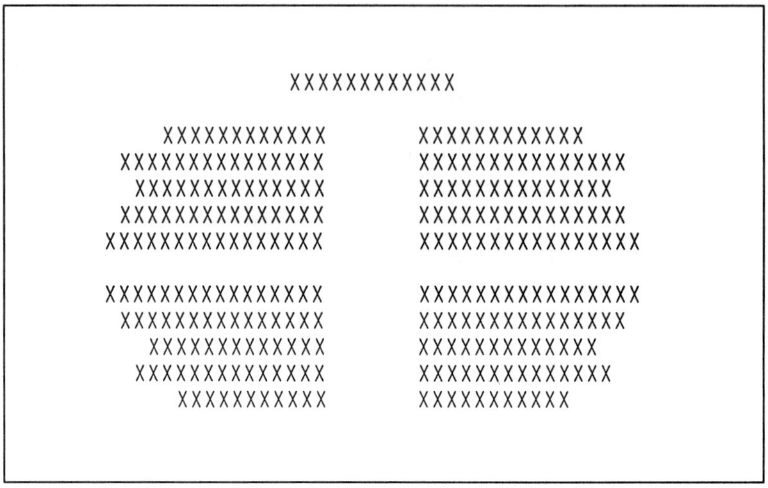

```
                    XXXXXXXXXXX

          XXXXXXXXXXXX          XXXXXXXXXXXX
        XXXXXXXXXXXXXX          XXXXXXXXXXXXXX
          XXXXXXXXXXXX          XXXXXXXXXXXX
          XXXXXXXXXXXX          XXXXXXXXXXXX
        XXXXXXXXXXXXXX          XXXXXXXXXXXXXX

        XXXXXXXXXXXXXX          XXXXXXXXXXXXXX
        XXXXXXXXXXXXXX          XXXXXXXXXXXXXX
          XXXXXXXXXXXX          XXXXXXXXXXXX
          XXXXXXXXXXXX          XXXXXXXXXXXX
            XXXXXXXXXXX          XXXXXXXXXXX
```

SYMMETRY

```
    XXXXXXXXXXX

    XXXXXXXXXXXX
    XXXXXXXXXXXXXX
    XXXXXXXXXXXX
    XXXXXXXXXXXXX          XXXXXXXXXXXX
    XXXXXXXXXXXXXX
    XXXXXXXXXXXXXXXX      XXXXXXXXX
    XXXXXXXXXXX
    XXXXXXXXXXXXXX          XXXXXXXXXXXX
      XXXXXXXXXXXXX
    XXXXXXXXXXXXXX        XXXXXXXXXX
      XXXXXXXXXXXX
    XXXXXXXXXXXXXX        XXXXXXXXXXXXXX
    XXXXXXXXXXXXXXX
    XXXXXXXXXXXXXX        XXXXXXXXXXXXXX
```

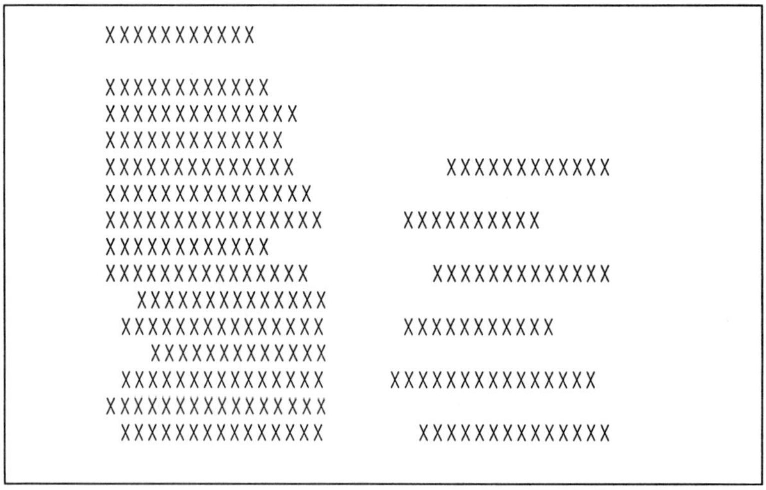

ASYMMETRY

Figure 4.4   Predictability (vs. spontaneity).

An order or plan that is highly conventional and consistent.

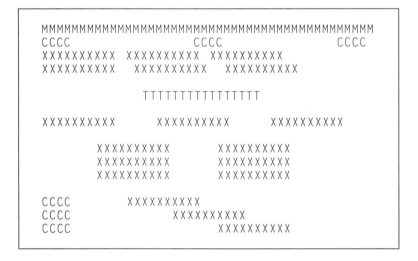

PREDICTABILITY

SPONTANEITY

Figure 4.5 Economy (vs. intricacy).

A visual arrangement that is frugal and judicious in the utilization of elements.

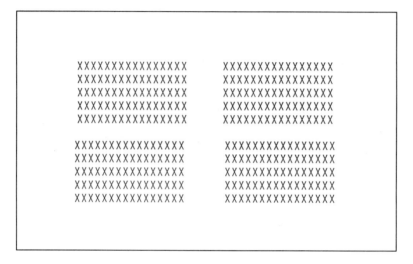

ECONOMY

INTRICACY

Figure 4.6   Sequentiality (vs. randomness).

A systematic, logical, and obvious ordering, usually a rhythmic pattern.

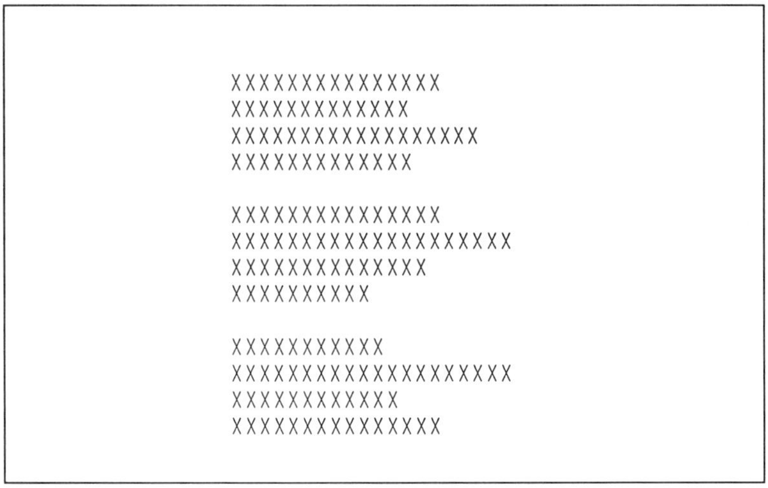

```
                XXXXXXXXXXXXXXX
                XXXXXXXXXXXXX
                XXXXXXXXXXXXXXXXXX
                XXXXXXXXXXXXX

                XXXXXXXXXXXXXXX
                XXXXXXXXXXXXXXXXXXXX
                XXXXXXXXXXXXX
                XXXXXXXXX

                XXXXXXXXXXX
                XXXXXXXXXXXXXXXXXXXXX
                XXXXXXXXXXX
                XXXXXXXXXXXXXX
```

SEQUENTIALITY

```
              XXXXXXXXXXXXXX

        XXXXXXXXXXXXX      XXXXXXXXXXXXXXXXX
                              XXXXXXXXXXXX
                              XXXXXXXXXXXX
        XXXXXXXXXXXXXXXXXXXXX

              XXXXXXXXXXXXX
        XXXXXXXXX
                                    XXXXXXXXXX
        XXXXXXXXXXXXXXXXXXXXX    XXXXXXXXXX

              XXXXXXXXXXXXX
```

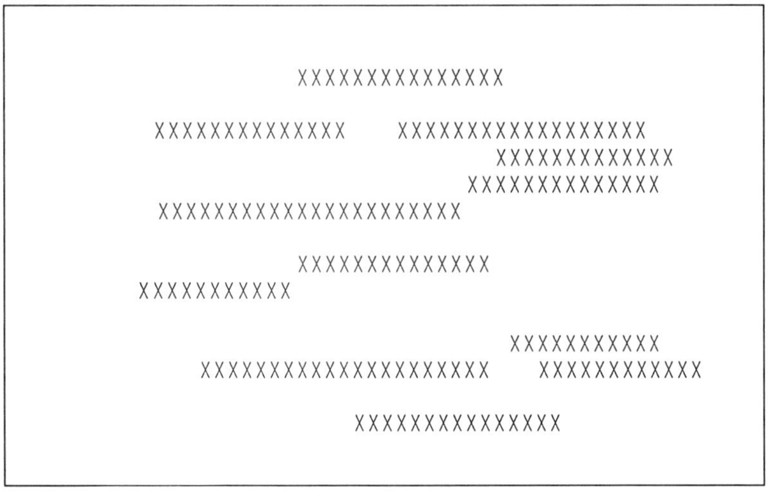

RANDOMNESS

Figure 4.7   Unity (vs. fragmentation).

The proper balance of all elements into a totality that is visually all one piece.

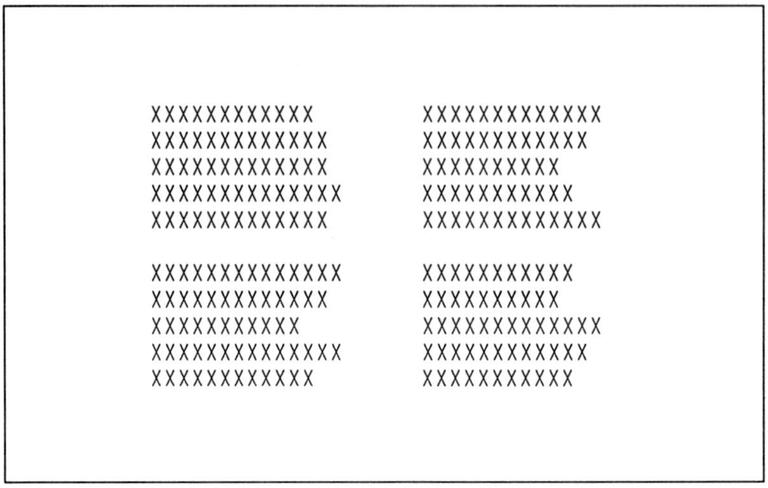

```
        XXXXXXXXXXXX          XXXXXXXXXXXXX
        XXXXXXXXXXXXX         XXXXXXXXXXXX
        XXXXXXXXXXXXX         XXXXXXXXXX
        XXXXXXXXXXXXXX        XXXXXXXXXXX
        XXXXXXXXXXXXX         XXXXXXXXXXXXX

        XXXXXXXXXXXXXX        XXXXXXXXXXX
        XXXXXXXXXXXXX         XXXXXXXXXX
        XXXXXXXXXXX           XXXXXXXXXXXXX
        XXXXXXXXXXXXXX        XXXXXXXXXXXX
        XXXXXXXXXXXX          XXXXXXXXXX
```

UNITY

```
XXXXXXXXXXXX                            XXXXXXXXXXXX
XXXXXXXXXXXXX                           XXXXXXXXXX
XXXXXXXXXXXXX                           XXXXXXXX
XXXXXXXXXXXXXX                          XXXXXXXXXX
XXXXXXXXXXXXX                           XXXXXXXXXXXX



XXXXXXXXXXXXXX                          XXXXXXXXXX
XXXXXXXXXXXXX                           XXXXXXXXX
XXXXXXXXXXX                             XXXXXXXXXXXX
XXXXXXXXXXXXXX                          XXXXXXXXXX
XXXXXXXXXXXX                            XXXXXXXXX
```

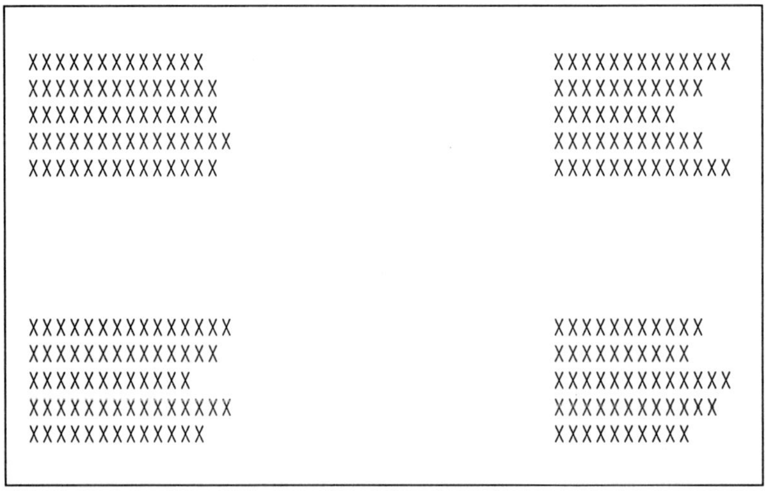

FRAGMENTATION

Simplicity (Complexity)

- Optimize the number of elements on a screen, within limits of clarity.
- Minimize the alignment points, especially horizontal or columnar.

Simplicity. Simplicity, illustrated in Figure 4.8, is directness and singleness of form, a combination of elements that results in ease in comprehending the meaning of a pattern. The opposite pole on the continuum is complexity. The scale created may also be considered a scale of complexity, with extreme complexity at one end and minimal complexity at the other.

Tullis (1983) has derived a measure of screen complexity based on the work of Bonsiepe (1968), who proposed a method of measuring the complexity of typographically designed pages through the application of information theory (Shannon and Weaver, 1949). This measure involves the following steps:

1. Draw a rectangle around each field on the screen, including captions, data, title, etc.;
2. Count the number of fields and horizontal alignment points (the number of columns in which a field, inscribed by a rectangle, starts);
3. Count the number of fields and vertical alignment points (the number of rows in which a field, inscribed by a rectangle, starts).

This has been done for the screens illustrated in Figures 4.9 and 4.10. These screens are examples from the earlier study by Tullis (1981) described in the introduction. They are an original inquiry screen (Figure 4.9) from the screens whose mean search time was 8.3 seconds, and a redesigned screen (Figure 4.10) from the screens whose mean search time was 5.0 seconds. A complexity calculation using information-theory for each screen is as follows:

- Figure 4.9 (original):
  - 22 fields with 6 horizontal (column) alignment points = 41 bits
  - 22 fields with 20 vertical (row) alignment points = 93 bits
  - Overall complexity = 134 bits
- Figure 4.10 (redesigned):
  - 18 fields with 7 horizontal (column) alignment points = 43 bits
  - 18 fields with 8 vertical (row) alignment points = 53 bits
  - Overall complexity = 96 bits

The redesigned screen is thus about 28 percent simpler than the original screen.

An easier method of calculation, yielding similar results, is to count the following: 1) the number of fields on the screen, 2) the number of horizontal

Figure 4.8   Simplicity (vs. complexity).

- A directness and singleness of form.
- Based upon knowledge of location of some elements, the location of others should be predictable.
- Complexity is a combination of elements that results in difficulties in establishing meaning in the pattern.

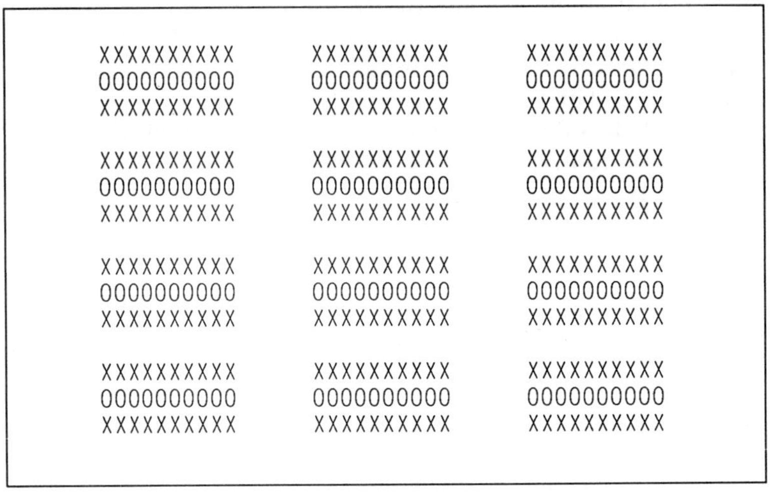

```
XXXXXXXXXX     XXXXXXXXXX     XXXXXXXXXX
0000000000     0000000000     0000000000
XXXXXXXXXX     XXXXXXXXXX     XXXXXXXXXX

XXXXXXXXXX     XXXXXXXXXX     XXXXXXXXXX
0000000000     0000000000     0000000000
XXXXXXXXXX     XXXXXXXXXX     XXXXXXXXXX

XXXXXXXXXX     XXXXXXXXXX     XXXXXXXXXX
0000000000     0000000000     0000000000
XXXXXXXXXX     XXXXXXXXXX     XXXXXXXXXX

XXXXXXXXXX     XXXXXXXXXX     XXXXXXXXXX
0000000000     0000000000     0000000000
XXXXXXXXXX     XXXXXXXXXX     XXXXXXXXXX
```

SIMPLICITY

```
    XXXXXXXXXX   XXXXXXXXXX    0000000000
    XXXXXXXXXX        0000000000      0000000000
    XXXXXXXXXX             XXXXXXXXXX
      XXXXXXXXXX
    0000000000         XXXXXXXXXX        0000000000
                       XXXXXXXXXX   XXXXXXXXXX
    XXXXXXXXXX   XXXXXXXXXX
                            XXXXXXXXXX
    0000000000
    XXXXXXXXXX                              XXXXXXXXXX
         XXXXXXXXXX        XXXXXXXXXX
      0000000000        0000000000     0000000000
    XXXXXXXXXXX                     XXXXXXXXXX
              XXXXXXXXXX          XXXXXXXXXX
    XXXXXXXXXX   XXXXXXXXXX     XXXXXXXXXX
    0000000000 0000000000 0000000000   XXXXXXXXXX
```

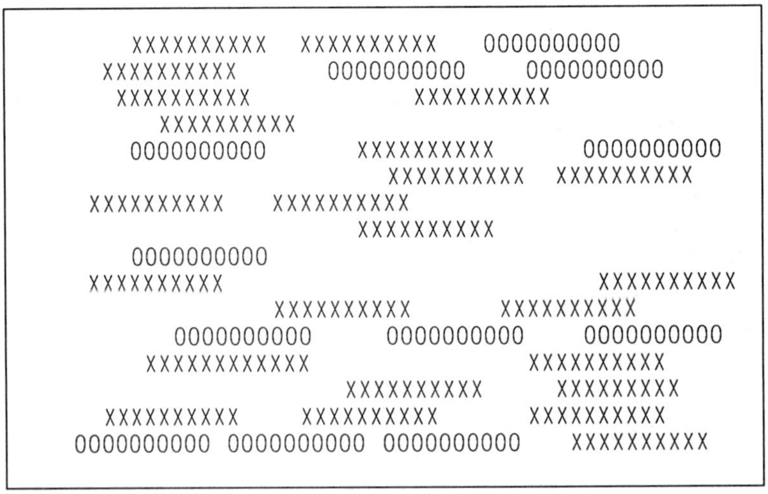

COMPLEXITY

Figure 4.9   Original screen, from Tullis (1981) with title, captions, and data inscribed by rectangles.

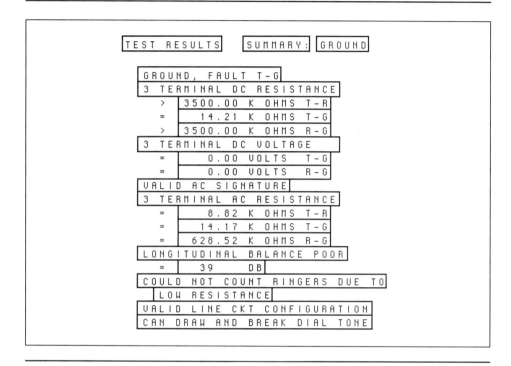

Figure 4.10   Redesigned screen, from Tullis (1981) with title, captions, and data inscribed by rectangles.

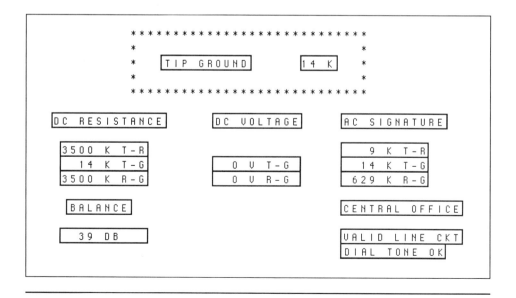

(column) alignment points, and 3) the number of vertical (row) alignment points. The sums for the original and redesigned screens are

- Figure 4.9 (original):
    - 22 fields
    - 6 horizontal (column) alignment points
    - 20 vertical (row) alignment points
    - 48 = complexity
- Figure 4.10 (redesigned):
    - 18 fields
    - 7 horizontal (column) alignment points
    - 8 vertical (row) alignment points
    - 33 = complexity

By this calculation the redesigned screen is about 31 percent simpler than the original screen.

Complexity.   By both calculations the redesigned screen has a lower complexity measure than the original screen. In the Tullis (1981) study the redesigned and faster-to-use screens had lower complexity measures. This leads to the following complexity guidelines:

- Optimize the number of elements on a screen, within limits of clarity.
- Minimize the alignment points, especially horizontal or columnar.

Obviously, the way to minimize screen complexity is to reduce the number of fields displayed. Fewer fields will yield lower complexity measures. This is unrealistic, however, since ultimate simplicity means nothing is there, which obviously does not accomplish very much. Indeed, Vitz (1966) has found that people have subjective preferences for the right amount of information, and too little is as bad as too much. The practical answer, then, is to optimize the amount of information displayed, within limits of clarity. What is optimum must be considered in light of guidelines to follow, so a final judgment must be postponed.

What can be done, however, is to minimize alignment points, most importantly horizontal or columnar alignment points. Fewer alignment points will have a strong positive influence on the complexity calculation. Tullis (1983) has also found, in a follow-up study of some other screens, that fewer alignment points were among the strongest influences creating positive viewer feelings of visually pleasing composition.

Groupings

- Organize the screen into functional, semantic groups.
- Provide "spatial" groupings, conforming to visual "chunks":
    - leave space lines about every 5 rows, but not exceeding 7 rows;

— confine line widths to about 11 to 15 characters;
— the space between groups should be less than the margins.

Grouping.   Grouping elements on a screen aids in establishing structure and meaningful form. In addition to providing aesthetic appeal, grouping has been found to aid recall (Card, 1982) and result in a faster screen search (Dodson and Shields, 1978; Haubner and Neumann, 1986; Tullis, 1983; Triesman, 1982).

The perceptual principles of proximity, closure, similarity and matching patterns foster visual groupings. But the search for a more objective definition of what constitutes a group has gone on for years. Tullis, in his 1981 study, described an objective method for establishing groups, based on the work of Zahn (1971) using the Gestalt psychologists' law of proximity. For the Tullis (1981) screens shown in Figures 4.9 and 4.10:

1. Compute the mean distance between each character and its nearest neighbor. Use a character distance of 1 between characters adjacent horizontally and 2 between characters adjacent vertically (between rows).
2. Multiply the mean distance derived by 2.
3. Connect with a line any character pair that is closer than the distance established in step 2.

Figure 4.11 Original screen, from Tullis (1981) with grouping indicated.

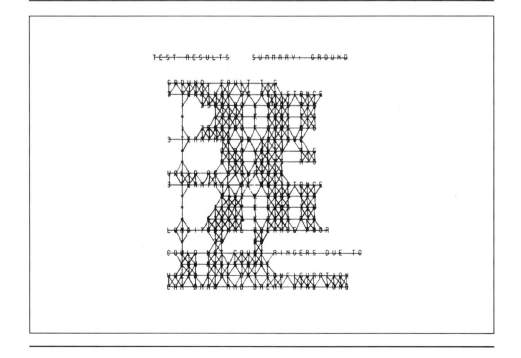

Figure 4.12 Redesigned screen, from Tullis (1981) with grouping indicated.

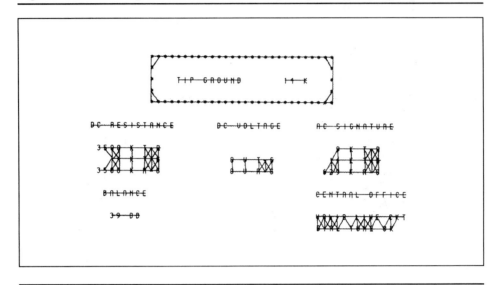

This has been done for these inquiry screens, as illustrated in Figures 4.11 and 4.12.

- Figure 4.11 (original):
  — Mean distance between characters = 1.05
  — Twice mean distance = 2.10
  — A line is drawn between characters 1 or 2 apart, not 3 or more
  — Resulting number of groups = 3
- Figure 4.12 (redesigned):
  — Mean distance between characters = 1.09
  — Twice mean distance = 2.18
  — A line is drawn between characters 1 or 2 apart, not 3 or more
  — Resulting number of groups = 13

A simplification of this formula involves doing the following. Connect with a line all characters on the screen separated by no more than one space horizontally and no blank lines vertically. Groupings will become immediately obvious.

Another grouping measure was calculated by Tullis: the average size of each screen's group. The average size of the 3 groups in the original screen is 13.3 degrees, whereas the 13 groups on the redesigned screen average 5.2 degrees. The redesigned screen group size, interestingly, closely matches the 5-degree visual acuity screen chunk described in Chapter 3. It seems that groups 5 degrees or less in size can be scanned with one eye fixation per group. Therefore screens with these size groupings can be searched faster. Groupings larger than 5 degrees require more eye fixations per grouping, slowing down screen scanning time. So, in addition to complexity the Tullis redesigned screens differ from the original screens by some grouping measures. The more effective redesigned screens have a greater number of smaller size groups.

Tullis, in his 1983 follow-up study, also found that groupings were the strongest determinant of a screen's visual search time. If the size of a group on a screen increased, or the number of groups increased, search time also increased. Number and size of groups have an opposite relationship, however; if the number increases, size usually decreases. If the size increases, number usually decreases. What proves to be most effective is a middle-ground solution—a medium number of medium-sized groups.

Based upon this and other research, the grouping guidelines described above are presented.

Functional, semantic groups are those that make sense to the user. Related information should be displayed together. A logical place to "break" a screen is between functional groups of information, but a massive grouping of information should be broken up into smaller groups. The most reasonable point is every five rows. A six- or seven-row grouping may be displayed without a break, if necessary, but do not exceed seven rows.

The 11- to 15-character width limitation must take into consideration the data to be displayed. Confining data to this width makes no sense if it thus suffers a reduction in legibility. Legibility and comprehension are most important.

To give unity to a display, the space between groups should be less than that of the margins. Fortunately, most cathode ray tubes have a fairly wide built-in margin. The most common and obvious way to achieve spacing is through white or blank space, but there are other ways. Alternatives include contrasting display features such as differing intensity levels, image reversals (dark characters on a light background versus light characters on a dark background), borders and color. Spacing, however, appears to be stronger than color. Two studies (Haubner and Benz, 1983; Haubner and Neumann, 1986) found that adequate spacing, not color, is a more important determinant of ease of use for uncluttered, highly structured inquiry screens.

Perceptual Principles and Functional Grouping

- Use visual organization to create functional groupings.
  - — Proximity: 000   000   000
  - — Similarity: AAABBBCCC
  - — Closure: [ ]   [ ]   [ ]
  - — Matching patterns: >>   < >

- Combine visual organization principles in logical ways.
  - — Proximity and similarity: AAA   BBB   CCC
  - — Proximity and closure: []   []   []

—Matching patterns and closure: ( )   < >   { }
—Proximity and ordering: 1234   1   5
                                                2   6
                                       5678   3   7
                                                4   8

- Avoid visual organization principles that conflict.
    —Proximity opposing similarity: AAA   ABB   BBC   CCC
    —Proximity opposing closure:] [   ] [   ] [
    —Proximity opposing ordering: 1357   1   2
                                                 3   4
                                        2468   5   6
                                                 6   8

Perceptual principles can be used to aid screen functional groupings.

Use visual organization to create functional grouping.   The most common perceptual principle used in screen design to aid visual groupings has been the proximity principle. The incorporation of adequate spacing between groups of related elements enhances the "togetherness" of each grouping. Space should always be considered a design component of a screen. The objective should never be to get rid of it.

The similarity principle can be used to call attention to various groupings through displaying them in a different intensity, font style, or color. The closure and matching patterns principles involve using lines, borders, and unique symbols to identify and relate common information.

Combine visual organization principles in logical ways.   Visual organization principles can be combined to enhance groupings. Proximity, being a very strong perceptual principle, can guide the eye through an array of information to be scanned in a particular direction. Scanning direction can also be made obvious through similarity (color, intensity, etc.) or matching patterns (lines or borders).

Avoid visual organization principles that conflict.   Principles may not always be compatible, however. When incompatibilities are encountered by the viewer confusion results. In the examples above proximity destroys similarity, proximity overwhelms closure, and proximity overwhelms logical ordering.

Grouping Using Borders and Backgrounds

- Consider incorporating line borders for relating groups of related information.

— Broken lines using standard keyboard keys.

```
------------------------
========================
```

— Solid lines.

— Do not exceed three line thicknesses or two line styles on a screen, however.
• Consider incorporating a screened background for related information.
— The background should not have the "emphasis" of the screen component that should be attended to. Consider about a 25 percent gray screening.
— Reserve higher contrast or "emphasized" shades for screen components to which attention should be drawn.
• Consider incorporating a different color background for related information. (See Chapter 10, Color in Screen Design.)

Line borders can greatly enhance groupings of information and direct the viewer's eye in the required direction of information scanning. Thacker (1987) found that displayed information with a border around it was reported to be easier to read, better in appearance, and preferable. On simple alphanumeric terminals, a row of dashes (– – –) or equal signs (= = =) can create a horizontal line. Vertical lines can be established using keys displaying solid (|) or broken (¦) lines. Avoid using asterisks for lines as they are too heavy visually. On a graphics terminal, solid lines can easily be created. Avoid too much use of lines, or too many kinds of lines, however, as they can cause visual clutter.

On monochromatic terminals, screened backgrounds for related elements can highlight the needed groupings. Care must be taken, however, that the background does not visually detract from the information of interest on the screen. Figure 4.13 illustrates a background detracting from the data because of the ragged-right edge created. In Figure 4.14 the attention-getting, ragged-right side is eliminated, allowing attention to be more easily directed to the information needed or presented.

Figure 4.13   Background with ragged-right edge.

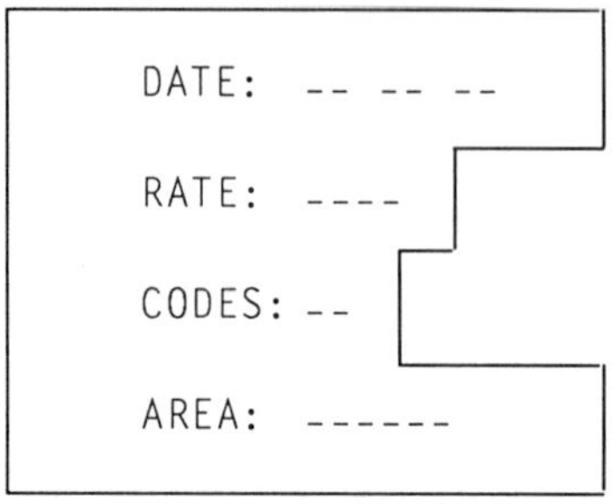

```
DATE:   __ __ __

RATE:   ____

CODES: __

AREA:   _____
```

Figure 4.14   "Blocked" background.

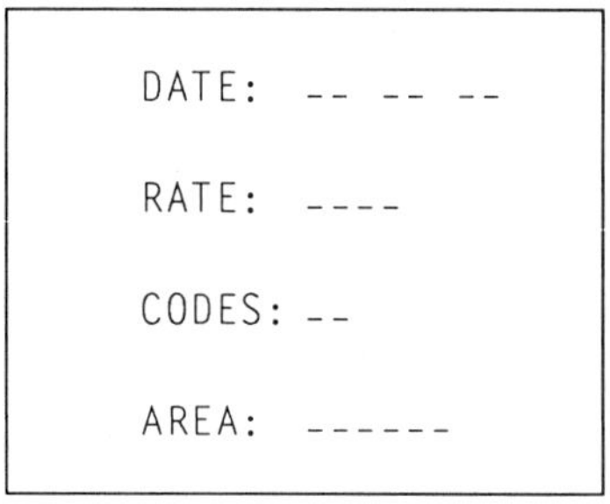

```
DATE:   __ __ __

RATE:   ____

CODES: __

AREA:   _____
```

Color backgrounds can also be incorporated into screens. Care must be exercised in choosing the right background and foreground colors, however. Effective use of color will be addressed in Chapter 10.

WHAT INFORMATION TO PLACE ON A SCREEN

- Provide only information that is essential to making a decision or performing an action. Do not flood a user with information.
- Provide all data related to one task on a single screen. The user should not have to remember data from one screen to the next.
- Maintain overall density levels of less than about 25 to 30 percent.

What information to place on a screen requires a determination of how much should be there.

Screens should provide only relevant information because the more infor-mation, the greater the competition among the screen components for a person's attention. Visual search times will be longer and meaningful patterns more difficult to perceive if the screens "flood" a viewer with too much information.

Providing all related data on a single screen will reduce the memory load on the user—an obvious benefit.

Density

An objective measure of "how much" is density. Density, by definition, is a calculation of the proportion of display character positions in the screen, or an area of the screen containing something.

Density is clearly related to complexity, for both measure "how much is there." Complexity looks at fields, density at characters, so they should rise and fall together.

In general, studies show that increasing the density of a display increases the time and errors in finding information (Callan et al., 1977; Dodson and Shields, 1978; Triesman, 1982). There are actually two types of density to be calculated on a screen: overall and local.

Overall density is a measure of the percentage of character positions on the entire screen containing data. Danchak (1976) stated that density (loading, as he called it) should not exceed 25 percent. Reporting the results of a qualitative judgment of "good" screens, he found their density was on the order of 15 percent. Tullis, in his 1981 study, reported that the density of screens from an up and running successful system ranged from 0.9 to 27.9 percent, with a mean of 14.2 percent. Using this and other research data, he concluded that the common upper-density limit appears to be on the order of 25 percent.

Thacker (1987) compared screens with densities of 14 percent, 29 percent, and 43 percent. Response time increased significantly as screen density increased. He found, however, that the time increase between 14 percent and 29 percent was much smaller than the time increase between 29 percent and 43 percent. He also found increased error rates with greater density, the 43 percent density screens showing significantly more errors.

Local density is a measure of how "tightly packed" the screen is. A measure of local density derived by Tullis is the percentage of characters in the 88-character visual acuity circle described in Chapter 3, modified by the weighting factors illustrated below.

```
       012222210
     0123445443210
   023456777654320
   1235679+9765321
   023456777654320
     0123445443210
       012222210
```

For every character on the screen, a local density is calculated using the above weighting factors, and then an average for all characters on the screen is established.

Figures 4.15 and 4.16 are the original and redesigned screens from the 1981 Tullis study again. Density measures for these screens are:

- Figure 4.15 (original):
  - overall density = 17.9 percent
  - local density = 58.0 percent

- Figure 4.16 (redesigned):
  - overall density = 10.8 percent
  - local density = 35.6 percent

In both cases the more effective redesigned screen had lower density measures. In his 1983 follow-up study, Tullis found a lower local density to be the most important characteristic creating a positive "visually pleasing" feeling.

The research does suggest some density guidelines for screens. Maintain

Figure 4.15   Original screen, from Tullis (1981).

```
          TEST RESULTS    SUMMARY: GROUND

          GROUND, FAULT T-G
          3 TERMINAL DC RESISTANCE
             >  3500.00 K OHMS T-R
             =    14.21 K OHMS T-G
             >  3500.00 K OHMS R-G
          3 TERMINAL DC VOLTAGE
             =     0.00 VOLTS  T-G
             =     0.00 VOLTS  R-G
          VALID RC SIGNATURE
          3 TERMINAL RC RESISTANCE
             =     8.82 K OHMS T-R
             =    14.17 K OHMS T-G
             =   628.52 K OHMS R-G
          LONGITUDINAL BALANCE POOR
             =    39    DB
          COULD NOT COUNT RINGERS DUE TO
             LOW RESISTANCE
          VALID LINE CKT CONFIGURATION
          CAN DRAW AND BREAK DIAL TONE
```

Figure 4.16   Redesigned screen, from Tullis (1981).

```
        *********************************
        *                               *
        *      TIP GROUND      14 K      *
        *                               *
        *********************************


    DC RESISTANCE         DC VOLTAGE         AC SIGNATURE

      3500 K T-R                                 9 K T-R
        14 K T-G            0 V T-G              14 K T-G
      3500 K R-G            0 V R-G             629 K R-G


       BALANCE                               CENTRAL OFFICE

        39 DB                                VALID LINE CKT
                                             DIAL TONE OK
```

overall density levels no higher than 25 to 30 percent. This upper overall density recommendation should be interpreted with extreme care. Density, by itself, does not affect whether or not what is displayed "makes sense." This is a completely different question. Density can always be reduced through substituting abbreviations for whole words. The cost of low density may be illegibility and poorer comprehension. Indeed, poorly designed screens have been redesigned to achieve greater clarity and have actually ended up with higher density measures than the original versions. How it all "hangs together" can never be divorced from how much is there.

A screen with an overall density of 30 percent is illustrated in Figure 4.17.

HOW TO PLACE INFORMATION ON A SCREEN

Following are general guidelines for how to place information on screens. They include some general considerations: the use of case—upper and mixed, words, text and special symbols, captions and data, messages, the command field, and function keys.

Figure 4.17 An overall density of 30 percent.

```
                                                              XXXXX
                        XXXXXXXXXX

XXXX:          00000000000         XXXXXXX:         00000000000
XXXXXXX:       0000000000000       XXXXXXXXXXX:     00
XXXX:          000000              XXXXXXXXXXXXXXX:  0000
XXXXXXXXXXXX:  00000000000000      XXXXXX:          0000000
XXXXXXXXX:     000000000           XXX:             000

XXXXX:         000000000           XXXX:            00000000000
XXXXXXXXXXX:   00                  XXXXXXXXXXXX:     000000000
XXXXXXXXX:     00000000000000      XXXXXXXX:        000
XXXXXXXXXXXX:  000                 XXXXXXXX:        000000
XXX:           0000                XXXXXXXXXX:      000000000000

XXXXXXXXXXXX:  0000000000          XXXXXX:          000000000
XXXXXXXXX:     00000               XXXXXXXXXX:      000000000000
XXXXXXXXXX:    00                  XXXXX:           0000
XXXXXX:        000000              XXXX:            0000000000000
```

General

- Present information in a directly usable form. Do not require reference to documentation, translations, transpositions, interpolations, etc.
- Use contrasting display features (different intensities and character sizes, underlining, reverse images, etc.) to call attention to:
  — different screen components,
  — items being operated upon, and
  — urgent items.
- Guide a user through the screen with implicit or explicit lines formed by display elements.
- Make visual appearance and procedural usage consistent.

Screen information should be presented in a directly usable form. Reference to documentation for interpretation should never be required. Contrasting display features should be used to call attention to different screen components, items being operated upon, or urgent items. Features chosen should aid in screen component identification so that attention may be quickly and accurately focused. Some recommended uses of display features are found in the following section on software considerations.

The eye should be guided horizontally or vertically through the screen, with lines formed through use of white space and display elements. More complex movements may require the aid of display contrasts. Eye movement direction may also be communicated to the viewer through the actual drawing of horizontal and vertical lines. This is an effective technique in situations where a great deal of information must be displayed on a single screen. Display methods chosen should be consistent in visual appearance and procedural usage.

Upper- and Mixed-Case Font

- Use mixed case for:
  - Text
  - Messages
  - Action/menu bar actions
  - Button descriptions
  - Screen ID
- Use upper case or capitalization for:
  - Title
  - Section headings
- Use either upper or lower case for:
  - Subsection headings
  - Captions
  - Data
  - Completion aids
  - Function key descriptions
  - Command field caption

The screen designer often has the choice of whether to display screen components in mixed-case or upper-case letters. Upper-case means all capital letters. Mixed case usually implies a predominance of lower-case letters with occasional capitalization as needed (initial letter of first word, acronyms, abbreviations, proper nouns, etc.).

The research on textual material is clear. For example, Tinker (1955), in a study of reading from hard-copy materials, found that mixed-case text is read significantly faster than upper-case text. Rehe (1974) found a 13 percent advantage in reading speed for mixed-case text. Moskel et al. (1984) found even larger advantages of mixed-case text compared to upper case in comprehension and reading of screen materials. The advantage of mixed-case text is that it gives a word a more distinctive shape. Upper-case letters are all the same height; lower-case letters have different heights. These differences aid comprehension.

The research on screen captions, however, leans another direction. Vartabedian (1974) established that screens with captions containing upper-case characters are searched faster than those using mixed-case characters. Williams (1988) found identical results with menu choice descriptions.

Why this difference? The materials finding superiority for mixed-case appear to be of a longer textual-style nature. The caption materials appear to be single words or short phrases. It may be that the superiority of mixed case does not exhibit itself until text of an extended nature is read. Why short upper-case captions were actually superior to mixed case is unknown. In light of this research, the following is recommended.

Use mixed-case for text, messages, action bar actions, and pull-downs, pushbuttons, and the screen identifier. Text and messages in mixed case reflects the years of research on readability. The action/menu bar in mixed case will provide contrast with the nearby upper-case title.

Buttons in mixed case will provide case compatibility with the component of similar function, the action bar. The screen ID in mixed case will deemphasize it slightly in relation to the screen title.

Use upper case for the title and section headings. Both will be emphasized, but not overly so.

The remainder of the screen elements may be displayed either way. Short captions in upper case may have some advantages according to the research. Displaying them in mixed case, however, will aid differentiating them from section headings. Longer, more narrative-style captions would probably benefit from mixed case. Data is easier to key in upper case and would contrast better with mixed-case captions. Larger data elements would be more recognizable in mixed case. Function key descriptions and the command field in mixed case provide usage compatibility with the similar action bar and pushbuttons. Function key descriptions and the command field in upper case, however, provide better differentiation with adjacent messages.

IBM's SAA CUA Design Guides present everything in mixed case, as illustrated in Figure 4.18. That this is an extrapolation of the textual reading research to all written words can only be assumed. What the guide seems to forget, however, is that the mydrid of printed materials we see entirely in mixed case also benefits from different type sizes, styles, and boldnesses. Many screens do not yet have all the capabilities. Screen component visual differentiation needs capitalization (and research does not discount it). Compare Figure 4.18 with Figure 4.19. Capitalization of the title and section headings on Figure 4.19 aids component differentiation.

Mixed-Case Captions

• When using mixed-case captions, capitalize the first letter of each significant word.

When mixed-case field captions are used, capitalize the first letter of each significant word. A caption is not a sentence but the name for an area into

Figure 4.18   SAA CUA design guide screen example.

```
                    Change Session Profile

Type information.   Then press Enter.

   Security Control
      PC password . . . . . . . . . .  _____
      VM password . . . . . . . . . .  _____
      Local area network password . . .  _____

   Printers
      PC printer port . . . . . . . . .  _
      VM printer address . . . . . . .  _____

   Communication
      Line speed  . . . . . . . . . . .  _____
      Bits  . . . . . . . . . . . . . .  _
      Parity  . . . . . . . . . . . . .  _____
```

Figure 4.19   SAA CUA style guide example screen with upper-case title and section headings.

```
                    CHANGE SESSION PROFILE

Type information.   Then press Enter.

   SECURITY CONTROL
      PC password . . . . . . . . . .  _____
      VM password . . . . . . . . . .  _____
      Local area network password . . .  _____

   PRINTERS
      PC printer port . . . . . . . . .  _
      VM printer address . . . . . . .  _____

   COMMUNICATION
      Line speed  . . . . . . . . . . .  _____
      Bits  . . . . . . . . . . . . . .  _
      Parity  . . . . . . . . . . . . .  _____
```

which information will be keyed. This makes it a proper noun. When a caption is phrased as a question, then it is a sentence, and only its initial letter should be capitalized. Never begin a caption or sentence with a lower-case letter. A capital letter makes it easier for the eye to identify the start of each caption.

Unfortunately, SAA CUA does not follow the significant word capitalization principle of only using a capital letter for the initial letter of the caption.

Comparing paper to screen reading.   Printing technology has been evolving for several centuries. Factors such as type size and style, character and line spacings, and column and margin widths have been the focus of research for a good part of that time. The product of this research is highly readable and attractive printed materials. Conversely, CRT-based characters are a relatively new innovation, with many technical limitations. The result is a displayed character that often lacks the high quality a paper medium can provide. This disparity in quality has resulted in performance differences when paper and screen reading of materials have been compared. Various researchers have found slower screen reading speeds, as much as 40 percent (Gould and Grischkowsky, 1984; Kruk and Muter, 1984; Muter et al., 1982; and Wright and Lickorish, 1983), and more errors (Gould and Grischkowsy, 1984; and Wright and Lickorish, 1983).

More recent research indicates that as display resolution improves, the reading speed differences can be reduced, if not entirely eliminated (Harpster, et al., 1989). For extended reading, hard-copy display of material still has significant advantages, however.

Special Symbols

- Consider special symbols for emphasis.
- Separate symbols from words by a space.

Special symbols.   Special symbols should be considered to emphasize or call attention to elements on a screen. An error message, for example, can be preceded by asterisks (**), or the "greater than" sign can be used to direct attention (AMOUNT >>). Symbols should be separated from words by one space.

Field Captions/Data Fields

- Identify fields with captions or labels.
- Differentiate field captions from field data by using:
  —contrasting features, such as different intensities, separating colons, etc.:

```
SEX FEMALE                    SEX: FEMALE
RELATION DAUGHTER        RELATION: DAUGHTER
```

— consistent physical relationships:

```
SEX:
FEMALE                          SEX: FEMALE
RELATION: DAUGHTER              RELATION: DAUGHTER
```

- For single data fields, place the caption to the left of the data field:

```
PRODUCER
                                PRODUCER: 770117
770117
```

- For repeating data fields, place the caption above the data fields:

```
PRODUCERS: 770117        PRODUCERS
           589136        770117
           642210        589136
                         642210
```

- Separate captions from data fields by at least one blank space:

```
CITY:CHICAGO             CITY: CHICAGO
```

Many screens contain information that must be identified by a caption or label. Captions must be complete, clear, easy to identify, and distinguishable from other captions and data fields.

Identify fields with captions.   All screen data fields should be identified by captions. The context in which data is found in the world at large provides cues as to the data's meaning. A number on a telephone dial is readily identifiable as a telephone number; the number on a metal plate affixed to the back of an automobile is readily identified as a license number. The same data displayed on a screen, being out of context, may not be readily identifiable.

There are, however, some exceptions to this rule on inquiry screens. The structure of the data itself in some cases may be enough to identify its meaning. The most obvious example is name, street, city, state, and zip code. Date may be another possibility. Elimination of these common captions will serve to further clean up inquiry screens. Before eliminating them, however, it should be determined that all screen users will be able to identify these fields all the time.

Differentiate field captions from data.   Captions and data should be visually distinguishable in some manner so that they do not have to be read in context to determine which is which. A common failing of many screens is that the captions and data have the same appearance and blend into one another when the screen is filled. This makes differentiation difficult and increases caption and field data search time. Methods to accomplish differentiation include using contrasting display features and consistent positional relationships.

Caption Positioning.   Captions can be, and have been, positioned at all major points of the compass around a data field. Carried to the extreme is the screen illustrated in Figure 4.20. It contains four field captions, each located in a different spatial position to its data fields. A thank you to its designer for providing such a succinct example of all possible positions.

Figure 4.20   A screen illustrating captions to the left, above, to the right, and below data fields.

```
                *** ON SPOT PROCESSING OPTIONS ***

                        ACCOUNT NUMBER

                          .....      [ <X> to EXIT ]

      PATIENT CHARGES? --->      YNY        <--- ACCOUNT REQUIRED?
                                  ^
                                  |
                                  |

                        PAYMENT?
```

The most common, and practical, ways to relate a caption to its data field are to position the caption either above or to the left of the data field.

For single data fields, place the caption to the left of the data field and separate the two with a colon (:).   This author recommends the colon (:) as the symbol to separate single captions and data fields oriented horizontally, or left to right. The colon is unobtrusive, does not physically resemble a letter or number, and is grammatically meaningful, "a punctuation mark used chiefly to direct attention to matter that follows" (Webster).

The IBM SAA CUA Basic Interface Design Guide (1989) also recommends left-to-right orientation but uses leader dots (. . .) to connect captions and fields, "so users can easily move their eyes from one side of the screen to the other." It continues by instructing to use a minimum of two dots on a line and align the dots. It also states that dots are not needed for the longest caption in a group of aligned captions. The practical effect of this recommendation is to move the data fields further from the captions, thus extending the eye movement necessary to move between the two.

Most of their examples in their design guide have at least two or more dots between all captions and data fields, as illustrated in Figure 4.18, thereby extending the distance between the two. Not placing leader dots after the longest caption gives the appearance of "something missing." As far as dots fulfilling the role of an "eye ruler" is concerned, space lines between groups of

Figure 4.21   SAA CUA basic design guide screen example illustrating colons
before protected fields.

```
                      Print Options

Type and select.  Then press Enter.

   Document name  . . . : mydoc

   Type style . . . . . : Prestige elite

   Number of copies . . . ___     1-999

   Left margin  . . . . . __      1-25

   Start page number  . . ___     1-999

   One or both sides  . . _ 1. One side
                            2. Both sides

   Keep print file  . . . _ 1. Keep
                            2. Delete

   Classification   . . . _ 1. None
                            2. Personal
```

Figure 4.22   SAA CUA style guide example screen with leader dots removed
and colon (:) caption delimiters.

```
                    CHANGE SESSION PROFILE

Type information.   Then press Enter.

      SECURITY CONTROL
        PC password:               _____
        VM password:               _____
        Local area network password: _____

      PRINTERS
        PC printer port:           _
        VM printer address:        _____

      COMMUNICATION
        Line speed:                _____
        Bits:                      _
        Parity:                    _____
```

about five items are more than adequate for that purpose. Leader dots also add unneeded density to a screen.

The SAA CUA guide does recommend colons to be placed just before output or protected text, as illustrated in Figure 4.21. The value of this is questionable since the system will not, in any circumstances, permit this data to be changed by the screen user. Protected and unprotected (or changeable) data will always be ascertainable by the user.

Figure 4.22 illustrates removal of the leader dots and substituting the recommended colons for the screen illustrated in Figure 4.18. Removing the dots reduces screen density and positions the data fields closer to the captions. It also carries forward the capitalized title and section headings from Figure 4.19.

Horizontal orientation for single data fields, (A) in Figure 4.23, is preferable to the caption-above approach, (B) in the same figure, for the following additional reasons:

- It conforms to the normal left-to-right reading pattern.
- It permits easier field alignment, facilitating visual scanning and field location, and reducing the screen complexity measure. The scanning advantage will be addressed more fully in the discussion on inquiry screens.
- It provides the best compromise between caption clarity and screen space utilization. The horizontal example (A) in Figure 4.23 consumes 59 character positions, while the caption-above approach (B) consumes 74 positions. The B approach allows only 12 lines of data on a 24-line

Figure 4.23   Caption/data field relationship.

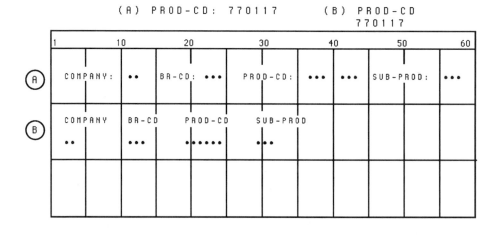

screen, while the A approach accommodates 24 lines of data. An approach screen designers often take to make B more efficient is to reduce the length of the caption to equal that of the data field below it. The result is often screens that look like that illustrated in Figure 4.24. Captions become very cryptic, and it is frequently difficult to tell where one caption stops and the next starts. The horizontal (A) approach requires that neither caption nor data be dependent on the other in the screen design process. Figure 4.25 is an example of the fields in Figure 4.24 restructured into the caption-preceding-data-field approach. While consuming 5 lines on the screen, caption lengths have been greatly expanded. To increase slightly the size of just a few of the captions in Figure 4.24 would have necessitated going to at least 6 lines. The caption-preceding approach (A) often permits longer caption sizes within the same space on the screen.

Figure 4.24   Example of screen fields using caption-above-data style (Approach B).

```
BEN   FROM      TO DATE  OCC BILLED     N/C AMT   CD MDCR PD    B/DED  B/PAID

----  --/--/--  --/--/-- ---  ---------  --------  -- ---------  ------  -------

INS EXA  MAT DED  MM ELIG  MM DEA   COI MM PAID  PROV    DCN       O  P  E

-------  -------  --------  --------  ---  --------  -------  --------  -- -- --
```

- Viewed in relationship to source document design, the best fit between a form and a screen created in the form's image is the horizontal (A) approach. Following good form design principles, an $8\frac{1}{2}$-by-11 source document line of fields is usually filled up before the screen line. That is, a line on paper $8\frac{1}{2}$ inches wide holds fewer characters than an 80-character screen line with appropriate spacing. (Galitz, 1975). This means that the horizontal (A) approach results in more efficient screen utilization than the caption-above (B) approach, since the latter tends to fill in less of each line, while using more lines.
- On a completely filled screen, the horizontal format (with colons) provides better visual discrimination between captions and data, as shown in Figure 4.26. On large or crowded screens, the caption-above format can cause captions and data to visually merge. This can be alleviated only by differentiating captions and data through a contrasting display technique. In the horizontal approach the colon serves as a flag allowing positional discrimination to be achieved.

Figure 4.25   Fields from Figure 4.24 restructured into the caption-preceding-
data style (Approach B).

```
BEN-CD: _____        FR-DATE: __/__/__  TO-DATE: __/__/__    OCC: ___

BILLED: _____     N/C-AMT: _____    N/C-CD: __      MDCR-PD: _____

BASE-DED: _____     BASE-PD: _____   INS-EXA: _____   MT-DED: _____

MM-ELIG: _____      MM-DED: _____      COINS: _____     MM-PD: _____

   PROV: _____      DCN: _____    OV-CD: __       POOL: __ EOB: __
```

Figure 4.26   Visual discrimination of captions/data fields.

```
(A)     EMPLOYER: CNA    DEPARTMENT: SERVICES    JOB: ANALYST
             SEX: M       EMPLOYEE#: A65449      DATE: 07/21/80

(B)     EMPLOYER    DEPARTMENT      JOB
        CNA         SERVICES        ANALYST
        SEX         EMPLOYEE#       DATE
        M           A65449          07/21/80
```

For repeating fields, place the caption above the data field. Captions
should be placed above a stack of data fields that are repeated two or more
times. Using horizontal caption formats for single fields and a columnar caption
orientation for repeating fields will also provide better discrimination between
single and repeating fields. The single-field caption will always precede the
data, and captions for repeating columnar fields will always be above the top
data field.

Field Caption/Data Field Justification

1. First Approach

  • Left-justify both captions and data fields.
  • Leave one space between the longest caption and the data field column.

```
            DIVISION:      _____
            DEPARTMENT:x_____
            TITLE:         _____
```

2. Second Approach

  • Left-justify data fields and right-justify captions to data fields.
  • Leave one space between each.

```
      DIVISION:x_____
   DEPARTMENT: _____
        TITLE: _____
```

Justification of single captions and data fields can be accomplished in several ways. These include:

A. Left-justifying captions; data field immediately follows caption.

```
   BUILDING: _____
   FLOOR: ___
   ROOM: _____
```

B. Left-justifying captions; left-justified data fields; colon (:) associated with captions.

```
   BUILDING: _____
   FLOOR:    ___
   ROOM:     _____
```

C. Left-justifying captions; left-justifying data fields; colon (:) associated with data field.

```
   BUILDING: _____
   FLOOR   : ___
   ROOM    : _____
```

D. Right-justifying captions; left-justifying data fields.

```
   BUILDING: _____
      FLOOR: ___
       ROOM: _____
```

Alternatives A and C are not recommended. Alternative A, left-justified aligned captions with data fields immediately following, results in poor alignment of data fields and increases the screens' complexity. It is more difficult to find data when searching data fields. Alternative C, while structurally sound, associates the colon (:) primarily with the data field. The strongest association of the colon should be with the caption.

The two most desirable alternatives are B and D. Alternative B, left-justified captions and data fields, is the first approach illustrated in the guideline. Alternative D, right-justified captions and left-justified data fields, is the second approach illustrated in the guideline.

Left-justified captions and data (1).   A disadvantage to this approach is that the caption beginning point is usually farther from the entry field than the right-justified caption approach. A large mix in caption sizes can cause some captions to be far removed from their corresponding data field, greatly increasing eye movements between the two and possibly making it difficult to accurately tie caption to data field. Tying the caption to the data field by a line of dots (. . . . .) solves the association problem but adds a great deal of noise to the screen. This does not solve the eye movement problem. Eye movement inefficiencies can be addressed by abbreviating the longer captions. The cost is reduced caption clarity.

An advantage to this approach is that section headings using location positioning as the key element in their identification do stand out nicely from the crisp left-justified captions.

Right-justified captions and left-justified entry fields (2).   A disadvantage here is that section headings using location positioning as the identification element do not stand out as well. They tend to get lost in the ragged left edge of the captions.

Advantages are that captions are always positioned close to their related data fields, thereby minimizing eye movements between the two, and that the screen takes on a more balanced look.

There is no universal agreement as to which is the better approach. Experimental studies have not provided any answers.

Examples to follow in this and succeeding chapters reflect both styles. This is done to enable the reader to see and evaluate each. Whichever the method chosen, however, should be consistently followed in a system's screen design.

The IBM SAA Design Guides only recommend left-justified captions, approach 1. Approach 2, right-justified captions is not considered.

Distinct and Meaningful Captions

- Choose distinct and meaningful captions that can be easily distinguished from other captions. Minimal differences (one letter or word) cause confusion.

Captions that are similar often repeat the same word or words over and over again. This increases the potential for confusion, adds to density, and often adds to screen clutter. A better solution is to incorporate the common words into headings, subheadings, or group identifiers.

The SAA CUA screen illustrated in Figure 4.18 suffers from this kind of redundancy. Note the repeating of the words "password" in the top grouping captions and "printer" in the second grouping. A screen eliminating this redundancy is illustrated in Figure 4.27. The triple-inscribed "password" is removed from the captions and incorporated in the section heading instead. "Printer," since it is already in the section heading, is removed from the captions. Other techniques to accomplish this redundant-caption reduction are described in the chapters addressing specific kinds of screens.

Screen captions should also be distinct from one another. One or two letter or word differences between captions can cause confusion.

Figure 4.27   SAA CUA style guide example with redundant words removed from the captions.

```
                          CHANGE SESSION PROFILE

       Type information. Then press Enter.

           SECURITY PASSWORD
                PC:                   ----------
                VM:                   ----------
                Local area network:   ----------

           PRINTERS
                PC port:              -
                VM address:           ------

           COMMUNICATION
                Line speed:           ------
                Bits:                 -
                Parity:               ------
```

Words

- Do not use jargon, words, or terms
    - — unique to the computer profession.
    - — with different meanings outside of the computer profession.
    - — made up to describe special functions or conditions.
- Use
    - — standard alphabetic characters to form words or captions.
    - — short, familiar words.
    - — complete words; avoid contractions, short forms, suffixes, and prefixes.
    - — positive terms; avoid negative terms.
    - — simple action words; avoid noun strings.
    - — the "more" dimension when comparing.
- Do not
    - — stack words.
    - — hyphenate words.
    - — include punctuation for abbreviations, mnemonics, and acronyms.

Words displayed on screens should be easily comprehended, with minimum ambiguity and confusion. Some ways to achieve this are given below.

Do not use jargon.   Jargon consists of several forms. It may be words or terms that are unique to the computer profession such as Filespec or Abend; words with different meaning outside of data processing such as Boot or Abort; or made-up words to describe special functions or actions such as Ungroup or Dearchive.

Use standard alphabetic characters.   Standard alphabetic characters are most familiar to screen viewers. Never use restricted alphabetic sets. Symbols should be used only if they are familiar to all who are using the screen. Common symbols that may be considered as substitutes for alphabetic characters are # for number, % for percent, and $ for dollar. Again, all potential screen users must be familiar with a symbol if it is used as a substitute for alphabet characters.

Use short, familiar words.   Shorter words tend to be used more often in everyday conversation, and so they are more familiar and easier to understand (of course, there are exceptions). The most important factor is familiarization, not length. A longer but familiar word is better than a short, unfamiliar word.

Use complete words.   A complete word is better understood than a contraction or short form. Thus, "will not" is better than "won't," "not valid" is better than "invalid."*

Words can also be more difficult to understand if they contain suffixes and prefixes, like "un-," or "-ness." Comprehension often involves decomposing such complex terms to establish their basic root meaning and then modifying the meaning to account for the various suffixes and prefixes (Wright, 1984). Structural complexity hinders comprehension.

Use positive terms.   It is generally easier to understand positive, affirmative information than the same information expressed in a negative way. Therefore, avoid the prefixes "ir-," "in-," "dis-," and "un-." Implicitly negative terms, such as "decrease," should be replaced with positive terms, such as "increase."

Use Simple Action Words.   Substitute noun strings with simple action words. Instead of saying, for example, PROJECT STATUS LISTING, say LIST PROJECT STATUS.

Use the "more" dimension when comparing.   When using comparative terms, the "more" dimension is easier to deal with. The opposite of the "more" is usually considered the "negative." So, use "longer" rather than "shorter," "bigger" rather than "smaller." (Barnard and Wright, 1975; Clark & Card, 1969.)

*"Invalid" has come into such widespread usage in computer systems that one may ask whether this should be an exception to this rule. Maybe, but what happens in a medical system where screens are developed for use about, or by, invalids?

Do not stack words.   Text is more readable if the entire statement is on one line.

Do not hyphenate words.   Again, for better readability, never break a word between two lines.

Abbreviations, mnemonics, and acronyms should not include punctuation.   This permits better readability and avoids confusion between the punctuation and data fields.

Messages

Messages are communications provided on the screen to the screen viewer. Several different types of messages exist and they may be displayed in different forms and places. A message should possess the proper tone and style and be consistent within itself and with other messages.

Types.   Screen messages fall into two broad categories: system and prompting. System messages are generated by the system to keep the user informed of the system's activities. They reflect the state of the system as it exists at that moment in time. Prompting messages are instructional messages provided on a screen.

System messages are of several kinds. *Notification / status / informational* messages provide information about the state of the system when it is not immediately obvious to the user. They may confirm nonobvious processing is taking place or is completed. They may also be used to provide intermediate feedback when normal feedback is delayed. No user actions are normally necessary with these kinds of messages, although confirmation that the message has been seen can be requested.

Warning messages call attention to a situation that may be undesirable to the user. The user must determine whether the situation is in fact a problem and may be asked to advise the system whether or not to proceed. A deletion request by a user is a common action that generates a warning message. When a user requests a deletion, a message asking for confirmation of the deletion is usually presented.

Action / critical messages call attention to conditions that do require a user action before the system can proceed. An error message is an action/critical message.

Question messages ask a question and offer a choice of options for selection. It is not a CUA SAA standard but may be used when there is a question to be asked and the message does not appear to be suited to the above described types.

The second category of messages, **prompting** messages, are instructional messages that tell the user how to work with, or complete, the screen displayed. They may be permanently affixed to a screen, or they may appear as the result of a help request. Prompting messages are of most benefit to the novice or casual system user.

Structure Location and Layout

Structure

- Use mixed-case letters.

Location

- Always use the message line for messages that must not interfere with screen information.
- Pop-up windows may be used for all kinds of messages, if available.
- Pop-up windows should be used for action/critical messages.

Layout

- In a message area:
  - Left-justify the message.
  - Allow space for the longest message.
- In a pop-up window:
  - Include an icon to the left of the text for each message type, if feasible.
    - Notification/Status/Informational—Lower-case *i* within a circle.
    - Warning—Exclamation point within a circle.
    - Action/Critical—Stop Sign (STOP within a hexagon).
    - Question—A question mark symbol within a circle.
  - Follow other relevant guidelines for window display.

Messages should consist of mixed-case letters following normal sentence-style capitalization. They may be displayed either in the message line or in pop-up windows. All action/critical messages should be displayed in a window if one is available. If windows are used, and the creation of an icon is possible, also include with the message text a unique icon for each type of message. This icon will immediately identify to the user the kind of message being presented.

Examples of the various system messages, derived from SAA CUA are illustrated in Figure 4.28. Included in each message window is the icon, the message text, and one or more pushbuttons for user acknowledgements and actions.

The notification/status/informational message window contains an OK pushbutton for confirmation that the message has been read. When OK is selected, the message is removed. SAA CUA also recommends a HELP button should be included in this window. The Warning message window provides OK and CANCEL, or YES and NO pushbuttons, depending on the message content. When an action is selected, the window is removed. A HELP button is again also recommended. The Action window includes RETRY, CANCEL, and HELP pushbuttons. RETRY assumes some action has been taken to correct the problem and directs the system to attempt to continue. With CANCEL the system does not take any further action. The HELP button is optional. The question window might include OK, CANCEL, and HELP pushbuttons.

Figure 4.28   Message pop-up windows with icon, text, and buttons.

Notification/Status/Informational

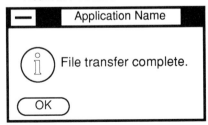

Warning

Action/Critical

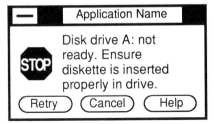

Question

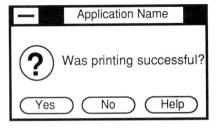

Sequence Control Guidance

- Consider providing a guidance message telling how to continue at points in the dialogue where
  — a decision must be made.
  — a response needs to be made to continue.
- Consider indicating what control options exist at points in the dialogue where several alternatives may be available.
- Permit these prompts to be turned on or off by the user.

Consider providing prompts telling the user how to continue when a decision, and response, must be made to continue. For example, it might be indicated that:

> Information is current through August 26, 1991.
> Press ENTER to continue.

Where several control options exist, consider providing a prompt such as

> Press S to Save, D to Delete, or P to Print.
> Type C to create a new file or E to edit a new file: _

For experienced users these kinds of prompts can become noise. Allow users to turn them on or off as needed.

Tone and Style

Sentences

- Sentences must be
  — brief, simple, and clear;
  — directly and immediately usable;
  — affirmative;
  — in an active voice;
  — nonauthoritarian;
  — nonthreatening;
  — nonanthropomorphic;
  — nonpatronizing;
  — in the temporal sequence of events;
  — structured so that the main topic is near the beginning;
  — cautious in the use of humor; and
  — nonpunishing.

Other Considerations

- Abbreviated, more concise versions of messages should be available.
- Something that must be remembered should be at the beginning of the text.

A message must minimize ambiguity and confusion, allowing easy, correct, and fast interpretation. It must also have the proper tone; threatening, rude, or impolite messages can evoke negative response.

The following guidelines will lead to easy, correct, and fast message interpretation and acceptance.

Schneiderman (1982B), in restructuring messages along such guidelines, found higher success rates in problem resolution, lower error rates, and improved user satisfaction.

Sentences

Use brief, simple sentences.   A message that has to be explained does not communicate. It fails as a message. Brief, simple sentences are more readily understood than longer sentences containing multiple clauses. Break long sentences into two or more simple sentences if this can be done without changing the meaning.

Roemer and Chapanis (1982) created messages at three levels of reading ability (fifth, tenth, and fifteenth grade) and tested them on people of varying verbal abilities. The fifth-grade version was found to be best for all levels. People of high verbal ability did not perceive the fifth-grade version as insulting as some have feared.

Provide directly and immediately usable sentences.   Searching through reference material to translate a message is unacceptable, as are requirements for transposing, computing, interpolating, or mentally translating messages into other units.

Use affirmative statements.   Affirmative statements are easier to understand than negative statements. For example, "Complete entry before returning to menu" is easier to grasp than "Do not return to menu before completing entry" (Herriot, 1970; Greene, 1972).

Use active voice.   Active voice is usually easier to understand than passive voice. For example, "Send the message by depressing TRANSMIT" is more understandable than "The message is sent by depressing TRANSMIT" (Herriot, 1970; Greene, 1972; Barnard, 1974).

Be nonauthoritarian.   Imply the system is awaiting the user's direction, not that the system is directing the user. For example, phrase a message "Ready for next command" not "Enter next command."

Nonthreatening.   Negative tones or actions, or threats, are not very friendly. Since errors are often the result of a failure to understand, mistakes, or trial-and-error behavior, the user may feel confused, inadequate, or anxious (Shneiderman, 1987). Blaming the user for problems can heighten anxiety, making error correction more difficult and increasing the chance of more errors. Therefore, harsh words like "illegal," "bad," or "fatal" should be avoided.

It is also suggested to avoid the word "error" in messages when it implies a user error (Paradies, 1991). "Error" tends to focus the attention on the person involved rather than on the problem. For example, instead of saying "Error— Numbers are illegal," say, "Months must be entered by name." Since the computer does not have an ego to be bruised, an excellent design approach would be to have it to assume the blame for all miscommunications.

Be nonanthropomorphic. Having the computer "talk" like a person should be avoided for several reasons. An attribution of knowledge or intelligence will, first, imply a much higher level of computer "knowledge" than actually exists, creating shattered user expectations. Second, this attribute eliminates the distinction that actually exists between people and computers. People "control" computers; they "respect the desires" of other human beings. Third, many people express anxiety about using computers by saying things like "they make you feel dumb." The feeling of interacting with another person who is evaluating your proficiency can heighten this anxiety (Shneiderman, 1987). There is some research evidence that a nonanthropomorphic approach is best, being seen as more honest (Quintanar et al., 1982), more preferred (Spiliotopoulos and Shackel, 1981), and easier to use (Gay and Lindward, in Shneiderman, 1987).

So, do not give a human personality to a machine. Imply that the system is awaiting the user's direction, not vice versa. Say, for example, "What do you need?" not "How can I help you?"

Be nonpatronizing. Patronizing messages can be embarrassing. "Very good; you did it right" may thrill a fourth-grader but would be somewhat less than thrilling to an adult. Being told "You forgot again" once may be acceptable, but being told three or four times in one minute is another story. A commonly available video golf game, after a particularly bad hole, returns with the suggestion to "try another sport." A golf professional who played this game took great offense to this advice and walked away. A person may disagree with patronizing conclusions, so why risk the offense?

Order words chronologically. If a sentence describes a temporal sequence of events, the order of words should correspond to this sequence. A prompt should say, "Complete address and page forward" rather than "Page forward after completing address" (Clark & Clark, 1968).

Messages that begin with a strange code number do not meet the user's needs. A code number, if needed at all, is only necessary after reading the message and should therefore be placed in parentheses at the end of the message.

Avoid humor and punishment. Until an optimal computer personality is designed, messages should remain factual and informative, and should not attempt humor or punishment. Humor is a transitory and changeable thing. What is funny today may not be funny tomorrow, and what is funny to some may not be to others. Punishment is not a desirable way to force a change in behavior, especially among adults.

Other Considerations

Display abbreviated versions of messages when requested. People are impatient with noninformative or redundant computer messages. A problem, however, is that the degree of computer-to-person message redundancy depends on the person's experience with the system. And it may vary with different parts of a system. So the availability of abbreviated or detailed messages allows tailoring of the system to the needs of each user. During system training and early implementation stages, detailed versions can be used. Individuals can switch to abbreviated versions as their familiarity increases, but they should always be able to receive detailed messages.

Place information that must be remembered at the beginning of text. One can remember something longer if it appears at the beginning of a message. Items in the middle of a message are hardest to remember.

Some words to forget. Words should be meaningful and common to all, not just to the designers. Language perceived as "computerese" may confuse or intimidate some users (Loftus et al., 1970; Wason and Johnson-Laird, 1972). The vocabulary of the designer often finds its way into messages or system documentation. While not always bad, some words have particularly harsh or vague meanings to many users. These words, which are summarized in Table 4.1, should be avoided whenever possible. Suggested alternative words are presented (derived from IBM, 1984).

Table 4.1   Some words to forget.

AVOID	USE
Abend	End, Cancel, Stop
Abort	End, Cancel, Stop
Access	Get, Ready, Display
Available	Ready
Boot	Start, Run
Execute	Complete
Hit	Press, Depress
Implement	Do, Use, Put Into
Invalid	Not Correct, Not Good, Not Valid
Key	Type, Enter
Kill	End, Cancel
Output	Report, List, Display
Return Key	Enter, Transmit
Terminate	End, Exit

Content

- Establish conventions for referring to
  - — individual keyboard keys.
  - — keys to be pressed at the same time.
  - — field captions.
  - — names supplied by users or defined by the system.
  - — commands and actions.
- Provide progress messages or graphics to indicate
  - — processing is delayed.
  - — proportion of processing completed.
  - — when processing is completed.

In messages and text it is often necessary to refer to keyboard keys, field captions, file names, commands, or actions. These components should be described in the same manner whenever referenced. Keyboard keys should always be referenced as they are inscribed on the keyboard. (They usually appear in a mixed-case text format.) A useful convention for referring to keys that should be pressed at the same time is a plus (+) sign between the key descriptions (Alt+F10). Names may be enclosed in quotes ("Pending").

The user should always be kept informed of system's processing status through messages or graphics. A "Please wait . . ." message can be presented to indicate more complex processing has been delayed or is continuing. An indication of the percentage of processing that has been accomplished can be given through a message ("22 of 27 transactions have been processed"), or graphics such as an hourglass or rectangular processing bar as illustrated in Figure 4.29. Processing being completed that is not visible to the user should also always be acknowledged ("Search complete, Jones not found").

Figure 4.29   Processing progress indicators.

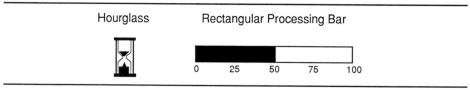

Text

Presentation

- Include no more than 40–60 characters on each line.
  - — A double column of 30–35 characters separated by 5 spaces is also acceptable.
- Do not right-justify.

- Use headings to introduce a new topic.
- Separate paragraphs by at least one blank line.
- Start a fresh topic on a new page.
- Emphasize important things by:
  — Positioning.
  — Boxes.
  — Bold typefaces.
  — Indented margins.
- Use lists to present facts.
- Use paging (not scrolling).
- Provide a screen design philosophy consistent with other parts of the system.

The typical screen is a little too wide for comfortable reading of text. It is difficult for the eye to keep its place as it moves from the end of one line to the beginning of the next line. Rehe (1974) recommends that a text line should contain no more than 40–60 characters. Lichty (1989) suggests the line width should be even less, 1.5 lower-case alphabets or 39 characters. For greater screen efficiency, it may be desirable to consider two columns of text, each about 30–35 characters wide.

Rehe also found that non-right-justified (or ragged-right edge) text lines are just as legible as justified text lines. Large spaces in right-justified text interrupt eye movement and impede reading.

Another study found that the reading speed of right-justified text was 8 to 10 percent slower than non-right-justified text (Trollip and Sales, 1986). Lichty states that non-right-justified text has advantages in word hyphenation not being required and the visual interest it generates. It is best for very narrow columns of text. Full left and right justification, Lichty says, is familiar, predictable, and orderly. It is best for long works that require continuous reading and concentration, long text, newspapers, and novels.

Headings to introduce new topics provide breaks or pause points for the reader. They provide obvious closure points. Starting new topics on new pages reinforce the needed breaks. Separating paragraphs by a blank line will result in more cohesive groupings and alleviate the impression of a dense screen.

Emphasize important points by placing them in unusual places, drawing boxes around them, using bold typefaces, or providing indented left and right margins. In addition to their emphasizing capabilities, they make the screen more interesting.

Use lists to present facts. Lists are convenient, simple, and uncluttered. Designate items in a list with a "bullet," a lower-case letter *o*, or a dash (—).

Paging through screens, rather than scrolling, has been found to yield better performance and to be preferred by novice system users (Schwarz et al., 1983). Expert users were found to perform satisfactorily with either paging or scrolling. A severe disadvantage of scrolling for novices is loss of orientation. While experts can handle scrolling, the best choice if all users are considered is paging.

If scrolling is going to be used, the preferred approach is "telescoping" in which the window moves around the data. This method is more natural and causes fewer errors than the "microscope" approach, in which the data appears to move under a fixed viewing window (Bury et al., 1982).

Writing

- Use short sentences composed of familiar, personal words.
  - Cut the excess words.
  - Try to keep the number of words in a sentence under 30.
- Cut the number of sentences.
- Keep the paragraphs short.
- Use the active writing style.
- Use the personal writing style, if appropriate.
- Write as you talk.
- Use subjective opinion.
- Use specific examples.
- Read it out loud.

Simple words and short sentences are the cornerstone of good writing. Keeping sentences under 30 words can be achieved. Long sentences often result from trying to express more than one idea in the sentence. They also result from trying to give a list of items and from the use of unnecessary words. Use separate sentences for separate ideas. Put multiple items in a list format, and delete all unnecessary words. Short paragraphs provide breaking points and make the page look less threatening.

The active writing style is easier to read and understand. It almost always uses less words and leaves no unanswered questions (contrast the passive "The customer name should be typed" with the active "Type the customer name").

The personal style, the use of "you" and "I" ("Now you must press the Enter key"), keeps the writing active, makes writing directly relevant to the reader, and is more interesting. Materials read by a wide variety of people for informational purposes only should not use the personal style, however.

Write in the way you would say something to the reader. Also, use subjective opinion ("This screen is not used very often") to reinforce the users' understanding of what they are reading. It does not tell anything specific but reinforces facts already read or about to be read. Do not overuse subjective opinion and make sure it is correct. Overuse makes facts harder to find, and an incorrect opinion casts suspicion on all the facts being presented.

The best way to explain a general rule is to show how it applies through examples. Examples should be short, relevant, and easy for the reader to relate to. They should also be visually different from the main text, either through indention, boxing, or some other technique.

Finally, read what you have written out loud to yourself. If it sounds wordy, stilted, or difficult, it will to the reader, too. Rewrite it.

Command Field

- The caption should consist of the word "command" followed by one (1) space and a right-pointing arrow consisting of three equal (=) signs and the great-than symbol (>).

```
COMMAND ===>
```

- The caption may be displayed in a mixed- or upper-case font.
- The entry field should be designated by underscores.
- Preferably, the entry field should follow the caption, separated by one (1) space.

```
COMMAND ===>  _____
```

- Alternatively, the caption may be positioned above the arrow and entry field.

```
COMMAND
===>  _____
```

A command field, when necessary, should consist of the caption "command," a right-pointing arrow, and an entry field designated by underscores. The caption may be displayed in mixed or upper case. Capitalization will provide some emphasis to the field and aid in differentiation from other screen components that are predominately in mixed case. Whichever style is chosen should be consistently followed. The preferred positioning is horizontal with the caption, arrow, and entry field on one line. Placing the caption above the arrow and entry field should be avoided unless horizontal space on the screen is at a premium.

IBM's SAA CUA Design Guide recommendations are identical to those above. SAA CUA, consistent with its recommendation for all screen components, recommends only mixed case as the caption style.

Function Keys

Uses

- For frequent and important actions.
- When the number of choices are limited.

Operation

- Require single action only.
- Do not display actions that are not applicable.
- If double keying is necessary, provide a list of options upon request.

Labels

- Provide informative descriptions.
- Describe the keyboard keys in the letter case used on the keyboard. (Usually mixed case.)
- Describe the actions to be performed in mixed-case letters.
- If multifunctional, describe the active function.
- Display in normal intensity or moderate emphasis.

Location and Layout

- Arrange in logical groupings.
- Make location compatible with importance
- Orient descriptions to match keyboard layout.
- If arranged horizontally,
  — Display in bottom line.
  — Indent first description one (1) character position from the left margin.
  — Relate key labels to actions through an equal (=) sign.
  — Separate descriptions by at least two (2) spaces.
  — If the descriptions do not fill up the line, center the descriptions in the line.
  — Separate the descriptions from the screen body through a blank line or a solid line.

```
Enter  F1=PROMPT  F2=RETRIEVE  F3=REFRESH  F6=CANCEL  F7=HELP  F8=EXIT
```

  — For multiple-row listings,
    — Expand the description area upward.
    — Align descriptions vertically.
    — Orient for top-to-bottom reading, where possible.

```
Enter       F2=RETRIEVE    F4=FORWARD    F6=CANCEL      F8=EXIT
F1=PROMPT   F3=REFRESH     F5=BACKWARD   F7=HELP
```

Consistency

- Use a common meaning and location discipline across all applications.

Function keys are advantageous because they reduce memory requirements, permit faster entry (fewer keystrokes), and reduce errors. Therefore, they are commonly included on many screens.

Uses. Function keys are ideal for a limited number of actions that are basic and frequent. Candidates include functions for navigating, processing, editing, or formatting, as described in the next section.

Operation.   Require only single actions to activate function keys. Avoid two-handed simultaneous operations or multiple-key depressions. Shift-key operations are especially prone to error. Hammond et al., (1980b) found that about one-third of the errors in a computer system were mistyping, and half of these were due to using the correct key with the wrong shift. Do not display function keys that are not applicable.

Labels.   Provide informative descriptions that clearly describe the key's purpose. Keyboard key descriptions should be inscribed in the letter case used on the keyboard. This is commonly mixed case. The actions themselves should be described in mixed-case letters. If a key is multifunctional, always display the current function. Function key descriptions should be moderately emphasized.

Location and Layout.   Provide logical groupings of keys based upon an analysis of their sequence of use, frequency of use, function, and importance. In establishing key meanings and locations, keep eye–hand movements to a minimum, and position the most frequently used keys in the most prominent locations. The most accessible locations for two common keyboard function key arrangements are shown in Figure 4.30. Orient the key descriptions to spatially match the keyboard layout. Bayerl et al., (1988) found that performance was 12 percent faster when the screen descriptions spatially matched the keyboard layout. They also concluded that the fastest combination was the horizontal array where function keys are spread across the top of the keyboard and across the bottom of the screen.

When arranging key descriptions horizontally, display them in the bottom line using an equal sign to relate the key to the action. Separate the descriptions from the screen body through a blank line or a solid line. The message line or command line may serve as the separation line between key descriptions and the screen body. If the function key descriptions consume more than one row, expand the description area upward. The message and command line will have to shift upward accordingly. Align the equal signs vertically, and orient them for the more efficient top-to-bottom scanning.

IBM's SAA CUA has established standard function key positions for screens that support the described action. These actions and key positions are:

F1 = Help
F2 = Display keys
F3 = Exit
F4 = Prompt
F5 = Refresh
F6 =
F7 = Backward
F8 = Forward
F9 = Retrieve/Command (F9 = Retrieve if the command area is in the
      primary window; F9 = Command if the command area will be
      provided in a pop-up.)
F10 = Actions
F11 =

Figure 4.30 Most accessible function key locations.

MOST ACCESSIBLE ——▶	F1	F2	F3	——▶ ACCESSIBLE
	F4	F5	F6	
	F7	F8	F9	
ACCESSIBLE ——▶	F10	F11	F12	——▶ ACCESSIBLE

MOST ACCESSIBLE ——▶ F1 F2 F3 F4 F5 F6 F7 F8 F9 F10 F11 F12 ——▶ ACCESSIBLE

F12 = Cancel
F13 =
F14 =
F15 =
F16 = Mark
F17 = Unmark
F18 =
F19 = Left
F20 = Right
F21 =
F22 =
F23 = Undo
F24 =

HARDWARE CONSIDERATIONS

- Important hardware considerations include
  — display screen size limits,
  — keyboard character population, and
  — character generation method and resolution.

Screen design is limited by the physical characteristics of the display terminal itself. Important characteristics include the display screen size, the characteristics of its associated keyboard, and the character generation method and screen resolution.

Display screens come in a variety of sizes and shapes. One of the most common is the 24-line, 80-column display encompassing 1920 character positions. Larger and smaller display screens will also be found. Some systems may impose smaller limits than the display terminal is physically capable of supporting. The CNA Insurance data entry utility DEBUT II, for example, restricts a designer from using 5 of the available 24 lines, leaving only 19 lines (1520 characters) for development of screen bodies (Galitz, 1979). The restricted lines are used for displaying such things as error messages and keying transaction commands. Before beginning any screen design activity, absolute limits and working areas must be identified.

In appearance and layout most keyboards resemble a standard typewriter keyboard with alphabetic and numeric characters, symbols, and punctuation marks. Typical symbols and punctuation marks are illustrated in Figure 4.31.

The keyboard character population is important because it defines the family of characters available for display on many screens. Operator guides will generally provide this exact information. Before beginning any design activity, however, it should be ascertained whether all these symbols are available for general use. Certain symbols may have predefined functions or may be unavailable.

The character-generation method and screen resolution are important in new graphics systems. Newer bitmap displays permit presenting text in different font sizes as well as graphics. A high-resolution display is necessary to achieve good legibility of characters and clear icons.

Figure 4.31 Typical displayable symbols and punctuations marks.

|	=	logical OR, vertical bar	_	=	underscore
!	=	exclamation point	+	=	plus sign
@	=	at sign	:	=	colon
#	=	number sign	"	=	quotation mark
$	=	dollar sign	<	=	less than sign
%	=	percent sign	>	=	greater than sign
¢	=	cent sign	?	=	question mark
−	=	minus sign	=	=	equals sign
&	=	ampersand	¬	=	logical NOT sign
*	=	asterisk	;	=	semicolon
(	=	left parenthesis	'	=	apostrophe
)	=	right parenthesis	,	=	comma
.	=	period	/	=	slash

SOFTWARE CONSIDERATIONS

Software considerations include how fields are defined on display terminals, the display techniques available to the screen designer, and concerns for edit and storage efficiency.

Field Characteristics

- A field is an area on the screen format possessing certain predefined characteristics.
- A field may encompass as little as one character position on the screen or cover the entire screen.
- The predefined characteristics of a field are normally established by a
  — control character that immediately precedes the field, or
  — control character within the field.
- This control character is called an attribute character. The attribute is invisible to the user.

The basic building block of the screen format is the *field*. A screen may consist of only one field or upwards of two hundred. Most terminals define a field's characteristics through use of a control character. This control character, commonly called an *attribute* character, occupies one screen character position immediately preceding the field. It is invisible to the user, appearing as a blank space.

Some terminals define a field's characteristics by other methods, not imposing restrictions on how certain screen character positions must be used. The attribute character is actually embedded within the field. From a practical standpoint, however, most screen fields will always include one or more blank spaces preceding a field for visual clarity requirements. So this imposed software restriction to allow for attributes has no practical consequences. It is also prudent to leave an attribute position on all screens for reasons of flexibility. If the screen is designed for use on systems not imposing this requirement, and at some point it must be converted to one requiring attributes, screen redesign will not be necessary.

For purposes of this handbook, screens are considered to use the attribute method of field specifications. For simplicity we will illustrate a field definition terminology employed by many terminal vendors. The field concepts described, however, can be generalized to most other terminals, since they encompass the basic kinds of fields necessary to lay out screens.

Fields on a screen format, then, can be visualized as follows:

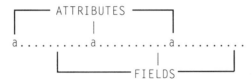

The letter *a* signifies an attribute character position.

Field Types

- Fields may be designed to contain the following types of data.
  - — captions or nonchanging material,
  - — variable and changeable keyed data, and
  - — variable but nonchangeable data.

Captions are descriptive identifiers of the information contained in an associated data field. Nonchanging materials are such things as titles or instructions. These kinds of fields are also often referred to as *literals*, *labels*, or *prompts*.

Variable and changeable keyed data fields are data entry screen fields into which data may be keyed. Variable but nonchangeable data fields frequently contain the contents of computer files. They are usually found on inquiry screen formats.

These field types are commonly related on screen formats, as illustrated below:

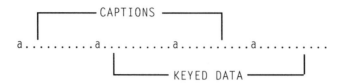

```
                ┌──────── CAPTIONS ────────┐
                │                          │
   a..........a..........a..........a.........
                └──────── KEYED DATA ──────┘
```

For example:

```
aEFF-DATE:a.....aEXP-DATE:a.....
```

Defining Field Characteristics

- The characteristics of a field's attribute specify the type of data contained in a field.
- An attribute's characteristics are determined by selecting one alternative condition in each of a series of conditions.
- Common alternative conditions are:
  1. Protected or Unprotected:
     — Protected—will not permit keying of data into field; field content is for viewing only;
     — Unprotected—permits keying of data into field.
  2. Numeric or Alphanumeric
     — Numeric—only permits keying of numeric data (0–9, decimal point, and minus sign) into field, if used in conjunction with unprotected condition. If used with protected condition, activates "auto skip" cursor movement function over field;
     — Alphanumeric—permits keying alphanumeric data into field, if used in conjunction with unprotected condition. If used with protected condition, requires operator manual tabbing to move cursor over the field.
  3. Normal intensity, high intensity or nondisplay:
     — Normal intensity—information in the field is displayed at a normal intensity;
     — High intensity—information in the field is displayed at a brighter than normal intensity;
     — Nondisplay—information in the field is not visible to the operator.

For each screen field one value must be selected from each of the alternative conditions 1, 2, and 3. The most common field definitions in screen layout follow.

Common Field Definitions

- *Data entry of alphanumeric data*—unprotected/alphanumeric/high intensity.
- *Data entry of numeric data*—unprotected/numeric/high intensity.

- *Caption (manual tabbing required)*—protected/alphanumeric/normal intensity.
- *Caption (auto skip required)*—protected/numeric/normal intensity.
- *Descriptive or nonchangeable information*—protected/alphanumeric/normal intensity.

Manual tabbing requires operator depression of the keyboard tab key to move the cursor over a protected field to the next unprotected field. Auto skip results in the cursor automatically moving over the protected to the next unprotected field if the previous unprotected field is fully completed. Nondisplay is typically reserved for "security" fields such as passwords.

Many terminals allow the designer much more flexibility than this, permitting such things as reverse video (dark characters on a light background), underlining, and blinking. These techniques and some recommended uses are described in the next section.

Because screen format layout is addressed in the following chapters, attribute specification is not a topic of discussion. Positions are allowed on the screen where the proper attribute can be specified. The screen designer must be aware of existing conventions and specifications methodologies for the terminals being used and see that all fields are defined as desired and in the required manner.

Monochromatic Display Features

High Brightness

- Good attention-getting capability.
- Least disturbing features.
- Provide two levels only.
- Suggested uses:
  — data fields,
  — items in error.

Mixed Case

- Moderate attention-getting capability.
- Use for textual information.

Upper Case

- Moderate attention-getting capability.
- Use for section headings and title.

Reverse Video

- Good attention-getting capability.
- Can reduce legibility.

- Can increase eye fatigue.
- Use in moderation.
- Suggested uses:
  - items selected,
  - error messages,
  - fields in error,
  - information being acted upon,
  - information of current relevance.

Underlining

- Poor attention-getting capability.
- May reduce legibility.
- Use to emphasize (e.g., title or headings).

Blinking

- Excellent attention-getting capability.
- Reduces legibility.
- Distracting.
- Provide two levels only (on and off).
- Blink rate should be 2–5 hz with minimum on interval of 50 percent.
- Suggested uses:
  - urgent situations,
  - situations where quick response required.
- Turn off when person has responded.

Multiple Fonts

- Moderate attention-getting capability.
- Use to differentiate screen components, with larger, bolder letters to designate higher-level pieces such as title and headings.

Thin/Thick/Double Rulings and Line Borders

- Suggested uses:
  - break screen into pieces,
  - guide eye through screen.

80/132 Columns

- 132 columns may reduce legibility.
- Avoid 80 and 132 columns for textual material.
- Confine text to 40 to 60 characters.
- Consider double and triple columns for displaying text.

Scrolling

- Not appropriate for novice users.
- Use "smooth" movement.

Phosphor Color

- At the standard viewing distance, white, orange, or green are acceptable colors.
- At a far viewing distance, white is the best choice.
- Over all viewing distances, from near to far, white is the best choice.

Windows

- To provide access to multiple sources of information.
- To combine multiple sources of information.
- To perform more than one task.
- To provide reminders.
- To monitor tasks or activities.
- To present multiple representations of the same task.

Today's monochromatic displays provide a wide range of techniques to aid the screen design process. Few terminals will have all the features described, but the more that do exist, the more flexibility the designer will have. Effective screen design can be accomplished, though, even with only a small number of features available.

Before beginning screen design, the designer must be aware of the capabilities existing on the terminal where the screen will be displayed. It is important to note whether the various features are available on an individual field basis, or whether they must be incorporated on a screen-wide basis. (For example, can any one caption be displayed at high intensity or must all captions be displayed at high intensity?) The latter will, of course, allow less flexibility in design.

Often these features will be used to call attention to various items on the display. The attraction capability of a mechanism is directly related to how well it stands out from its surroundings. Its maximum value is achieved when it is used in moderation. Overuse is self-defeating, as contrast with the surroundings is reduced and distraction may even begin to occur.

Not all display features are ideal for all situations. Following are some recommended uses and limitations that currently exist.

High brightness. High brightness has a good attention-getting quality and no disturbing features. It is frequently used to indicate fields in error on data entry screens and is an excellent vehicle for calling attention to data fields on inquiry screens. It may be used for data fields on data entry screens if an alternative method such as reverse video is available to call attention to errors. If it has a fault, it is that terminals with improperly set manual screen contrast controls can diminish its effectiveness, even causing it to disappear. This can be a major problem for terminals placed in exceptionally bright viewing conditions.

Mixed case. Mixed case should be used for textual information since it is read faster than upper case. However, use it only if the character set contains true descenders (the line dropping from a *g* or *p* that makes it lower than an *a* or *o*) or ascenders (the upward line on a *b* or *d*). Words composed of characters without true ascenders and descenders (the bottom of the *p* is not longer than the bottom of the *o*) are harder to read than upper case since the structure of the word fits no pattern we have memorized. Without true ascenders and descenders, it is better to use upper case exclusively.

Upper case.   Upper case is used for captions, headings, title, and data fields, unless the data fields are heavily text oriented.

Reverse video.   Reverse video is a display feature that permits a screen to resemble the normal printed page (dark letters on a light background). Rooms with overhead lighting can cause disturbing screen reflections, a problem that is significantly reduced by reverse video because the reflection is masked by the light screen background. However, reverse video should be used with caution. Some potential problems are:

- Excessively bright display caused by the large area of emitted light from the electron gun. The result is best described as "dazzle" to one's eyes that can be fatiguing. Paper viewing is accomplished by reflected light, which is not subject to this phenomenon (although a light source positioned close to a piece of paper can create reflected glare that also creates viewing problems).
- Light emitted by the display screen tends to bleed into the dark surrounding area, as perceived by the viewer's eyes. Therefore a display with a light background results in the background bleeding into the characters displayed. Light characters bleed into a dark background. Thus, a light character on a dark background will actually look larger to the viewer than do dark characters on a light background. If character size and resolution are not adequate, the reverse video characters may not be as legible as the light-on-dark characters.
- For a normal light character on dark background display, a display refresh rate of 60 cycles per second must be maintained so the viewer does not perceive a display flicker (which can be fatiguing to the eye). A full reverse video display is much more susceptible to the perception of flicker, and the refresh rate must be increased to 90 to 100 cycles per second to eliminate it. If reverse video is used on a display being refreshed at 60 cycles per second, flicker can become a problem.

Several studies comparing reverse video screens to the more prevalent light character on dark background screens have found no performance differences (Cushman, 1986; Kühne et al., 1986; and Zwahlen and Kothari, 1986) and no differences in eye-scanning behavior and feelings of visual fatigue (Zwahlen and Kothari, 1986). One study did find reverse video more visually fatiguing (Cushman, 1986), while another (Wichansky, 1986) found green and orange phosphor reverse video screens easier to read but found no differences in white phosphor readability.

Given the above potential problems and conflicting study results reverse video should be used with discretion. Before implementing it on a full-screen basis, it is necessary to verify whether or not these problems do actually exist. Some terminals will be fully acceptable, others will not. The number of different display terminals in existence makes it impossible to specify any all-encompassing conclusions. The safest general conclusion is to use reverse video in moderation. Calling attention to fields in error or using in error messages are two practical uses. Another is to highlight actions such as program function key alternatives. If reverse video is used to identify certain fields or highlight certain kinds of information, some additional cautions are warranted:

- If reverse video is used to identify one kind of field such as data entry, avoid what can best be described as the crossword puzzle effect—the haphazard arrangement of elements on the screen creating an image that somewhat resembles a typical crossword puzzle. An arrangement of elements might be created that tries to lead the eye in directions that the designer has not intended or causes elements to compete for the viewer's attention. The cause of this problem is using reverse video for too many purposes or by poor alignment and columnization of fields selected for this emphasis.

  Conservative use and alignment and columnization rules, to be described in the sections on designing specific kinds of screens, will minimize this effect.

- If reverse video is used to highlight information such as error messages or actions to be taken, allow an extra reversed character position on each side of the field. This will leave a margin around the information in the field, giving it a more pleasing look. This will also eliminate any degradation in information legibility caused by lines made up of wide characters being placed too close to the edge of the field.

Underlining.   Underlining can reduce legibility, so it should be used with caution. One possibility is to emphasize titles or headings. Use underlining only if some space exists between the underlining and the word being underlined. On some terminals the underline is part of the character itself, thereby reducing word legibility.

Blinking.   Blinking has a very high attention-getting capability, but it reduces character legibility and is disturbing to most people. It often causes visual fatigue if excessively used. Therefore, it should be reserved for urgent situations and when quick response is necessary. A user should be able to turn off the blinking once his attention has been captured. The recommended blink rate is 2–5 hz with a minimum "on" time of 50 percent. An alternative to consider is creating an "on" cycle considerably longer than the "off," a "wink" rather than a "blink."

Multiple Fonts. Multiple fonts have moderate attention-getting capability. Their varying sizes and shapes can be used to differentiate screen components. Use larger, bolder letters to designate higher-level screen pieces, such as titles and headings.

Thin/thick/double rulings and line borders. Use horizontal rulings as a substitute for spaces in breaking a screen into pieces. Use vertical rulings to convey to the screen viewer that a screen should be scanned from top to bottom. Line or graphical borders can also be drawn around elements to be grouped. Figure 4.32 illustrates identical screens with and without borders. While many groupings are obvious without borders, borders certainly reinforce their existence.

80/132-column screens. A 132-column screen is an increasingly popular alternative to the traditional 80-column screen. Some terminals are capable of displaying either width. If the terminal is capable of both widths, verify that the 132-column screen does not degrade character legibility. This can happen because, in many cases, 132 columns are created by compressing the 132 characters into an 80-column width.

Avoid using the full 80 and 132 columns for display of textual material. Confine text to 40–60 characters per line.

Scrolling. Scrolling is a technique to move data across or through the screen. Scrolling is not appropriate for novice users (Schwarz et al., 1983). Scroll movement should be "smooth"; it should not use the "jump" method that is bothersome to most people.

Phosphor color. In a study by Hewlett-Packard (Wichansky, 1986), at the standard screen viewing distance (18–24 inches), no performance differences were found between white, orange, and green phosphor in either polarity (light characters on a dark background, or dark characters on a light background). Subjective ratings of ease of reading were highest for green and orange reverse video screens as compared to normal video (light character screens), while no differences in ease of reading were found for either polarity with white phosphor at this distance. At a far viewing distance (4–5 feet), orange and green phosphor reverse video screens could be seen more clearly than normal video screens, while white screens were equally legible in either polarity. More errors were found with green phosphor than the other two.

Green phosphor caused red or pink afterimages for 35 percent of the screen viewers; orange phosphor yielded blue afterimages for 20 percent; and white phosphor yielded afterimages for 5 percent. A 35 percent green phosphor afterimage for viewing was also found by Galitz (1968).

Some conclusions are:

- At standard viewing distances, no significant performance differences exist for white, orange, or green. All are acceptable. Subjective prefer-

Figure 4.32   The effect of line or graphical borders.

```
BASIC    Tournament              Get note to Roger        MURPHY'S LAW
DRAPE    Scores                  on solution to    ) _ +
COLOR      Ralph       67        Park District's   0 - =  If it can go
CODES      Stanley     76        tree problem.     { }    wrong it will
blk 0      Bob         77                          [ ]    go wrong.  It
bro 1                               A S D F G H J K L : "  can and it
red 2    24 tables                  a s d f g h j k l ; '  really did!
orn 3    96 Chairs                  Z X C V B N M < > ?
yel 4    16 Beds                    z x c v b n m , . /
grn 5
blu 6                                                      CUSTOMER: ACME
pur 7                                                      improvement due to
gry 8                               Dinner at 7:30.        these
wht 9                                                             This is an
                                                                  illustration
                         FORECAST                         TRIP of the effect
                         Today, partly cloudy, high       Lugga that the use
FIB CONTRACT             about 90.  Tonight, colder,       Suit of graphical
Change paragraph         increasing clouds, heavy   ICING  Water boundaries
to reflect the n         snow possible.             -10 $ 44  Golf has on the
purchase agreeme                                    -99   41  Tenni perception of
of 9/3/91.                                          100+  37        groups on a
                                                                   screen.
```

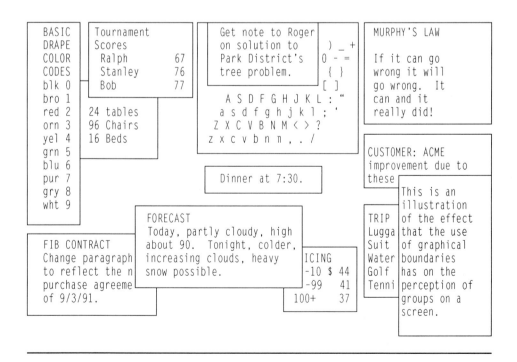

ences may vary, however, so providing the viewer a choice of any of these colors is desirable.

- At far viewing distances, white is the more legible color and therefore the best choice.
- Over all viewing distances, white phosphor is the best choice.
- White phosphor has the lowest probability for creating afterimages.

Windows. A window is a technique in which only a portion of the display screen is used for a particular interaction or task. In effect, two or more "miniscreens" are available to the viewer. A window may be small, a single message, or it may be large, consuming most of the display space available. Windows are a relatively recent innovation in the evolving human-computer interface. They were created to allow the "display workspace" to more closely mirror the "desk workspace."

The value of a window is that it reduces short-term memory loads. The ability to do mental calculations is limited by how well one keeps track of one's place, interim products, and results. The window acts as an external memory that is an extension of one's internal memory (Card, et al., 1984). Windows also provide access to more information than would normally be available on a single screen of the same size. This is done by overwriting or placing more important information on top of information that is less important at that moment. While all the advantages and disadvantages of windows are still not well understood, they do seem to be useful in the following ways.

Providing access to multiple sources of information. Independent sources of information may have to be accessed at the same time. For example, information to solve a problem may be stored in a Help function. This information may be presented on the screen alongside the problem, greatly facilitating its solution. Or, a writer may have to refer to several parts of text being written at the same time. Or, a travel agent may have to compare several travel destinations for a particularly demanding client.

Combining multiple sources of information. Text from several documents may have to be reviewed and combined into one. Pertinent information is selected from one window and copied into another.

Performing more than one task. More than one task can be performed at one time. While waiting for a long, complex procedure to finish, another can be performed. Tasks of higher priority can interrupt less important ones. The interrupted task can then be resumed with no "close down" and "restart" necessary.

Reminding. Windows can be used to remind the viewer of things likely to be of use in the near future. Examples might be menus of choices available, a history of the path followed or command choices to that point, or the time of an important meeting.

Monitoring.   Changes, both internal and external, can be monitored. Data in one window can be modified and its effect on data in another window can be studied. External events, such as stock prices, out of normal range conditions, or system messages can be watched while another major activity is carried out.

Multiple representations of the same task.   The same thing can be looked at in several ways—for example, alternative drafts of a speech, different versions of a screen, or different graphical representations of the same data.

Windows are described in much more detail in Chapter 10.

Edit Requirements

- The three basic types of edits are

  Field   — verification that the data contained within a field is within predefined limits, or present when required;

  Cross-Field   — verification that the data contained within two or more fields on one screen format is consistent;

  Cross-Screen   — verification that the data contained within two or more fields on two or more screen formats is consistent.

- Field edits are performed faster and more efficiently than cross-field edits.
- Cross-field edits are performed faster and more efficiently than cross-screen edits.

Transaction processing time can be lessened to the extent that edits (validation or checking the correctness of the entered data by the computer) can be reduced to the lowest level, as follows: (1) field, (2) cross-field, (3) cross-screen.

For many years edits have been a technical consideration receiving much attention by screen designers. As a result, edits have been a major cause of the frequent mismatches between the computer subsystem and the manual subsystem. Whereas the organization of screens is weighted heavily toward screen edits, the organization of information as it flows through the manual subsystem has usually not reflected screen edit needs. Therefore, the data has often arrived at the display terminal organized differently than the system has structured it for entry. The organization of information in the manual subsystem should reflect the needs of the system edits. The system and screen, however, should not expect the data to be organized in a way that is not meaningful to the users of the system. So, screens should be organized for edit ease on the basis of what makes sense to the data provider.

Storage Capabilities

- Do not define identical screens as separate screen formats.
- For functions with similar requirements, try to utilize one screen format.

Identical screen formats should not be defined as separate screen formats. This is an unnecessary waste of screen format file storage space. Similarly, it may be possible to develop one screen format to handle two separate but similar functions. Again, screen format storage benefits accrue.

A point of caution, however. Storage should not be optimized at the expense of screen clarity and ease of use.

APPLICATION CONSIDERATIONS

- Screen design must reflect the objectives of the system for which the screens are designed.

Screens consist of data elements. These data elements must incorporate the requirements of the application for which this system is being developed, in order that the purpose of the system can be fulfilled. This last consideration can be stated briefly, but it is the cornerstone of all screen design activity.

Data Entry Screens 5

Data entry screens are those onto which data is keyed. Also called data collection screens, their purpose is to capture information quickly and accurately. Quite often this data is edited on-line so that errors can be corrected quickly.

This class of screens encompasses applications that frequently include large numbers of data elements. Several screens may be required to complete one transaction, and a system may comprise many transactions. The traditional definition given to this kind of application has been the term *data entry*. The definition of screens discussed on these pages, however, applies to all screens onto which data is keyed. This includes the newer office automation applications such as electronic mail, executive calendars, and so forth.

The design style of a data entry screen can also be characterized as "form fill-in." The screen itself should provide the cues necessary to permit an inexperienced user to easily and accurately determine what must be keyed, enter the required information, and then later review it if necessary. That the novice user of a computer performs better with, and prefers, this kind of screen to a command dialogue was experimentally ascertained by Ogden and Boyle (1982). Nevertheless, while helping the novice user, the design of the data entry screen should not inhibit the experienced person.

The most important variable in data entry screen design is the availability of a specially designed source document from which data is keyed. If such a document is used, and if it has been designed in conjunction with the screen, the primary visual focus of the user will be toward the document, with the screen assuming a secondary role in the keying process. If a special source document is not developed, the user's primary visual focus is usually the screen, and the data source assumes a less important role in the overall design.

This distinction is important because it determines whether keying aids are built into the screens or into source documents. With a dedicated source document, the document itself can include keying aids. But without a dedicated source document, the screen format must incorporate aids. The resulting screens will have fundamental conceptual differences in data organization, content, and structure.

Due to the fundamental differences in these kinds of screens, they are addressed in three separate sections in this chapter.

Section 5-1 reviews the guidelines that are common to both kinds of screens. These guidelines are not affected by screen type. Subjects include information grouping techniques, transaction organization rules, keying procedures, the structure of keyed data, and data editing guidelines. Section 5-2 is devoted to guidelines for screens used with a dedicated source document, and section 5-3 details screen guidelines for which a dedicated source document is not available.

SECTION **5-1**

Data Entry Screens—General

INFORMATION GROUPING TECHNIQUES

- *Conventional*—grouping items of information in generally accepted or customary orders.
- *Sequential*—grouping items of information in the order in which they are commonly received or transmitted, or by natural groupings.
- *Frequency of use*—grouping together items that are used most frequently.
- *Function*—grouping items according to the function they perform.
- *Importance*—grouping items of information according to how important they are to the task or transaction.
- *General to specific*—locating items more general in nature before those that are more specific.

This arrangement may be based on what is customary, a logical sequence, frequency, function, importance, or the generality/specificity of the elements.

Conventional. Through convention and custom, some ordering schemes have evolved for certain elements. Examples are days of the week, months of the year, and one's name and address. These elements should be ordered in the customary way.

Sequence of use. Sequence of use grouping involves arranging information items in the order in which they are commonly received or transmitted, or in natural groups. An address, for example, is normally given by street, city, state, and zip code. Another example of natural grouping is the league standings of football teams, appearing in order of best to worst records.

Frequency of use. Frequency of use is a design technique based on the principle that information items used most frequently should be grouped at the beginning, the second most frequently used items grouped next, and so forth.

Function. Function involves grouping information items according to their purpose. All items pertaining to insurance coverages, for example, may be placed in one location. Such grouping also allows convenient group identification for the user.

Importance. Importance grouping is based on the information's importance to the task being performed. Important items are placed in the most prominent positions.

Screen design normally reflects a combination of these techniques. Information may be organized functionally but, within each function, individual items may be arranged by sequence or importance. Numerous permutations are possible.

General to specific. If some data elements are more general than others, the general elements should precede the specific elements. This will usually occur when there is a hierarchical relationship among data elements.

TRANSACTION ORGANIZATION

- Optimize system editing by grouping edit-related items on the same screen.
- Minimize cursor positioning movements by locating required elements toward the top of screens or at the beginning of lines.
- Structure the transaction to consist of as few screen formats as possible, but not at the expense of visual clarity.
- Break screens at logical or natural points, such as
  — between different kinds of information,
  — between sections of a source document,
  — at the end of a source document page, or
  — at breaking points between reference sources.

Availability of a dedicated source document will have little impact on overall organization of data entry transactions. The guiding concept here is to minimize the number of screens required to complete a transaction by incorporating required data elements (those always completed during data entry) in the earliest screens and in upper screen positions. This permits concluding transactions without displaying all transaction screens, and ending screens without having to tab through all screen elements. Incorporating on one screen items to be edited against one another will yield faster and more efficient transaction editing than placing such fields on different screens.

Structuring a transaction to consist of as few screens as possible will also reduce user "wait" periods between screens. For example, 100 fields split between two screen formats will yield a faster data entry rate (in terms of characters per second) than the same number of fields split between four screen formats. In the two-screen scenario, user inactivity occurs only once—between screens one and two. In the four-screen scenario, three inactive periods occur.

An important word of caution, however. Development of a transaction must be based on the logical order of data collection (especially if a source document is involved). Transaction organization rules should be implemented with the understanding that the organization must make sense to the person providing or collecting the data. Screen design must never dictate source document design. Form design must be the controlling factor.

KEYSTROKES

---

* Do not focus on minimizing keystrokes without considering other factors such as
  — keying rhythm,
  — the goals of the system.

A sought-after goal in many data entry applications is to minimize key-strokes. Fewer keystrokes have been synonymous with faster keying speeds and greater productivity in the minds of many. But this is not always true. Fewer keystrokes may actually decrease keying speeds and reduce productivity in many cases.

One example is found in Galitz (1972), who compared auto skip with manual tabbing in a data entry application. Auto skip, while requiring fewer keystrokes, was found to result in longer keying times and more errors than manual tabbing because it disrupted keying rhythm. This study is described in more detail in the following section.

Another example is a study by Springer and Sorce (1984), who, in an information retrieval task, compared input keystrokes to resulting output evaluation time. They found that more keystrokes yielded more precise outputs, which resulted in faster problem solving.

So, the number of keystrokes must be considered in light of keying rhythms and the objectives to be achieved as a result of the keying. Fewer is not always better.

KEYING PROCEDURES

Manual Tab versus Auto Skip

---

* Define fields to permit manual tabbing.

Auto skip is a display terminal feature that causes a cursor to automatically move to the beginning of the next entry field once a field is completely

Figure 5.1   Data entry using auto skip.

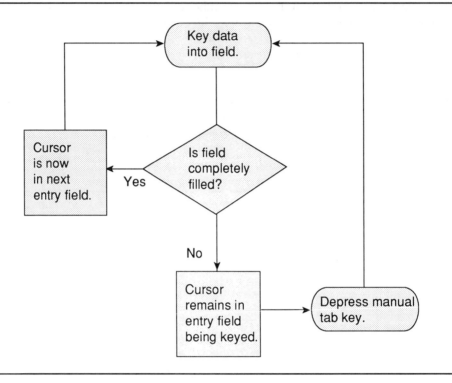

filled. Auto skip obviates manual tabbing and requires fewer keystrokes to complete a screen. Theoretically, keying speeds should increase with auto skip. In practice, however, they do not always do so.

Rarely are many entry screen fields completely filled with data. When an entry field is not full, the user must still depress the tab key to move the cursor to the next entry field. Figure 5.1 illustrates the auto skip function.

Auto skip, therefore, imposes decision-making and learning requirements. After keying data in each field, one must determine where the cursor is and whether to depress the manual tab key. Only then can the next keying action be performed. As illustrated in Figure 5.2, manual tabbing requires extra keystrokes, but no decisions need be made. The data entry task is rhythmic and consistent. Galitz (1972) summarizes operator performance data from a study of both auto skip and manual tabbing. In that study manual tabbing resulted in faster performance and fewer keying errors.

Auto skip can delay detection of one particular human error. If an extra character is inadvertently keyed into a field, the cursor will still move automatically to the next entry field and keying can continue. The error will not be immediately detected, and the spacing in subsequent fields may also be one position off, at least until the tab key is depressed. Were this situation to occur while using manual tabbing, the keyboard would lock as soon as the entry field

Figure 5.2   Data entry using manual tabbing.

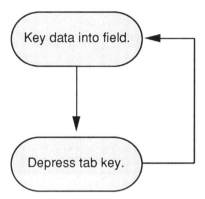

was full or when an attempt was made to key the extra character. The error would be immediately obvious.

But auto skip, despite its limitations, can be useful if a system's screens are easily learned or if all screen fields are always completely filled. Nevertheless, most large-volume data entry applications would not appear to meet these criteria.

Cursor-Rest Position

- Maintain a cursor-rest position at the end of each display line.

While manual tab control is in use, and when an entry field is completely filled, the cursor will move to the first character position of the next protected field to await a manual tab command. This command will direct the cursor to the first character position of the next entry field. After a line of data is keyed, the user can also depress the return key to direct the cursor to the first entry field of the next line. If an entry field extends into the next-to-last or last column in a line, however, depression of the return key can put the cursor in the wrong location. Figure 5.3 illustrates how this happens. Restricting the end-point of an entry field to the second-to-last column in a line will prevent the situation in example B, thus eliminating a potential error and establishing a consistent data entry procedure.

Keying Rules

- Do not require recoding, changing, omitting, or including data based on special rules or logical transformations.

Figure 5.3 The need for a cursor-rest position.

Example A
1. The cursor (a block) is positioned in column 78 awaiting the last key entry in the field.

2. A 7 is keyed and the cursor moves to column 80 awaiting a tab or return key depression.

3. A tab or return key depression moves the cursor to the first position of the next entry field.

Example B
1. The cursor is positioned in column 79 awaiting the last entry in the field.

2. A 7 is keyed, and the cursor moves to the next available position to await a tab or return key depression. It is now in column 1 of the next line.

3. The return key is depressed and the cursor moves down to the first entry position of the next line. A situation has thus been created that will allow an error to occur.

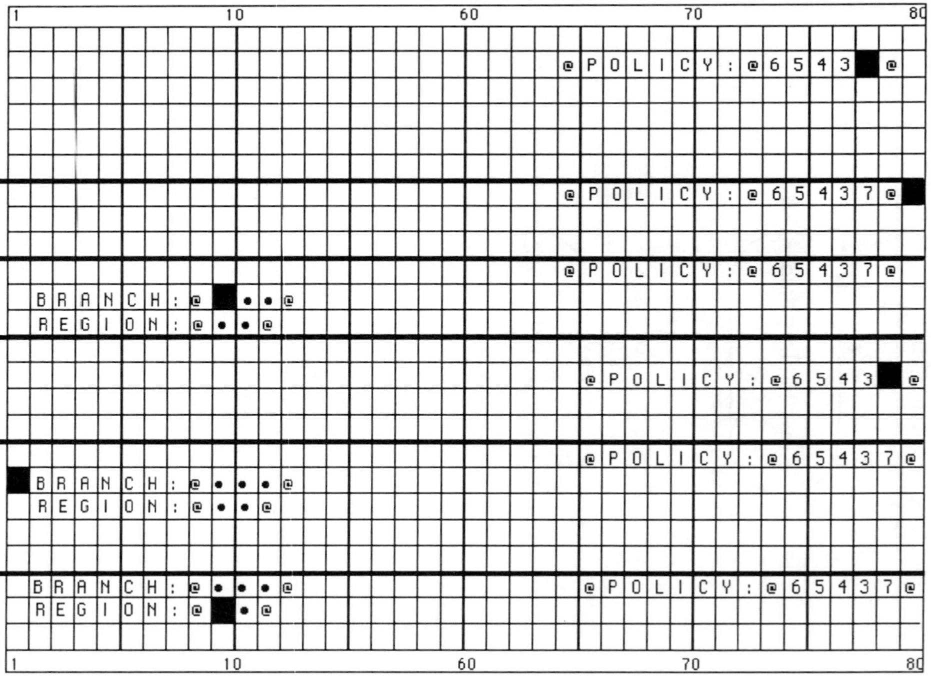

Note: The @ is an attribute character that defines the field's characteristics (protected, entry, etc.).

136

Slower data entry keying speeds and increased error probability result if users must make such decisions as

- Should this data always be keyed?
- If that field is keyed, should this one be keyed?
- If the data is X, then should I be keyed in the field?
- If a 4 goes here, where should other figures be keyed?

Such keying decisions impose learning requirements on users. Except in the most simple systems, this learning will never reach a satisfactory level. The fewer rules and decisions involved in keying, the faster and more accurate data entry will be. Coding, omitting, changing, and including data by special rules or transformations as a group represent probably the greatest single decrement to data entry speed.

Cursor Positioning

- Position the cursor at the first character location of the first entry field upon initial presentation of a screen.

Upon presentation of a screen, the cursor should be positioned for quick and easy start of the keying process. Never require a user to move the cursor manually to the proper location before keying can start.

Character Entry

- Key entry should be accomplished by direct character replacement (of underscores, previous entries, default values, or blanks).
- Keyed entries should always appear on the display (except for passwords or other secure entries).
- Data should be keyed without separators or delimiters such as dashes (—) or slashes(/).
- Data should be keyed without dimensional units (such as "$", "mph", etc.).
- Right or left justification of keyed data for variable-length fields should not be required.
- Key entry of leading zeros should not be required.
- Removal of unused underscores for variable-length fields should not be required.
- Areas of the screen not containing entry fields (i.e., protected fields) should be inaccessible, not requiring repeated key depressions to step through.

The above guidelines will speed the key entry of data on the screen and minimize the potential for errors.

ENTRY FIELDS

- Identify the entire entry field by underscores.

```
CITY:  _ _ _ _ _ _ _ _ _ _ _ _ _
```

- Alternatively, consider using boxes in a contrasting background or color.

```
Billing ID: ⌈          ⌉
```

An entry field should possess the following qualities.

- It should draw a person's attention to the fact that information must be keyed into it.
- It should not detract from the legibility of the characters keyed into the field.
- It should provide some indication of the nature of the desired response.
- It should indicate the appropriate number of characters for the entry.

Savage (1980), in an opinion study comparing reverse video and underscore field indicators with no indicators at all, found that users overwhelmingly preferred indicators to no indicators in the entry field.

In a follow-up study, several entry field techniques, including broken line underscores, a reverse video box, pointed brackets (<< >>), and two column separation methods (a dot or a line between each character position), were compared by Savage et al. (1982). They found that while it was not superior in every quality, the best delimiter overall was the underscore. More details on this study are given in following chapters.

The underscore has an added advantage in that it visually resembles an entry field line on a paper form (as the reverse video box resembles a paper form box, though the underscore doesn't have the readability problems).

Entry Field Separators and Delimiters

If the attribute convention does not require a reserved character position on the screen,

- incorporate separators or delimiters (such as slashes (/) or dashes (—) within the entry field.

```
DATE:  _ _ / _ _ / _ _
```

If the attribute convention requires a reserved character position on the screen,

- incorporate spaces where separator or delimiter characters would normally occur within the entry field.

```
DATE:  __  __  __
```

Separators and delimiters are often included with common data elements such as date and telephone number. Incorporated within an entry field on the screen, they permit much easier visual checking of the data keyed within that field. On a screen whose conventions do not require attribute character positions to be reserved on the screen itself, these separators or delimiters should be included in the entry field, as illustrated in the first example above.

When the screen attribute convention requires that attribute character positions be reserved on the screen, incorporating separators or delimiters is wasteful of screen space and lacks visual closure, as illustrated below.

```
DATE:  __ / __ / __
```

In this case the most reasonable alternative is to break the entry field into pieces by defining each component normally separated by a delimiter into separate unprotected fields. The attribute character positions will create spaces between data components, as illustrated in the second example above. The cursor will auto skip between the separate entry fields that have actually been created. To the user, however, what will visually appear is one field with the necessary structure to aid visual checking.

Default Values

- Current default values should be displayed in their appropriate entry fields upon transaction initiation. Do not rely on a user to remember them.
- Acceptance of a default value should be accomplished easily, such as by
  — a single confirming key entry,
  — a tab past the default field.
- Replacement of a default value should be accomplished without changing the default's current definition.

Incorporation of default values can also speed the data keying process, as long as the above guidelines are followed.

Screen Transmission

- Transmission of screens containing multiple data entry fields should be accomplished by a single explicit action when all entries are completed. Separate entry of fields should not be required or performed.

- Transmission should be accomplished through an explicitly labeled EN-TER or TRANSMIT key.
- An action requesting transmission of keyed data on a screen should result in transmission of all items on that screen, regardless of where the cursor is currently positioned on the screen.

Often the choice exists to transmit keyed data to the computer by either 1) a field-by-field basis, or 2) the entire screen at one time (commonly referred to as "block mode").

Full screen, or block mode, entry is thought to have these advantages:

- greater speed,
- easier review and correction of errors,
- more obvious logical groupings and more obvious relationships of elements, and
- more efficient cross-field edits.

Field-by-field entry is thought to have these advantages:

- less dense screens because they do not have to display optional elements unless necessary,
- faster error correction, and
- fewer errors due to early detection of errors that could trigger cross-field errors if detected later.

One study comparing these two modes of entry is Romano and Sonnio (1984). They found that the full screen (block) mode was significantly faster, though no error differences existed between the two modes.

It would seem that in cases of large amounts of data and source document-oriented entry, the block mode advantages are substantial, and this is the recommended mode in these cases. In other cases—smaller volumes of data, where speed is not critical, and non-source document-oriented entry—either mode is satisfactory. For very casual system users, a field-by-field mode has the greatest advantages.

ABBREVIATIONS

- Truncation has been found to be the most consistent abbreviation method for encoding.
- No significant abbreviation method differences exist for decoding.
- Teach users the abbreviation method to be used.
- Train users with full words, not abbreviations.
- Develop a standard dictionary of abbreviations.

Computer systems often require the creation of abbreviations, for field captions, data, or commands. A variety of studies have addressed optimum abbreviation strategies, good summaries being found in Ehrenreich (1985) and Grudin and Barnard (1985). A dozen or so abbreviation methods that have been described, the most common being:

- natural—subjective judgments of what is a good representation of the full word;
- contraction—the first and last letter of the word are retained, some letters in between are deleted;
- vowel deletion—all vowels in the word are deleted;
- truncation—the first few letters of the word are retained, the remainder deleted.

The studies have concluded that for encoding, or creating abbreviations, the truncation method has yielded the most consistent results. In general, it has been found that people have great difficulties in reconstructing consistent abbreviations for the same words. Word lengths and letter selection rules vary considerably. For decoding, understanding the abbreviation, no method has been found to be superior to any other.

Teaching users the abbreviation rule to be followed will result in more consistent abbreviations. Train them with the full word or words first to aid word–abbreviation association. Users who learn only abbreviations, it has been found, often do not know what they stand for. Because of the problems in creating and remembering abbreviations, a standard dictionary of abbreviations is a valuable aid in any screen design activity.

DATA EDITING

When

- Data should be edited as close to its source as possible.
- Data should be automatically edited after entry of all fields on a screen has been keyed, not on an item-by-item basis.
- Correction of errors should be permitted immediately after an error is detected.

How

- Computer data editing should always be performed. Never rely upon the operator to make correct entries.
- Inability to correct an error should not prevent initiation of another transaction. The capability should exist for the storage and later retrieval of the transaction with an error.

Data should always be edited as close as possible to its source. When errors occur, and they will, the correction process will thus be much more efficient. Data should also be edited on a screen basis, not an item basis. An experienced data entry operator will find stopping for errors disruptive to the keying rhythm.

DATA STRUCTURE

Data Size

- Restrict all alphabetic codes to four or fewer characters.
- Restrict all numeric codes to six or fewer characters.
- Keep code length and format constant throughout any single category.

As the length of a field increases, errors in using it also increase. Figure 5.4 shows mean error rates for various field lengths. Smaller data fields will pay dividends in lower error rates.

Data Content

- Do not intersperse letters with numbers.
- Use alpha combinations that are
  — meaningful,
  — distinctive,
  — predictable.
- For alphabetical data entry, do not use restricted alphabetic sets.
- If special characters are selected for keying (e.g., =, /, @, etc.) choose those that will not require frequent shifts between upper and lower case.

Codes based on common English usage (words, contractions, abbreviations, acronyms, quantities, etc.) are the most easily used because they require minimum learning. Arbitrary codes require extensive learning and are seldom easy to use. Keying errors decrease when people learn familiar letter sequences and patterns. They can also detect and correct inconsistencies and inaccuracies more easily.

Figure 5.4   Error percentage for varying field lengths.

Average Number Characters per Field	Percent of Fields in Error
3	1.4
5	2.0
7	2.6
9	3.1
11	3.6

If abbreviated codes are chosen for entry, make sure they are as distinctive as possible. This will minimize potential confusions due to similarity. BAM vs. BAN, for example, is bad. BAM vs. PRV is good.

Codes containing predictable letter sequences can be keyed more rapidly. The letter combinations "TH" and "IN" are much more predictable than "YX" or "JS," and can be keyed faster.

Many keying errors are caused by incorrect SHIFT key usage. Shifts take longer to accomplish and can severely disrupt the keying rhythm.

Data Legibility

- Break long codes (seven or more characters) into three- or four-character groups.
- Present source data visually, not with auditory devices, such as telephones or dictating machines.
- Eliminate frequently confused characters and character pairs from code vocabularies.
  — Eliminate the letters *O* and *I* from alphanumeric code vocabularies.
  — Do not use the letters *Y, N, V, Z, Q, U,* and *G* in hand printing.

Figure 5.5 shows the most frequent character substitutions.

Figure 5.5   Frequency of character substitutions.

Characters:

Characters:	Substitution Frequency	
I	24%	} 47%
O	23%	
8	9%	} 70%
0	5%	
Z	5%	
B	4%	

Character Pairs:

Characters:	Cumulative Frequency
I-1	25%
O-0	50%
B-8	60%
Z-2	70%

Figure 5.6   Illegibility of hand-printed characters.

(ranked from highest to lowest probability of being printed illegibly)

1.	Y						
2.	N	24%					
3.	V		50%				
4.	Z						
5.	Q						
6.	U						
7.	G						
8.	J	18.	5	28.	H		
9.	C	19.	4	29.	Z		
10.	X	20.	I	30.	R		
11.	O	21.	A	31.	P		
12.	T	22.	F	32.	0		
13.	E	23.	6	33.	7		
14.	D	24.	L	34.	3		
15.	K	25.	W	35.	8		
16.	S	26.	M	36.	1		
17.	B	27.	9				

About half of all coding errors could be eliminated if *O* and *I* were not in the alphanumeric code vocabulary. And about two-thirds of all errors could be eliminated if *I*, *O*, *8*, *0*, and *B* were not used as codes.

The two worst legibility offenders in hard hand printing, as shown in Figure 5.6, are *Y* and *N*. Removal of the first 7 offending characters would delete about 50 percent of the characters causing legibility errors.

People prefer to handle codes in small chunks. A 6-character code may be perceived as two 3-character codes, and a 7-character code as a three-four pair. For example, the telephone number 2155847053 is commonly handled as 215 584 7053. Lengthy codes should be structured in 3- or 4-character groupings.

Legibility problems could be greatly reduced by training people to write big, closed loops; to use simple shapes; to connect lines; to block print rather than scrawl; and not to link characters together.

SECTION **5-2**

Data Entry Screens Used With a Dedicated Source Document

SCREEN ORGANIZATION

- The screen must be an image of its associated source document.

Skipping around a source document to locate data adds time to the data entry process. It also imposes learning requirements on users, since they must master the order and location of fields. Having the source document and screen in the same sequence can eliminate these problems. Cursor location on the screen is then always known because it corresponds with the user's position on the source document. Proper sequence also allows the user's eyes to move easily ahead of his hands—another design objective of data entry.

Ideally, keying should never require eye movement from the source document to the screen. Theoretically (and frequently, if the design is proper), the user should be able to key an entire screen without glancing at it. Often, however, eye movements between document and screen are necessary to check for possible keying errors and to correct edit-detected errors. This eye movement will be most efficient (and natural) if fields on the screen and the document are in the same relative position. These considerations lead to this cardinal rule for developing data entry systems: *Develop screens that are exact images of source documents.* Fields on a screen should be located on the same line and in the same order as fields on the source document. This factor is more important than absolute visual clarity.

The rule should not be interpreted literally, however; different caption sizes and the number of fields included on one line can cause minor distortions. Thus, the goal should be relative positioning, since the eye will not detect minor distortions in the exact image relationship.

If a source document contains nonentry fields, ink screening techniques can maintain the image relationship. If a source document contains a large number of these fields, the positioning of data entry fields on the screen may appear awkward. For consistency, however, the relative positioning rule must be maintained. The only exception would be a revised scheme that could eliminate the awkwardness while maintaining consistency within the application and the ability to locate specific fields easily.

Screens of this kind and their associated source documents cannot be developed separately. Constraints imposed by source document design considerations must be reflected in screen format design and vice versa. In fact, as was mentioned earlier, source document design is usually a greater restriction in the design process than screen design (Galitz, 1975). Design guidelines for source document design are discussed in Chapter 13.

CAPTIONS

Structure and Size

- Captions should use abbreviations and contractions.
- Captions should not exceed eight characters.
- Abbreviations should not exceed three or four characters.
- Separate two or more abbreviations by hyphens.
- Display captions in normal intensity.

Formatting

- Single fields:
  - — locate caption to left of entry field;
  - — right-justify caption to enter field;
  - — separate from entry field by a unique symbol (such as a colon) and one space.

```
    ORG : X---------    ---------------
```

- Multiple-occurrence fields:
  - — row orientation—
    locate caption to left of entry fields;
    separate from entry field by a unique symbol (such as a colon) and one space;
    separate entry fields by a unique symbol with one space on each side of it.

```
    CDS: -----X : X----- : ----- : ----- : -----
```

—columnar orientation—
  locate caption one line above column of entry fields;
  left-justify caption above first position of entry fields;
  precede entry fields by a unique symbol (such as a colon) separated
  from entry fields by one space (if no underscores displayed).

```
ORD-NO
-------------
-------------
-------------
-------------
```

Structure and size.   When a dedicated source document is used for keying, field captions are normally needed only for error detection or correction, or to find one's exact place on the screen when momentarily confused. Thus, captions have a supportive rather than a primary function in the data entry process, and abbreviations and contractions should be used.

The caption size limit is 8 characters. This is a compromise between screen space utilization and clarity. It results in a good fit between standard (8½ by 11) documents and 80-character-wide screens (Galitz 1975), while maintaining an exact image relationship. Learning requirements do exist, but they are minimal. Since screen captions are derived from associated fields on the source document, the document provides a constant reference to aid in caption interpretation and learning.

The 8-character limitation should not be considered an absolute, since a longer caption may occasionally be needed to achieve clarity. Since caption pieces are small, hyphens should be used to tie them together visually. This will minimize misinterpretations and erroneous associations.

Formatting.   Single data field captions should be located to the left of the entry field and separated by a unique symbol. The colon (:) is recommended for this purpose, because it provides a definitive and yet unobtrusive break between the two. The recommended approach for multiple occurring (repeating) fields is the columnar orientation. The caption should be placed above the data field and justified above the data field's first character entry position. This above-entry-field positioning will aid in distinguishing the single from multiple occurring fields. Components of larger captions should not be stacked above one another when the columnar approach is used. Maintain the caption on one line. If underscores are used as entry field delimiters for multiple occurring fields, the colons defining the beginning point of the field are not necessary. Colons are only necessary if entry field designators are not used, since they then become the only way a user has to determine how many occurrences of a field exist.

ENTRY FIELDS

Structure

- Optimally:
  —identify entire field by underscores;

  ```
  ACCT:x_____
  ```

  —break up long fields through incorporation of slashes (/), dashes (-), other common delimiters, or spaces;
  if attribute character does not consume a character position:

  ```
    DT:  __/__/__
  TEL-NO:  (___) ___-____
  ```

  if attribute character consumes a character position:

  ```
    DT:  __ __ __
  TEL-NO:  ___ ___ ____
  ```

- Minimally, identify starting point of fields with unique symbols (separated by one space).

  ```
   NM:x
  STR:x
  ```

  —Optionally, identify ending point of long nonunderscored fields with a unique symbol (such as a semicolon). Separate symbol by one space.

  ```
  STR:x
  ```

Highlighting

- Call attention to entry fields through a highlighting technique.

Structure. An entry field for this kind of screen should possess the following qualities:

- It should draw a user's attention to the fact that information must be keyed into it.
- It should not detract from the legibility of the characters keyed into the field.

As mentioned previously, Savage (1980) found that users overwhelmingly preferred something to indicate entry fields, and a follow-up study (Savage et al., 1982) found that the best alternative for defining an entry field appears to be the broken line underscore, which possesses an added advantage in that it visually resembles an entry field line on a paper form. It is also a desirable alternative in the next class of data entry screens where estimation of field length is more important. Thus, consistency between different kinds of screens is maintained.

To make entry fields more readable, it is desirable to break them up into logical pieces. If the attribute character does not consume a character position, slashes and dashes may easily be inserted into the entry field as illustrated above. If the attribute character does consume a character position, however, the best alternative is to break it logically through the use of spaces, which are actually unprotected attribute character positions. The entry field then becomes segments separated by auto skip cursor movements. This allows the keyer to still visualize the field as one entry field. To use slashes and dashes in this situation latter condition would be wasteful of space, as numerous attribute characters may be needed to break the field into segments.

If underscores are not possible, the caption symbol (such as the colon) used to signify the starting point of an entry field is acceptable. The entry field will usually start immediately after the symbol and one blank space. Absolute identification of field length is not essential if the system is operating with manual tabbing, because the terminal will identify the end by locking the keyboard.

Highlighting.   If any field on this kind of data entry screen is highlighted, it should be the entry field not the caption, since entry fields are the strongest tie between source document and screen. A common highlighting technique is high intensity display of the field. The method chosen, however, should permit fields in error to be found quickly. Possible ways to call attention to error fields are to display them in reverse video or to turn off the highlighting when system edits are invoked.

FIELD ALIGNMENT

- Maintain image relationship with source document through placement of entry fields (not captions).

When a dedicated source document is used, the document/screen image relationship is maintained through placement of entry fields on the screen, as illustrated in Figure 5.7. Captions need not be aligned. Note that the third field in the second line of the form (F-Medical Payments-Each Accident) is a nonentry field. It is shaded on the form and does not appear on the screen.

Figure 5.7 Maintaining a document/screen image relationship.

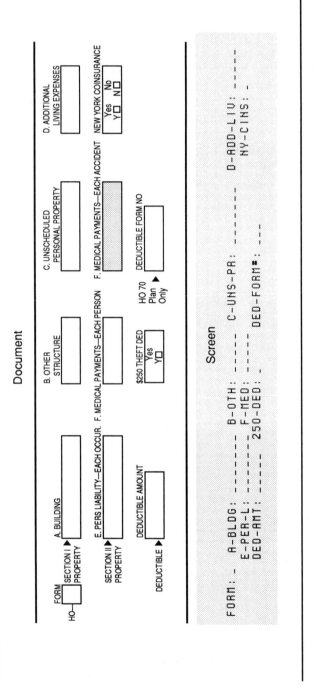

SPACING

Horizontal

- Optimally, leave a minimum of three spaces between one entry field and the caption of the following field. One space is acceptable if space constraints exist.

```
EFF-DT: __ __ __xxxEXP-DT: __ __ __xxx
```

Vertical

- Incorporate space lines where "visual" breaks or spaces occur on the source document.

When using a source document with horizontally arranged fields, it is preferable to leave three blank spaces between the last character of one field and the caption of the next. If space constraints exist, however, one blank space is acceptable.

Vertical spacing between rows of fields on a screen will follow the spacing conventions of the source document. If source document rows are single spaced, the screen rows will be single spaced also. If a gap between source document rows appears, there should be a gap between screen rows. This is another method of maintaining an image relationship between document and screen.

It is important to keep in mind that this spacing is relative. Some source documents may be designed for purposes of clarity, with what appears to be a space line between rows of document fields. From a screen design standpoint, these wider-spaced document rows should be considered as consecutive rows and the screen spacing accomplished accordingly. Leave a space line on a screen only when a wider than usual gap exists on the document.

COMPLETION AIDS AND PROMPTING

Completion Aids

- None necessary.

Prompting

- None necessary.

Completion aids are a form of guidance on the structure of data to be keyed within a field. Prompting messages are instructions to the user on what to do with, or how to work with, the screen being presented. Neither should be necessary on this kind of screen. With a dedicated source document, the structure is obvious from the design of the form. The data keyed is simply that coded on the document.

HEADINGS

Section Headings

- Locate section heading directly above its associated data fields.
- Indent related field captions or row headings a minimum of three spaces from the beginning of the section heading.
- Spell out fully.

```
           CUSTOMER INFORMATION

               NAME:  _____

           xxxBTH-DT:  __ __ __

                OCC:  _____
```

Most source documents will contain section headings identifying related groups of document fields. These section headings may be incorporated on the screen following the rules given above. Note that with varying size captions, the three-space indention is to the longest caption.

This indention of captions and spelling out of the section heading is intended to make the heading visually distinguishable from the captions on the screen. They will be obvious to the screen user by their size and location. Other techniques may, of course, be used to achieve the same objective without resorting to positional cues. These techniques might be double-size characters or underlining. Whichever method is chosen should always permit easy discrimination of the section headings from other components of the screen.

Subsection or Row Headings

- Optional.
- Locate to left of associated entry fields.
- Spell out fully.
- If directly adjacent to entry field, separate from entry field by a unique symbol (such as a colon) and one space.

```
                 INV-CD
              1:x_____
              2:x_____
              3:x_____
```

- If adjacent to field caption, indent related caption a minimum of three (3) spaces and incorporate "greater than" (>>) symbols.

```
PROPERTY >>        BLDG: --------
LIABILITYx>>xxx    MED:  --------
```

Some source documents contain one or more row subsection or headings to describe the subject of the entry fields in that row. These headings may be included on screens if space permits.

A meaningful convention to designate row headings is two "greater than" symbols (>>). They direct attention to the right and indicate that everything that follows refer to this category. In the example above, the caption BLDG: and all fields that follow on that line refer to PROPERTY.

This convention can also be used to clean up a line of captions containing redundant words. The redundant word within each caption is removed and incorporated into the row heading as, for example, DATES >>.

Field Group Headings

- Center field group heading above the captions to which it applies.
- Relate to these captions by a broken dashed line ended by pointed brackets.
- Spell out fully.

Single-Occurrence Fields

```
< - - - - - - HOMEOWNERS - - - - - >
EFF-DT: __ __ __    EXP-DT: __ __ __
```

Multiple-Occurrence Fields

```
< - - - - - HOMEOWNERS - - - - - >
FORM        EFF-DT      EXP-DT
-------     __ __ __    __ __ __
-------     __ __ __    __ __ __
-------     __ __ __    __ __ __
```

Occasionally a group heading above a series of related captions may be needed. It may be centered above the captions to which it applies and related to them through a broken dashed line ended by pointed brackets ("greater" and "less than" symbols). This provides closure to the grouping. Field group headings will normally be spelled out fully.

TITLE

- Create a short, simple, clear, and distinctive title describing the purpose of the screen.
- Locate the title in a centered position at the top of each screen.
- Spell out fully using an upper-case font.

The title should be short, simple, clear, distinctive, and truthful. It should immediately orient the viewer to the screen's content and purpose. It is normally made up of two parts, a subject and function such as INSURANCE (subject) APPLICATION (function). There may be some single-word exceptions (such as INVOICE or STATEMENT). Do not include words such as FORM or SCREEN in the title, and eliminate connecting words such as "of" unless absolutely necessary. The title should be centered at the screen's top for balance and displayed using capital letters for emphasis.

SCREEN IDENTIFIER

- Place a screen identifier, page number, or other reference information in a consistent location in the upper right-hand corner.
  — For screens containing several pieces of screen identification information, both the left-hand and right-hand upper corners may be used.

Screen identification or other reference information warrants only occasional viewer interest. Therefore it should be located in a less prominent position on the screen. When included, the preferred location is the upper right corner. For a series of screens, a page-numbering convention should be included to allow users to know their exact location. The paging convention may simply be "page n of x" or it may incorporate a mnemonic code that is a contraction of the screen title, for example, "POL02" or "AUTO03," the last two digits indicating the number of the screen in the series.

When the screen identifier includes additional information (such as date, time), a more efficient use of the screen body and better screen balance can be achieved by splitting the information between the upper left and upper right corners. All elements should maintain consistent locations on all screens.

Every screen must have a way of being uniquely identified through its titling- and/or screen-numbering convention.

MESSAGES AND NAVIGATION TECHNIQUES

- Uniquely identify informational, warning, and status messages through
  — a consistent location such as
    — a designated line at the bottom of the screen,
    — in a window.

— use of contrasting display features such as
  — reverse video,
  — highlighting,
  — different font style,
  — preceding each message type by a unique symbol
— display in a mixed-case font.
- Uniquely identify the screen navigation technique (command field, function keys, action bars, etc.) through
  — a consistent location,
  — separating from the body of the screen.

Recommended locations and display methods for messages and navigation techniques have been described in Chapter 4. They must attract the viewer's attention and be easily discernible from the screen body and other screen components. This is accomplished most effectively by locating them outside the screen body (or in windows) using consistent locations, contrasting display features, and special symbols. Again, each type must be identified by its structure and location without actually having to be read.

Example 1. A portion of a source document and its associated screen. Note the left and right justification and alignment of entry fields (not captions) to maintain the document/screen image relationship.

```
                                                                        CHG01
                    CHANGE / ENDORSEMENT

POLICY IDENTIFICATION

    EFF-DT: ------                                    POL #: -----------
    INSD-NM: ------------                             ACCT #: --------
    AGCY-NM: ------------       BR-CD: ---           PROD-CD: ------

SECTION I  ENDORSEMENTS

48: - IDES: ---------- ------                  ADDL-LIM: ------     48-PR: ------
    2DES: ---------- ------                    ADDL-LIM: ------
    3DES: ---------- ------                    ADDL-LIM: ------
49: - 2LIM: ------  PR-GR: --  C/O: -  TER: --   F&E: ------  P-C: ---
    3LIM: ------  PR-GR: --  C/O: -  TER: --   F&E: ------  P-C: ---
50: - 2LIM: ------                       3LIM: ------                 PR: ------
51: - LIM: ------                                                  50-PR: ------
69: - LIM: ------                                                  51-PR: ------
216: - TYPE: -                                                     69-PR: ------
                                                                  216-PR: ------
```

Example 1. Continued

CHANGE/ENDORSEMENT WORKSHEET

POLICY IDENTIFICATION ▶

CHANGE EFFECTIVE DATE
MO   DAY   YEAR

INSURED NAME

AGENCY NAME

POLICY NUMBER

ACCOUNT NUMBER

BRANCH CODE   PROCEDURE CODE

SECTION I ENDORSEMENTS ▶

DESCRIPTION

1.

2.

3.

| | LIMIT OF LIABILITY | PREM GRP. | C/O GRP. | TERR | FIRE AND E.C. RATE | ADDITIONAL LIMIT OF LIABILITY | | PROT. CLASS |

2ND RES.

3RD RES.

TOTAL LIMIT OF LIABILITY

2ND RES.

TOTAL LIMIT OF LIABILITY

3RD RES.

TOTAL LIMIT OF LIABILITY

LIMIT OF LIABILITY

TYPE   Central Station Alarm   Fire or Police Alert Alarm   Local Alarm
              C   A   L

OTHER
STRUCTURES   HO-48
             ▲ A D C

BUILDING
ADDITIONS AND
ALTERATIONS HO-49
             ▲ A D C

INC. LIMITS ON
PERS. PROPERTY —
OTHER RESIDENCES HO-50
             ▲ A D C

BUILDING ADDITION
AND ALTERATIONS
INCREASED LIMITS HO-51
                A D C

DENTISTS, DOCTORS
AND VETERINARIANS HO-65
             ▲ A D C

PREMISES ALARM
SYSTEM   HO-216
             ▲ A D C

HO-48 PREMIUM

HO-49 PREMIUM

HO-50 PREMIUM

HO-51 PREMIUM

HO-69 PREMIUM

HO-216 PREMIUM

157

Example 2. Again, a portion of a source document and its associated screen. Note the several nonentry fields on the document that have not been included on the screen.

```
                    PERSONAL AUTOMOBILE - SUPPLEMENT                              PASUP


APPLICANT INFORMATION
   AP-NM: --------------                                              POL#: --------------
DRIVER INFORMATION
   DR-NM: ----------- BTH-DT: ----- SEX: - OCC: --------
   MR-ST: - LIC#: ------------ ST: -- YR-LIC: -- GD-ST: - DR-TR: - IMP: -
VEHICLE INFORMATION
   VEH-YR: -- N/U: - MAKE: ----------- ID#: ----------- HP: - SYM: -----
   USE: -- MILE: -- AV/MI: ----- MOD: - DAM: - CLS: ---- YR: --
LIENHOLDER INFORMATION
   VEH#: -
   LN-NM: ------------------------
   LN-NM2: ------------------------
   ML-AD: ------------------------
   CITY: ------------ ST: -- ZIP: -----
PAYOR INFORMATION
   PY-NM: ------------------------              ACCT#: -------
   Y-NM2: ------------------------              TEL#: --- --- ----
   PY-AD: ------------------------
   CITY: ------------ ST: -- ZIP: -----
```

Example 2. Continued

Personal Automobile Application—Supplement

APPLICANT INFORMATION

APPLICANT NAME

POLICY NUMBER

DRIVER INFORMATION

DRIVER NAME (from license)

MARITAL STATUS

DRIVERS LICENSE NUMBER

DATE OF BIRTH
MO   DAY   YEAR

STATE   YEARS LICENSED

SEX

GOOD STUDENT

OCCUPATION (if student miles from home)

DRIVER TRAINING

IMPAIRED DRIVER

VEHICLE INFORMATION

YR/PUR   VEH.YR   NEW/USED?
No☐ Yes☐

MAKE MODEL AND BODY STYLE

VEHICLE IDENTIFICATION NUMBER

HP

SYMBOL   CYL   DRIVER

USE   MILES   ANN.MI

ALTERNATE GARAGE

MODIFIED
No☐ Yes☐

DAMAGE
No☐ Yes☐

CLASS

YEAR   GARAGED
No☐ Yes☐

CAR CAR CAR

LIENHOLDER INFORMATION

VEHICLE NUMBER

LIENHOLDER ACCOUNT #

LIENHOLDER NAME

MAILING ADDRESS

CITY   STATE   ZIP CODE

PAYOR INFORMATION (Complete only if policy payor is other than the insured.)

PAYOR NAME

PAYOR ACCOUNT NUMBER

PAYOR TELEPHONE NUMBER

PAYOR ADDRESS

CITY   STATE   ZIP CODE

Example 3. A columnar-organized document and screen with row headings. Again note the nonentry fields.

```
                          FARM / FIRE SCHEDULE                              FA/FI

           PREM    CNS    DED    W-DED   AMT-INS   CNST

  FIRE  >  -----   --     -----
    EC  >  -----          -----   ----     ----      --
  V&MM  >  -----          -----
   AOP  >  -----   --     -----            ----
SPEC-EC >  ------  --     -----            ----       --
```

Example 3. Continued

FARM/FIRE SCHEDULE DATA ENTRY WORKSHEET

Data Entry Screens Used Without a Dedicated Source Document

SCREEN ORGANIZATION

- The screen should provide optimum visual clarity and represent the organization of the world from which data is collected.

If data entry screens must be developed without dedicated source documents, their design should be based on the organization of the manuals, documents, papers, or notes from which the data is keyed. If the data is being provided by a person, such as a customer or sales agent, it must be organized in a manner meaningful to that person. Since these information organization variables cannot always be controlled, an exact correspondence between source material and screen isn't usually achievable. Thus, the screen format must be the controlling force in the development. A person usually identifies a field on the screen and then seeks data or information for keying from appropriate source materials or people. The rules for optimizing screen visual clarity should be applied here. Data entry will be enhanced by visual "anchor points" built into the screen that permit easy and efficient eye movements back and forth between the screen and source materials. Data entry will also be enhanced by minimizing required visual references to the screen. Every attempt should be made to reflect in the screen format the organization of the world from which entry data is taken.

If the sequence of data collected for entry is arbitrary or cannot be predicted, it may be preferable to develop a command language dialogue to identify each entry rather than have a user remember and reorder items to conform to the screen. The data then may be keyed in the order in which it is received, each field being identified by a unique keyed label.

CAPTIONS

Structure and Size

- Fully spell out in a meaningful language to the user.
- Display in normal intensity.
- Use an upper-case or mixed-case font:

Formatting

- Single Fields:
  — locate caption to left of entry field;
  — separate caption from entry field by a unique symbol and one space. The colon (:) is the recommended symbol.

```
        Organization:x_____
```

- Multiple Occurrence Fields:
  — row orientation—
    — locate caption to left of entry fields;
    — separate from entry field by a unique symbol (such as a colon) and one space;
    — separate entry fields by a unique symbol (such as a colon) with one space on each side of the symbol.

```
    Codes:  _____x:x____ : _____ : _____ : _____
```

  — columnar orientation—
    — locate caption one line above column of entry fields;
    — left-justify caption above first position of entry fields;
    — precede entry fields by a unique symbol (such as a colon) separated by one space (if no underscores displayed).

```
        Order Number
        _____
        _____
        _____
        _____
```

Structure and size. Since a dedicated source document does not exist, screen captions are used to identify what information must be keyed into a field. Normal entry requires that the screen user read the caption, find the information in source materials or through conversation with someone else (or perhaps even create the entry from memory), and then key the information. Since data to be keyed must be identified from the screen, captions must clearly and concisely describe the information required.

Captions should be fully spelled out in the user's natural language.

Captions that are ambiguous, imprecise, or unclear will impair performance until they are learned. In general, abbreviations and contractions should not be used. To achieve the alignment recommendations to be discussed shortly, an occasional abbreviation or contraction may be necessary. If so, choose those that are common in the everyday language of the application or those that are meaningful and easily learned.

Formatting.   Formatting conventions will be identical to those for source document-oriented data entry screens. For single fields the caption will precede the entry field; for multiple occurring fields the caption will be above. The colon (:) will be the symbol to break caption from data.

ENTRY FIELDS

Structure

- Optimally:
  — identify entire field by underscores;

  ```
             Account:x--------
  ```

  — break up long fields through incorporation of slashes (/), dashes (-), other common delimiters, or spaces—
  - if attribute character does not consume a character position:

    ```
              Date: __/__/__
      Telephone Number: (___) ___-____
    ```

  - if attribute character consumes a character position:

    ```
              Date: __ __ __
      Telephone Number: ___ ___ ____
    ```

- Minimally, identify starting point of field with unique symbol (separated by one space).

  ```
            Name:x
          Street:x
  ```

  — Optionally, identify ending point of long nonunderscored fields with a unique symbol (such as a semicolon). Separate symbol by one space.

  ```
          Street:x;
  ```

Highlighting

- Call attention to entry fields through a highlighting technique.

Structure.   In addition to possessing the qualities described for data entry screens with source documents (attracting attention; not detracting from entry legibility), entry fields for this class of screens should

* provide some indication of the nature of the desired response,
* indicate the appropriate number of characters for the entry.

The Savage et al. (1982) study concluded that the broken underscore is a good technique for estimating field size. Pointed brackets (<>) were found to create the most errors in estimating field lengths, and column separators (a dot between each character position) to take the longest time to estimate field length.

To make entry fields more readable, again it is desirable to break them up into logical pieces. If the attribute character does not consume a character position, slashes and dashes may be easily inserted into the entry field as illustrated above. If the attribute character does consume a character position, the best alternative is to break it logically with spaces.

Highlighting.   While the caption initially fulfills a more important role on this kind of screen than in the other kinds, to maintain consistency between all screen kinds, it is recommended that the entry field receive the highlighting. Again, high intensity may be used for this purpose, but the method chosen must be visually different from that used to communicate errors to the screen user.

FIELD ALIGNMENT

---

* Vertically align entry fields and captions into columns.

```
        Policy Number:      _ _ _ _ _ _ _ _ _ _
        Account Number:     _ _ _ _ _ _ _ _
        Effective Date:     _ _  _ _  _ _
        Expiration Date:    _ _  _ _  _ _
        Policy Status:      _ _ _ _ _ _ _ _
```

To aid users in finding their position quickly, fields should be columnized. Space constraint tradeoffs will sometimes result in two or even three columns of fields on one screen. It is important to remember that if the screen cursor moves from left to right and from top to bottom, related columnized fields will be placed *adjacent* to one another. A terminal whose cursor can be programmed to move down a column will result in a more efficient entry process, though, as eye movements between fields are greatly reduced and finding one's place is easier.

This is because the visual "anchor point" remains at about the same place on the screen as the eye moves back and forth between successive fields and source materials. If left-to-right field orientation is maintained, the anchor point jumps from side to side in a less efficient manner. So, columnize the organization of elements for top-to-bottom entry whenever possible.

FIELD JUSTIFICATION

1. First Approach

- Left-justify both captions and entry fields.
- Leave one space between the longest caption and the entry field column.

```
Policy Number:    ----------
Account Number:   --------
Effective Date:   -- -- --
Expiration Date:x -- -- --
Policy Status:    --------
```

2. Second Approach

- Left-justify entry fields and right-justify captions to entry fields.
- Leave one space between each.

```
       Corporation:x -------------
             Title:x -------------
Social Security No:x --- -- ----
```

Field justification can be accomplished in either of two ways. Approach 1 results in both captions and entry fields left-justified into columns. Approach 2 right-justifies the captions up against the left-justified column of entry fields (see examples above). Each approach has advantages and disadvantages, as previously discussed in Chapter 4. Whichever method is chosen should be consistently followed in a system's screen design.

Again, examples at the end of this and succeeding chapters reflect both styles to enable the reader to see and evaluate them.

KEYING ORDER

Cursor Moves from Left to Right

- For a large number of data fields, order sequentially from left to right.

```
First Prize: ---------    Second Prize: ---------
Third Prize: ---------    Fourth Prize: ---------
Fifth Prize: ---------    Sixth Prize:  ---------
```

- For a small number of data fields (about 15 or less) order sequentially from top to bottom.

```
           First Prize:    ----------
           Second Prize:   ----------
           Third Prize:    ----------
           Fourth Prize:   ----------
           Fifth Prize:    ----------
           Sixth Prize:    ----------
```

Cursor Can Move in Any Direction

- Order sequentially from top to bottom.

```
            First Prize: ----------
           Second Prize: ----------
            Third Prize: ----------
           Fourth Prize: ----------
            Fifth Prize: ----------
            Sixth Prize: ----------
```

Ordering data fields for keying will be determined by the screen's cursor movement requirements as well as the amount of information to be keyed. For screens whose cursor moves left to right, ordering will, of course, have to be left to right. However, if there are few enough data fields to permit top-to-bottom movement, this should be done. Eye movements and the keying process will be more efficient in a top-to-bottom orientation.

For screens whose cursor can be programmed to move in any direction, top-to-bottom ordering is always recommended. If more than one column of elements exist on the screen, cursor movement will be from the bottom of one column to the top of the next.

SPACING

Horizontal

- Leave a minimum of five spaces between the longest entry field in one column and the leftmost caption in an adjacent column.

```
    First  Prize:  ----------xxxxxSecond  Prize:   ----------
    Third  Prize:  ----------     Fourth  Prize:   ----------
    Fifth  Prize:  ----------     Sixth   Prize:   ----------
```

Vertical

- Leave at least one space line between columnized "groups" of related information.

```
Driver Name:      ------------------------
License Number:   ----------------
Restrictions:     ----------
Expires:          --  --  --

Vehicle Type:     -------------
Model Year:       ----
Horsepower:       ---
Plate Number:     ----------
```

- For long columns of related elements, leave a space line after every fifth row. (If space permits, leave a space after every third row.) Never exceed seven rows without leaving a space line.

```
Policy Number:     -----------
Account Number:    --------
Effective Date:    --  --  --
Expiration Date:   --  --  --
Policy Status:     --

Policy Form:       --
Property:          -------
Liability:         -------
Deductible:        ----
Endorsement:       -------

Model
--------
--------
--------
--------
--------

--------
--------
--------
--------
--------
```

To separate columns visually, leave a minimum of five spaces between the longest entry field in one column and the leftmost caption in the next column. To improve readability of field rows, leave a blank line after every fifth row; if space permits, leave a blank line after every third row.

Optimum spacing between columns of elements will be affected by the weighting of the elements within each column. The objective is for captions to be visually tied to their related entry fields and columns of elements to be visually broken up. Thus, spacing between columns should be enough to meet this objective.

COMPLETION AIDS AND PROMPTING MESSAGES

Completion Aids

- Incorporate completion aids on a screen as necessary, in a manner that visually distinguishes them, such as:

```
1)        Date (MMDDYY):      __ __ __
          Rate (NN.N):        ____
          Codes (AB,CD,EF):   __
          Area (Square Feet): _____

2)        Date: MM DD YY
          Rate: NN.N

3)        Date:   __ __ __      (MMDDYY)
          Rate:   ____          (NN.N)
          Codes:  __            (AB,CD,EF)
          Area:   _____        (Square Feet)
```

Prompting Messages

- Incorporate prompting messages on a screen, as necessary.
  - In a position just preceding the part, or parts, of a screen to which they apply.
  - Using mixed-case letters.
  - In a manner that visually distinguishes them, such as
    - Beginning at least three (3) spaces to the left of the left-most heading or field caption.
    - Using a different type style.

```
The following are necessary for changes only.
             Kind:  _____
           Amount:  _____
   Effective Date:  __ __ __
```

Completion aids and prompting messages must be easily discernible from the body of the screen. This is accomplished most effectively by using contrasting display features, special symbols, and consistent locations. The message must stand out as an instruction or prompt by its size, shape, and/or location without it actually having to be read.

Before incorporating completion aids or prompting messages into a screen, make sure they are really needed since they can quickly become visual noise. In most cases a frequently used screen, or a frequently used system, might not require them.

Completion aids.   Field completion aids can be used to provide some indication of the kind of data to be encoded within a field. Some methods are illustrated above. Approach 1, the completion aid within the caption, suffers from excess noise in the visual field once the field structures are learned. Because the aid is placed within the area normally consumed by the caption, the caption itself is also moved farther away from the entry field to which it relates. This can cause longer, and unnecessary, eye movements. Approach 2 puts the completion aid in the data field itself, and the key entry simply replaces it. The disadvantage here is that the aid is erased during data entry and is not available should the screen user ever question an entry's correctness. Approach 3 is advantageous in that it removes noise from the primary visual focus of attention (caption and entry field) for the experienced person but may be easily found by one who is inexperienced. Its disadvantage is that it still leaves noise on a screen, and care must be exercised to design the screen so that the completion aids are properly associated with the correct entry field. All things considered, approach 3 is the one that is recommended.

Required fields may be indicated on a screen by a special character such as the asterisk (*) illustrated in the RATE field. Again, use required field indicators with discretion, since the system edits will quickly let a user know if any are omitted.

Prompting.   Prompting messages are instructions to the screen user on what to do with, or how to work with, the screen being presented. They are analogous to instructions on filling out a paper form. Prompting messages should be positioned just preceding that part of the screen to which they apply. They should be visually distinguishable, using a lower-case font style.

HEADINGS

Section Headings

- Locate section headings on line above related screen fields.
- Indent captions a minimum of five spaces from the start of the heading.
- Fully spell out in an upper-case font.
- Display in normal intensity.

```
COVERAGES
xxxxxDwelling:      _____
        Outbuildings: _____
        Liability:   _____
```

The indention of captions makes the section headings visually distinguishable from the captions on the screen. They will be obvious to the screen user by their location. If the right-justified caption-to-entry-field approach is used, indention greater than five spaces may be necessary. Other techniques than positional cues may, of course, be used to set off section headings, such as double-size characters or underlining. The method chosen, however, should always permit easy discrimination of the section headings from other components of the screen.

Subsection or Row Headings

- Locate to the left of topmost row of associated data fields.
- Fully spell out in an upper-case font style.
- Display in normal intensity.
- Separate from the adjacent caption through use of a unique symbol, such as "greater than."
- Separate symbol from heading by one space and from caption by three spaces.

```
ANIMALSx>>xxxElephants: _____    Kangaroos:     _____
              Camels:    _____    Polar Bears:   _____

   BIRDS >>   Kiwis:     _____    Cockatoos:     _____
              Eagles:    _____    Hawks:         _____
```

- If both section and subsection, or row, headings are included on a screen, the subsection, or row, heading should be indented a minimum of five character positions beneath the section heading.

```
ZOO POPULATION
xxxxxANIMALS >>     Elephants: _____    Kangaroos:     _____
                   Camels:    _____    Polar Bears:   _____
```

A meaningful convention to designate subsection, or row, headings is the "greater than" symbol (>). It directs attention to the right and serves to indicate that everything that follows refer to this category. The subsection is broken by a space line.

Like captions, these subsection, or row, headings may also be right-justified instead of left-justified as illustrated below:

```
                      ANIMALS >>
                        BIRDS >>
```

Field Group Headings

- Center field group headings above the captions to which they apply.
- Relate to these captions by a broken dashed line ended by pointed brackets.
- Spell out fully in an upper-case font.
- Display in normal intensity.

```
    < - - - - - - - -AUTOMOBILE - - - - - - - - >

    Driver                        License Number
    ----------------------        ----------------
    ----------------------        ----------------
    ----------------------        ----------------
```

Occasionally a group heading above a series of related captions may be needed. It may be centered above the captions to which it applies and related to them through a broken dashed line ended by pointed brackets ("greater" and "less than" symbols). This provides closure to the grouping. Field group headings will normally be fully spelled out.

BORDERS

- Create borders around groups of related information to guide the viewer's eye.

```
 --------------------------------------------------------------------
|                                                                    |
|   ANIMALS >>    Elephants: ------    Camels:       ------          |
|                 Kangaroos: ------    Polar Bears: ------           |
|--------------------------------------------------------------------|
|                                                                    |
|    BIRDS >>     Cockatoos: ------    Eagles:       ------          |
|                 Hawks:     ------    Kiwis:        ------          |
|                                                                    |
 --------------------------------------------------------------------
```

Borders inscribed on data entry screens will enhance the perception of groupings and guide the viewer's eye in the direction the cursor moves. Do not overuse lines, however.

TITLE

- Create a short, simple, clear, and distinctive title describing the purpose of the screen.
- Locate the title in a centered position at the top of each screen.
- Spell out fully using an upper-case font.

The title should be short, simple, clear, distinctive, and truthful. It should immediately orient the viewer to the screen's content and purpose. It is normally made up of two parts, a subject and function such as INSURANCE (subject) APPLICATION (function). There may be some single-word exceptions (such as INVOICE or STATEMENT). Do not include words such as FORM or SCREEN in the title, and eliminate connecting words such as "of" unless absolutely necessary. The title should be centered at the screen's top for balance and displayed using capital letters for emphasis.

SCREEN IDENTIFIER

- Place a screen identifier, page number, or other reference information in a consistent location in the upper right-hand corner.
  — For screens containing several pieces of screen identification information, both the left-hand and right-hand upper corners may be used.

Screen identification or other reference information warrants only occasional viewer interest. Therefore it should be located in a less prominent position on the screen. When included, the preferred location is the upper right corner. For a series of screens, a page numbering convention should be included to allow users to know their exact location. The paging convention may simply be "page n of x" or it may incorporate a mnemonic code that is a contraction of the screen title, for example, "POL02" or "AUTO03," the last two digits indicating the number of the screen in the series.

When the screen identifier includes additional information (such as date, time), a more efficient use of the screen body and better screen balance can be achieved by splitting the information between the upper left and upper right corners. All elements should maintain consistent locations on all screens.

Every screen must have a way of being uniquely identified through its titling- and/or screen-numbering convention.

MESSAGES AND NAVIGATION TECHNIQUES

- Uniquely identify informational, warning, and status messages through
  - a consistent location such as
    - a designated line at the bottom of the screen,
    - in a window.
  - use of contrasting display features such as
    - reverse video,
    - highlighting,
    - different font style,
    - preceding each message type by a unique symbol
  - display in a mixed-case font.
- Uniquely identify the screen navigation technique (command field, function keys, action bars, etc.) through
  - a consistent location,
  - separating from the body of the screen.

Recommended locations and display methods for messages and navigation techniques have been described in Chapter 4. They must attract the viewer's attention and be easily discernible from the screen body and other screen components. This is accomplished most effectively by locating them outside the screen body (or in windows) using consistent locations, contrasting display features, and special symbols. Again, each type must be identified by its structure and location without actually having to be read.

Example 1. This example uses the same data elements as illustrated in Section 5-2, example 2 for "with source documents." Because a source document is now not presumed to exist, the fields have been columnized and expanded into two screens for visual clarity. Both captions and fields are left-justified. The cursor moves left to right and the captions are in mixed case.

```
                PERSONAL AUTOMOBILE - SUPPLEMENT                        PASP01

APPLICANT
    Name: _____         Policy #: _____

DRIVER
    Name: _____
    Occupation: _____         Birth Date: __ __ __
    Sex: _                                 Marital Status: _

LICENSE
    License #: _____         State: __
    Yrs Licensed: __                       Impaired: _
    Training: _                            Good Student: _

VEHICLE
    Year: __                               New/Used: _
    Make: _____         ID #: _____
    Horsepower: _                          Symbol: ____
    Use: __                                Miles Work: __
    Annual Miles: _____                    Modified: _
    Damaged: _                             Class: ____
    Territory: __
```

175

Example 1. Continued

```
                                                                    PASP02


                            PERSONAL AUTOMOBILE - SUPPLEMENT


        LIENHOLDER
            Vehicle #:  -
            Name 1:     --------------------------
            Name 2:     --------------------------
            Street:     --------------------------
            City:       ------------- St: -- Zip: ----- ----

        PAYOR
            Name 1:     --------------------------
            Name 2:     --------------------------
            Street:     --------------------------
            City:       ------------- St: -- Zip: ----- ----

            Account #:  ----- ----
            Telephone #: --- --- ----
```

Example 2. This example uses the same data elements as illustrated in Example 1. It assumes top-to-bottom cursor movement and includes line borders. Captions are right-aligned and in mixed case.

```
                    PERSONAL AUTOMOBILE SUPPLEMENT                    PASP01

APPLICANT
              Name: -------------------
           Policy #: ----------

DRIVER
              Name: -------------------
         Occupation: -------------------
         Birth Date: -- -- ----
                Sex: -
      Marital Status: -
LICENSE
         License #: -------------------
              State: --
       Yrs Licensed: --
           Impaired: -
           Training: -
       Good Student: -

VEHICLE
               Year: --
          New/Used: -
               Make: -------------
               ID #: -----------
        Horsepower: -
             Symbol: -----
               Use: --
         Miles Work: --
       Annual Miles: -----
           Modified: -
            Damaged: -
             Class: -----
          Territory: --
```

Example 2. Continued

```
                          PERSONAL AUTOMOBILE - SUPPLEMENT                    PASP02


LIENHOLDER
     Vehicle #: -
        Name 1: --------------------------
        Name 2: --------------------------
        Street: --------------------------
 City/State/Zip:------------------ : -- : -----


PAYOR
        Name 1: --------------------------
        Name 2: --------------------------
        Street: --------------------------
 City/State/Zip:------------------ : -- : -----

     Account #: ----------
   Telephone #: --- --- ----
```

Example 3. This screen illustrates right-justified captions, subsection headings, and completion aids.

```
                                                                 ANMCAT


                   ANIMAL CATALOGUE


       NAME >>        Common: -----------------------
                   Scientific: -----------------------


DESCRIPTION >>         Color: ------------
                      Height: ------
                      Length: ------
                      Weight: -----


   HABITAT >>  Activity Times: -                    (D,N)
                     Terrain: ------------
                        Food: ------------


 OFFSPRING >>         Number: --
              Season of Year: ---              (SPR,SUM,FAL,WIN)
```

Example 4. This example illustrates a group of multiple-occurrence fields in a columnar orientation with field group headings (ITEM and COST). Section headings (CUSTOMER and CREDIT CARD) follow the "above-fields" approach. Captions are left-aligned and capitalized.

```
                         CATALOG ORDER

CUSTOMER
  NAME:       ------------------------
  ADDRESS:    ------------------------
  CITY:       ------------  STATE: --  ZIP: -----
  TELEPHONE:  -- --- ----

            <- - - - - ITEM - - - - ->   <- - - COST - - - ->
  PG  #   CATLG #   QTY  SIZE  DESCRIPTION   WGT    ITEM   MAIL   TOTAL

  ---     -------   ---  ---   -----------   ---    ----   ----   -----
  ---     -------   ---  ---   -----------   ---    ----   ----   -----
  ---     -------   ---  ---   -----------   ---    ----   ----   -----

  ---     -------   ---  ---   -----------   ---    ----   ----   -----
  ---     -------   ---  ---   -----------   ---    ----   ----   -----

                                            HANDLING:  ------
                                               TOTAL:  ------

CREDIT CARD
  KIND:            --
  NUMBER:          ------
  EXPIRATION DATE  ------
```

Example 5. This example illustrates left-aligned, lower-case captions and line borders. The cursor moves top to bottom.

```
                        PERSONAL  BANKING  APPLICATION                      PBAPP
 ---------------------------------------------------------------------------------
 CUSTOMER
    Name:            -----------------------------
    Street:          -----------------------------
    City/State/Zip:  ------------------  --  -----

    Telephone:       ----'-'----
 --------------------------------|------------------------------------------------
 CHECKING ACCOUNT                | LOAN
    Totally Free:  -             |    Home:     -
    Interest:      -             |    Auto:     -
    Plus:          -             |    Boat:     -
    Market Rate:   -             |    Personal: -
                                 |
 SAVINGS ACCOUNT                 | MISCELLANEOUS
    Passbook:          -         |    Cert of Deposit: -
    Statement:         -         |    Visa Card        -
    Insured Fund:      -         |    Master Card      -
    Prem Insured Fund: -         |
 ---------------------------------------------------------------------------------
```

Inquiry Screens 6

Inquiry screens are used to display the results of an inquiry request or the contents of computer files. Their design objective is human ease in locating data or information. Thus, they should be developed to optimize human scanning. Scanning is made easier if eye movements are minimized, required eye movement direction is obvious, and a consistent pattern is followed.

SCREEN ORGANIZATION

- Only display information necessary to perform actions, make decisions, or answer questions.
- Group information in a logical or orderly manner, with the most frequently requested information in the upper left corner.
- For multiscreen transactions, locate most frequently requested information on the earliest screens.
- Do not pack the screen. Use spaces and lines to perceptually balance the screen.
- Columnize, maintaining a top-to-bottom, left-to-right scanning orientation.

Information contained on an inquiry screen should only be what is relevant. Forcing a user to wade through volumes of data is time consuming, costly, and error prone. Unfortunately, relevance is most often situation specific. A relevant item one time a screen is displayed may be irrelevant another time it is recalled.

Inquiry screen organization should be logical, orderly, and meaningful. When information is structured in a manner that is consistent with a person's organizational view of a topic, more information is comprehended (Kintish, 1978).

Finding information on an inquiry screen can be speeded by a number of factors. First, if information is never used, do not display it. Limit a transaction or screen to what is necessary to perform actions, make decisions, or answer questions.

Second, for multiple-screen transactions locate the most frequently sought information on the earliest transaction screens and the most frequently sought information on a screen in the upper left-hand corner.

Third, to aid in locating any particular item, provide easily scanned and identifiable groupings of information and, within each group, easily scanned and identifiable data fields. This is done through columnization with a top-to-bottom, left-to-right orientation. This means permitting the eye to move down a column from top to bottom, then moving to another column located to the right and again moving from top to bottom. This also means, if the situation warrants it, permitting the eye to move easily left to right across the top of columns to the proper column, before beginning the vertical scanning movement.

Top-to-bottom scanning will minimize eye movements through the screen and enable human perceptual powers to be utilized to their fullest. Inquiry screens are often visually scanned not through the captions but through the data fields themselves. A search for a customer name in a display of information often involves looking for a combination of characters that resembles the picture of a name that we have stored in our memory. The search task is to find a long string of alphabetic characters with one or two gaps (first name, middle initial, last name, perhaps). A date search might have the user seeking a numeric code broken by slashes. Other kinds of information also have recognizable patterns and shapes. Field captions usually play a minor role in the process, being necessary only to differentiate similar looking data fields. This leads to two key requirements in the design of inquiry screens: call attention to data fields, and make the structural differences between data fields as obvious as possible. Differences are most noticeable in a columnar field structure, since it is easier to compare data fields when one is above the other.

Data entry screens have been designed to achieve other objectives and seldom yield good inquiry screens. The left-to-right cursor movement results in a screen organization incompatible with the organization that is best for fast scanning.

CAPTIONS

Structure and Size

- Fully spell out in a meaningful language to the user.
- Display in normal intensity.
- Use an upper-case or mixed-case font.

Formatting

- Single Fields:
  — locate caption to left of entry field;

— separate caption from entry field by a unique symbol and one space— the colon (:) is the recommended symbol.

```
Organization: MARKETING
```

- Multiple-Occurrence Fields:
  — locate caption one line above column of data fields;
  — center caption above column of data fields.

```
         City
    PHILADELPHIA
    PHOENIX
    PITTSBURGH
    PORTLAND
```

Structure and size.   Captions on inquiry screens, while supporting the data itself, must still clearly and concisely describe the information displayed. They are important for inexperienced screen users and for identifying similar-looking data or infrequently used data. As such, they should be fully spelled out in the natural language of the user. In general, abbreviations and contractions should not be used. To achieve the alignment recommendations to be discussed shortly, an occasional abbreviation or contraction may be necessary, but choose those that are common in the everyday language of the application or those that are meaningful and easily learned.

Captions for commonly used fields obvious to all screen users may, optionally, be left off inquiry screens. The most obvious example is name, address, city, state, and zip code. The shape and structure of the data itself is sufficient to identify it. This will give the screen a cleaner look and eliminate some potential noise. Never leave a caption off, however, unless all screen users can identify the data all the time.

Formatting.   Caption formatting rules are most similar to those for data entry screens without source documents. For multiple-occurrence fields the caption will be *centered* above its related data field, however.

DATA FIELDS

- Provide visual emphasis to the data fields.
- Display directly usable information:
  — fully spell out all codes;
  — include natural splits or predefined breaks in displaying data.

```
338302286            072179            162152

338-30-2286          07/21/79          16:21:52
```

- Display data in mixed-case or upper-case.
  - —display data strings of five or more numbers or alphanumeric characters with no natural breaks in groups of three or four characters with a blank between each group.

~~K349612094~~   K349 612 094

- Left-justify text and alphanumeric formats.

```
Name:   JOHN SMITH
Street: 612 PINE ST.
```

- Right-justify lists of numeric data.

```
Basic:        965
Surcharge:     82
Total:      1,047
```

- Identical data should be consistent despite its origin.

~~Company: 71~~   Company: ATLAS STEEL
~~Company: ATLAS STEEL~~   Company: ATLAS STEEL
~~Company: AS~~   Company: ATLAS STEEL

- Consider not displaying captions or data for fields whose values are "none," "zero," or blank.
- Consider creating "data statements" where the caption and data are combined.

~~Elephants: 4,163~~   4,163 Elephants
~~Camels: 982~~   982 Camels

Visually emphasize data fields. Data fields should be visually emphasized to attract attention. This will enable the screen user to immediately find and begin scanning the display for the relevant information. High intensity is recommended to accomplish this.

Display directly usable information. Whereas data on a data entry screen is often keyed in the form of a code, data on the inquiry screen should be displayed fully spelled out. An entry code, for example, might be keyed "AS," but the inquiry screen should display "Atlas Steel." Again, this will reduce learning requirements for the screen viewer.

A data display should also reinforce the human tendency to break things into groups. People handle information more easily when it is in chunks.

Justification.   In general, columnized text and alphanumeric data should be left-justified, and numeric data should be right-justified. In aligning data fields, keep in mind how the fields will look in relation to one another when they contain information. The visual scan should flow relatively straight from top to bottom. This may require that some data fields be right-justified in the column that is created, not left-justified.

Consistency.   Identical data taken into the system in different formats should be displayed in the same formats on inquiry screens.

Consider not displaying fields containing no data.   Optional fields on data entry screens occasionally do not have data keyed into them. When displayed on an inquiry screen the data field may be blank or contain a value such as zero or none. In some situations it may not be important to the screen viewer to know that the field contains no data. In these cases consider not displaying both captions and data for these fields. Display on the screen only the fields containing data, thereby creating less cluttered screens.

If this alternative is chosen, space on the screen must be left for situations in which all fields contain data. In order to avoid large blank screen areas, a useful rule of thumb is to allow enough space to clearly display all data for about 90 percent of all possible screens. For screens containing an excessive amount of filled-in optional fields, paging to a second screen will be necessary.

This "nondisplay" alternative should only be considered if it is not important that the viewer know something is "not there." If it is important that the viewer know that the values in a field are zero or none, or that the field is blank, then the fields must be displayed on the inquiry screen.

Consider displaying "data statements."   The traditional way to display data on an inquiry screen is the "caption: data" format, for example, "Autos: 61." Another alternative is to create data statements where the caption and data are combined: "61 Autos." This format improves screen readability and slightly reduces a screen's density. If this data statement format is followed, consider the statement as data and highlight it entirely.

DATA ORGANIZATION

- Organize data in accepted and recognizable orders.

```
SANDY SCHMIDT                      8:30 AM
1422 WHEELER RD                   10:56 AM
KIRKLAND, IL 60146                 2:06 PM
                                   4:33 PM
```

- In lists where there is no obvious frequency, pattern, or order, and in long lists (more than seven items), arrange information in alphabetic order.
- For long lists leave a space line between groups of related data, or about every five rows. Never exceed seven rows without inserting a space line.

```
ADAMS
BARNWELL
CHARLES
DENTON
EDWARDS

FRANKHAUSER
GOLDEN
HAMMER
INGOLDBY
JACKSON
```

Data must always be organized to be meaningful and consistent with human expectations.

FIELD ALIGNMENT

- Vertically align captions and data fields into columns.

```
Policy Number:   HGB-9011
Account Number:    796624
Effective Date:  02/01/88
Expiration Date: 02/01/91
Policy Status:   ACTIVE
```

Columnization is necessary for efficient visual scanning and ease in finding the desired information. Since the scan will be downward, information organization will flow from top to bottom.

FIELD JUSTIFICATION

1. First Approach

- Left-justify both captions and data fields.
- Leave one space between the longest caption and the data field column.

```
Name:       WILLIAM L. HASKIN
Title:      VICE PRESIDENT
Department: ENGINEERING
```

2. Second Approach

- Left-justify data fields and right-justify captions to data fields.
- Leave one space between each.

```
      Name: WILLIAM L. HASKIN
     Title: VICE PRESIDENT
Department: ENGINEERING
```

Again, field justification can be accomplished in either of two ways. Approach 1 results in both captions and entry fields left-justified into columns. Approach 2 right-justifies the captions up against the left-justified column of entry fields (see examples above). Each approach has advantages and disadvantages, as previously discussed in Chapter 4. Whichever method is chosen should be consistently followed in a system's screen design.

Again, examples at the end of this and other chapters reflect both styles, to enable the reader to see and evaluate them.

HEADINGS

Section Headings

- Locate section heading on line above related screen fields.
- Indent captions a minimum of five spaces from the start of the heading.
- Fully spell out in an upper-case font.
- Display in normal intensity.

```
COVERAGES
xxxxxDwelling:     200,000
     Outbuildings:  15,000
     Liability:  1,000,000
PREMIUMS:
     Basic:            335
     Endorsement:       64
     Total:            399
```

This indention of captions is intended to make the section heading visually distinguishable from the captions on the screen. They will be obvious to the screen user by their location. If the right-justified caption-to-entry-field approach is used, indention greater than five spaces may be necessary. Other techniques besides positional cues may, of course, be used to achieve the same objective. Alternatives might be double-size characters or underlining. The method chosen, however, should always permit easy discrimination of the section headings from other components of the screen.

Subsection or Row Headings

- Locate to the left of top-most row of associated data fields.
- Fully spell out in an upper-case font style.
- Display in normal intensity.
- Separate from the adjacent caption through use of a unique symbol such as "greater than."
- Separate symbol from heading by one space and from caption by three spaces.

```
ANIMALSx>>xxxElephants:    4,163
               Camels:      982
               Kangaroos:  1,411
               Polar Bears:    59

   BIRDS >>    Cockatoos:    136
               Eagles:         3
               Hawks:      3,612
               Kiwis:        141
```

- If both section and subsection, or row, headings are included within a screen, the subsection or row heading should be indented a minimum of five character positions beneath the section heading.

```
   ZOO POPULATION
   xxxxxANIMALS >>   Elephants:    4,163
                     Camels:        982
                     Kangaroos:   1,411
                     Polar Bears:     59

        BIRDS >>     Cockatoos:     136
                     Eagles:          3
                     Hawks:       3,612
                     Kiwis:         141
```

Again, the "greater than" symbol (>) is a good way to designate subsection or row headings. It directs attention to the right and serves to indicate that everything that follows refer to this category. The subsection is broken by a space line.

Like captions, these subsection or row headings may also be right-justified instead of left-justified, as illustrated below:

```
                    ANIMALS >>
                      BIRDS >>
```

Field Group Headings

- Center field group heading above the captions to which it applies.
- Relate to these captions by a broken dashed line ended by pointed brackets.
- Spell out fully in an upper-case font.
- Display in normal intensity.

```
        < - - - - - - - -AUTOMOBILE - - - - - - - - >

            DRIVER                LICENSE NUMBER
        MARY GRABOWSKI            G433 5857 6445
        JON GRABOWSKI             G433 8990 9051
        HAROLD GRABOWSKI          G433 8990 9590
```

Occasionally, a field group heading above a series of related captions may be needed. It may be centered above the captions to which it applies and related to them through a broken dashed line ended by pointed brackets ("greater" and "less than" symbols). This provides closure to the grouping. The heading should be spelled out fully.

SPACING

Horizontal Spacing—Single Fields

Without Section Headings

- Leave at least five spaces between the longest data field in one column and the leftmost caption in an adjacent column.

```
        Make:  OLDSMOBILE         List Price:  $18,424
        Model: NINETY-EIGHTxxxxxDown Payment:    4,000
        Doors: 2                 Balance Owed:   14,424
```

With Section Headings

- Leave at least five spaces between the longest data field in one column and the section heading in an adjacent column.

```
                          Financing
Automobile
    Make:  OLDSMOBILE              List Price:   $18,424
    Model: NINETY-EIGHTxxxxx       Down Payment:   4,000
    Doors: 2                       Balance Owed:  14,424
```

Lines Substituted for Spaces

- Where space constraints exist, vertical lines may be substituted for spaces.

```
                          |
    Make:  OLDSMOBILE      | List Price:   $18,424
    Model: NINETY-EIGHTx|xDown Payment:   4,000
    Doors: 2              | Balance Owed:  14,424
                          |
```

To visually separate columns, leave a minimum of five spaces between the longest entry field in one column and the leftmost caption in the adjacent column.

Optimum spacing between columns will ultimately be affected by the weighting of the elements within each column. Captions should be visually tied to their related entry fields, and columns of elements should be visually broken apart. Thus, spacing between columns should be enough to achieve this.

Where space constraints exist, an excellent way to provide visual separation is to incorporate a line between adjacent columns, as illustrated above. This is also clearly conveys to the screen viewer that the desired scanning motion is downward.

Horizontal Spacing—Multiple Occurrence Fields

Without Group Headings

- Leave at least three spaces between the columns of fields.

```
        Make        Model      Year
     CHRYSLERxxxNEW YORKER   1987
     FORD        TAURUS      1988
     PONTIAC     BONNEVILLExxx1988
```

With Group Headings

- Leave at least three spaces between columns of related fields.
- Leave at least five spaces between groupings.

```
< - - - - - OWNED - - - - - >    < - - - - - LEASED - - - - ->
    Make       Model      Year      Make       Model      Year
 CHRYSLERxxxNEW YORKER   1987xxxxxTOYOTA      COROLLA     1988
 FORD       .TAURUS      1988     CADILLAC    FLEETWOOD   1986
 PONTIAC    BONNEVILLExxx1988     MERCURY     COUGAR      1987
```

Multiple-occurrence fields must also provide adequate visual separation of columns of fields. Again, these are minimum guidelines and greater separation may be necessary.

Vertical Spacing

- Leave at least one space line between columnized "groups" of related information.

```
          Name: WILLIAM BRADFORD
           Age:  34
        Height:   6 Ft., 2 In
        Weight: 194

          Occupation: DIVER
    Years Experience:  11
              Degree: M.S.
               Major: ACCOUNTING
```

- For long columns of related elements, leave a space line after every fifth row. (If space permits, leave a space after every third row.) Never exceed seven rows without inserting a space line.

```
         AMERICA'S LARGEST CITIES
              First:   NEW YORK
              Second:  LOS ANGELES
              Third:   CHICAGO
              Fourth:  PHILADELPHIA
              Fifth:   SAN FRANCISCO

              Sixth:   DETROIT
              Seventh: BOSTON
              Eighth:  HOUSTON
              Ninth:   WASHINGTON
              Tenth:   DALLAS
```

To permit the eye to move easily across the screen data fields, to reduce screen density, and to satisfy the human need for groupings, space lines must be left on screens. This is accomplished in the ways shown above.

BORDERS

- Create borders around groups of related information to guide the viewer's eye.

```
┌──────────────────────────────┬──────────────────────────────┐
│                              │                              │
│ ANIMALS >>   Elephants: 4,163 │ BIRDS >>   Cockatoos:    136 │
│              Camels:      982 │            Eagles:         3 │
│              Kangaroos: 1,411 │            Hawks:      3,612 │
│              Polar Bears:  59 │            Kiwis:        141 │
│                              │                              │
└──────────────────────────────┴──────────────────────────────┘
```

Borders inscribed on inquiry screens will enhance the perception of groupings and guide the viewer's eye in the desired direction.

MULTIPAGE DISPLAYS

- Where data or lists extend beyond a single screen, provide an indication that the information is continued on a following screen.

When data or lists consume more than one screen, inform the user of this fact. Display at the bottom of the page:

```
Continued next page.
```

Or, include as part of the title or screen identifier:

```
Page ___ of ___.
```

For scrolled data, the current and ending locations can be displayed:

```
Line ___ of ___.
```

TITLE

- Create a short, simple, clear, and distinctive title describing the purpose of the screen.
- Locate the title in a centered position at the top of each screen.
- Spell out fully using an upper-case font.

The title should be short, simple, clear, distinctive, and truthful. It should immediately orient the viewer to the screen's content and purpose. It is normally made up of a subject and function such as INSURANCE (subject) APPLICATION (function). There may be some single-word exceptions (such as INVOICE or STATEMENT). Do not include words such as FORM or SCREEN in the title, and eliminate connecting words such as "of" unless absolutely necessary. The title should be centered at the screen's top for balance and displayed using capital letters for emphasis.

SCREEN IDENTIFIER

- Place a screen identifier, page number, or other reference information in a consistent location in the upper right-hand corner.
  - For screens containing several pieces of screen identification information, both the left-hand and right-hand upper corners may be used.

Screen identification or other reference information warrants only occasional viewer interest. Therefore it should be located in a less prominent position on the screen. When included, the preferred location is the upper right corner. For a series of screens, a page numbering convention should be included to allow users to know their exact location. The paging convention may simply be "page n of x" or it may incorporate a mnemonic code that is a contraction of the screen title, for example, "POL02" or "AUTO03," the last two digits indicating the number of the screen in the series.

When the screen identifier includes additional information (such as date, time), a more efficient use of the screen body and better screen balance can be achieved by splitting the information between the upper left and upper right corners. All elements should maintain consistent locations on all screens.

Every screen must have a way of being uniquely identified through its titling- and/or screen-numbering convention.

MESSAGES AND NAVIGATION TECHNIQUES

- Uniquely identify informational, warning, and status messages through
  - a consistent location such as
    - a designated line at the bottom of the screen,
    - in a window.
  - use of contrasting display features such as
    - reverse video,
    - highlighting,
    - different font style,
    - preceding each message type by a unique symbol
  - display in a mixed-case font.
- Uniquely identify the screen navigation technique (command field, function keys, action bars, etc.) through
  - a consistent location,
  - separating from the body of the screen.

Recommended locations and display methods for messages and navigation techniques have been described in Chapter 4. They must attract the viewer's attention and be easily discernible from the screen body and other screen components. This is accomplished most effectively by locating them outside the screen body (or in windows) using consistent locations, contrasting display features, and special symbols. Again, each type must be identified by its structure and location without actually having to be read.

Example 1. The "personal automobile" data elements illustrated in Section 5-2, example 2, and Section 5-3, examples 1 and 2, are now columnized for easy visual scanning on an inquiry screen. Section headings are included and captions follow the left-justified approach. Captions are in mixed case and data in uppercase. Visual separation of the left and right sides of the screen is aided by a vertical broken line. Data elements within sections are organized into logical groupings. The name and address fields on screen 2 are only briefly captioned as Name.

```
                PERSONAL AUTOMOBILE - SUPPLEMENTAL INFORMATION              PAGE 1 OF 2

POLICY                               |   VEHICLE
   Name:            LESTER ANDERSON  |      Year:            1987
   Policy #:        556 904          |      New/Used:        NEW
DRIVER                               |      Make:            MERCEDES
   Name:            KIMI ANDERSON    |      ID #:            S988 6702
   Occupation:      MODEL            |      Horsepower:      160
   Birth Date:      09/21/63         |
   Sex:             FEMALE           |      Symbol:          K
   Marital Status:  SINGLE           |      Use:             WORK
LICENSE                              |      Miles Work:      13
   License #:       G432 6689 5543   |      Annual Miles:    15,000
   State:           ILLINOIS         |      Modified:        NO
   Yrs. Licensed:   10               |      Damaged:         NO
   Impaired:        NO               |
   Training:        YES              |      Class:           6
   Good Student:    YES              |      Territory:       13
```

197

Example 1. Continued

PERSONAL AUTOMOBILE — SUPPLEMENTAL INFORMATION

LIENHOLDER

Vehicle #: 1

Name: NORTHERN LIGHTS BANK
       800 DIAMOND BLVD.
       ANCHORAGE, AK 99515

PAYOR

Name: LESTER ANDERSON
       644 HAPPY WAY
       KUALAPUU, HI 96757

Account #: NONE
Telephone #: (808) 555-4601

Example 2. The "personal automobile" data from the previous example. The captions are in upper case right-justified, the data in mixed case. Line borders are included to emphasize groupings and guide the eye.

PERSONAL AUTOMOBILE — SUPPLEMENTAL INFORMATION

POLICY

```
          NAME: Lester Anderson
      POLICY #: 556 904
```

DRIVER

```
          NAME: Kimi Anderson
    OCCUPATION: Model
    BIRTH DATE: 09/21/63
           SEX: Female
MARITAL STATUS: Single
```

LICENSE

```
     LICENSE #: G432 6689 5543
         STATE: Illinois
 YRS LICENSED: 10
      IMPAIRED: No
      TRAINING: Yes
  GOOD STUDENT: Yes
```

VEHICLE

```
          YEAR: 1987
      NEW/USED: New
          MAKE: Mercedes
          ID #: S988 6702
    HORSEPOWER: 160

        SYMBOL: K
           USE: Work
    MILES WORK: 13
  ANNUAL MILES: 15,000
      MODIFIED: No
       DAMAGED: No

         CLASS: 6
     TERRITORY: 13
```

199

Example 2. Continued

PERSONAL AUTOMOBILE — SUPPLEMENTAL INFORMATION

LIENHOLDER

    VEHICLE #: 1

        NAME: Northern Lights Bank
              800 Diamond Blvd.
              Anchorage, AK 99515

PAYOR

        NAME: Lester Anderson
              644 Happy Way
              Kualapuu, HI 96757

   ACCOUNT #: None
 TELEPHONE #: (808) 555-4601

Example 3.   A one-column inquiry screen with left-justified captions using the subsection heading concept. Captions and data are in mixed case.

```
----------------------------------------------------------------
                          INVOICE                          INV

CUSTOMER >>      Name:         Reginald Jones
                 Address:      44 Dolphin Way
                               Claxton, GA 30417

                 Telephone:    (314) 555-5672

ITEM >>          Catalog #:    762J
                 Quantity:     1
                 Size:         Extra Large
                 Description:  Golf Glove
                 Color:        White

CHARGES >>       Item:      $   9.95
                 Mail:          .79
                 Handling:     1.50
                 Total:     $  12.24

CREDIT CARD >>   Kind:         Amex
                 Number:       3700 690 5432
                 Exp. Date:    5/93
----------------------------------------------------------------
```

Example 4. This example uses the data elements found on the Personal Banking Application screen in example 5 in Section 5-3. It reflects the nondisplay of fields containing no data or not applicable, and uses "data statements" to describe amounts. The amounts are indented to show their dependencies. Section headings are to the right and left-aligned. Grouping borders are also included.

```
                                                              PBAS
                    PERSONAL BANKING ACCOUNT SUMMARY
 ┌──────────────────────────────────────────────────────────────────┐
 │                                                                    │
 │         CUSTOMER >>      Reginald Smith                            │
 │                         3 Oceanview Drive                          │
 │                         Tortilla Flat, AZ 85290                    │
 │                                                                    │
 │                         (602) 555-6789                             │
 │                                                                    │
 ├──────────────────────────────────────────────────────────────────┤
 │                                                                    │
 │         ACCOUNTS >>      Totally Free Checking                     │
 │                              $    764.13 Balance                   │
 │                                                                    │
 │                         Passbook Savings                           │
 │                              $ 4,523.76 Balance                    │
 │                                                                    │
 │            LOANS >>      Boat                                      │
 │                              $ 9,124.00 Paid                       │
 │                              $ 4,876.00 Due                        │
 │                                                                    │
 │    MISCELLANEOUS >>      Visa Card                                 │
 │                              $    167.22 Due                       │
 │                              $ 5,000.00 Limit                      │
 │                                                                    │
 └──────────────────────────────────────────────────────────────────┘
```

Multipurpose Screens

7

Information is entered into a system through a data entry screen, and the contents of the system are viewed through an inquiry screen. Sometimes, however, it may seem desirable to use a single screen for more than one purpose—perhaps to initially enter data into the system (data entry) and then call it back to see what is there (inquiry), or to view the contents of the system's database (inquiry) and then make changes or corrections (data entry). Is a combination or multipurpose screen a viable alternative?

From a human perspective a multipurpose screen does make sense if a person needs to deal with different classes of screens at different times. Learning will be aided because only one organization of elements will be confronted. The problem is that the organization of the screen often cannot be optimized for both situations. The left-to-right movement of the cursor for data entry is not compatible with the desired top-to-bottom scanning of the screen during inquiry. What, then, is the sensible approach concerning multipurpose screens?

IMPLEMENTATION

- If different people will be using screens for different reasons, create separate screens to achieve their intended purposes.
- If the same people will be using screens for different reasons, consider creating multipurpose screens. Structure these multipurpose screens in the direction of their most frequent usage.

Since a screen usually cannot be created that satisfies both data entry and inquiry needs, develop separate screens for users who will be using them in only one way. If there is a group within an organization whose job is to enter data into the system, fashion data entry screens for this group. If there is another group whose purpose is to review computer records (such as customer service), develop screens following the inquiry screen guidelines presented above. The usability objectives of each group will be best served by this approach.

If the same groups will be using screens for different reasons, however, consider creating multipurpose screens. Structure them in the direction of their most frequent usage based on an analysis of what the most frequent usage is. If, for example, a screen will be used to change or correct a computer record, and few items of information are changed at a time, the optimum arrangement is the inquiry screen approach. Scanning will be optimized to aid in finding elements to be changed. When the field is located, the cursor is moved to it before the change can be made. While the left-to-right movement of the cursor may be across unrelated fields, this illogical movement is less important than making it easy to find what must be changed.

If screens will be heavily used in a variety of ways, and creation of a multipurpose screen may severely affect usability in one or more of those ways, the best alternative is to create separate screens, each optimized for its intended purpose. This will result in more far-reaching benefits than those achieved by the reduced learning requirements of the multipurpose screen.

Question and Answer Screens

A question and answer screen is characterized by short alternating communications between a user and a system. Normally the system will provide a thought or prompt and the user will respond; or the user will make a short request and the system will respond. The dialogue proceeds on this basis, each participant sharing in a continual step-by-step interaction. This may be contrasted with the kinds of screens previously described where the communication is on a full screen basis—the screen using the entire available display area and the user being able to work with it before sending a response to the system.

A question and answer screen does not necessarily perform unique functions. They may be used for data entry or to display the results of inquiries. They are, however, not very efficient in performing these functions extensively because of the excessive amount of communication needed and the slowness of the process.

Question and answer dialogues are especially valuable when a system user has little or no training and a fast computer response time is expected. They can supplement full screen display techniques in the log-on process or when providing guidance and assistance.

DEVELOPMENT RULES

- Limit computer communication to one idea or question.
- Phrase questions as concisely as possible.

- Require short user responses.
- Display previous user answers for related questions.

In a question-and-answer dialogue, questions to the user should be displayed separately. Never require him to answer several questions at once. Computer questions and user responses should be as short and concise as possible. If questions are related, or if a user response is based on answers to previous questions, make sure the previous messages are visible, not having "scrolled" out of view. The proper context for answering the current question must be maintained.

FIELD FORMATTING

- Maintain field widths within a range of 25 to 40 characters.
- Locate in a left-centered position on the screen.

For reading ease field widths should not exceed 40 characters. For visual balancing purposes the fields should be located in a left-centered position on the screen. (On an 80-character-wide display, a 40-character-wide field should begin in about column 15.)

FIELD CHARACTERISTICS

- Provide a means to visually distinguish computer messages from keyed entries. For example:
  - always display computer message at high intensity, key entry at normal intensity,
  - display computer message in lower case, key entry in upper case;

```
          Applicants name:
          CAROL FORESTER
```

  - indent key entry several spaces to right of start of computer message;

```
          APPLICANTS NAME:
                CAROL FORESTER
```

  - precede key entry by a unique symbol;

```
          APPLICANTS NAME:
          ==>  CAROL FORESTER
```

— if questions are generally short, position key entry to right of question and align beyond longest expected caption.

```
APPLICANTS NAME:        CAROL FORESTER
```

Key entries and computer messages should be easily distinguishable from one another. This can be accomplished by using various display components, contrasting features, or variable spacing techniques summarized above.

TITLE

- Optional.
- Locate in a centered position at the top of the screen.
- Separate from first screen field by at least one blank line.

The necessity of a title should be based on the kind of question and answer screen created, following the guidelines described in the chapters on data entry screens and inquiry screens.

Example 1. Computer messages are distinguished from key entries by letter case. Computer messages are in lower case, key entries in upper case.

```
Driver's name:
KARIN ROEPEL
Sex:
F
Birth date:
11 18 61
Marital status:
M
Occupation:
OFFICE MANAGER
Driver's license number:
T6994 334 556A
State:
OK
```

Example 2. Computer messages are distinguished from key entries by spatial positioning. Key entries are indented five character positions.

```
DRIVER'S NAME:
     KIMI ANDERSON
SEX:
     F
BIRTH DATE:
     09 21 63
MARITAL STATUS:
     S
OCCUPATION:
     MODEL
DRIVER'S LICENSE NUMBER
     G543 569 4453
STATE:
     IL
```

Example 3. Computer messages are distinguished from key entries by a unique symbol preceding them.

```
DRIVER'S NAME:
==>  BARRY MITCHELL
SEX:
==>  MALE
BIRTH DATE:
==>  JULY 17, 1959
MARITAL STATUS:
==>  SINGLE
OCCUPATION:
==>  FARMER
DRIVER'S LICENSE NUMBER:
==>  M432 6775 988
STATE:
==>  ILLINOIS
```

Example 4. Aligned key entries following computer messages.

```
DRIVER'S NAME:        LISA RENCH
SEX:                  F
BIRTH DATE:           08 05 61
MARITAL STATUS:       M
OCCUPATION:           STUDENT
DRIVER'S LICENSE NO:  R668 9870 254
STATE:                NC
```

Menu Screens

A system will often contain large amounts of data and perform a variety of functions. Regardless of its purpose, the system must provide some means to tell users about the information it possesses or the things it can do. This is accomplished by displaying a screen listing the choices or alternatives the user has at appropriate points while using the system, or creating a string of screens that lead a user from a series of general descriptors on the first screen through increasingly specific categories on following screens until the lowest level screen is reached. This lowest level screen provides the desired choices. The common name for these kinds of screens is *menu screens*.

Menu screens are effective because they utilize the more powerful human capability of recognition rather than the weaker recall. Working with menus reminds users of available options and information that they may not be aware of or have forgotten.

Menu screens are not without problems, however. New system users might find learning larger systems difficult because information must be integrated across a series of displays (Engel and Granda, 1975; Dray et al., 1981; Billingsley, 1982; and Miller, 1981). As each menu is viewed in isolation, relationships between menus are difficult to grasp. Words and phrases with multiple meanings may be interpreted incorrectly because of the inability to see relationships (Bower et al., 1969). Ambiguities may be resolved on the basis of assumptions about menu structure that are incorrect (Cuff, 1980; Durding et al., 1977). The frequent result is that users make mistakes and get lost in the hierarchical structure.

Experienced system users, while finding menus helpful at first, may find them tedious as they learn the system. Continually having to step through a series of screens to achieve the desired objective can be time consuming and frustrating.

Therefore, the design of menu screens must consider the conflicting needs of both inexperienced and experienced users.

This discussion of menu screens begins with a categorization of the kinds of menus typically found on screens. Topics to follow include menu organization, ordering, selection, identification, and navigation techniques. Finally, some specific rules concerning caption wording, alignment, justification, spacing, and other considerations are presented.

KINDS OF MENUS

Shneiderman (1987) has identified three basic kinds of menus to be found on screens: single, linear sequence, and multipath. (See Figure 9.1.) Both single and multipath menu categories contain several subclasses.

Single Menus

A single menu is generally confined to one screen. It may encompass the whole screen or just a portion of it. In some instances it may extend beyond a single screen. Single menu subclasses are as follows.

Figure 9.1   Kinds of menus.

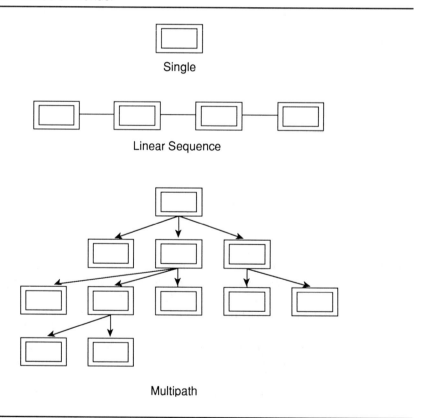

Single

Linear Sequence

Multipath

Binary choice.   A binary menu simply asks the user to select from a pair of choices, yes/no, true/false, and so forth. Binary menus are commonly found in computer games.

Multiple item.   A multiple-item menu presents the user with more than two choices. Several or more options may be displayed, and the user must select the proper alternative.

Extended.   In an extended menu a lengthy list of options is presented that extends beyond one screen. The last choice presented on the first screen leads to the second screen. The user, not finding the desired choice on the first screen, goes to the second screen and continues searching. To achieve efficiency, extended menus often have the more common choices on the first screen and less frequent choices on the second.

Pop-up.   Through use of windowing techniques, a pop-up, pull-out, or pull-down menu may appear on demand in a portion of the screen. Possible actions or choices that can be made at that moment are displayed. Because they cover other information on the screen, they tend to be small. These kinds of menus are also discussed in Chapter 10, Graphic Screens.

Permanent.   A permanent menu shows commands that can be applied to a displayed object or in the current situation. They are usually permanently displayed in a reserved area on the screen. Function key choices or labels in the bottom line of a screen reflect this approach. Action bars are also classified as permanent menus.

Multiple selection.   A multiple selection menu permits more than one choice from the list of alternatives displayed.

Embedded.   An embedded menu permits a selection from choices within the data itself. A paragraph of text may have highlighted words that, when selected, provide additional information about the word or topic selected. Whereas the other kinds of single menus are explicit, an embedded menu is implicit, a by-product of another function.

Linear Sequence Menus

Linear sequence menus are a series of choices requiring two or more screens to complete. For example, setting the parameters for document printing may involve a number of decisions that must be made. These kinds of menus guide a complex decision-making process by presenting one choice at a time.

Multipath Menus

When the number of choices grows too large for easy comprehension, a semblance of order is established by categorizing alternatives and providing "paths" of choices to achieve the desired results. How the user is permitted to move through these paths, which together resemble a tree, gives each subclass its name. (See Figure 9.2.)

Figure 9.2 Multipath menus.

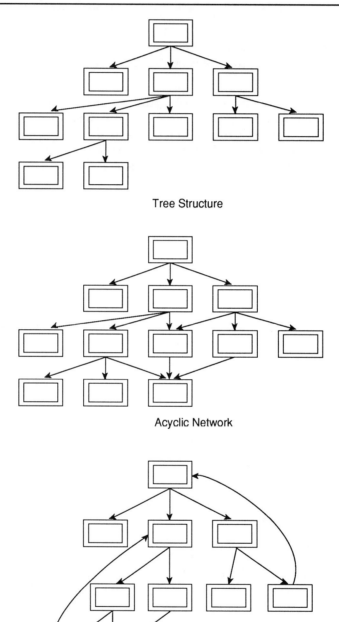

Tree Structure

Acyclic Network

Cyclic Network

Tree structure.   A simple tree structure multipath menu permits the user to make a series of choices that takes him down through succeedingly lower level menus until his destination is reached. Movement back up a path is not permitted, nor is movement between paths.

Acyclic network.   An acyclic network menu is a tree structure that permits downward movement between tree paths.

Cyclic network.   A cyclic network menu is a tree structure that permits downward and upward movement between tree paths.

Multipath menu systems can make large numbers of choices easily available. On the other hand, they are very easy to get lost in.

DISPLAY

- If continual or frequent reference to menu options are necessary, permanently display the menu in an area of the screen that will not obscure other screen data.
- If only occasional reference to menu options are necessary, the menu may be presented on demand.
    — Critical options should be continuously displayed, however.

Whether to display a menu continually, or on demand, is determined by the menu's frequency of use. Always permanently display menus that are frequently referenced, while occasionally needed menus may be presented on request via pop-ups or pull-downs. Critical options should always be continuously displayed.

ORGANIZATION

- Provide a general or main menu.
- Display:
    — All relevant alternatives.
    — Only relevant alternatives.
        — If nonavailable options must be displayed, they must be visually distinguishable from available options.
- Minimize number of menu levels within limits of clarity.
    — Without logical grouping of options, limit choices per screen to 4–8.
    — With logical grouping of options, 9 or more choices per screen may be displayed.
- If rapid menu search time is critical, place as many options on a single screen as possible.

Provide a general menu.   The top level menu in a hierarchical menu scheme should be a general or main menu consisting of basic system options. This will provide a consistent starting point for all system activities and a "home-base" to which the user may always return.

Relevant alternatives.   A menu screen, or screens, should provide all relevant alternatives, and only relevant alternatives, at the point at which it is displayed. Including nonrelevant choices on a menu screen increases learning requirements and has been found to interfere with performance (Baker and Goldstein, 1966). There are two exceptions to this rule, however. Alternatives that are conditionally nonactive may be displayed along with the conditionally active choices, if the active choices can be visually highlighted in some manner (such as through high intensity or reverse video). A recent study (Francik and Kane, 1987), however, found that completely eliminating nonactive alternatives on a menu resulted in faster choice access time, when compared to leaving nonactive alternatives on a menu but displayed in a subdued manner. Eliminating conditionally nonactive choices from a menu appears to be the best approach. Options to be implemented in the future may also be displayed if they can be visually marked in some way (through a display technique or some other annotation).

Minimize number of levels within limits of clarity.   The issue that must be addressed in creating a multipath menu structure is determining how many items will be placed on one menu (its breadth) and how many levels it will consume (its depth). In general, the more choices contained on a menu (greater breadth) the less will be its depth; the fewer choices on a menu (less breadth), the greater will be its depth.
   The advantages of a menu system with greater breadth and less depth are

- fewer steps, and shorter time, to reach one's objective. (Seppala and Salvendy, 1985),
- fewer opportunities to wander down wrong paths,
- easier learning by allowing the user to see relationships of menu items.

A broad menu's disadvantages are

- a more crowded screen that reduces the clarity of the choice wording,
- increased likelihood of confusing similar choices because they are seen together,
- difficulties in displaying choices in the same area of the screen, which is preferred to displaying choices in different areas of the screen (Baker and Goldstein, 1966).

The advantages of greater depth are

- less crowding on the screen,
- fewer choices to be scanned,

- easier hiding of inappropriate choices,
- easier display of all information in the same area of the screen,
- less likelihood of confusing similar choices since there is less likelihood that they will be seen together.

Greater depth disadvantages are

- more steps, and longer time, to reach one's objective (Seppala and Salvendy, 1985),
- more difficulties in learning since relationships between elements cannot always be seen,
- more difficulties in predicting what lies below resulting in increased likelihood of going down wrong paths or getting lost,
- higher error rates (Tullis, 1985; Snowberry et al., 1983; Kiger, 1984; Seppala and Salvendy, 1985).

A good number of studies have looked at the breadth–depth issue in recent years. Some have concluded that breadth is preferable to depth in terms of either greater speed or fewer errors (Landauer and Nachbar, 1985; Tullis, 1985; Wallace, 1987), that a low number of levels (2 to 3) and an intermediate number of choices (4 to 8) results in faster, more accurate performance as opposed to fewer or greater numbers of levels and choices (Miller, 1981; Kiger, 1984), and that 4 to 8 choices per menu screen is best (Lee and MacGregor, 1985). Another study found that one level was easiest to learn (Dray et al., 1981), and a couple of studies have concluded that a menu could contain up to 64 items if it were organized into logical groups (Snowberry et al., 1983; Paap and Roske-Hofstrand, 1986). The least desirable alternative in almost all cases was deep-level menu screens that simply presented the user with a binary choice (select one of two alternatives) on each screen.

Paap and Roske-Hofstrand (1988) also have recently reviewed studies addressing the breadth–depth issue. They conclude that if a system under development has even a couple of the following properties, one should be reluctant to consider a hierarchical structure with more than two levels.

- The labels and/or descriptors for some screens will have to be quite general or abstract.
- The top-level menu screens will be more error prone than those at lower levels.
- There is little opportunity for insulation, or hiding choices that are not likely or not valid.
- Most users will often be navigating down unexplored or new pathways.
- System response time is long and/or the task places a premium on fast responses.
- Users must recover from mistakes by backtracking one step at a time.
- The task requires the synthesis of information located on more than one branch or pathway.

The conclusion that one might derive from these studies is this. Fewer levels of menus aid the decision-making process, but trying to put too many choices on a single screen also has a negative impact. The final solution is a compromise: Minimize the number of levels within limits of clarity. What is clarity? The studies seem to indicate that if the choices to be displayed cannot be segmented into logical categories, then confine the number of alternatives displayed to 4 to 8 per screen. If logical categorization is possible, and meaningful, logical category names can be established, then a larger number of choices can be presented, perhaps as many as 64. The maximum number of alternatives will, however, be dependent upon the size of the words needed to describe the alternatives to the user. "Wordy" captions will greatly restrict the number of alternatives capable of being displayed.

GROUPING

- Provide hierarchical groupings of elements into categories that
  - — contain logically similar options.
  - — cover all alternatives.
  - — do not overlap.
- If meaningful categories cannot be developed and more than eight options must be displayed on a screen, create arbitrary visual groupings that
  - — consist of about four or five, but never more than seven, options.
  - — are of equal size.
- Provide immediate access to critical or frequently chosen alternatives.

Hierarchical groupings. A large number of alternatives should be structured in a multipath format, with the primary or main choices on the top screen and secondary choices on lower level screens. Undifferentiated strings of choices should be avoided.

Items displayed on menus should be logically grouped to aid learning and speed up the visual search process (Card, 1982).

Liebelt et al. (1982) have demonstrated that logically categorized menus are easier to learn and result in faster and more accurate performance. McDonald et al. (1983) have found similar results comparing versions of a 64-item menu either structured into logical categories, arranged alphabetically, or randomly arranged. They speculate that a categorical organization may facilitate the transition from novice to expert user because information is visually represented in the way people think about it.

Shneiderman (1987) states that in addition to containing logically similar items, groupings should cover all the possibilities and contain items that are nonoverlapping. While some collections of information will be easily partitioned into logical groups, others may be very difficult to partition. Some users may not understand the designer's organizational framework, and there may be differences among users based on experience. Thus, no perfect solution may exist for all, and extensive testing and refinement may be necessary to create the most natural and comprehensible solution.

Visual groupings.   Noncategorized large menus should be broken into arbitrary visual groupings through the use of space or lines. Groups should be of as equal size as possible and consist of about four or five options. Groupings should never exceed more than seven options.

Finally, choices that are critical or frequently chosen should be accessible as quickly and through as few steps as possible.

ORDERING

- Order lists of choices by their natural order, or
- For lists with a small number of options (seven or less), order by
  — sequence of occurrence.
  — frequency of occurrence.
  — importance.
- Use alphabetic order for
  — long lists (eight or more options).
  — short lists with no obvious pattern or frequency.
- If option usage changes, do not reorder menus.
- Maintain a consistent ordering of options on all related menus.
  — For variable-length menus, maintain consistent relative positions.
  — For fixed-length menus, maintain consistent absolute positions.

Within categories included on a menu, or in menus in which categories are not possible, options must be ordered in meaningful ways. When a menu contains categories of information, category ordering will follow these same principles.

Natural ordering.   If items have a natural sequence, such as chapters in a book, months in the year, or physical properties such as increasing or decreasing sizes or weights, the ordering scheme should follow this natural sequence. These ordering schemes will have already been well learned by the screen viewer.

Small number of options.   For groupings with a small number of options (about seven or less), sequence of use, frequency of use, or importance of the item is the best ordering scheme.

Alphabetic order.   For a large number of options, alphabetic ordering of alternatives is desirable. Alphabetic ordering is also recommended for small lists where no frequency or sequence pattern is obvious.

It has been found that alphabetically ordered menus can be searched much faster than randomly ordered menus (Card, 1982; McDonald et al., 1983;

Perlman, 1984). Card, for example, found that an 18-item alphabetic menu was visually searched four times faster than a randomly organized menu. Search time was a function of saccadic eye movements through the display. Search patterns were random, but fewer eye movements were required with the alphabetic arrangement. After twenty trials, however, only one eye movement was required for all conditions and search time was the same. Learning does take place, but it will be greatly aided by the ordering scheme.

Do not reorder menus.   Adaptivity is thought to be a desirable quality of a computer system. This may not be so for menu option ordering. Mitchell and Shneiderman (1989) compared static or fixed menus with dynamic menus whose options were continually reordered based upon the frequency in which they were chosen. Dynamic menus were slower to use and less preferred than static menus. The continual reordering interfered with menu order learning, which occurred quickly.

Consistency between menus.   Options found on more than one menu should be consistently positioned on all menus. If menus are of variable length, maintain relative positioning of all item options (for example, place EXIT at the bottom or end of the list). If menus are of fixed length, place options in the same physical position within the list.

INITIAL CURSOR POSITIONING

- If one option has a significantly higher probability of selection, position the cursor at that option.
- If repeating the previously selected option has the highest probability of occurrence, position the cursor at this option.
- If no option has a significantly higher probability of selection, position the cursor at the first option.

When a menu is first displayed, position the cursor at the most likely option to be chosen, or the first option in the list.

CONTROL

- Permit only one selection per menu.
- When hierarchic levels of menus are used, provide one simple key action to
  — return to the next higher level menu.
  — return to the main menu.
- Where access of a lower-level menu is possible through multiple pathways, provide these pathways.

One selection per menu.   Requiring more than one choice per displayed menu can be confusing to the novice user.

Simple key actions.   Navigation through menu levels should be accomplished through simple key actions. It should always be very easy to return to the next higher level menu and the main or general menu.

Provide multiple pathways.   If it is logical to access levels within a menu structure by meaningful and relevant multiple pathways, provide for access through such pathways.

MENU NAVIGATION AIDS

- To aid menu navigation and learning, provide
  — menu maps.
  — lists of options selected.
- Present these aids
  — in documentation.
  — in a help function.
  — permanently on the menu screen.
  — on demand in a pop-up window.

Provide menu maps.   It is often difficult to maintain a sense of position or orientation as one wanders deeper into a multipath menu system. The result is that "getting lost" in the menu maze is quite easy to do. The value of a menu map in reducing disorientation has been demonstrated in three studies (Billingsley, 1982; Parton et al., 1985; Kaster and Widdell, 1986). In all cases, providing a graphic representation of the menu in map form, either in hard copy or on-line, resulted in fewer errors or wrong choices, faster navigation, and/or greater user satisfaction when compared to no guides or simply providing indexes or narrative descriptions of the menu structure. Kaster and Widdell also found that being able to view on the screen just the "path" one was following improved performance and learning.

So, menu maps or graphic representations of the menu structure are desirable. These maps should be included in the system documentation and also should be available through a HELP function. In addition, it is advantageous to either display on a menu screen the path of choices that has led to the current position, or make this path easily available through a pull-down window.

Paap and Roske-Hofstrand (1988) suggest that the display of a list of choices selected is especially valuable if the system has many levels and the user frequently has to navigate down new pathways. Maps of the menu structure, they say, are very useful when there is high ambiguity at high-level choice points.

CAPTIONS

Content

- Provide familiar, fully spelled-out descriptions of alternatives and choices available.
- Use concise and consistent phrasing.
- Use distinctive wording.
- If the option represents
  - — an action, state it as a verb.
  - — an object, state it as a noun.
  - — both an action and object, use a verb-noun syntax.
- Use high-imagery key words.
- Begin the caption with the key word or main topic.

Font

- Use either an upper- or mixed-case font.

Spacing

- If captions are placed in columns,
  - — double-space the captions if no more than seven or eight noncategorized options exist.
  - — single-space the captions if more than eight options exist, or if options are categorized.

Other Considerations

- Word option captions as commands to the computer; do not present yes/no choices.
- If menu options will be used in conjunction with a command language, the capitalization and syntax of the captions should be consistent with the command language.
- If a menu option leads to another menu, include the word "menu" in the caption.

Content. Menu captions, like captions on other screens, should comprise familiar, fully spelled-out words. While abbreviations may occasionally be necessary, they should be kept to a minimum. Captions should also be concise, containing as few words as possible, and distinctive, constructed of words that make a caption's intent as clear as possible. One way to improve caption distinctness is to avoid repeating the same word, or words, in a list of captions. Repeated words often signal the need for menu categorization.

If an option name represents an action, state it as a verb. If it represents an object, state it as a noun. If an option name represents both an action and an object, use a verb-noun syntax.

Use high-imagery key words, words that elicit a mental image of the object or action. Avoid low-imagery key words, words more general in connotation. For example, when obtaining a printout of a screen, the term "print" is much more descriptive than "list."

Arrange the caption so that the descriptive and unique words appear at its beginning. This optimizes scanning and recognition while the user is learning the menu. Caption phrasing and wording should also be consistent across all menus to further aid learning.

In creating menu choice captions or descriptions, never assume the caption chosen by the designer will have the same meaning to the user. Furnas et al. (1984) found that the probability of two people choosing the same name or description for something ranged from 8 to 18 percent. Names chosen by experts were no better than nonexperts. Therefore, iteratively test and refine the choices to achieve as much agreement as possible.

Font.   In general, research has shown that mixed-case text is read faster than text in all upper case. Williams (1988), however, found some reading speed and user preference advantages for capitalized menu options over mixed-case options. The captions were fairly short (the longest average length being 11 characters), so perhaps the advantage found for mixed case over upper case in text had not yet begun to show. The conclusion that can be drawn is that either upper case or mixed case may be acceptable. Whichever style is chosen, however, should be consistently followed.

Spacing.   Williams also examined single-spaced versus double-spaced menus and found that double-spacing yielded significantly shorter search times and was preferred by 85 percent of the study participants. The maximum number of options he studied was eight, however. Double-spacing does seem desirable for short menus of no more than seven or eight options. Where there are more than seven or eight options, screen space constraints and the inability to create visual groupings will necessitate single-spacing of options.

Other considerations.   Captions for menu options should be worded as commands to the computer, not questions to the user. For example, a menu phrased as a question to the user might be:

```
        Do you want to exit without saving?
            Yes
            No
```

A similar request worded as a command to the computer would be:

```
        Choose one.
            Save and exit
            Exit without saving
```

Wording options as questions to the user implies the dialog initiative is with the computer and can be confusing. Requests worded as commands to the computer implies the initiative is with the user and is clearer in intent. It also permits the development of mnemonic codes for options, which facilitates learning commands and bypassing menus as system familiarity is achieved. If menus are intended to be used in conjunction with a command language, then the capitalization and syntax of the option name should be consistent with the command language.

Menu options leading to other menus should clearly indicate that fact. The most common way is to include the word "menu" in the caption. If, however, the majority of options lead to another menu, consider only designating the exceptions.

OPTION CAPTION ALIGNMENT, JUSTIFICATION, AND POSITIONING

Menus As Complete Screens

- Align alternatives or choices into columns.
- Left-justify captions.

```
                              CREATE
                              COPY
                              DELETE
                              EDIT
                              PRINT
                              EXIT
```

- Position in the center of the screen.

Menus Included on Other Screens

- Distinguish from other screen components through
  — consistent positioning,
  — using a distinctive display technique to contrast with the remainder of the screen, and
  — setting off with lines.
- Align alternatives or choices into columns, if possible.
- If a single-row (horizontal) orientation must be maintained, organize for left-to-right readings.

```
    CREATE       COPY       DELETE      EDIT       PRINT       EXIT
```

- If two or more rows are available
  — organize for top-to-bottom, left-to-right reading,

— left-justify captions.

```
     CREATE      DELETE      PRINT
     COPY        EDIT        EXIT
```

Menus as complete screens. For scanning ease, options should be left-justified and aligned into columns. Parkinson et al. (1985) and Backs et al. (1987) have found columnar menus searched significantly faster than horizontally oriented menus. Position the aligned items in the center of the screen.

Menus included on other screens. When menus are included on other screens, such as with pop-up or permanent menus, space constraints often exist and the menu must somehow be easily differentiated from other screen components. This can be accomplished by always presenting the menu in the same location and using distinctive display techniques to contrast the menu with the remainder of the screen. Display techniques must, of course, be compatible with those used for other purposes on the remainder of the screen. A good way to set a menu off from the remainder of the screen is to enclose it in a box or, if it is at the screen's top or bottom, separate it with a horizontal line. Techniques chosen should be consistent throughout the system.

Choices should always be aligned in columns if possible. If a single-row (horizontal) orientation is necessary, organize for left-to-right reading based on one of the ordering principles described earlier. If two or more rows are available for displaying choices, organize for top-to-bottom, left-to-right reading to facilitate visual scanning.

OPTION IDENTIFICATION METHODS

- Menu items may be identified by
    - an ordinal code,
    - a mnemonic code,
    - or be unidentified.

Ordinal Identification

- Use numbers starting with one, not zero.

```
          1   CREATE
          2   COPY
          3   EDIT
          4   ERASE
          5   PRINT
```

Mnemonic Identification

- Use a mnemonic or abbreviation that meaningfully describes the alternative.

— Each mnemonic must be unique.
— Create mnemonics using a consistent, easily learned rule.
— Simple truncation is the preferred primary method.
— When the primary rule results in duplicate designators, apply a secondary rule such as vowel deletion.

```
CR   CREATE
CO   COPY
ED   EDIT
ER   ERASE
PR   PRINT
```

No Identification

- The caption serves to identify the item.

```
CREATE
COPY
EDIT
ERASE
PRINT
```

Identification of choices on a menu may take one of several forms. The common methods are the following.

Ordinal identification.   With ordinal identification the identifier has no meaningful relationship with the item it describes. The advantage of an ordinal code is that it provides a simple and unique way to identify a choice, and few keystrokes are needed to communicate the selection.

The disadvantage of the ordinal code is that it makes remembering choices on other menu screens much more difficult. Alternative "3" on eight different menus will usually mean eight different things. Ordinal codes also cause problems when items are added to menus. If the original menu has items arranged in some logical order (such as sequence of use), adding a new alternative in its logical location in the listing of choices will cause a renumbering of alternatives appearing below it. This problem often results in menu listings on expanding systems not being ordered in some meaningful way because the designer chooses not to renumber and simply adds to the list at the bottom.

Ordinal codes commonly found on screens have been made up of letters of the alphabet or numbers. The advantages of sequential lettering are that 26 choices can be communicated with one keystroke and fewer errors occur because the letters are more spread out. Disadvantages include longer times to find choices (especially for those not familiar with a typewriter keyboard) and the potential for fostering erroneous associations. That is, letters of the alphabet associated with captions comprising letters can create associations that were not intended and that interfere with menu learning.

Using numbers as ordinal codes has the following advantages. Numbers are grouped more logically from both a spacing and ordering perspective, aiding visual scanning and making it easier to find the relevant key. Thus, selection speed is improved. Numbers also permit function keys to be substituted for typewriter key activation, and they exactly identify how many choices are available. Disadvantages of numbers are the necessity for making two keystrokes when more than nine choices exist and that numbering may imply an ordering or preference (number 1 is most important) that does not exist.

In a study comparing these two ordinal coding schemes, Perlman (1984) found that numbered ordinal codes were searched about twice as fast as lettered codes.

In consideration of the arguments above, the recommended ordinal code is numeric digits beginning with one (1). Never start with zero (0). While computers may start counting with zero, people never do.

Mnemonic identification.   A mnemonically identified alternative has a meaningful relationship with the item it identifies. Mnemonics are extremely advantageous in that they aid the menu users' learning of the system choices, thereby facilitating the transition to a command language and avoiding the need to always step through a series of menu screens. Thus, the transition from novice to expert user is aided. Mnemonics also permit easy reordering of menu listings as items are added. They may be inserted in their proper places without renaming identifiers.

A disadvantage of a mnemonic scheme is that uniqueness must be maintained throughout the entire menu structure. This can create large identifiers that require more keystrokes to communicate a command to the system.

Three studies (Perlman, 1984; Shinar et al., 1985; Shinar and Stern, et al., 1987) have demonstrated that mnemonically coded menus can be searched significantly faster than menus with ordinal numeric codes. Mnemonic codes are preferable to ordinal codes, whenever they are possible.

No identification.   Of course, items may not be identified at all, which implies that a user has to select an alternative by pointing at it with the screen cursor (using the keyboard or a control like the "mouse"), or by touching it with his finger. A problem with this method is that a transition to a command language is impossible.

OPTION IDENTIFICATION CODE POSITIONING

Numeric Codes

- Position code to the left of its associated caption and separate from the caption by two (2) blank spaces.

• Right-align the codes.

```
 1xxCREATE
 2   COPY
 3   EDIT
 4   ERASE
 5   PRINT
 "      "
 "      "
10   EXIT
```

Mnemonic Codes

• If displayed as a separate code,
  — position the code to the left of its associated caption and separate from the caption by two (2) blank spaces.
  — left-align the codes.
  — do not display in mixed case.

```
CRxxCREATE
CO   COPY
ED   EDIT
ER   ERASE
PR   PRINT
 "      "
 "      "
EX   EXIT
```

• If incorporated within the option caption,
  — display the code in a visually distinctive manner.
    — Underlining the mnemonic letters is the recommended method.

```
CREATE
COPY
EDIT
ERASE
PRINT
  "
  "
EXIT
```

Horizontal Arrangements

• For horizontally arranged captions with space constraints, visually relating caption to code may be necessary:
  — use an equal (=) sign as the delimiter.

```
1=CREATE   2=COPY   3=EDIT   4=ERASE   5=PRINT
```

When codes are positioned to the left of the options, they should be distinguishable from, but visually related to, the options. A two-space separation should be sufficient to accomplish this. Mnemonic codes displayed separately should be entirely in upper case or lower case, not mixed case. If the code is incorporated within the option name, the code letters should be visually distinct from the option name. Best distinctiveness, without impacting readability of the option, is achieved through underlining the code.

On screens where space to display a menu is restricted, such as with pop-up or permanent menus, visually tying the code to the caption may be necessary. A good symbol to accomplish this is the equal sign (=).

CATEGORY HEADINGS

- Incorporate menu category headings whenever possible.
- Categories of menu items should
  — contain logically similar items,
  — cover all possibilities,
  — not overlap.
- Distinguish the category heading from the choices by
  — displaying it in an upper-case font.
  — positioning it in the line above its related choice captions and starting the category heading five spaces to the left of the aligned listing of choice captions, choice codes, or multiple-selection entry fields.

```
            CUSTOMER
                1  Account
                2  Information
                3  Status
```

  — positioning the category heading to the left of the caption, code, or multiple-selection entry field, separated by a "greater than" sign (>) and three spaces.

```
            CUSTOMERx>xxx1  Account
                        2  Information
                        3  Status
```

Category headings should be included whenever possible. They will reflect the hierarchical groupings recently discussed. Therefore, they should contain logically similar items, cover all possibilities, and not overlap. They should be easily distinguishable from the alternatives but should not detract attention from choices to be scanned. The recommended approach is the second one illustrated above: positioning the category heading to the left of the first item in the group and separating it with a "greater than" (>) sign. The first approach, indention of the category heading above the column of choices, is most practical and efficient on multicolumn menus or on menus where horizontal spacing constraints exist.

SPACING

Vertical Spacing

- Leave a blank line between categories of information.

```
CUSTOMER                    CUSTOMER >    1   ACCOUNT
    1   ACCOUNT                           2   INFORMATION
    2   INFORMATION                       3   STATUS
    3   STATUS
                            TRANSACTION > 4   HISTORY
TRANSACTION                               5   NUMBER
    4   HISTORY                           6   TYPE
    5   NUMBER
    6   TYPE
```

- For long lists of alternatives, leave a blank line after every fifth item. Do not exceed seven items without inserting a space line.

```
                    BILL
                    CANCEL
                    CORRECT
                    DISPLAY
                    ENDORSE

                    FILE
                    ISSUE
                    PRINT
                    QUOTF
                    RENEW
```

- Alternatively, separate the groupings with solid lines.
  - Left-align the lines with the start of the captions (or selection codes if displayed).
  - Extend the lines as far left as the longest caption in the column of options.

```
                    BILL
                    CANCEL
                    CORRECT
                    DISPLAY
                    ENDORSE
                    ───────
                    FILE
                    ISSUE
                    PRINT
                    QUOTE
                    RENEW
```

Horizontal Spacing

- For multicolumn arrangements on full screens, leave a minimum of five spaces between the longest item caption in one column and the first character position of the adjacent column category heading, code, or multiple selection field.
- Center the double column on the screen.

```
        BILL       FILE
        CANCEL     ISSUE
        CORRECTxxxxxPRINT
        DISPLAY    QUOTE
        ENDORSE    RENEW

     1  BILL       6  FILE
     2  CANCEL     7  ISSUE
     3  CORRECT    8  PRINT
     4  DISPLAY    9  QUOTE
     5  ENDORSExxxxx10  RENEW
```

- Where horizontal space constraints exist, consider separating columns by a dashed line.

```
        BILL     | FILE
        CANCEL   | ISSUE
        CORRECT  | PRINT
        DISPLAY  | QUOTE
        ENDORSE  | RENEW

     1  BILL     | 6  FILE
     2  CANCEL   | 7  ISSUE
     3  CORRECT  | 8  PRINT
     4  DISPLAY  | 9  QUOTE
     5  ENDORSE  | 10  RENEW
```

- Where horizontal orientation of choices is necessary, leave a minimum of two spaces between adjacent captions, three spaces if available.

```
     CREATExxCOPY  DELETE  EDIT  PRINT  EXIT

  1=CREATExx2=COPY  3=DELETE  4=EDIT  5=PRINT  6=EXIT

  1=CREATExxx2=COPY  3=DELETE  4=EDIT  5=PRINT  6=EXIT
```

Vertical spacing.   The vertical spacing guidelines outlined above are necessary to achieve visual groupings and separation. Parkinson et al. (1985) found that spacing between groups of information reduced menu search time. It is not desirable to leave space lines between elements within a group because they hamper visual perception of the group as a separate entity. If space is available on the screen, consider leaving an extra space line between groups instead. If a logical grouping contains six or seven items, a space line may be left after the last one instead of after five items, as recommended above. Do not, however, go beyond seven items within the logical grouping without including a space line.

Horizontal spacing. Horizontal spacing guidelines are intended to achieve visual separation and to convey the necessity of columnar scanning. Thus, these separation requirements should be considered minimums, and more space should be left between columns if available. Lengthy captions will usually require greater between-column spacing than that described above (unless a vertical line is drawn).

OPTION SELECTION

Methods

- Options may be selected by
  — one entry field per screen (single selection field).
  — one entry field for each option (multiple selection fields).
  — pointing at the option (with cursor, mouse, finger, etc.)
  — Function keys.

Single Selection Fields

- Locate the selection field directly underneath the column of option codes (or under the first column if a multicolumn menu screen).
- Separate the selection field from the options by a blank line.
- Identify with a unique or descriptive caption such as SELECTION or OPTION.

```
         9   PRINT              PR   PRINT
        10   EXIT               EX   EXIT


    SELECTION: __             SELECTION:  __
```

Multiple Selection Fields

- Identify selection fields by an underscore.
- Position the selection field to the left of the option.
- Leave two (2) spaces between the selection field and the caption.

```
            _xxCREATE
            _   COPY
            _   EDIT
            _   ERASE
            _   PRINT
```

- If option codes are included, leave two (2) blank spaces between the selection field and the code.

```
_xx1xxCREATE
_  2  COPY
_  3  EDIT
_  4  ERASE
_  5  PRINT
```

- Visually distinguish single- and multiple-choice menus.

Pointing

- Select the choice through pointing at it with a pointing mechanism such as the cursor, light pen, or finger.
- Indicate:
  — Which options are selectable.
  — When the option is under the pointer and can be selected.
- Visually distinguish single- and multiple-choice menus.

Function Keys

- Use the function keys available on the keyboard to select the choice.

Techniques

Cursor Key Movement

- The up and down arrow keys should move the cursor up or down vertically oriented menu options.
- The left and right cursor keys should move the cursor left or right between horizontally oriented menu options.

Selection/Execution

- If keyboard typing into a single selection field is the selection method used,
  — option codes should be acceptable in upper, mixed, or lower case.
- If keyboard typing into a multiple selection field is the selection method used,
  — the recommended value to be keyed is Y.
- If cursor pointing is the selection method used,
  — the selectable target area should be at least twice the size of the active area of the pointing device, or displayed pointer. In no case should it be less than six (6) millimeters square.
  — adequate separation must be provided between adjacent target areas.
- If the finger pointing is the selection method used,
  — the touch area must be a minimum of 20 to 30 millimeters square.
  — the touch area must encompass the entire caption plus one (1) character around it.

- Provide separate actions for selecting and executing menu options.
- Indicate the selected choice through either
  — highlighting it with a distinctive display technique.
  — modifying the shape of the cursor.
  — displaying the choice in the command field.
- Permit unselecting choice before execution.
  — If a multiple-choice menu, permit all options to be selected before execution.

Combining Techniques

- Permit alternative selection techniques to provide flexibility.

Methods

Items on a menu screen may be selected in a variety of ways. One entry field may be provided on a screen, the single-selection field method; an entry field may be associated with each option, the multiple-selection field method; the item may be pointed at by moving the cursor to the option desired; or the keyboard's function keys may be used. Each method has advantages and disadvantages.

Single selection field. One entry field may be incorporated on a menu screen into which the code for the selective alternative is keyed. Single selection fields should be located in a consistent position at the bottom of the screen and must be identified with a unique and descriptive caption. The recommended location is at the bottom of the column of menu options. The inexperienced user's eyes are permitted to scan down the column of alternatives until the desired alternative is found. The eyes then continue downward until the selection field is found. Eye movement from keyboard back to selection field to verify that the entry is correct is also minimized by this location. The experienced user who does not rely on scanning the menu listing to find a choice, but relies on memory instead, will also find this location acceptable, as it is consistent and minimizes the visual distance between the keyboard and the field itself. If command or choice stacking or "typeahead" is permitted (which is desirable as it permits the expert user to override the display of menus in a string), this selection field must be large enough to permit keying as many choices as needed.

On multicolumn menu screens position the entry field at the bottom of the first column of options. This will provide the most location consistency in systems containing menus of varying numbers of option columns.

Multiple-selection fields. With multiple-selection fields the screen user moves the cursor to an entry field associated with an item and keys a value to indicate the item has been selected. For screens containing a small number of items, this method can be used quite efficiently. As the number of items on a menu increases, however, it becomes less efficient as the cursor must be moved greater distances. Where the single-selection field method can become more efficient is difficult to say. As a rule of thumb, confine this technique to menus where one item must be selected from no more than five or six.

The multiple-selection field method may also be effectively employed where more than one item must be selected from a large number of items. That is, the user may wish to select 3 or 4 items at one time from a list of 10 or 12 choices. Menus containing a larger number of choices may use this method, since distances between choices will, on the average, remain short. (If about 4 items are selected from 12 alternatives, approximately 1 in every 3 entry fields will have a value keyed into it.) Again, a rule of thumb would be to restrict the method to situations where on the average 1 item is selected for every several alternatives displayed.

Other advantages of the multiple-selection field approach are that codes to identify alternatives are not necessary and that fewer opportunities exist for making typing errors. A disadvantage is that command stacking, or "typeahead," is not permitted.

Pointing.   The pointing approach to choice selection resembles the multiple-selection field approach, except that a value need not be keyed. Instead, the cursor is moved to the designated item through use of the cursor movement (arrow) keys, or an alternative control mechanism such as a "mouse"; or the user's finger is used to make the selection (if the screen is touch sensitive). Depressing a key such as TRANSMIT or ENTER or a mouse button signals the choice to the computer. Indicate which options are selectable and when the option is under the pointer and can be selected. Visually distinguish single- and multichoice menus.

Other advantages and disadvantages to pointing are similar to those of the multiple-selection field approach. One study (Shinar et al., 1985) compared cursor pointing to single-field entry of a one-character mnemonic code, and found that keying a mnemonic code was faster than pointing for more than five choices.

Francik and Kane (1987) found a single field entry superior to pointing using cursor keys for menus ranging in length from 8 to 15 options. Shinar and Stern (1987) found cursor selection slightly better than typed letter entry for menus containing two to four options. It appears that if there are fewer than five options, cursor pointing is faster.

Function keys.   Menu alternatives may also be selected through use of function keys. Item identification on the screen can incorporate the key number, and a choice is made by pressing the applicable key. The advantage of this approach is that it requires only one key stroke to implement a choice. Disadvantages are that usually fewer alternatives are available (some terminals may have few, if any, function keys) and that command stacking for the experienced user is not possible.

Techniques

Cursor key movement.   The up and down arrow keys should move the cursor up and down a vertical column of menu options. The left and right arrow keys should move the cursor left and right across a horizontal array of options.

Selection/execution.   In typing codes into a single-selection field, the codes should be acceptable in any case (upper, lower, and mixed). If keying of an option is permitted on a screen other than the menu screen where the options are listed, fully spelled-out captions should be permitted as well as their corresponding mnemonic codes.

In typing into a multiple-selection field the recommended value to be keyed is "*Y.*" It possesses a high association value (Yes, I would like to choose this alternative), and the letter *Y* is located at a convenient place on the standard typewriter keyboard (middle of top alphabetic row).

If cursor pointing is the selection method used, an adequate target area should be provided. This area should be at least twice the size of the active area of the pointing device or the displayed pointer. In no case should it be less than six (6) millimeters square. To avoid unintended activation of the wrong option, provide adequate separation between selectable areas. Highlighting of the selected choice will also provide indication of an incorrect choice.

If finger pointing is the selection method used, an even larger touch area must be provided, a minimum of 20–30 millimeters. Single-character positions on a screen make poor targets for most fingers. Also, keep in mind that using a finger to signify a choice can be taxing on arm muscles, so this approach should only be used in casual or infrequent use situations.

Provide separate actions for selecting and executing menu options. For example, require typing the option code to select and then pressing the enter or return key to execute. Or, with a mouse, require moving the cursor to the option to select and then "clicking" to execute. Always permit erroneous selections to be unselected and, in a multiple-choice menu, all options to be selected before execution.

The item selected should be highlighted in some way through a distinctive display technique such as reverse polarity. An alternative is to change the shaping of the pointer itself. These methods provide direct visual feedback that the proper choice has been selected, reducing the probability of errors in choice selection.

Combining techniques.   Permit alternative selection techniques to provide flexibility. If a pointing method is used, also provide a keyboard alternative to accomplish the same task. Pointing will probably be easier for the novice, but many experts prefer the keyboard alternative.

An example of combining techniques is described by Goodwin (1983). In the system described, called MENUS, several alternatives are implemented concurrently, including numbered ordinal identification codes, function keys, and mnemonic-like commands. An example of a menu from this system is

Figure 9.3   An example of a standard MENUS system menu.

```
-------------------------------------------------------------

                    OFFICE SUPPORT TOOLS (O)
                        (parent:  MAIN)

    PF KEY       COMMAND      DESCRIPTION

      1            OM         Mail System
      2            OP         Personal Appointments (Calendar)
      3            OR         Reminder Files

      9            RMM        Return to MAIN Menu
     10            RPM        Return to Previous Menu (F)
     11            LVE        Leave MENUS
     12            LOG        Logoff of CMS


-------------------------------------------------------------

ENTER YOUR SELECTION:
```

From Goodwin, N. C., "Designing a Multipurpose Menu Driven User Interface to Computer Based Tools," in *Proceedings of the Human Factors Society-27th Annual Meeting (1983)*, p. 820. Santa Monica, Calif.: Human Factors Society, Inc. Reproduced by permission of the publisher.

illustrated in Figure 9.3. Each menu contains a numbered listing corresponding to the number of the function key associated with this option. A system user may press the appropriate function key or key the one-digit number into the selection field. Since this does not allow the expert user to go directly to the wanted screen, a command code has also been provided through the creation of meaningful path names derived from one- and two-character alphabetic codes added to the command as the several levels of menus are navigated. To go from one menu to the next simply requires keying the meaningful code displayed on that menu. As code structures are learned, they may be strung together (stacked) to go directly to the menu or screen needed. Thus, all system users may use the approach with which they are most comfortable at any time.

BORDERS

- Incorporate a line border to enhance menu distinctiveness.
  - Keep the border simple using medium-size lines.
  - Entirely surround the menu.

— Provide adequate separation from the menu content.
— Leave a minimum of two (2) spaces left and right between the side borders and the widest menu text.
— Leave a minimum of one (1) space line between the bottom border and the menu text.
— A space line between the title and top border is desirable but not required if space constraints exist.
— Attempt to create equal-size box borders for a family of menu screens.

```
┌───────────────────────────────────────┐
│                                       │
│          DISPOSITION                  │
│                                       │
│          Bill                         │
│          Cancel                       │
│          Correct                      │
│          Display                      │
│          Endorse                      │
│                                       │
│          File                         │
│          Issue                        │
│          Print                        │
│          Quote                        │
│          Renew                        │
│                                       │
│                                       │
└───────────────────────────────────────┘
```

• Create impenetrable borders for faster selection speed.

Line borders.   A line border completely surrounding the menu will make the menu more distinctive. As some kinds of menus (pop-ups, pull-downs) must have borders, incorporating borders around all menus will create a common look. In order to not detract from the options, keep borders consistent and simple, using medium-size lines. If color is used, the border should be of the same color as the option characters. The border should entirely surround the menu and be sufficiently separated from the menu content. Keeping menu box borders of equal size also will aid in menu recognizability.

Impenetrable borders.   Impenetrable borders are borders that the cursor cannot move past. Walker and Smelcer (1990) found that option selection speed was significantly faster when the cursor, and choices, were placed within a pop-up menu window whose borders were impenetrable. Impenetrable borders permit faster movement to the top and bottom of the menu list because the user does not have to worry about "overshooting" the target.

Walker and Smelcer also compared movement times for options columnized in a pop-up window with options horizontally arrayed in an action bar. Movement time was shorter to the action bar option than to the window option, in spite of the fact that the distance of the movement to the action bar was longer. This faster speed is attributed to the fact that the top border of the action bar was impenetrable and movements to all the options could be more ballistic in nature (again, no worry of overshooting the target). A vertical move within a window was only stopped above the top option and below the bottom option, with movements to other options having to be more precise.

MENU NAVIGATION TECHNIQUES

- Permit typeahead—the keying of following menu screen codes on the displayed menu screen.
- Permit direct access—the keying of the desired menu screen name on the displayed screen.
- Permit menu macros—regularly used menu paths to be stored and keyed as commands.
- Permit one simple action to return to
  — the next-higher-level menu,
  — the general or main menu.
- Provide alternative selection methods for selecting options.
- Provide a way to combine selection and execution.
- Provide and display keyboard accelerators
  — to the right of the option caption.
  — right-aligned.
  — enclosed in parentheses.

```
            Print              (Alt+P)
```

A criticism of many menu systems concerns is the long and tedious path that may have to be traversed to reach one's objective. This is extremely bothersome if menus are several levels deep and/or response times are somewhat slower than desirable. These problems can be alleviated if users are permitted to go directly to their destination, avoiding intermediate stops along the way. Shneiderman (1987) has outlined three ways to improve menu navigation: typeahead, direct access, and menu macros.

Typeahead.   Typeahead is command or choice "stacking." As paths through the menu system are learned, the needed choice codes can be keyed on higher level menus, and the destination screen will be directly displayed. If choice codes are mnemonics, the strings can achieve a mnemonic value themselves. The transition from novice menu user to expert command user can be gradual and graceful. As the user becomes experienced, he learns and remembers deeper paths. Infrequently used paths can still be supported by menus, as can the occasional memory lapse.

Typeahead requires a single-entry field, which must be large enough to accommodate the deepest path that can be covered.

Direct access. If a name is assigned to each menu, it can be keyed on any menu and then its menu will be directly displayed. Again, learning is gradual and graceful, with full menu paths always available when needed.

This approach is most useful if there are only a few destinations that have to be remembered. Unique names must also be created for all menus.

Menu macros. Regularly used paths can be recorded as menu macros; that is, a command name can be established to cause the desired path to be traversed whenever the command is executed. In addition to simplifying access, this permits individual customization of the system.

Other methods to enhance menu navigation are:

Upward movement. One simple key action should be all that is necessary to return to the next-higher-level menu and the main or general menu.

Alternative selection methods. Alternative selection methods, pointing and alphanumeric key entry, should be allowed to satisfy the needs of all users.

Combine selection and execution. For experts, allow the chosen option to be executed immediately after the first letter is typed. If an undesirable consequence can occur, an "undo" must be provided.

Keyboard accelerators. If keyboard accelerators are possible, display the accelerator to the right of the menu choice. Refer to keys as they are engraved on the keyboard and enclose them in parentheses to indicate that they are a prompt.

TITLE

- Create a short, simple, clear, and distinctive title reflecting the nature of the choice to be made or the menu's purpose.
- Locate the title in a centered position at the top of each screen.
- Spell out fully using an upper-case font.
- In a menu hierarchy, repeat the option name selected in the menu above in the title of the menu to which it leads.

The title should immediately orient the viewer to the menu's content and purpose. It should be centered at the top for balance and displayed using upper-case letters for emphasis.

SCREEN IDENTIFIER

- Place a screen identifier, page number, or other reference information in a consistent location in the upper right-hand corner.
  - For menus containing several pieces of screen identification information, both the left-hand and right-hand upper corners may be used.

Screen identification or other reference information warrants only occasional viewer interest. Therefore it should be located in a less prominent position on the screen. When included, the preferred location is the upper right corner. For a series of menus, a page-numbering convention should be included to allow users to know their exact location. The paging convention may simply be "menu n of x" or it may incorporate a mnemonic code that is a contraction of the menu title.

When the screen identifier includes additional information (such as date, time), a more efficient use of the screen body and better screen balance can be achieved by splitting the information between the upper left and upper right corners. All elements should maintain consistent locations on all screens.

Every menu must have a way of being uniquely identified through its titling- and/or screen-numbering convention.

MESSAGES

- Uniquely identify informational, warning, and status messages through
  - a consistent location such as
    - a designated line at the bottom of the screen.
    - in a window.
  - use of contrasting display features such as
    - reverse video,
    - highlighting,
    - different font style,
    - preceding each message type by a unique symbol
  - display in a mixed-case font.

Recommended locations and display methods for messages have been described in Chapter 4. They must attract the viewer's attention and be easily discernible from the screen body and other screen components. This is accomplished most effectively by locating them outside the screen body (or in windows) using consistent locations, contrasting display features, and special symbols. Again, each type must be identified by its structure and location without actually having to be read.

Example 1. A menu containing separate mnemonic codes, category headings to the left, mixed-case options, and a single-selection field.

```
          COUNTRIES OF THE WORLD

     AFRICA >    CH   Chad
                 KE   Kenya
                 LI   Liberia
                 MO   Mozambique
                 UG   Uganda

       ASIA >    BR   Brunei
                 HO   Hong Kong
                 IN   Idonesia
                 SI   Singapore
                 TH   Thailand


     SELECTION:  __
```

Example 2. A menu containing ordinal codes, category headings above the options, mixed-case options, and a single-selection field.

```
        FAMOUS AMERICAN ATHLETES

        BASEBALL PLAYERS
             1   Joe DiMaggio
             2   Willie Mays
             3   Stan Musial
             4   Ted Williams

        FOOTBALL PLAYERS
             5   Sammy Baugh
             6   Elroy Hirsch
             7   Walter Payton
             8   Bob Waterfield

     SELECTION:  _
```

Example 3. A menu containing multiple-selection fields and mixed-case options.

Example 4. A menu containing upper-case "pointing" options and a line to separate groups.

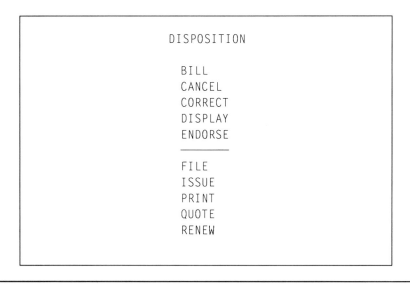

Example 5. A menu containing "pointing" options with accelerators, upper-case options, and a line to separate groups.

```
               DISPOSITION

         BILL       (Alt+B)
         CANCEL     (Alt+C)
         CORRECT    (Ctrl+C)
         DISPLAY    (Alt+D)
         ENDORSE    (Alt+E)
         ────────────────
         FILE       (Alt+F)
         ISSUE      (Alt+I)
         PRINT      (Alt+P)
         QUOTE      (Alt+Q)
         RENEW      (Alt+R)
```

Example 6. A menu containing mnemonic codes within the option descriptions, upper-case options, and a single-selection field.

```
           FURNITURE STYLES

              CHIPPENDALE
              COLONIAL
              DUNCAN PHYFE
              EARLY AMERICAN
              EMPIRE

              FRENCH PROVINCIAL
              HEPPLEWHITE
              JACOBEAN
              LOUIS XIV
              VICTORIAN

       SELECTION:  __
```

Graphical Screens

10

The expanded capabilities of graphic terminals permit a richer, more varied, screen interface. Whereas a traditional screen maintains a one-dimensional, text-oriented, form-like quality, graphic screens can assume a three-dimensional look. Information can "float" in windows, small rectangular boxes seeming to rise above the background plane. Windows can also float above other windows. Information can appear, and disappear, as needed, and in some cases text can be replaced by symbols representing objects or actions. These symbols are commonly referred to as "icons."

The graphical interface is permissible today because of the vast improvement in the quality of the display and greatly increased computer power. This enables the user's actions to be reacted to quickly, dynamically, and meaningfully. These improvements have been paired with new easy-to-use input devices that use pointing, not the keyboard, as the input mechanism. This new interface is often characterized as representing one's "desktop" with scattered notes, papers, and objects such as files, trays, and trash cans arrayed around the screen.

Graphic presentation of information utilizes a person's information processing capabilities much more effectively than other presentation methods. Properly used, it minimizes the necessity for perceptual and mental recoding and reduces short-term memory loads. It also permits faster information transfer between computer and user by permitting more visual comparisons of amounts, trends, or relationships; more compact representation of information; and simplification of the perception of structure. Graphics can also reduce errors, as well as the necessity for training and practice, and has also been shown to enhance problem solving (Polya, 1957) and improve retention (Wertheimer, 1959).

Nevertheless, graphics may not be the best alternative in all situations. Some studies have found textual presentation of information (Shneiderman, 1977, 1982A; Stern, 1984) or tabular display of information (Tufte, 1983) superior to graphics. So, it is the content of the graphic that is critical to its usefulness. The wrong information or a cluttered presentation may actually lead to greater confusion, not less.

SCOPE OF GRAPHICS

Graphics has added many new concepts to the screen interface. Information can be displayed in the aforementioned windows and in a pictorial or iconic form. Screen navigation and commands can be executed through action/menu bars and pull-downs. Menus may "pop-up." In the screen body, selection fields such as radio buttons, check boxes, list boxes, and value sets coexist with the reliable old entry field. More sophisticated entry fields with attached or drop-down menus of alternatives are also available. Screen objects and actions may be selected through use of pointing mechanisms such as the mouse or joystick instead of the traditional keyboard.

GRAPHICS COMPLEXITY

Graphics, then, while supporting a person's memory and needs much better than text-based single-screen technology, does increase the potential for even greater visual clutter and user confusion because of its variety and complexity. How the elements and techniques available to the graphic screen designer far outnumber those that have been at the disposal of the text-based screen designer can easily be seen by comparing the typical, but nonexhaustive, listings in Table 10.1. This "more" may not necessarily be better, unless it is carefully, thoughtfully, consistently, and simply applied. Since graphics is often applied with color, the advantages and problems of color must also be considered. With graphics the skill of the designer is increasingly challenged.

The graphical user interface is also burdened today by a lack of experimentally derived design guidelines and inconsistencies in technique and terminology between various system providers. Tremendous "look and feel" differences exist between different systems, making learning much more difficult than it need be. Graphical guidelines and standards are one of the topics of attention of some worldwide standards organizations, as previously detailed in Chapter 3. Like many aspects of computer systems, some of these inconsistencies will be resolved in the years ahead. These problems will be more fully addressed in the pages that follow.

DESIGN OBJECTIVES

Properly applied, graphics can assist in achieving these design objectives already described for text-based screens:

- Distinguishing or differentiating the various screen components.
- Helping the viewer to recognize classes or groups of information

By itself, graphics provides these additional benefits to the screen user interface:

- Adds appeal or charm.
- Permits greater customization to create a unique corporate style.

Table 10.1   A representative listing of typical textual and graphical screen
elements and techniques.

Textual Screens	*Graphical Screens*
Title	Title
Screen ID	Screen ID
Headings	Action/Menu Bars
Captions	Pull-Downs
Entry/Data Fields	Pop-up Menus
Function Key Listings	Buttons
Command Fields	Window Style
Messages	Direct Manipulation
Blinking	Indirect Manipulation
Scrolling	Scrolling
High/Low Intensity	Headings
Upper/Mixed-Case Characters	Captions
Normal/Reverse Video	Entry/Data Fields
Underlining	Radio Buttons
	Check Boxes
	Value Sets
	List Boxes
	Spin Lists
	Attached Menu Boxes
	Drop-Down Menu Boxes
	Messages
	Mice
	Icons
	High/Low Intensity
	Highlighting/Lowlighting
	Upper/Mixed-Case Characters
	Multiple-Character Styles
	Multiple-Character Sizes
	Normal/Reverse Video
	Thin/Thick/Double Rulings
	Foreground Colors
	Background Colors
	Color Lightness Differences
	Proportion
	Oval Shapes
	Rectangular Shapes
	Scalloped Corners
	Beveled Edges
	Drop Shadows
	Shrinking/Growing
	Motion

OVERVIEW.

This chapter begins with a set of general appearance principles for the graphical user interface. Topics discussed include depth and layering, separation, proportion, and typeface styles. Then the components of graphical screens are defined, including action/menu bars, pull-downs, pop-up menus, buttons, windows, and the screen body. The screen body discussion looks at entry fields, selection fields, screen composition, borders, titles, and messages.

Other graphical topics are addressed in subsequent chapters. The design and use of icons is addressed in Chapter 11, graphics of a statistical nature are described in Chapter 12, and color will be detailed in Chapter 13.

SPATIAL IMAGES AND GENERAL GRAPHICS CONSIDERATIONS

The appearance of a graphical screen is enhanced, and visual clutter is minimized, if the following are true:

- Its components are adequately separated or set off from one another,
- The depth or levels of information are obvious,
- The classes of information are obvious,
- The varieties or variations in the elements building the screen are restricted,
- The shapes of elements or windows conform to desirable proportional relationships.

Separation of Screen Components

The test described at the start of Chapter 4—can all screen components be identified without reading any words—also applies in a graphics environment. Component identification is aided by locating elements consistently, using the available display techniques sparingly and consistently, and adequately separating the elements. Consistent locations and several display techniques were reviewed in Chapter 4. Some additional considerations will be addressed in the following pages.

Component separation is especially critical in a graphics environment because of the spatial layering that can occur. Separation is enhanced through the use of lines, borders, and frames comprised of space.

Lines, Borders, and Space Frames

- Incorporate rules or lines to create groupings of related information.
- For action/menu bar pull-downs and windows,
    - incorporate surrounding borders.
    - leave a space frame, preferably two blank spaces but minimally one blank space, between the pull-down or window text and the border.
- Restrict line and border weights to a maximum of three variations.
- Create lines consistent in height and length.
- Use rules and borders sparingly.

Rules. Lines or rules assist in focusing attention on related information. They also aid in separating groupings of information from one another. Rules also serve to guide the viewer's eye in the desired direction. Use a standard hierarchy for rules, the thickest to differentiate major components, the thinnest for minor separation.

Borders and space frames. Surrounding borders aid in focusing attention on action/menu bar pull-downs and windows. They also isolate the contents of these elements. Include a line border around an element of a screen when it is presented and attention must be directed to it. Simple background differences in color or shade by themselves are not as effective in drawing attention. Line borders also make a screen appear less complicated.

Provide "breathing space" around text in pull-downs and windows. A common problem with windows is that the text within a window has no outer margins. The text from one window runs directly into the text from an underlying window, making reading more difficult and giving the screen a cluttered look. Preferably, leave a minimum of two spaces (but at least one space) between a window's text and its borders.

Minimize line thickness variations. Too many variations in line thicknesses on a screen create clutter and are distracting. Use no more than three line weights at one time.

Consistent line widths and heights. Similarly, variations in line widths and heights are distracting. Create horizontal lines of equal widths across the screen and vertical lines of equal height whenever possible.

Use lines and borders sparingly. Too many lines and borders on a screen also creates clutter and can be distracting. Like any display technique, lines and borders must be used sparingly.

Conveying Depth of Levels

The spatial composition of a graphics screen, and currently important screen elements, can be emphasized by making them appear to be closer to the viewer. Techniques to accomplish this include overlapping, drop shadows, highlighting and lowlighting, growing and shrinking, and beveled edges (Marcus, 1988).

Overlapping, Shadows, Highlighting, Growing, and Beveled Edges

Overlapping

- Fully display windows where viewer attention must be directed.
- Partially hide windows not currently the focus of attention.

Drop Shadows

- Include a heavier shaded line along the bottom and right side of a pull-down or window where viewer attention must be directed.

Highlighting and Lowlighting

- Highlight windows where viewer attention must be directed.
- Lowlight windows not currently the focus of attention.

Shrinking and Growing

- Enlarge windows where viewer attention must be directed.
- Shrink windows not currently the focus of attention.

Beveled Edges

- Create beveled edges for action bar choices, buttons, windows, or icons.

Overlapping. Fully display the window or screen element of current relevance and partially hide beneath it other screen windows or elements, as illustrated in Figure 10.1. The completeness or continuity of outline of the relevant element will make it appear nearer than those partially covered.

Drop shadows. To further aid the impression of the placement of a pull-down above a screen, or a window above a screen or another window, locate a

Figure 10.1   Overlapping screen elements.

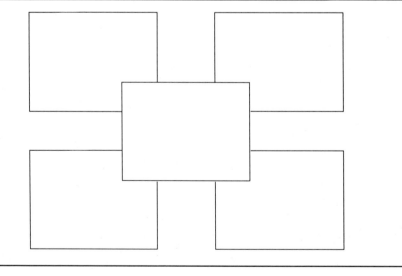

Figure 10.2   Drop shadow.

heavier line along the bottom and right edges of the pull-down or window, as illustrated in Figure 10.2. This creates the impression of a shadow caused by a light source in the upper left corner of the screen, reinforcing the nearness of the important element. The light source should always appear to be upper left, the shadow lower right.

Highlighting and lowlighting.   Highlighted or brighter screen elements appear to come forward while lowlighted or less bright elements recede. Attention will be directed to the highlighted element.

Shrinking and growing.   Important elements can be made to grow in size while less important remain small or shrink. An icon, for example, should expand to a window when it is selected. The movement as it expands will focus attention upon it.

Beveled edges.   A beveled edge (non-right-angle lines to the screen element borders) will also give the impression of depth. With beveled edges, windows, buttons, and action bar choices will appear to arise from the screen, as illustrated in Figure 10.3. To strengthen the three-dimensional aspect of the screen element, give it a drop shadow by shading the bottom and right sides with either a tone of gray or a darker shade of the basic screen color.

Figure 10.3   Beveled edges.

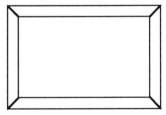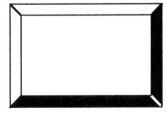

Other Ways To Convey Depth

Texture Change

- Display nonapplicable elements in a less dense texture.
- Display applicable elements in a more dense texture.

Color Change

- Display applicable elements in a saturated color.
- Display nonapplicable elements in a hazy, less saturated color.

Size Change

- Display applicable elements larger.
- Display nonapplicable elements smaller.

Clarity Change

- Display applicable elements clearly.
- Display nonapplicable elements fuzzy or blurred.

Vertical Location

- Display applicable elements in the lower part of the screen.
- Display nonapplicable elements in the upper part of the screen.

Spacing Change

- Display applicable elements widely spaced.
- Display nonapplicable elements narrowly spaced.

Receding Lines

- Display parallel lines receding to a vanishing point.

Motion Differences

- Move close objects at a faster rate.
- Move distant objects at a slower rate.

Other ways to establish the perception of depth on a screen, and to call attention to more important screen windows or elements, include the following (Hall, 1982 in Marcus, 1988). Often two or more of these techniques are combined.

Texture change.   Increased density of an object implies a further distance. Increase the density of nonapplicable screen elements, display currently relevant elements less densely.

Color change.   Objects farther away appear hazy and less saturated. Increase haziness as screen element importance diminishes; display currently relevant elements more vividly.

Size change.   Objects farther away appear smaller. Decrease the size of nonapplicable screen elements; display currently relevant elements larger.

Clarity change.   Objects not at the eye's focus distance appear fuzzy or blurred. Display nonapplicable elements blurred and currently relevant screen elements clear.

Vertical location.   The horizon appears higher, objects up close lower. Present currently applicable screen elements at the bottom of the screen, nonapplicable elements at the screen's top.

Spacing change.   Faraway objects appear more closely spaced, closer objects more widely spaced. Display nonapplicable elements more closely spaced, currently applicable screen elements more widely spaced.

Receding lines.   Parallel lines receding to a vanishing point imply depth.

Motion change.   Objects moving at uniform speeds appear slower the farther away they are.

Typefaces—Styles and Sizes

Variations in typeface, weight, and size can be used to emphasize the structural relationship of graphical screen components. These variations should be limited, however, since too many display methods leads to clutter and the impression of confusion.

Typeface

- Use simple, readable fonts such as Times Roman or Helvetica.

Style

- Use no more than two styles of the same family.
- Use no more than two weights, regular and bold.

Size

- Use no more than three sizes.

Consistency

- Establish a consistent hierarchy and convention for using typefaces, styles, and sizes.

Typeface.   Visually simple, readable fonts are needed for clarity on screens. Ornate fonts should be avoided because they reduce legibility. Generally, sans serif typefaces are recommended (serifs are the small cross strokes that appear on the arms of some letters) if the type is less than 8 points in size or if the display environment is less than ideal. The serifs can wash out under these conditions. Types with serifs, it is felt, provide better links between letters in a word, provide a horizontal guideline for the eye, and help in distinguishing one letter from another. Helvetica is a sans serif typeface, while Times Roman is characterized by very small serifs.

Style.   A typeface exists in a family of styles designed to complement one another, creating unity in design. Styles include italics, outlines, and shadows, and different weights, regular and bold. An example of a family is that of Times illustrated in Figure 10.4.

Never use more than two styles at one time. A regular type and its italics is a good combination. Also, restrict a type to two weights, regular and bold for example.

Similar typefaces are grouped into what are called races. One kind of race is called *roman* which contains the Times typeface illustrated as well as the Bookman, Schoolbook, and Palatino typefaces. A second race is *sans serif* where the typefaces Helvetica and Avant Garde reside. Another race is named Old English. An effective design can almost always be achieved by staying within one typeface race.

Figure 10.4   The Times family of type.

Times Roman

Times Italic

Times Bold

Times Bold Italic

Times Outline

Times Shadow

If it is necessary to mix typeface families on a screen, Lichty (1989) recommends the following:

- Never mix families within the same race. Typographic noise is created.
- Assign a separate purpose to each family. A sans serif typeface for the title and headings and a roman typeface for the body is a good combination.
- Allow one family to dominate.

For a much more detailed discussion of typefaces, see Lichty.

Sizes.   Type sizes are described by points, the distance between the top of a letter's ascender and the bottom of its descender. One point equals $\frac{1}{72}$ inch. Variations in type sizes should also be minimized, no more than three being the maximum to be displayed at one time on a screen.

Consistency.   Apply typeface, style, and size conventions in a consistent manner to all screen components. This will aid screen learning and improve screen readability.

Proportion

Down through the ages, people and cultures have had preferred proportional relationships. What constitutes beauty in one culture is not necessarily considered the same by another culture, but some proportional shapes have stood the test of time and are found in abundance today.

- Create windows and groupings of data or text with aesthetically pleasing proportions.

Marcus (1988) describes the following shapes, illustrated in Figure 10.5, as aesthetically pleasing.

Square (1:1).   The simplest of proportions, it has an attention-getting quality and suggests stability and permanence. When rotated it becomes a dynamic diamond, expressing movement and tension.

Square root of two (1:1.414).   A divisable rectangle yielding two pleasing proportional shapes. When divided equally in two along its length, the two smaller shapes that result are also each a square root of two rectangles. This property only occurs with this proportion and is often used in book design. An open book has the same outside proportion as the individual pages within it. The square root of two has been adopted as a standard paper size in many countries of the world (the United States excluded).

Figure 10.5   Pleasing proportions.

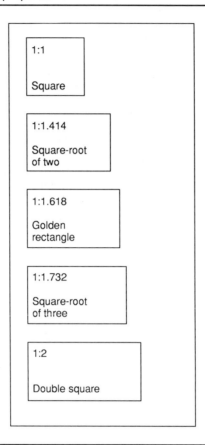

Golden rectangle (1:1.618).   An old (fifth century B.C.) proportion is the golden rectangle. Early Greek architecture used this proportion, and a mathematical relationship exists between this number and growth patterns in plant and animal life. This "divine division of a line" results when a line is divided such that the smaller part is to the greater part as the greater part is to the whole. The golden rectangle also has another unique property. A square created from part of the rectangle leaves a remaining area with sides also in the golden rectangle proportion.

Square root of three (1:1.732).   Used less frequently than the other proportions, its narrowness gives it a distinctive shape.

Double square (1:2).   Frequently seen in Japan, the tatami mat used for floor covering usually comes in this proportion. Rectangles more elongated than this one have shapes whose distinctiveness are more difficult to sense.

While these pleasing shapes have passed the test of time, not everything we encounter conforms to these principles. The American letter paper size has a ratio of 1:1.29, a typical American television screen a ratio of 1:1.33, and CRT screens typically have ratios in the range of about 1:1.33 to 1:1.50.

In screen design, aesthetically pleasing proportions should be considered for major components of the screen, including windows and groups of data or text.

SOME CURRENT GRAPHIC SYSTEMS

In the last decade a number of graphic systems have been introduced and are available in the marketplace. In the discussion that follows, an occasional reference will be made to some of them. These systems are briefly introduced in the following paragraphs. The reader in need of detailed information concerning their design and operation is referred to their design documentation. Another source of information is Marcus (1992) who provides a comparative evaluation of the operational characteristics of several of those listed.

Xerox Star.   The first of the graphical interfaces, it was the product of extensive studies at the Xerox PARC research center. It introduced pointing, selection, manipulation, and the mouse to the office.

Macintosh.   Introduced in 1984 by Apple, it was the first mass-marketed, widely accepted graphic system providing the interaction style referred to as direct manipulation. Its success is attributed to its consistent and user-oriented interface. Its simplicity makes its easy to learn but limits the flexibility available to the expert user.

NeXTStep.   Introduced in 1988 by NeXT, it was the first to present a simulated three-dimensional appearance for its components. Like the Macintosh, its simplicity and user-oriented interface is oriented toward inexperienced and nontechnical users. It provides a very good set of end-user customization tools.

OPEN LOOK.   OPEN LOOK was developed as the standard operating environment for UNIX System V.4 by AT&T and Sun Microsystems. Providing more functionality than Macintosh or NeXTStep, it provides more power and flexibility for the expert user at the cost of increased learning requirements for the inexperienced user. It possesses many innovative appearance and behavioral characteristics in order to avoid potential legal challenges, and it also provides an excellent functional specification and style guide.

DECwindows.   An interface for workstation software, it was announced in 1987. One of its goals was to achieve a consistent interface across operating systems, including VMS and UNIX, and across different input and screen configurations. A resulting product for achieving consistency is the XUI (X User Interface) style guide and toolkit.

OSF/Motif.   A window-manager and user interface toolkit, it was developed by Digital Equipment Corporation and Hewlett-Packard for the Open Software Foundation (OSF). Its appearance and behavior are based upon OS/2 Presentation Manager. Customization is encouraged, and some stylistic guidance is provided through a style guide (Open Software Foundation, 1991). Like NeXTStep, it presents a simulated three-dimensional appearance.

Microsoft Windows.   Created in 1985 as a graphics-oriented alternative to MS-DOS, it opened the door to graphics-oriented software on the PC. Initially limited by the design characteristics of DOS, it has recently been enhanced. The user interface is relatively easy for inexperienced users, and its extensive use of keyboard equivalents is intended to ease the transition for experienced DOS users.

OS/2 Presentation Manager.   Developed jointly by Microsoft and IBM in 1987, it is intended as the graphics operating system replacement for MS-DOS. It will become the standard operating environment for IBM and compatible microcomputers in the 1990s. It is largely indistinguishable from Microsoft Windows in appearance and behavior. A joint style guide exists for Microsoft Windows and Presentation Manager.

ELEMENTS OF GRAPHICAL SCREENS

Graphical screens are composed of a variety of different elements. In one category are the techniques for the user to communicate commands or actions to the computer: action or menu bars, pull-downs, pop-up menus, and buttons. Another element is the window through which the user can obtain a view of some portion of the computer, or through which the user's dialogue with the computer is carried out. Finally are a category of techniques through which the user and computer communicate concerning the application: entry fields, selection fields, and display fields.

COMMAND/ACTION TECHNIQUES

Command and action techniques are screen navigation components used to present alternatives or choices to the screen user. These choices may be commands or they may be properties that apply to an object in the screen itself. They are presented to the user at appropriate times in the dialogue in a preestablished manner. The user simply selects the desired alternative from those presented. Command and action techniques may take the form of action or menu bars, pull-downs from this bar, pop-up menus, or buttons.

ACTION/MENU BARS

A series of choices displayed horizontally across the top of a screen are most commonly referred to as action bars or menu bars. These bars often consist of a

Figure 10.6   Action/menu bar comprised of text.

| File | Edit | Options | Window | Help | Exit |

Figure 10.7   Action/menu bar comprised of buttons.

| File | | Edit | | Options | | Window | | | Help |

series of textual words as represented in Figure 10.6. Examples of this textual approach are illustrated by Macintosh, Presentation Manager, and Windows 3.0.

Some products have placed the choices within buttons as represented in Figure 10.7. An example of this approach is Sun Microsystems's *Open Look*, which calls them "menu buttons."

There are also combinations of both. OSF/Motif presents a list of textual choices, but when one is selected, it resembles a button. Motif refers to these as "cascade buttons."

Although visual differences may exist, action/menu bars should possess the following qualities.

Location

- Position choices horizontally over the entire row at the top of the screen, just below the screen title.
  - A large number of choices may necessitate display over two rows.

Choices should be positioned horizontally across the top of the screen below the screen title. A typical bar is comprised of about seven or eight choices, although more or less are sometimes seen. Due to screen space constraints, and human information processing capabilities, a maximum of seven or eight is reasonable. In the event more are needed, a second line of choices may be added.

Content

- Use mixed-case letters to describe choices.
- Use single-word choices whenever possible.

Choices should be composed of mixed-case single words. Typically, only the first letter of the choice is capitalized. Acronyms, abbreviations, or proper nouns that are normally capitalized may be capitalized. Choices should never be numbered.

IBM's SAA CUA has defined three common actions for all action/menu bars: File, Edit, and Help.

Organization

- Order choices left-to-right with
  - most frequent choices to the left.
  - related information grouped together.
- Choices found on more than one action bar should be consistently positioned.
- Left-justify choices within the line.
- When choices can be logically grouped, provide visual logical groupings, if possible.

- Help and/or Exit, when included, should be located as follows:
  - Exit—Justified to the right side of the bar.

File	**Edit**	**Options**	**Window**		**Exit**

  - Help (with Exit included)—Justified to the right side of the bar, but positioned to the left of Exit.

File	**Edit**	**Options**	**Window**	**Help**	**Exit**

  - Help (without Exit)—Justified to the right side of the bar.

File	**Edit**	**Options**	**Window**		**Help**

Order all choices left-to-right, with most frequently elected choices to the left and related information grouped together. Choices found on more than one action/menu bar should be consistently positioned.

Left-justify all choices within the line (as opposed to centering when there are not enough choices to completely fill the line). However, always locate Exit, when included, to the far right side. Help, when included with Exit, should be positioned just to the left of Exit. When Exit is not included and Help is, locate the Help to the far right side. Right-side positioning will always keep Help and Exit in a consistent location within the bar. Also, provide visual groupings of all related choices, if space permits on the bar.

IBM's SAA CUA's ordering recommendation is: File, Edit, application-specific choices, and Help.

Layout

- Indent the first choice one (1) space from the left margin.
- Leave at least three (3) spaces between each of the succeeding choices (except Help and/or Exit which will be right-justified).
- Leave one (1) space between the final choice and the right margin.

xTabsxxx**Justification**   **Spacing**   **Left**   **Right**   **Carriage**   **Help**   **Exit**x

---

The spacing recommendations above are intended to provide clear delineation of choices, leave ample room for the selection cursor, provide a legible selected choice, and provide efficiency in bar design.

Separation

- Separate the bar from the remainder of the screen by
  — a different background, or
  — solid lines above and below.

In addition to being identified by its location at the top, the bar should be identifiable by a contrasting display technique. The most effective way to do this is through use of a different background, either reversed polarity (black on white for the bar contrasted with white on black for the screen body), or a color different from the adjacent title and screen body. When a color is used, it must be chosen in conjunction with good color principles in Chapter 13, Color in Screen Design. Affecting the background color choice will be the foreground or choice description color, the selection indicator to be described next, and the screen body background color. The contrast of the bar to the remainder of the screen should be moderate, neither too vivid nor too subtle.

Mnemonic Code Keyboard Accelerators

- Provide unique mnemonic codes by which choices may be selected through the keyboard whenever possible.
- Indicate the mnemonic code by underlining the proper character.

F̲ile	E̲dit	O̲ptions	W̲indow		H̲elp	E̲xit

Enabling the user to select action/menu bar choices through the type-writer keyboard provides flexibility and efficiency in the dialogue. To do this, provide single-character mnemonic codes which, when typed, will also cause the choice to be invoked. Mnemonic codes can be visually indicated in a number of ways. The suggested method is an underline beneath the proper character within the choice, as is done, for example, on OSF/Motif, and on Presentation Manager and Windows 3.0. Other possible methods, displaying the relevant character of the word in a different color or intensity, or displaying the relevant character with a contrasting color bar, are visually more complex. These approaches are not recommended.

Selection Indication

Keyboard Cursor

- Use a reverse video, or reverse color, selection cursor to surround the choice.
- Cover the entire choice, including one (1) blank space before and after the choice word.

File	Edit	Options	Window		Help	Exit

Pointer

- Use reverse video, or reverse color, to highlight the selected choice.

When using the keyboard, the selection cursor should be indicated by a contrasting reverse video or reverse color bar surrounding the choice. The cursor should extend at least one space to each side of the choice word. When using a pointer, use a reverse video or reverse color to highlight the choice when it is selected.

The recommended reverse color combination is to simply reverse the foreground and background colors of the nonselected choices. Colors chosen must be those that are completely legible in either polarity. Some good combinations would include: black-white, blue-white, and black-cyan.

Other contrasting-color combinations may, of course, also be used. Since limitations exist in the number of colors that may be used on a screen, however, the colors chosen for action/menu bars must be performed in conjunction with the colors of other screen components. Since an action/menu bar can be easily identified by its location, the use of a completely different color to identify it will

Figure 10.8   Action/menu bar pull-down.

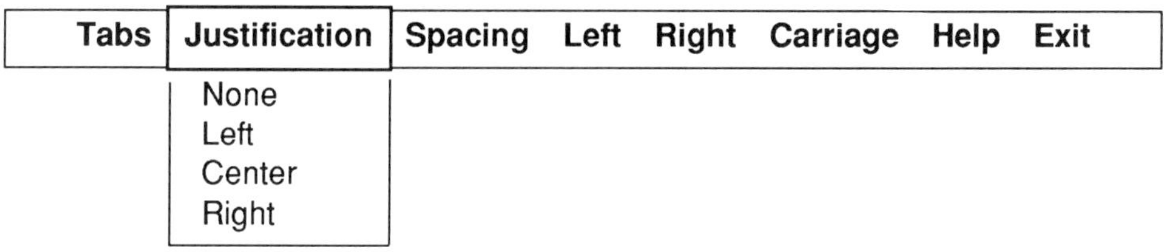

Tabs	Justification	Spacing	Left	Right	Carriage	Help	Exit
	None						
	Left						
	Center						
	Right						

be redundant and unnecessary. It is more practical to reserve the use of color for other less identifiable screen components. For more information on the use of color, see Chapter 13.

PULL-DOWN MENU

Selection of an alternative from the action/menu bar may require a series of further choices to be made by the user. These choices are frequently displayed as a vertically arrayed listing that appears to "pull-down" from the bar. Hence, these listings, as illustrated in Figure 10.8, are typically referred to as pull-downs. Other terms are occasionally used, however. For example, OSF/Motif refers to them as "cascades."

Location

- Position the pull-down directly below the selected action/menu bar choice.

The pull-down will be located directly below the action/menu bar choice by which it is selected. A typical pull-down is comprised of about 5 to 10 choices, although more or less are sometimes seen. Because of their vertical orientation, there is space for more choices containing longer descriptions than on an action bar, and they can easily be positioned on one screen.

Content

- Use mixed-case letters to describe choices.
    - If the choices can be displayed graphically, such as fill-in patterns, shades, or colors, textual descriptions are not necessary.
- Do not
    - use scrolling in pull-downs.
    - place instructions in pull-downs.

Choices should be composed of mixed-case letters. Typically, only the first letter of the choice is capitalized. For multiword-choice descriptions, capitalize the first letter of each significant word. Acronyms, abbreviations, or proper nouns that are normally capitalized may be capitalized. If the choices can be displayed graphically, such as fill-in patterns, shades, or colors, textual descriptions are not necessary. Do not use scrolling in, or place instructions within, a pull-down.

Organization

- Align choices into columns, with
  - most frequent choices toward the top.
  - related choices grouped together.
  - choices found on more than one pull-down consistently positioned.
- Left-align choice descriptions.

Align all pull-down choices into columns with their descriptions left-aligned. Locate most frequently chosen alternatives toward the top and group-related choices together. Choices found on more than one pull-down should be consistently positioned.

Layout

- Leave the action bar choice leading to the pull-down highlighted in the selected manner (reverse video or reverse color).
- Align the first character of the pull-down descriptions under the second character of the applicable action bar choice.
- Horizontally, separate the pull-down choice descriptions from the pull-down borders by two (2) spaces on the left side and at least two (2) spaces on the right side.
  - The left-side border will align with the left side of the action bar highlighted choice.
  - The right-side border should extend, minimally, to the right side of its highlighted action bar choice.

Tabs	Justification	Spacing	Left	Right	Carriage	Help	Exit
	None						
	Left						
	Center						
	Right						

  - Pull-downs for choices on the far-right side of the action bar, or long pull-down descriptions, may require alignment to the left of their action bar choice to maintain visibility and clarity.

Page	Source	Destination	Init-String	Margins	Name	Other	Exit

Space-Compression
Attributes
Format
Top-Labels
Left-Labels
No-Labels

The action/menu bar choice leading to the pull-down should remain highlighted in the selected manner. Pull-down columnized descriptions should be aligned beginning under the second character position of the applicable bar choice. Pull-down borders should be positioned for balance and for maximum legibility and clarity of the choice descriptions. Leave two spaces to the left of the descriptions to align the left pull-down border with the left border of the selected action/menu bar choice. Leave a minimum of two spaces after the longest description and the right pull-down border. Minimally, the right pull-down border should extend to the right border of the highlighted action bar choice. Action/menu bar choices located at the far right, or long pull-down choice descriptions, may require alignment to the left of the applicable action bar choice, however.

Groupings

- Provide groupings of related pull-down choices by incorporating a solid line between the groupings.
  — Left-justify the lines under the first letter of the columnized choice descriptions.
  — Right-justify the lines under the last character of the longest choice description.
  — Display the solid line in the same color as the choice descriptions.

Maintain
———————
Select
Combine
Eliminate
Condense
———————
Display
Print

Indicate groupings of related choices by inscribing a line between each group. The line, or lines, should only extend from the first character of the

Figure 10.9   Border to border grouping lines.

Maintain
Select Combine Eliminate Condense
Display Print

descriptions to the end of the longest description, as shown above. SAA CUA recommends that the line extend from pull-down border to border. Many other system pull-downs also follow this border-to-border approach, as illustrated in Figure 10.9. This extended line, however, results in too strong a visual separation between pull-down parts. The parts should be separated but not too strongly.

Dynamic Pull-Downs

- Do not display any conditionally active choices unless they are valid.
  - Alternatively, display any nonapplicable pull-down choices in a reduced or subdued intensity.
- To indicate a pull-down choice whose state is current or active, precede the choice with a check mark (✓).

If pull-downs can be dynamically changed to reflect a current condition, the preferred method is to not display choices when they are not valid. An alternative suggestion is to display any nonapplicable choices in a reduced or subdued (grayed) intensity. If the need exists to tell the user which choice is currently active, this may be done by preceding the choice description with a check mark (✓).

Pull-Downs Leading to Another Pull-Down

- If a pull-down choice leads to another pull-down,
  - place a right-pointing triangle (▶) after the choice description.
  - separate the triangle from the description by one (1) space.
  - display the triangle in the same color as the choice descriptions.

```
┌─────────────────────┐
│ Font ▶               │
│ Spacing ▶            │
│ Size ▶               │
│ Intensity ▶          │
│                      │
└─────────────────────┘
```

Occasionally a secondary or second level pull-down (or cascading pull-down as it is frequently called) may be desirable if the first pull-down leads to another short series of choices. Or, it may be desirable if the first pull-down has a large number of choices that are capable of being logically grouped. The existence of this second level, and hidden, pull-down should be indicated to the user on the first pull-down in a consistent manner. A simple way to do this is to include a right-pointing triangle to the right of the applicable choice description. These triangles can be seen displayed directly adjacent to their choice description, or they can be positioned aligned to the right side of the pull-down. The recommended method is adjacent for position consistency with the location of the pop-up window indicator to be described next. Displaying them adjacent to the choice text is IBM's SAA CUA recommended method, also.

Apple recommends that these secondary pull-downs not exceed one level. DECwindows suggests no more than three levels.

Pull-Downs Leading to a Pop-Up Window

- For pull-down choices leading to a pop-up window,
  — place an ellipsis (three dots) after the choice description.
  — do not separate the dots from the description by a space.
  — display the ellipsis in the same color as the choice descriptions.

```
┌─────────────────────┐
│ Change . . .         │
│ Delete . . .         │
│ Copy . . .           │
│ Move . . .           │
│                      │
└─────────────────────┘
```

When a pop-up window results from the selection of a pull-down choice, a visual indication of this fact is desirable. An ellipsis inscribed after the choice description is a good indicator that a window will appear.

Cascading Pull-Down Location and Structure

- Position the first choice in the cascading pull-down immediately to the right of the selected choice in the initial pull-down.

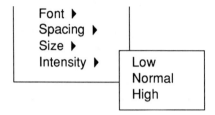

- Leave the previous pull-down choice leading to the cascading pull-down highlighted in the selected manner (reverse video or reverse color).
- Follow the relevant pull-down guidelines for organization, content, layout, separation, and selection cursor.

The second-level or cascading pull-down should be positioned to the right of the previous pull-down, beginning adjacent to the choice that uncovered it. The previous choice should remain highlighted in the selected manner. Follow all other design guidelines for pull-downs.

Keyboard Accelerators/Hot Keys

- Provide unique mnemonic codes by which choices may be selected through the typewriter keyboard.
  - Indicate the mnemonic code by underlining the proper character.
- Provide key alternatives for choice selection.
  - Identify the keys by their actual key top engravings.
  - Use a plus (+) sign to indicate two or more keys must be pressed at the same time.
  - Enclose the key names within parentheses ( ).
  - Right-align the key names, beginning three (3) positions to the right of the longest choice description.
  - Display the key alternatives in the same color as the choice descriptions.

```
┌─────────────────────────────────────┐
│  Maintain          (Alt+Backspace)  │
├─────────────────────────────────────┤
│  Select                (Shift+Ins)  │
│  Combine                            │
│  Eliminate                          │
│  Condense                           │
├─────────────────────────────────────┤
│  Display                            │
│  Print                              │
│                                     │
└─────────────────────────────────────┘
```

Figure 10.10   Typical non-subdued display of accelerator keys on a pull-down.

Maintain	Alt+Backspace
Select	Shift+Ins
Combine	
Eliminate	
Condense	
Display	
Print	

Enabling the user to select pull-down choices through the keyboard provides flexibility and efficiency in the dialogue. One method of doing this is to provide single-character mnemonic codes which, when typed, will also cause the choice to be invoked. Mnemonic codes can be visually indicated in a number of ways. The recommended method is an underline beneath the proper character within the choice. Other methods, a different character color, a different character intensity, or a contrasting color bar through the relevant character are visually more complex.

Another method is to assign one key, or a combination of keys, to accomplish the action. Identify these keys exactly as they are engraved on the keyboard, indicate simultaneous depression through use of a plus sign, and right-align and position to the right of the choice descriptions. Incorporating these key names within a parentheses indicates that they are prompts (which they actually are) and that they may easily be ignored when not being used. SAA CUA and most graphic systems do not place them within parentheses, giving them too strong a visual emphasis. See Figure 10.10.

Separation

- Separate the pull-down from the remainder of the screen, but visually relate it to the action/menu bar by
  — using a background color the same as the action bar.
  — displaying choice descriptions in the same color as the action bar.
  — incorporating a solid-line border completely around the pull-down in the same color as the choice descriptions.
- A drop shadow (a heavier shaded line along two borders that meet) may also be included.

In addition to being identified by its position below the action/menu bar, the pull-down should visually relate to the action bar and also visually contrast with the screen body. The most effective way to do this is to use the same foreground and background colors that are used on the action/menu bar but ensure that these colors adequately contrast with the screen body background. Because good contrasting background colors are often limited, a solid-line border of the same color as the choice descriptions will clearly delineate the pull-down border. A drop shadow, when included, will give the pull-down a three-dimensional effect.

Selection Cursor

- Use a reverse video, or reverse color, selection cursor the same color as the action/menu bar to surround the choice.
- Create a consistently sized cursor as long as the longest choice plus one (1) blank space before and after.

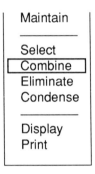

— If ellipses, right-pointing arrows, or keyboard accelerators are displayed, the cursor should extend one space beyond the longest one.

The selection cursor should be a contrasting reverse video or reverse color bar of a consistent size surrounding the selected choice, including ellipses, arrows, or keyboard accelerators. The reverse color combination should be the same as appears within the action/menu bar.

POP-UP MENUS

Alternatives or choices may also be presented on the screen through pop-up menus. They may be called to the screen in a variety of ways. Some systems present pop-up menus when a designated area of the screen is pointed at and selected. Others present them when this is done to a designated menu icon. Some systems may present a pop-up menu when the proper mouse button is depressed.

Pop-up menus are usually presented as vertically arrayed listings of alternatives. In looks, they resemble the just described action/menu bar pull-downs and the full-screen menus described in Chapter 9. Like pull-downs, they should be properly visually set apart from what underlies them; they may

Figure 10.11   Pop-up menu.

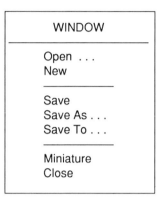

cascade and they may contain accelerators. Their distinguishing difference is much less in content, more in style. What distinguishes a pop-up menu from a full-screen menu is its appearance on demand in a window, overlaying the underlying screen and windows. What distinguishes it from a pull-down is that it is not associated with the higher-level series of textual menu choices contained in the action/menu bar. A pop-up menu is illustrated in Figure 10.11.

The guidelines presented in Chapter 9 for menus, and the guidelines for pull-downs, should be referenced in pop-up menu design. What follows are some additional considerations unique to pop-ups plus a summary of the most significant guidelines more fully explained in other parts of this text.

Location

- Position the pop-up directly beneath the pointer by which it was selected.

The pop-up menu should be located directly below the pointer used to request it. A typical pop-up is comprised of about 5 to 10 choices, although more or less are sometimes seen. Because of their vertical orientation, more choices containing longer description than an action bar can easily be positioned on one screen.

Title

- Include a title on all initial pop-up menus.
  - Locate in a centered position at the top.
  - Display in capital letters, or in mixed case in letters of a larger size or bolder than the choice descriptions.

All pop-up menus should possess a title clearly describing its contents. The title should be centered at the menu's top and displayed in either capital letters, or, if different letter sizes are available, in mixed-case letters of a larger size or bolder than the choices.

Cascading Pop-ups

- If the choice leads to a cascading menu, place a right-pointing triangle after the choice description.
- Either
    — position the first choice in the cascading menu immediately to the right of the selected choice.
        — Leave the choice leading to the cascading menu highlighted.
        — A title is not absolutely necessary on the cascading menu.

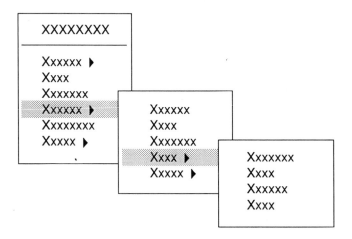

    — position the cascading menu to the right of the previous menu, aligned at the top.
        — Include a title on each menu.

XXXXXXXX	DXXXXX	JXXX
Axxxxxx	Gxxxxx	Lxxxxxx
Bxxx	Hxxxx	Mxxx
Cxx	Ixxxxxx	Nxxxxx
Dxxxxx	Jxxx	Oxxxx
Exxxxxxx	Kxx	
Fxxxx		

If a pop-up menu choice leads to a cascading menu, place a right-pointing triangle after the choice description as done with pull-downs. Cascading menus may be positioned in two ways.

First, succeeding pop-up menus may be positioned so that the first choice in the cascading menu is located immediately to the right of the selected choice on the previous menu. The choice leading to the cascading menu should remain highlighted so that the path to the latest pop-up is obvious. If this method of display is used, a title is only needed on the initial pop-up menu.

Alternatively, position the cascading menu to the right of the previous menu, aligned at the top. Include a title on each menu so that the menu path is obvious. Choices on each menu need not remain highlighted.

Other Guidelines

- Arrange logically organized and grouped choices into columns.
- Left-align choice descriptions.
- Use mixed-case letters to describe choices.
- Separate groups with a solid line the length of the longest choice description.
- If the choice leads to a pop-up window, place an ellipsis after the choice description.
- If keyboard accelerators are shown,
    - — indicate the mnemonic code by underlining the proper character.
    - — set apart key alternatives by placing them within parentheses.
- To separate the pop-up from the screen background,
    - — use a contrasting, but complementing, background.
    - — incorporate a solid line border around the pull-down.
- Use a reverse video, or reverse color, selection cursor slightly longer than the longest choice.

For more detail, see the relevant guidelines in Chapter 9, Menus, and in the section describing Pull-Downs in this chapter.

BUTTONS

A button, or pushbutton as it is sometimes called, resembles the pushbutton control commonly found on electrical or mechanical devices. Buttons are commonly placed within windows, and activating them causes the action or command inscribed upon them to be immediately performed. While buttons are usually rectangular in shape, they do come in a variety of styles, some of which are illustrated in Figure 10.12.

Figure 10.12 Examples of buttons.

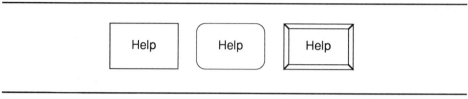

Structure

- Make the button a rectangular-shaped box with the caption inscribed inside. Design alternatives include
  — A square-cornered rectangle.

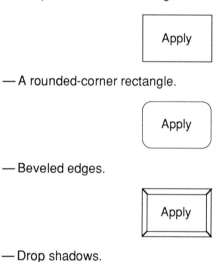

  — A rounded-corner rectangle.

  — Beveled edges.

  — Drop shadows.

- Maintain consistency in style through an application.

The shape of a button can vary. Generally, rectangular-shaped buttons are preferred because they provide the best fit for horizontally arrayed textual captions. Square-cornered rectangles are found in OSF/Motif and rounded-corner rectangles are found in OPEN LOOK, Presentation Manager, and suggested in IBM's SAA CUA. Drop Shadows will be found in OPEN LOOK and in NeXTStep. OSF/Motif uses beveled edges. The button style chosen is mostly a matter of preference. The button style chosen should be consistently maintained throughout an application, however.

Location

- Locate buttons horizontally in the lower part of the window.

— If the lower portion of the window is not available, position the buttons vertically along the right side.

The preferred button location is horizontally across the lower part of the window. This is consistent with one's top-to-bottom movement through the window. If the lower portion of the window is not available, locate the buttons vertically along the window's right side.

Content

- Provide fully spelled out, meaningful descriptions of the actions that will be performed.
- Use mixed-case letters to describe choices.
- Use single-word choices whenever possible.
- When a button action leads to another window, include an ellipsis (. . .) after the action text.
    - Do not leave a space between the text and the ellipsis.
- Provide standard names and uses for common actions.

Button captions should be clearly spelled out, meaningful descriptions of the actions that they cause to be performed. Choices should be composed of mixed-case single words. When a button leads to another window, include an ellipsis after the action text.

Common button functions should have standard names and uses. IBM's SAA CUA provides these standard names and definitions:

OK   — Any changed information in the window is accepted and the window is closed.

APPLY   — Any changed information in the window is accepted and again displayed in the window.

RESET   — Cancels any changed information that has not been submitted.

CANCEL   — Closes window without performing nonsubmitted changes.

HELP   — Displays, if available, contextual help for the item on which the cursor is positioned.
            — If no contextual help is available, help for the entire window is displayed.

Organization

- For buttons ordered left-to-right, place most frequent actions to the left.
- For buttons ordered top-to-bottom, place most frequent actions at the top.
- Keep related buttons grouped together.
- Buttons found on more than one window should be consistently positioned.

Buttons should be ordered logically, such as by frequency of use, sequence of use, or importance. For buttons arrayed left-to-right, start ordering from left-to-right. For buttons arrayed top-to-bottom, start ordering from top-to-bottom. Ordering, as recommended by IBM's SAA CUA, is

Application specific pushbuttons
OK
APPLY
RESET
CANCEL
HELP

Keep related buttons together, and the same buttons on different windows should always be consistently positioned.

Layout

- Horizontally arrayed buttons should be of the same height.
- Vertically arrayed buttons should be of the same width.
- Provide equal and adequate spacing (two or more spaces) between adjacent buttons.
- If the buttons can be logically grouped, provide visually logical groups, if possible.

- Center the buttons at the bottom of the screen.
  — Vertically positioned buttons should also be centered.

To create visual appeal, do the following. Make horizontally arrayed buttons the same height and vertically arrayed buttons the same width. Also, provide equal and adequate spacing (two or more spaces) between adjacent buttons and create logical visual groups whenever possible. Finally, center horizontal buttons at the bottom of the screen and vertical buttons along the right side of the screen.

Dynamic Buttons

- Do not display any conditionally active buttons unless they are valid.
  — Alternatively, display nonapplicable buttons in a reduced or subdued intensity.

If buttons can be dynamically changed to reflect a current condition, the preferred method is to not display buttons when they are not valid. An alternative suggestion is to display nonapplicable buttons in a reduced or subdued (grayed) intensity.

Keyboard Accelerators

- Provide unique mnemonic codes by which choices may be selected through the keyboard whenever possible.
- Indicate the mnemonic code by underlining the proper character.

Enabling the user to select button actions through the typewriter keyboard provides flexibility and efficiency in the dialogue. To do this, provide single-character mnemonic codes which, when typed, will cause the action to be performed. The suggested method to indicate the accelerator is by underlining the proper character in the button label.

Button Activation

Pointing

- Highlight the button in some visually distinctive manner when the pointer is resting on it and the button is available for selection.

Activation

- Call attention to the button in another visually distinctive manner when it has been activated or pressed.

Default

- When a window with buttons is first displayed, provide a default action.
- Indicate the default action by displaying the button with a bold or double border.
   — The default action should be a positive response such as "OK."
   — If a destructive action is performed (such as "DELETE"), the default should be "CANCEL."

Pointing. Highlight the button in some visually distinctive manner when the pointer is resting on it and the button is available for selection. This will provide the user feedback that the selection process may be performed. Some systems, such as Sun's OPEN LOOK, display a brighter button.

Table 10.2 Advantages and disadvantages of various command/action techniques.

ACTION/MENU BAR

+ Always visible, reminding user of existence.
− Take up space on screen.
− Requires looking away from main working area to activate.
− Requires moving pointer to select.

PULL-DOWN MENUS

+ Reminder of existence provided by action/menu bar.
+ No space on screen used when not needed.
− Requires looking away from main work area to activate.
− Requires moving pointer to select.

POP-UP MENUS

+ Permits user to continue viewing main work area.
+ No space on screen used when not needed.
+ No pointer movement needed, if selected by button.
− Existence must be learned and remembered.
− Extra step needed to display.

BUTTONS

+ Always visible, reminding user of existence.
− Take up space on screen.
− Requires looking away from main working area to activate.
− Requires moving pointer to select.

Activation.   Highlight the button in another visually distinctive manner when it has been activated or pressed to indicate that the action is successful. OPEN LOOK subdues or grays the button. OSF/Motif has raised beveled buttons that appear to sink into the screen when selected. Another alternative is to slightly move the button as if it had been depressed.

Default.   When a window with buttons is first displayed, provide a default action and identify the button through a bolder border. For example, DECwindows uses a double border to indicate the default button; IBM's SAA CUA recommends using a bold border. The default action should be a positive response such as "OK." If the default is a destructive action (such as "DE-LETE"), the default should be "CANCEL," requiring the user to change the selection in order to perform the destructive action.

WINDOWS

A window is an area of the screen, usually rectangular in shape, defined by a border that contains a particular view of some area of the computer or some portion of the user's dialogue with the computer. It can be moved, sized, and rendered independently on the screen. A window may be small, containing a short message or a single field, or it may be large, consuming most or all of the available display space. A display may contain one, two, or more windows within its boundaries.

A window is seen to possess the following characteristics:

- A name or title, allowing it to be identified.
- A location, relative to the display boundary and relative to other windows that may be located within the display. (It may appear beside another window, on top of another window, or beneath another window.)
- A size in height and width (which can vary).
- A state, whether it is accessible or active or not accessible. (Only active windows can have their contents altered.)
- Visibility—the portion that can be seen. (A window may be partially or fully hidden behind another window, or the information within a window may extend beyond the window's display area.)
- Management capabilities, methods for manipulation of the window on the screen.
- The application or task it is dedicated to.

The Attraction of Windows

The value of windowing is best seen in the context of the typical office job. An office worker performs a variety of tasks, often in a fairly unstructured manner. The worker is asked to monitor and manipulate data from a variety of sources, synthesize information, summarize information, and reorganize information. Things are seldom completed in a continuous time frame. Outside events such as telephone calls, supervisor requests, and deadlines force shifts in emphasis and focus. Tasks start, stop, and start again. Materials used in dealing with the tasks are usually scattered about one's desk, being positioned in the workspace to make handling the task as efficient as possible. This spatial mapping of tools helps people organize their work and provides reminders of uncompleted tasks. As work progresses and priorities change, materials are reorganized to reflect the changes.

Single-screen technology supports this work structure very poorly. Since only one screen of information can be viewed at one time, comparing or integrating information from different sources and on different screens often requires extensive use of one's memory. To support memory, the worker is often forced to make handwritten notes or obtain printed copies of screens. Switching between tasks is difficult and interrupting and later returning to a task requires an extensive and costly restructuring of the work environment.

The appeal of windowing is that it allows the "display workspace" to much more closely mirror the "desk workspace." This dramatically reduce one's short-term memory loads. A person's ability to do mental calculations is limited by how well one keeps track of one's place, one's interim conclusions and products, and, finally, the results. Windows act as external memories that are an extension of one's internal memory (Card, et al., 1984). Windows also make it much easier to switch between tasks and to maintain one's context, since one does not have to continually reestablish one's place. Windows also provide access to more information than would normally be available on a single screen of the same size. This is done by overwriting or placing more important information on top of that of less importance at that moment.

While all the advantages and disadvantages of windows are still not well understood, they do seem to be useful in the following ways.

Presentation of different levels of information.   Information can be examined in increasing levels of detail. A document table of contents can be presented in a window. A chapter, or topic, selected from this window can be simultaneously displayed in more detail in an adjoining window. Deeper levels are also possible on additional windows.

Presentation of multiple kinds of information.   Variable information needed to complete a task can be displayed simultaneously in adjacent windows. An order-processing-system window could collect a customer account number in one window and return the customer's name and shipping address in another window. A third window could collect details of the order after which another window presents factory availability and shipping dates of the desired items. Significant windows remain displayed so that details may be modified as needed prior to order completion. Low stocks or delayed shipping dates might require changing the order.

Sequential presentation of levels or kinds of information.   Steps to accomplish a task can be sequentially presented through windows. Successive windows are presented until all the required details are collected. Key windows may remain displayed but others appear and disappear as necessary. This sequential presentation is especially useful if the information-collection process leads down different paths. An insurance application, for example, will include different coverages. A requested coverage might necessitate the collection of specific details about that coverage. This information can be entered into a window presented to collect the unique data. The windows disappear after data entry and additional windows appear when needed.

Access to different sources of information.   Independent sources of information may have to be accessed at the same time. This information may reside in different host computers, operating systems, applications, files, or areas of the same file. For example, information to solve a problem may be stored in a Help function. This information may be presented on the screen alongside the problem, greatly facilitating its solution. Or, a writer may have to refer to several parts of text being written at the same time. Or, a travel agent may have to compare several travel destinations for a particularly demanding client.

Combining multiple sources of information.   Text from several documents may have to be reviewed and combined into one. Pertinent information is selected from one window and copied into another.

Performing more than one task.   More than one task can be performed at one time. While waiting for a long, complex procedure to finish, another can be performed. Tasks of higher priority can interrupt less important ones. The interrupted task can then be resumed with no "close down" and "restart" necessary.

Reminding.   Windows can be used to remind the viewer of things likely to be of use in the near future. Examples might be menus of choices available, a history of the path followed or command choices to that point, or the time of an important meeting.

Monitoring.   Changes, both internal and external, can be monitored. Data in one window can be modified and its effect on data in another window can be studied. External events, such as stock prices, out of normal range conditions, or system messages can be watched while another major activity is carried out.

Multiple representations of the same task.   The same thing can be looked at in several ways—for example, alternative drafts of a speech, different versions of a screen, or different graphical representations of the same data.

Constraints in Window System Design

Windowing systems, in spite of their appeal and obvious benefits, have failed to live up to their expectations, says Billingsley (1988) in her excellent review.

Benest and Dukic (1989) describe the overall user interface as "chaotic" because of the great amount of time users must spend doing such things as pointing at tiny boxes in window borders, resizing windows, moving windows, closing windows, and so forth. Billingsley attributes the problems with windowing systems to three factors: historical considerations, hardware limitations, and human limitations.

Historical considerations.   Historically, system developers have been much more interested in solving hardware problems than in user considerations. Since technical issues abound, they have received the strong focus of attention. There has been very little research addressing design issues and their impact on the useability of window systems. Therefore there are few concrete window design guidelines to aid designers.

This lack of guidelines makes it difficult to develop acceptable and agreeable window standards. While some companies are developing style guides, they are very general and limited in scope to their products. Standardization is also made more difficult by the complexity and range of alternatives available to the designer. Without user performance data, it is difficult to realistically compare the different alternatives, and design choices become a matter of preference.

Standardization of the interface is also inhibited by other factors. Some software developers, who are proud of their originality, see standards as a threat to creativity and its perceived monetary rewards. Some companies are wary of standards because they fear other companies are promoting standards that reflect their own approach. Finally, some companies have threatened, or brought, legal action against anyone who adopts an approach similar to their own.

The result, Billingsley concludes, is that developers of new systems create another new variation each time they design a product, and users must cope with a new interface each time they encounter a new windowing system.

Hardware limitations.   Many of today's screens are not large enough in size to take full advantage of windowing capabilities. As a result, many windows are still of "post-it" dimensions. There is some evidence (Cooper, 1985; Johnson-Laird, 1985) that many users on personal computers expand their windows to cover a full screen. Either seeing all the contents of one window is preferable to seeing small parts of many windows or the operational complexity of multiple windows is not wanted.

The slower processing speeds and smaller memory sizes of some computers may also inhibit use of windows. A drain on the computer's resources may limit feedback and animation capabilities, thereby reducing the system's useability. Poor screen resolution and graphics capability may also deter effective use of windows by not permitting sharp and realistic drawings and shapes.

Human limitations.   A windowing system, because it is more complex, requires the learning and using of more operations. Much practice is needed to master them. These window management operations are placed on top of other system operations, and window management can become an end in itself. This can severely detract from the task at hand. In a study comparing full screens with screens containing overlapping windows (Davies et al., 1985), task completion times were longer with the window screens, but the nonwindow screens generated more user errors. After eliminating screen arrangement time, however, task solution times were shorter with windows. The results suggest that the advantages for windows do exist, but they can be negated by excessive window manipulation requirements.

Benest and Dukic (1989) suggest that to truly be effective, window manipulation must occur implicitly as a result of user task actions, not as a result of explicit window management actions by the user.

Other limitations.   Other possible window problems include the necessity for window borders to consume valuable screen space, and small windows providing access to large amounts of information can lead to excessive, bothersome scrolling.

Window Presentation Styles

The presentation style of a window refers to its spatial relationship to other windows. There are two basic styles, usually referred to as tiled or overlapping. Most systems use one or the other style exclusively, seldom using both at the same time.

Tiled windows.   Tiled windows, illustrated in Figure 10.13, derive their name from the common floor or wall tile. Tiled windows appear in one plane on the screen and expand or contract to fill up the display surface. Most systems provide two-dimensional tiled windows, adjustable in both height and width. Some less powerful systems, however, are only one-dimensional, the windows being adjustable in only one manner (typically the height). Tiled windows, the first and oldest kind of window, are felt to have these advantages:

- The system usually allocates and positions windows for the user, eliminating the necessity to make positioning decisions.
- Open windows are always visible, eliminating the possibility of them being lost and forgotten.
- Every window is always completely visible, eliminating the possibility of information being hidden.
- They are perceived as less complex than overlapping windows, possibly because there are fewer management operations (Bury, et al., 1985) or they seem less "magical" (Smith, 1987).
- They are easier for novice or inexperienced people to learn and use (Bly and Rosenberg, 1986).
- They yield better user performance for tasks where the data requires little window manipulation to complete the task (Bly and Rosenberg, 1986).

Perceived disadvantages include the following:

- Only a limited number can be displayed in the screen area available.
- As windows are opened or closed, existing windows change in size. This can be annoying.
- As windows are opened or closed, existing windows change in position. This can also be annoying.
- As windows change in size or position, the movement can be disconcerting.
- As the number of displayed windows increases, each window can get very tiny.
- The changes in sizes and locations made by the system are difficult to predict.
- The configuration of windows provided by the system may not meet the user's needs.
- They are perceived as crowded and more visually complex because window borders are flush against one another. Crowding is accentuated if borders contain scroll bars and/or control icons. Viewer attention may be drawn to the border, not the data.
- They permit less user control because the system actively manages the windows.

Overlapping windows.   Overlapping windows, illustrated in Figure 10.14, may be placed on top of one another like papers on a desk. They possess a three-dimensional quality, appearing to lie on different planes. Users can control the height, width, and location of these windows, as well as the plane in which it appears. Most new systems use this style of window. They have the following advantages:

- Visually, their look is three-dimensional, resembling the desktop that is familiar to the user.
- Greater control allows the user to organize the window to meet his or her needs.
- Windows can maintain larger sizes.
- Windows can maintain consistent sizes.
- Windows can maintain consistent positions.
- Screen space conservation is not a problem, as windows can be placed on top of one another.
- There is less pressure to close or delete windows no longer needed.
- The possibility exists for less visual crowding and complexity. Larger borders can be maintained around window information, and the window is more clearly set off against its background.
- They yield better user performance for tasks where the data requires much window manipulation to complete the task (Bly and Rosenberg, 1986).

Figure 10.13   Tiled windows.

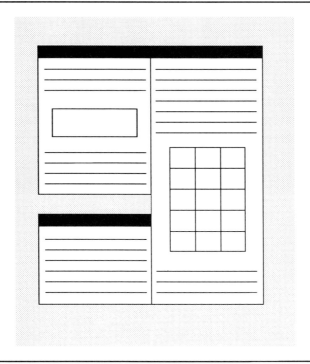

Figure 10.14   Overlapping windows.

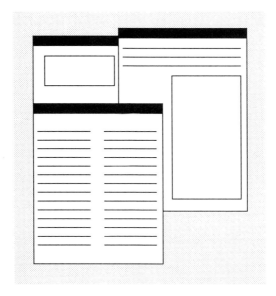

Disadvantages include the following:

- They are operationally more complex than tiled windows. More control functions require greater user attention and manipulation.
- Information in windows can be obscured behind other windows.
- Windows themselves can be lost behind other windows.
- Control freedom increases the possibility for poorly planned, inappropriate, inefficient, and disorganized screens.
- Control freedom increases the possibility for greater visual complexity and crowding. Too many windows, or improper setoff, can be visually overwhelming.

Cascading windows.   A special type of overlapping window has the windows automatically arranged in a regular progression. Each window is slightly offset from others, as illustrated in Figure 10.15. Advantages of this approach include the following:

- No window is ever completely hidden.
- Bringing any window to the front is easier.

Types of Windows

Windows may appear in a variety of forms to achieve a variety of purposes. Defining standard types is difficult because of the varying terminology and definitions used by different windowing systems. The following is an attempt to categorize the kinds of windows based upon common features. Any single system's windows may not behave exactly as described, or characteristics of separate windows may be combined to form one kind of window.

Figure 10.15   Cascading windows.

Application or primary window.   This window is the first that appears on a screen when an activity or action is started. It may itself contain data or provide a top-level context for one or more dependent windows to be created. It is variously referred to as the primary, main or application window. It may also be referred to as the "parent" window if one or more "child" windows exist.

Document, supplemental, or secondary window.   A window derived from the primary or application window, these "offspring" windows usually contain the actual data being processed. They are most often called document windows because they are typically associated with a single data object that can be modified, such as a text file. Their structure is similar to the application or primary window. Most systems permit the display of multiple-document windows, allowing the user to work with more than one file at one time.

Dialogue boxes.   Dialogue boxes are also child windows that are used to ask the user to complete an action within a limited spatial context. Therefore, they are associated with another window. Dialogue boxes may be of two kinds, modal or modeless.

A modal dialogue box presents information to which the user must respond before interaction with any other window can be continued. It will remain displayed until the appropriate action is taken, after which it is removed from the screen. One specific kind of modal dialogue box is the message box. Message boxes typically provide critical information that must be reacted to before continuation of the dialogue is permitted.

A modeless dialogue box permits the user to perform a parallel dialogue in addition to another dialogue. Switching between the modeless dialogue box and its associated window is permitted. Other work may be accomplished while the box is displayed, and it may be left on the screen after a response has been made to it. Actions leading to the modeless dialogue box can also be cancelled, causing the box to be removed from the screen. A modeless dialogue box may incorporate some basic window functions such as positioning and sizing.

Active window.   Most systems only permit interaction with one window at a time. The window that may be manipulated, and into which data may be keyed, is typically called the active window. The active window is usually identified in some visually distinctive way.

Window Interaction Styles

In a windowing system, like any other system, the user must communicate requests to the system and receive feedback from the system. Communication to the system is accomplished through a unique interaction style referred to as "manipulation." Manipulation is of two kinds, direct or indirect (or combinations of the two).

Table 10.3   Suggested uses for various types of windows.

APPLICATION OR PRIMARY WINDOW

- Performing primary application actions.
- Presenting constantly used window components.
- Performing simple actions.
- Performing complex actions.
- Presenting continually updated information.

SUPPLEMENTAL OR SECONDARY WINDOW

- Performing subordinate or supplementary actions.
- Presenting frequently or occasionally used window components.
- Performing simple actions.
- Performing complex actions.

DIALOGUE BOXES

- Performing subordinate or supplemental actions.
- Presenting seldom used window components.
- Performing complex actions.
- Presenting transient information, such as messages.

Direct manipulation.   The term "direct manipulation" was first used by Shneiderman (1982). Direct manipulation systems possess the following characteristics:

The system is portrayed as an extension of the real world.   It is assumed that the system user is already familiar with the objects and actions in his or her environment of interest. The system replicates them and portrays them on a different medium, the screen. The user has the power to access and modify these objects, among which are windows. The user is allowed to work in a familiar environment and in a familiar way, focusing on the data, not the application and tools. The physical organization of the system, which may be unfamiliar, is hidden and not a distraction.

Objects and actions are continuously visible.   Like one's desktop and office, objects are continuously visible. Reminders of actions to be performed are also obvious, labelled buttons and icons replacing complex syntax and command names. The physical connection between the window and the user is provided by a pointer, the selection cursor. The cursor serves as an electronic equivalent to the human hand, pointing at, selecting, and manipulating objects on the screen. Cursor action and motion occur in physically obvious and intuitively natural ways.

One problem in direct manipulation, however, is that there is no direct analogy in the desktop world for all windowing operations. A piece of paper on one's desk maintains a constant size, never shrinking or growing. Windows can do both. Solving this problem requires embedding a control panel, a familiar concept to most people, in the window's border. This control panel is manipulated, not the window itself.

Actions are rapid and incremental with visible display of results.   Since tactile feedback is not yet possible (as would occur with one's hand), the results of actions are immediately displayed on the screen in their new and current form. Auditory feedback may also be provided. The impact of a previous action is quickly seen and the evolution of tasks is effortless.

Incremental actions are easily reversible.   Actions, if not correct or not desired, can be easily undone.

Indirect manipulation.   In practice, direct manipulation of all screen objects and actions may not be feasible to implement because of the following:

- The operation may be difficult to conceptualize.
- The graphics capability of the system is limited.
- The amount of space available for manipulation controls in the window border may be limited.
- It may be difficult for users to learn and remember all the icons and actions.

When this occurs, "indirect manipulation" is often provided. Indirect manipulation substitutes words and text, such as pull-down or pop-up menus, for symbols, and substitutes typing for pointing. Many window systems are a combination of both kinds of manipulation. A menu may be accessed by pointing at a menu icon and selecting it. The menu itself, however, is a textual list of operations. When an operation is selected from the list, by pointing or typing, the system executes it as a command.

Which style of interaction—direct manipulation, indirect manipulation, or a combination of both—is best, under what conditions, and for whom remains an unanswered question.

Window Structure

The structure of a window also varies between systems. Most windows have a title bar and a screen body, sometimes called the screen content or client area (IBM's SAA CUA). The body is usually modifiable by the application. Windows may also possess command/action techniques such as action/menu bars, pull-down menus, pop-up menus, and buttons. Windows also have a border region where the window's manipulation controls are located. This border is controlled by the windowing system. An OS/2 Presentation Manager window is illustrated in Figure 10.16.

Figure 10.16   OS/2 Presentation manager.

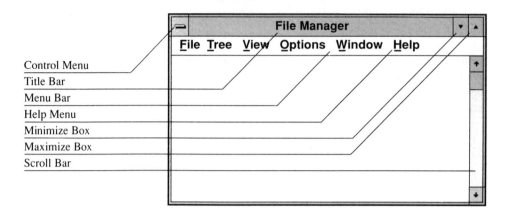

Window Manipulation Operations

Window manipulation requires performing a series of actions or operations upon the window. Across the many windowing systems in existence today, little consistency exists in operation naming or implementation procedures. Billingsley (1988) has attempted to identify, and name, a basic functional set of operations. She segments them into two basic categories, those associated with making windows "visible," such as opening and closing, and those associated with "working" with or changing a window's composition, such as moving and scrolling. These operations are summarized in Table 10.4. While not intended to be exhaustive, they do provide a useful categorization of operations.

Window Controls

Any window component that can be manipulated directly with a mouse or keyboard is commonly referred to as a control. Within this broad definition, action/menu bars, buttons, selection fields, and entry fields are considered controls. These screen components are described elsewhere in this chapter. Another type of control are those dealing with window management and manipulation.

Window manipulation controls.   The actions involved in window manipulation have attained a fairly high level of standardization. The steps to perform an action, and the look and availability of controls to perform the action, do, however, vary between systems. These user controls for window manipulation may exist as a command on a menu, a "hot" area or handle on a segment of the window, or a unique icon embedded in the window's border. Some common, but not exhaustive, listing of window actions and their controls are the following:

Table 10.4 Window manipulation operations.

OPENING AND CLOSING WINDOWS

CREATE	Displays an entirely new window.
DELETE	Removes a window from the screen.
OPEN	Replaces an iconic window with the full-size window it represents.
CLOSE	Replaces window with an iconic window.
BRING-TO-FRONT	Moves a window to the most forward plane of the screen (overlapping windows only).
PUSH-TO-BACK	Moves a window to the most rearward plane of the screen (overlapping windows only).

CHANGING WINDOWS

MOVE	Repositions a window in its two-dimensional plane.
RESIZE	Shows more or less of the data in a window by contracting the window or expanding it up to its maximum size.
ZOOM	Expands to maximum size with one action.
RESCALE	Shows more or less of the data in the window by changing the scale of the image in the window.
SCROLL	Selects a different portion of data for viewing without resizing.
NAME/RENAME	Defines or changes the name of a window.
MAKE ACTIVE	Designates a window as the one with which to communicate.

From Billingsley (1988)

System menu. To obtain a listing of the actions that may be performed on a window, a system menu icon is provided by many systems. Typically located in the upper left corner of the window, when the icon is selected a pull-down menu of actions is displayed. Examples of system menu icons are shown in Figure 10.17.

Minimize. Removes from the screen all windows associated with an application and places an application-defined icon on the screen. Typically accomplished by selecting an icon in the upper right corner of the window, some examples of minimize icons are illustrated in Figure 10.18.

Maximize. Enlarges a window to the largest possible size. Typically accomplished by selecting an icon in the upper right corner of the window, some examples of maximize icons are illustrated in Figure 10.19.

Figure 10.17   Representative system menu icons.

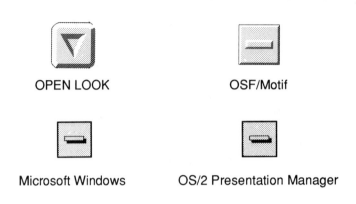

OPEN LOOK   OSF/Motif

Microsoft Windows   OS/2 Presentation Manager

Move.   Moves a window to a new location. Usually performed by using the mouse select button to drag while pointing within the title bar. OPEN LOOK permits dragging by either side border as well.

Resize.   Changing a window's size is accomplished in a number of different ways. The Macintosh provides a single sizing control in the lower right corner of the window. OPEN LOOK permits resizing from all four corners while Motif, Microsoft Windows, and OS2/Presentation Manager permit resizing from each corner and all sides.

Close.   Dismisses a window and closes its associated file. Typically accomplished by selecting an icon at the top of the screen. Some close icons are illustrated in Figure 10.20.

Figure 10.18   Representative minimize icons.

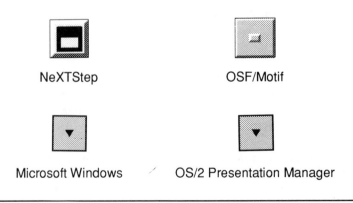

NeXTStep   OSF/Motif

Microsoft Windows   OS/2 Presentation Manager

Figure 10.19   Representative maximize icons.

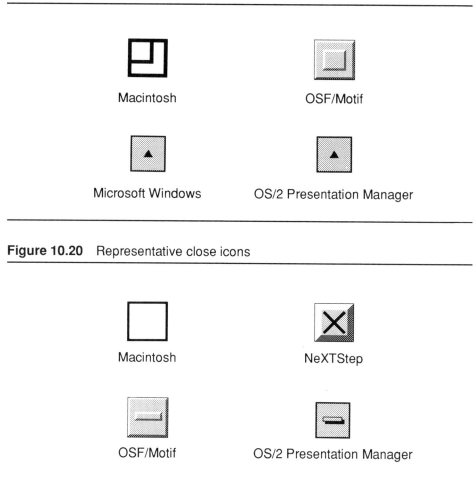

Macintosh   OSF/Motif

Microsoft Windows   OS/2 Presentation Manager

Figure 10.20   Representative close icons

Macintosh   NeXTStep

OSF/Motif   OS/2 Presentation Manager

Scrolling.   A scroll bar is needed when the entire contents of a file cannot be displayed within a window at one time. While scroll bars in various windowing systems assume different physical appearances, they are composed of the same basic elements: a scroll area or container, a slider box or scroll handle, and directional arrows. Vertical scroll bars are usually located at the right side of a window, horizontal scroll bars at the bottom of a window.

POINTING/INPUT DEVICES

To manipulate a graphics screen, and select alternatives and data, it is generally more efficient to use a pointing mechanism. The most frequently used device for this purpose is the mouse. Other mechanisms commonly employed are light pens, joysticks, trackballs, graphic tablets, and touch sensitive screens. As an alternative, keyboard keys may also, of course, be used for this purpose. Which devices work better for what tasks and under what conditions has been addressed by a number of investigators. A survey of the research literature comparing and evaluating different devices was done by Greenstein and Arnaut (1988). They provide the following summarization concerning tasks involving pointing and dragging:

- The fastest tools for pointing at stationary targets on screens are the devices that permit direct pointing, the touch screen and light pen. This is most likely due to their high level of eye-hand coordination and because they use an action familiar to people.
- In positioning speed and accuracy for stationary targets, the indirect pointing devices, the mouse, trackball, and graphic tablet, do not differ greatly from one another. The joystick is the slowest, although it is as accurate as the others. Of most importance in selecting one of these devices will be its fit to the user's task and working environment.
- A separate confirmation action that must follow pointer positioning increases pointing accuracy but reduces speed. The mouse offers a very effective design configuration for tasks requiring this confirmation.
- For tracking small, slowly moving targets, the mouse, trackball, and graphic tablet are preferred to the touch screen and light pen because the latter may obscure the user's view of the target.

Another common manipulation task is dragging an object across the screen. Using a mouse, graphic tablet, and trackball for this task, as well as pointing, was studied by MacKenzie et al. (1991). They report the following:

- The graphic tablet yielded best performance during pointing.
- The mouse yielded best performance during dragging.
- The trackball was a poor performer for both pointing and dragging, and it had a very high error rate in dragging.

Greenstein and Arnaut conclude that the selection of a proper pointing device for an application should consider the following:

- The characteristics of the task, users, and working environment.
- The characteristics of the hardware.
- The present and future demands of the application.
- The research that has been performed using the various devices.
- User preferences. While they may not always correspond to performance, it is important that the user be comfortable with the selected device.
- The characteristics of the device in relation to the application. Table 10.5, based upon a table presented by these authors, summarizes the characteristics and relative capabilities of the various devices.

Table 10.5 Advantages and disadvantages of the standard pointing/input devices (from Greenstein and Arnaut, 1988).

Legend: + Advantage
        o Neutral
        – Disadvantage

	Touch Screen	Light Pen	Graphic Tablet	Mouse	Trackball	Joystick
Eye-hand Coordination	+	+	o	o	o	o
Unobstructed View of Screen	–	–	+	+	+	+
Ability to Attend to Display	+	o	+	o	+	+
Freedom from Parallax Problems	–	–	+	+	+	+
Input Resolution Capability	–	–	+	+	+	+
Flexibility of Placement in Workplace	–	–	o	o	+	+
Minimal Space Requirements	+	+	–	–	+	+
Minimal Training Requirements	+	o	o	o	o	o
Comfort in Extended Use	–	–	+	o	+	+
Absolute Mode Capability	+	+	+	–	–	o
Relative Mode Capability	–	–	+	+	+	o
Capability to Emulate Other Devices	–	–	+	–	–	–
Suitability for:						
• Pointing	+	+	+	+	+	–
• Rapid Pointing	+	+	o	o	o	–
• Pointing with Confirmation	–	o	o	+	o	–
• Drawing	–	–	+	o	–	–
• Tracing	–	–	+	–	–	–
• Continuous Tracking of:						
— Slow Targets	o	o	+	+	+	–
— Fast Targets	–	–	o	o	o	+
• Alphanumeric Data Entry	–	–	+	–	–	–
Dragging (From MacKenzie, et al., 1991)	o	o	+	+	–	o

Mouse

The most common manipulation device, the mouse, comes in a variety of configurations, performs some basic functions, and is operated in several ways.

Configurations. A mouse may possess one, two, or three buttons. Most, but not all, windowing systems permit operation using all configurations. Buttons are used to perform the three functions to be described. When three mouse buttons are not available, the pointer location or keyboard qualifiers must be used to determine the function to be performed. A multibutton mouse permits a more efficient operation, but a person must remember which button to use to perform each function. A multibutton mouse may usually be configured for left- or right-hand use.

Functions. The functions performed by a mouse are select, menu, and adjust. The SELECT function is used to manipulate controls, select alternatives and data, and select objects that will be affected by actions that follow. Select is a mouse's most important function and is the function assigned to a one-button mouse. For a multibutton mouse, it is usually assigned to the leftmost button (assuming a right-handed operation).

The MENU function is typically used to request and display a pop-up menu on a screen. A menu appears when the button is depressed within a particular defined area of the screen. This area may be, for example, the entire screen, within a window, or on a window border. This button eliminates the need for a control icon, which must be pointed at and selected. The user, however, must remember that a menu is available.

The ADJUST function extends or reduces the number of items selected. It is the least used of the three functions and is usually assigned last and given the least prominent location on a mouse.

Operations. Five operations can be performed with any mouse button, point, click, double-click, press, and drag. The first operation, POINT, is the movement and positioning of the mouse pointer over the desired object or at the desired location on the screen. Once the pointer is positioned, to CLICK is to press and immediately release a button. To DOUBLE-CLICK is to perform two clicks within a predefined time limit. To PRESS is to press and hold the mouse button down and not release it. To DRAG is to press and hold the mouse button down, but, while keeping the button depressed, to move the pointer in the appropriate direction.

Pointer

- The shape of a pointer should clearly indicate its purpose and meaning.
- Use predefined shapes. Do not create new shapes for already-defined standard functions.
- Do not use a shape for any other purpose than its predefined meaning.

- The pointer itself should be easy to locate and see, not fostering visual clutter.
- The pointer hotspot should be easy to locate and see.
- The pointer location should not warp (change position). The user should always position the pointer so as not to lose track of it.
- The pointer gain (mouse-pointer move distance ratio) should not change.
- The pointer acceleration (temporary change in gain) should not change.

The focus of the user's attention in any mouse operation is most often the pointer. As such, the pointer image should be used to provide feedback concerning the function being performed, the mode of operation, and the state of the system. For example, the pointer shape image can be changed when it is positioned over a selectable object, signaling to the user that a button action may be performed. When an action is being performed, the pointer can assume the shape of a progress indicator such as a sand timer, providing an indication of processing status.

Keyboard Window Management

Using a mouse is the most efficient method for performing tasks requiring spatial manipulation. Some tasks, however, such as text or data entry and window shuffling are accomplished more efficiently using the keyboard. Frequent keyboard activities of this nature can result in the necessity for many shifts of hands between a mouse and a keyboard. This can be time consuming and inefficient, especially for a touch typist.

Inefficiencies in mouse usage can also occur in other ways. A mouse with a limited number of buttons will require use of the keyboard to accomplish some functions, possibly causing frequent shifting between devices. Operations that are being performed on very large screens may also find keyboard window management preferable to the long mouse movements frequently required. Therefore, to compensate for these possible inefficiencies, many windowing systems provide alternative keyboard operations for mouse tasks.

In a menu, keyboard alternatives are usually referred to as accelerators. Windowing systems providing menu accelerators usually display them to the right of the menu text. Some systems also permit navigation of a screen though use of keyboard keys like the space bar, arrows, tab, and enter.

WINDOW MANIPULATION GUIDELINES

Because of the paucity of research data, window manipulation guidelines are not as thorough and detailed as desired. Many of the recommendations are, indeed, more anecdotal and intuitive than scientific. A complete set of guidelines must await further research and experimentation.

Presentation Styles of Windows

- Use tiled windows for
  - — single task activities.
  - — tasks requiring little window manipulation.
  - — novice or inexperienced users.
- Use overlapping windows for
  - — switching between tasks.
  - — tasks necessitating a greater amount of window manipulation.
  - — expert or experienced users.

Use of tiled windows. Tiled windows seem to be better for single task activities. Bly and Rosenberg (1986) found that tasks requiring little window manipulation can be carried out faster using tiled windows. They also found that novice users performed better with tiled windows, regardless of the task.

Use of overlapping windows. Overlapping windows seem to be better for situations that necessitate switching between tasks. Bly and Rosenberg concluded that tasks requiring much window manipulation could be performed faster with overlapping windows but only if user "window expertise" existed. For novice users, tasks requiring much window manipulation were found to be carried out faster with tiled windows. Therefore, the advantage to overlapping windows comes only after a certain level of expertise is achieved.

Interaction Style

- Direct manipulation seems to be a faster and more intuitive interaction style than indirect manipulation for many windowing operations.

This conclusion is presented by Billingsley (1988), but it is based upon anecdotal evidence. She cautions that there is no empirical evidence to substantiate this observation and much research remains to be done.

Pointing, Selecting, Dragging, and Execution

Pointing

- Visually indicate the following in a unique and consistent manner:
  - — what objects or choices on the screen are selectable.
  - — when the object or choice is under the pointer and can be selected.

- If cursor pointing with a mouse or other similar pointing mechanism is the selection method used
    — the selectable target area should be at least twice the size of the active area of the pointing device. In no case should it be less than six (6) millimeters.
- If a touch screen with finger pointing is the selection method used
    — the touch area must be a minimum of 20–30 millimeters square.
    — the touch area must encompass the entire choice or object plus one (1) character surrounding it.
- Adequate separation must be provided between adjacent target areas.
- Pointer tracking with the mouse should be smooth and even.

Selecting

- Provide feedback concerning the operation to be performed.
    — If the action is a selection, highlight the object selected.
    — If the action is a movement, change the shape of the mouse pointer and highlight the object being moved.

Dragging

- Move the entire object as it is dragged.
- The object being moved should not lag behind the pointer.

Execution

- Provide separate steps for selecting and executing actions.
- Permit cancelling the choice before execution.
- Selection and the performance of actions should be accomplished in a consistent manner.

In a graphics environment, elements on a screen can be selected by pointing at them through movement of one of the pointing/input devices. The touch screen and light pen are called direct pointers because they are positioned directly on the screen. The others, graphic tablet, mouse, trackball, and joystick, are called indirect pointers because they exist in another plane, usually the desktop. A movement of these indirect pointers causes a pointer displayed on the screen to also move in the same direction. With most devices, an indication of an action to be performed requires pressing of one or more keyboard keys. Some devices, such as the mouse, signal actions by pressing one or more buttons located on the mouse itself.

Pointing

Visual indication. Visually indicate in a unique and consistent manner what objects or choices on the screen are selectable. This can be accomplished through highlighting selectable options or lowlighting nonselectable options.

Also indicate in another visually distinctive way when an object or choice is under the pointer and can be selected. This can be accomplished by highlighting (if not used for selectable options), reversing the item's polarity, or changing the shape of the cursor itself. Indicating when an item is under the pointer provides direct visual feedback that the proper choice has been selected, reducing the probability for errors in choice selection.

Cursor selection.   If cursor pointing with a mouse or other indirect pointing mechanism is the selection method used, the selectable target area should be at least twice the size of the active area of the pointing device. It should never be less than six (6) millimeters. Indirect device movements tend to be faster and more ballistic in nature than cursor movement through the keyboard. Larger target areas are needed to reduce the potential for errors.

Touch screens.   If a touch screen with finger pointing is the selection method used, the touch area must be larger, a minimum of 20–30 millimeters square. The touch area must encompass the entire choice or object plus one (1) character surrounding it. Again, this is needed to reduce the potential for errors.

Adequate separation.   Because of the faster, less precise movements associated with these devices, adequate separation must be provided between adjacent target areas to minimize unintended activation of the wrong item.

Smooth tracking.   The movement of the screen pointer with the mouse should be smooth and even.

Selecting

To indicate that an item on the screen has been selected, highlight it in another distinctive way. If the selection action also involves a movement, the shape of the mouse pointer may also be changed in a distinctive manner.

Dragging

In a dragging operation, show the entire object being moved on the screen. If movement of the entire object cannot be shown, minimally show the outline of the object being moved. The object being moved should not lag behind the pointer as it is dragged across the screen.

Execution

Separate actions.   Provide separate steps for selecting and executing actions. Using a mouse, for example, requires moving the cursor to the option to select and then pressing a button to execute.

Election cancelling.   Always permit erroneous selections to be cancelled or "undone" before execution. This will prevent unwanted actions.

Consistency.   All actions must be accomplished in a consistent manner with consistent results. Control actions that are inconsistent in procedure and result are very confusing.

Opening and Closing Windows

- When opening overlapping windows, do the following:
  - — Provide an iconic representation or textual list of available windows.
  - — Position in the most forward plane of the screen.
  - — Designate it as the active window.
  - — Set it off against a neutral background.
  - — If opening with an expansion of an icon representation, animate the icon expansion.
  - — Display iconic representations of open windows in a visually highlighted manner on the screen.
- When closing overlapping windows, do the following:
  - — When closing to an iconic representation of the window, animate the icon contraction.
  - — Display iconic representations of closed windows in a visually subdued manner on the screen.
- With tiled windows do the following:
  - — Provide an easy way to resize and move newly opened windows.

Opening and closing overlapping windows.   The open and close operations provide a way of temporarily setting aside a window without having to remove it from the screen. When no longer needed and closed, the window should be placed in a storage area of the screen and "shrunk" into a meaningful icon. These icons conserve screen space and serve as reminders of the window's existence. Closed-window icons should have some visual display different from that of open-window icons. This can be done by displaying them subdued or grayed. Typically, when windows are opened they are designated as active and positioned in the most forward plane of the screen so that they can be used immediately. To focus attention on the newly opened window, display the screen background behind the window in a neutral or subdued manner. To indicate that a window is open, maintain the iconic representation on the screen and highlight in some manner. Keeping the open iconic representations visible helps the user keep track of the kind and number of windows actually open. This also reminds users of a window's existence if it is hidden behind another window. When closing or opening windows to or from iconic representations, gradually contract or expand the window so that the movement is visible. This will aid association of the icon with the window in the mind of the viewer.

Opening tiled windows.   The first opened tiled window will consume the entire screen. Subsequent windows are usually positioned by defaults in the system. The system positioning of these subsequent windows may not always be consistent with the user's needs. The system should allow the user to change the default positions, or provide a way for the user to easily move and resize the system-provided windows.

Sizing Windows

- Provide a large enough window to
  - — not obscure important information.
  - — not cause crowding or visual confusion.
  - — minimize the need for scrolling.
- otherwise, make the window as small as possible.
  - — optimum window sizes are
    - — for text, about 12 lines.
    - — for alphanumeric information, about 7 lines.

Large enough windows should be provided to minimize the need for scrolling. Very small windows with a large number of scrollable items appear to increase decision-making time (Hendrickson, 1989). Procedural text in window sizes of 6, 12, and 24 lines were evaluated by Desaulniers et al. (1988). Fastest and most accurate completion occurred with the 12-line window. The retrieval of alphanumeric information was compared in 7- , 13- , and 19-line windows by Elkerton and Williges (1984). A 7-line window was found to be more than adequate.

Active Window

- Make moving to and designation of an active window as simple as possible.
- Visually differentiate the active window from other windows through
  - — a contrasting title bar,
  - — a different border,
  - — a different color background, and/or
  - — an "active" indicator.
- The visual cue should be moderate in intensity, not too powerful or too subtle.

Simple designation.   Most systems permit communication with only one window at a time. This window, the "active" window, may be designated by the system or the user. Many systems make a window active when it is the object of another windowing operation. It is assumed that if the user wishes to change one aspect of a window's structure, they also wish to change its contents. The user should be permitted to move to and make any window active with as few steps as possible. This can be accomplished by simply allowing the user to move the selection cursor to the window's interior and then signaling by pressing a key or button. For hidden windows, a menu of open windows might be presented from which the user selects a new open window.

In some situations it may be desirable to allow multiple open windows. Hendrickson (1989) compared a single open window with multiple open windows in performing queries and found multiple open windows were rated by people as more "natural." Performance was slower with multiple open windows, however. He concludes that if user acceptance is important, multiple open windows may be the better alternative. If speed of task handling is critical, a single active window is more desirable.

Visually differentiate the active window from other windows.   It is important that the user be able to quickly identify the active window. Methods to do this include a contrasting window title bar, border, or background color. An "active" indicator in the window border, which is turned on or off, may also be used. A combination of two or more of these visual cues may also be used. The visual cue selected should be of moderate intensity, not too powerful or too subtle. Powerful cues will be distracting; subtle cues will be easily overlooked.

Scrolling

Scroll Area or Container

- To indicate that scrolling is available, a scroll area or container should be provided.
  - It should be constructed of a filled-in bar displayed in a technique that visually contrasts with the window and screen body background.

Scroll Slider Box or Handle

- To indicate the location and amount of information being viewed, a slider box or handle should be provided.
  - It should be constructed of a moveable and sizeable open area of the scroll area displayed in a technique that contrasts with the scroll area.
  - It should indicate by its position, spatially, the relative location in the file of the information being viewed.
  - It should indicate by its size, proportionately, the percentage of the available information in the file being viewed.

Scroll Directional Arrows

- To indicate the direction that scrolling may be performed, directional arrows should be provided.
  - They should be constructed of arrows in small boxes with backgrounds contrasting with the scroll area.

Selection

- When the slider box/handle has been selected, highlight it in some visually distinctive way.

Location

- A vertical (top-to-bottom) scroll bar should be positioned to the right of the window.
- A horizontal (left-to-right) scroll bar should be positioned at the bottom of the window.

Size

- A vertical scroll bar should be the height of the scrollable portion of the window body.
- A horizontal scroll bar should be at least one-half the width of the scrollable portion of the window body.

Current State Indication

- Whenever the window size or information position changes, the scroll bar components must also change, reflecting the current state.
- Include scroll bars in all sizeable windows.
    — If no information is currently available through scrolling in a particular direction, the relevant directional arrow should be subdued or grayed.

Directional Preference

- Where the choice exists, vertical (top-to-bottom) scrolling is preferred to horizontal (left-to-right) scrolling.

A scroll bar provides a method to permit display of information that may not always fit within a window displayed on a screen. One should only be included when scrolling may be necessary.

Components. In today's systems, scroll bars come in a variety of styles, as illustrated in Figure 10.21. Scroll bars consist of three elements: a scroll area or container, a slider box or handle that moves within a track made by the scroll area/container, and directional scroll arrows.

Scroll area or container. The scroll area or, as it is sometimes called, the scroll container is an elongated rectangular-shaped bar. Its presence indicates scrolling is available. It usually is constructed of a filled-in area displayed in a technique that visually contrasts with the window and screen body background. The chosen display technique should be of moderate intensity, not too powerful or too subtle. A powerful technique will be distracting, a subtle technique may be overlooked.

Slider box or handle. To indicate the location and amount of information being viewed, a slider box or, as it is sometimes called, a scroll handle is included within the scroll area/container. It is constructed of a moveable and sizeable

Figure 10.21   Representative scroll bars.

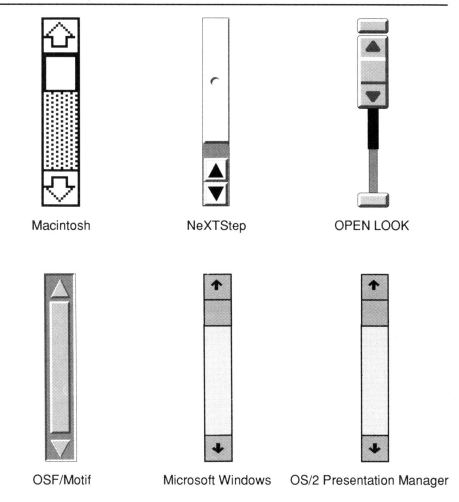

Macintosh   NeXTStep   OPEN LOOK

OSF/Motif   Microsoft Windows   OS/2 Presentation Manager

portion of the scroll area displayed in a technique that contrasts with the scroll area. It should indicate by its position, spatially, the relative location in the file of the information being viewed. It should indicate by its size, proportionately, the percentage of the available information in the file being viewed. The useability of the slider box or handle can be further enhanced by displaying within it the page number of page-organized material being viewed.

Directional or scroll arrows.   To indicate the direction that scrolling may be performed, directional or scroll arrows are also included. They are constructed of variously shaped arrows in small boxes with backgrounds contrasting with the scroll area/container. They are most often located at each end of the scroll bar, but some systems locate them adjacent to one another within the scroll area/container itself.

Placing directional arrows at opposite ends of the scroll bar, as is done by Macintosh, OSF/Motif, Microsoft Windows, and OS/2 Presentation Manager is conceptually the clearest. The mouse pointer is moved in the same direction, away from the current position, when either the scroll arrow or scroll handle is manipulated. The distance the directional arrows are separated, however, causes increased effort when a window's contents must be adjusted by scrolling in opposite directions.

NeXTStep solves the direction-switching problem by positioning the directional arrows adjacent to one another at one end of the scroll bar. While the forward-backward scrolling is made more efficient, the spatial correspondence between the beginning, middle, and end of the data is lost.

OPEN LOOK takes another approach, placing the directional arrows at opposite ends of the slider box/handle to maintain the desirable spatial correspondence while at the same time minimizing their separation. Since during a continuous scrolling operation the directional arrows move as the slider box/handle moves, OPEN LOOK automatically moves the mouse pointer to keep it aligned with the scroll arrow. This eliminates the need for the user to move the pointer during the continuous scrolling operation, but it requires that the user relinquish control of the mouse operation and may be disorienting.

All of the advantages and disadvantages of these different approaches to scrolling are still not well understood and can only be experimentally resolved.

Scrolling operation. The scrolling movement can be performed in several ways. The most common actions involve grabbing the slider box/handle and moving it in the desired direction, or selecting the proper directional arrow. Clicking a mouse button while selecting a directional arrow moves the contents of a window one line. Pressing the mouse button scrolls the window's contents continuously until the button is released. NexTStep also provides another more efficient process. A region of the scroll area/container can also be selected, automatically moving the slider box/handle to that point and displaying the proper window contents.

Based upon scrolling research (see page 110 and also Bury et al., 1982), movement of the window data usually follows the window-up or telescope approach, whereby the window moves around over data that appears fixed in location. This causes the data in a window to move in the direction opposite the one indicated by the directional arrow or the direction of movement of the scroll container/handle. Scrolling using window systems, however, seems to be especially mistake prone, users often assuming the arrows will move the data in the same direction as the directional arrow or scroll container/handle. In other words, it is sensed that the data moves under the window, not the window over the data (Billingsley, 1988). Why this happens is open to conjecture. Billingsley speculates that because windows are seen to physically "move" on screens, when data scrolls or moves in a window, people may conclude the data must be moving because the window remains still during the scrolling operation. Or, because of the close physical proximity of the directional arrows in scroll bars to the data, people may feel the arrows are acting on the data, not the window. The implication is that the scrolling procedure should be rethought and restudied. Some recent applications have devised scrolling methods through actually pointing at the window data.

Selection.   When the slider box/handle has been selected, highlight it in some visually distinctive way. Most systems do provide some visual feedback of this kind. NexTStep, however, does not.

Location.   While again no universal agreement exists, the majority of systems locate the vertical (top-to-bottom) scroll bar to the right of the window and the horizontal (left-to-right) scroll bar at the bottom of the window.

Size.   A vertical scroll bar should be the height of the scrollable portion of the window body. A horizontal scroll bar should be at least one-half the width of the scrollable portion of the window body.

Current state indication.   Whenever the window size or information position changes, the scroll bar components must also change, reflecting the current state of the scrolling process. Providing accurate information about the scrolling location facilitates user navigation and makes it easier to reposition the slider box/container. Include scroll bars in all sizeable windows.

  If scrolling cannot be performed in a particular direction, the relevant arrow box should be reduced in contrast or grayed.

  If all the information in a window is displayed and no information is available for scrolling, both directional arrows should be reduced in contrast or grayed. OPEN LOOK is one of the few systems that takes this action.

Directional preferences.   Where the choice exists, people prefer and deal better with vertical (top-to-bottom) scrolling rather than horizontal (left-to-right) scrolling.

Moving Windows

- Change cursor shape to indicate the move selection is successful.
- Move the entire window as the cursor moves.
  - If it is impossible to move the entire window, move the window outline while leaving the window displayed in its original position.
- Permit moving a window without making it active.

Change cursor shape and move entire window.   An indication that the move operation has been successfully selected, and that the move may begin, should be indicated to the user by changing the cursor's shape. This will provide the necessary feedback that it is safe to begin the move operation and avoid false starts. Ideally, the entire window should move along with the cursor. If the entire window cannot be moved, move the window outline while leaving the full window displayed on the screen. Displaying only the window's outline during the move operation, and not the window itself, may make it harder for the user to decide when the window has been repositioned correctly (Billingsley, 1988).

Permit moving without making a window active.   It may sometimes be necessary for a window to be moved without being active. This should be possible.

Resizing Windows

- Change the cursor shape to indicate the resizing selection is successful.
- The simplest operation is to anchor the upper left corner and resize from the lower right corner.
  - Permitting resizing from any point on the border is thought to be more complex for the user.
- Show the changing window as the cursor moves.
  - If it is impossible to show the entire window being resized, show the window outline while leaving the window displayed in its original position.
- When window size changes and the image remains the same size, do the following:
  - Clip (truncate) information arranged in some logical structure or layout.
  - Format (restructure) information when no layout considerations exist.
- When window size changes and image size also changes do the following:
  - Change image sizes proportionally as window size changes.
  - If resizing creates a window too small for easy use, do one of the following:
    - Clip when all components are at minimum size.
    - Remove less useful information, if it can be determined.
    - Replace information with a message that indicates the minimum size has been reached and that the window must be enlarged to continue working.

Change cursor shape and anchor point.   An indication that the resize operation has been successfully selected, and that the move may begin, should be indicated to the user by changing the cursor's shape. This will provide the necessary feedback that it is safe to begin the resizing and avoid false starts. The simplest operation for the user, conceptually, is to always resize from the lower right corner and "anchor" the window in the upper left corner. Resizing flexibility can be provided by permitting it to occur from any point on the border (the anchor is always opposite the pulling point) but conceptually this is more complex. Some people may have difficulty predicting which window sides or corners will be resized from specific pulling points (Billingsley, 1988).

Show the changing window.   Ideally, the entire window should move along with the cursor. If the entire window cannot be moved, move the window outline while leaving the full window displayed on the screen. Displaying only the window's outline during the move operation, and not the window itself, may make it harder for the user to decide when the window has been repositioned correctly (Billingsley, 1988).

Effect on data.   The effect of a resizing operation on the window's contents usually depends on the application. In enlarging, more data may be displayed, a larger image may be created, or blank space added around the image. In reducing, less data may be displayed, the image made smaller, blank space eliminated, or the data may be reformatted. When the window size changes and the image remains the same size, clip or truncate information arranged in some logical structure, format, or layout. When no layout considerations exist, such as for text, format or restructure the displayed information.

Positioning Windows

- Position a window so that it is completely visible.
- Position a window adjacent to information on the underlying screen or window it may relate to.
  - If it is the initial window
    - preferred positions, in suggested order of placement, are below-right, below, right, top-right, below-left, top, left, top-left.
  - If it is a second window on top of another window
    - position it offset below-right so the underlying window title is fully visible.
    - If this second window is the result of a selection made on the previous window, leave the description of this choice fully (or partially) visible on the underlying window.
- Do not allow the window to cover
  - needed underlying screen information.
  - underlying screen title.
  - navigation controls that may be needed.
- If the window does not relate to items on an underlying screen, center the window on the screen.
- Permit the user to move the window, if necessary.

Position adjacent.   Position a new window adjacent to the information on the underlying screen or window it may relate to. If the window is the initial window, preferred positions are essentially below and right. The suggested order of placement is below-right, below, right, top-right, below-left, top, left, top-left.

If it is a second window on top of another window, locate it offset below-right so the underlying window title is fully visible. If this second window is the result of a selection made on the previous window, leave the description of this choice fully (or partially) visible on the underlying window. This will provide a reminder about the origins of this window.

Do not cover needed information.   Information needed on underlying screens or windows should always be visible. This includes underlying screen title and any needed navigation techniques.

Window Shuffling

 • Window shuffling should be easy to accomplish.

Window shuffling should be easy to perform in as few steps as possible. OPEN LOOK, for example, permits toggling of the two most recent windows displayed. Microsoft Windows and Presentation Manager permit rapid window shuffling and swapping of the front window and the second or back window.

Keyboard Control/Mouseless Operation

 • Window actions should be capable of being performed through the keyboard as well as with a mouse.
 • Keyboard alternatives should be designated through use of mnemonic codes, as much as possible.
 • Keyboard designations should be capable of being modified by the user.

All window actions should be capable of being performed using the keyboard as well as the mouse. This will provide a more efficient alternative for applications that contain tasks that are primarily keyboard oriented, for users skilled in touch typing, and for any other situations in which frequent movement between keyboard and mouse may be required. The use of mnemonic codes to reflect window mouse actions will greatly aid user learning of the keyboard alternatives. To provide the user flexibility, all keyboard designations should be capable of being user modified.

Number of Windows to Display

 • Display no more than two or three windows at one time.

Guidelines concerning the maximum number of windows to display that appeared in early stages of window evolution were quite generous, a limit of seven or eight being suggested. As experience with windows has increased, these numbers have gradually fallen. One study (Gaylin, 1986) found the mean number of windows maintained for experienced users was 3.7. Today, based upon expressions of window users, a recommendation of no more than two or three at one time seems most realistic. The exact number of windows a person can effectively deal with at one time will ultimately depend on both the capabilities of the user and the characteristics of the task. Some users and situations may permit handling of more than three windows; for other users and situations, three windows may be too many.

SCREEN BODY

The screen body is the working area of the graphical screen. IBM's SAA CUA calls it the "client" area, the computer equivalent of a piece of paper. Others refer to it as the screen "content." Whatever name it goes by (this text uses the word body), it may possess a variety of looks. In a word processing application it may be presented blank for the creation of text. For many other types of applications the body is formatted, containing captions, entry or selection fields, messages, and other similar items. In an accounting application it may take the form of a spread sheet.

This section addressing the screen body begins with a reminder to provide visual clarity by leaving a margin around the body's contents. It next looks at screen organization. Then, the focus shifts to the kinds of fields available: entry fields, selection fields, and combination entry/selection fields. Each field type will be examined in terms of its components: captions, entry areas or choice descriptions, internal alignment, and spacing.

Finally, more general considerations including completion aids and prompting, multiple field alignment, headings, and borders will be addressed.

Separation

- For graphical screens with line borders, such as windows, provide visual clarity by
  - leaving at least two (2) blank character positions between the left and right borders and the widest element within the screen or window.
- Leave a space line between the title and other screen elements.

The information displayed within the body of a graphical screen or window will consist of entry fields, selection fields, messages, icons, and other textual information. These will be structured and organized following the relevant guidelines to follow. Never cramp the body of a screen or window. Always leave a sufficient margin on all sides. The screen will look much more appealing to the viewer.

Organization

- The screen should provide optimum visual clarity and reflect the organization of the world in which the information is collected or used.

A person organizes information internally in meaningful and expected ways. When the screen reflects these patterns and expectancies, it will be handled faster and be less prone to errors. The screen organization should always reflect the experiences and expectancies of its user.

ENTRY FIELDS

Entry fields are areas of the screen into which information may be typed. They usually possess identifying captions and their display and organizational principles are similar to those of text-based screens.

Captions

Structure and Size

- Fully spell out in a language meaningful to the user.
- Use a mixed-case font.
- Display in normal intensity or a color of moderate brightness.

Formatting

- Single Fields:
  — Locate the caption to left of entry field.
  — Separate the caption from the entry field by a unique symbol and one space. The colon (:) is the recommended symbol.

  Organization: ⎡＿＿＿＿＿＿＿＿＿＿＿＿⎤

- Multiple Occurrence Fields
  — For data entry fields:
    — Locate the caption left-justified one line above the column of entry fields.

  Office
  ⎡＿＿＿＿＿＿＿＿⎤

— For display or inquiry fields:
    — If the data field is fixed-length, or the displayed data is about the same length, center the caption above the displayed data.

Date

```
┌─────────────┐
│  01/26/89   │
│  07/21/90   │
│  11/18/91   │
└─────────────┘
```

    — If the data displayed is alphanumeric and quite variable in length, left-justify the caption above the displayed data.

City

```
┌────────────────────┐
│  Alice Springs     │
│  Darwin            │
│  Traralgon         │
│  Wagga Wagga       │
│  Whyalla           │
└────────────────────┘
```

    — If the data field is numeric and variable in length, right-justify the caption above the displayed data.

Balance

```
┌─────────────┐
│       1.26  │
│      53.98  │
│  45,345.00  │
│   2,509.04  │
└─────────────┘
```

Structure and size. Screen captions must be understandable to the screen user. Fully spell out all captions in a language meaningful to the user. In general, abbreviations and contractions should not be used. To achieve the alignment recommendations (to be discussed shortly), however, an occasional abbreviation or contraction may be necessary. If so, choose those that are common in the everyday language of the application or those that are meaningful or easily learned. Used mixed-case text in the caption, capitalizing only the first letter of each word (except for articles, conjunctions, and prepositions—a, the, and, for, etc.). Acronyms, abbreviations, or proper nouns that are normally capitalized, however, may be capitalized. If the caption is of a sentence-style nature, sentence-style capitalization should be followed. In this case, capitalize only the first letter of the first word of the caption.

    In relation to the entry field, the caption should be of normal intensity or consist of a moderately bright color. Visual emphasis should be given to the entry field.

Formatting. For single fields the caption should precede the entry field. Place a colon (:) directly following the caption to visually separate the caption from the data. IBM's SAA CUA, unfortunately, recommends breaking the caption from the data with a series of leader dots (. . .). Dots are visually "heavy" and push captions farther from the entry field, as discussed in Chapter 4.

For multiple-occurrence fields, the captions should be positioned above the columnized entry fields. The exact location of the caption will depend upon the kind of screen and the kind of data displayed. For data entry screens, the caption should be left-justified above the columnized entry fields. This will signal the starting point of the entry field and assure the caption is positioned directly above the keyed data.

For display or inquiry screens where information already exists in the entry field, positioning of the caption depends upon the kind of information displayed within the field. The goal is to center the caption over the data. If the field is fixed-length, or the information to be displayed within it usually fills, or almost fills, the field, center the caption above the data. If the information is alphanumeric and can be quite variable in length, left-justify the caption. This will keep the caption directly above the data when it appears in the field. Similarly, for numeric fields, right-justify the caption to keep it above the data that will be right-justified when it appears.

Entry Fields

Structure

- Identify entry fields by underscores or underlining

> Account: _____

or a rectangular box.

> Account: [_____]

- Break up long fields through incorporation of slashes (/), dashes (-), spaces, or other common delimiters.

> Date: __/__/__
> Telephone Number: (__) ___ ____

> Date: [/   /   ]
> Telephone Number: [(   )   -   ]

Size

- Entry fields for fixed-length data must be large enough to contain the entire entry.
- Entry fields for variable-length data must be large enough to contain the majority of the entries.
  - Where entries may be larger than the entry field, scrolling must be provided to permit keying into, or viewing, the entire field.

Highlighting

- Call attention to the entry fields through a highlighting technique.
  - If the entry field is indicated by an underscore or underline, display the data in a higher intensity or brighter color than the caption.
    - If color is used, choose one that contrasts well with the screen background.
  - If the entry field is indicated through a box, choose a box color that both complements the screen background and provides good contrast with the color chosen for the entry field data.

Structure.   Entry fields should attract attention, not detract from the entry legibility, provide some indication of the kind of desired response, and indicate the appropriate number of characters required for the entry. Savage et al. (1982) found that a broken underscore is a good technique for entry fields. Graphic terminals also permit the use of rectangular boxes. Both resemble the coding areas most frequently found on paper forms. To make the entry fields more readable, it is desirable to break them up into logical pieces. Slashes, dashes, and spaces should be inserted into the entry fields as illustrated above.

Size.   Entry fields for fixed-length data must be long enough to contain the entry. Variable-length entry fields should be large enough to contain the majority of the entries. The size of variable-length entry fields will be dependent upon field alignment, space utilization, and aesthetics. If an entry field is not large enough to key, or view, the entire entry, it must be scrollable. Scrolling, however, should be avoided whenever possible.

Highlighting.   Entry fields and data (as opposed to captions) are the most important part of a screen. Call attention to them through highlighting techniques. If an underline or underscore is the field delimiter, display them in high intensity with monochrome screens. With color screens, use the brightest colors. As will be described in Chapter 13, the brightest colors are white and yellow. If a box is the delimiter, choose a background color that complements the screen body background and provides good contrast with the color chosen for the entry field data. Again, see Chapter 13 for more detail.

Entry Field Alignment

- Vertically left-align entry fields into columns.

- If the entry field is numeric and is being used for display or inquiry purposes, right-align the field by its decimal point (or implied decimal point).

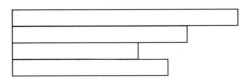

Fields should always be columnized. Left-align all entry fields. If a field is numeric and is used for inquiry or display purposes, right-align on the decimal point or implied decimal point. This will make the entry process more efficient by reducing eye movements and permitting reading of more than one piece of data at a time with one eye fixation. When reading screen data, this also makes it easier and faster to find and compare the data of interest. When space permits the creation of two or more columns on a screen, the entry process should flow in a columnar orientation, from top-to-bottom, then left-to-right. Top-to-bottom visual scanning is always more efficient than left-to-right scanning.

Caption Justification

1. First Approach
   - Left-align captions.
   - Leave one (1) space between the longest caption and the entry field column.

Name:
Organization:x
Location:
Building:

2. Second Approach
   • Right-align captions.
   • Leave one space between each caption and entry field.

```
      Name:x[                              ]
Organization: [                            ]
    Location: [              ]
    Building: [      ]
```

Field justification can be accomplished in either of two ways. Approach 1 results in both captions and entry fields being left-aligned into columns. Approach 2 right-aligns the captions up against the left-justified column of entry fields. Each approach has advantages and disadvantages, as previously discussed in Chapter 4. SAA CUA presents Approach 1 only, left-aligned captions. Whichever approach is chosen should be consistently followed in a family of screens.

Horizontal Spacing

   • Provide horizontal separation of columns of data by:
      — Leaving a minimum of five spaces between the longest entry field in one column and the leftmost caption in an adjacent column.

```
Make:  [            ]xxxxx Warranty: [            ]
Model: [            ]      Period:   [      ]
Year:  [      ]           Labor:    [          ]
Color: [        ]         Parts:    [          ]
```

      — Separating adjacent columns with a vertical solid line.

```
Make:  [            ] | Warranty: [            ]
Model: [            ] | Period:   [      ]
Year:  [      ]       | Labor:    [          ]
Color: [        ]     | Parts:    [          ]
```

Columns of data on a screen must be separated to maintain their own visual identity. This is done by separating adjacent columns by at least five spaces. To reinforce the vertical nature of entry and visual scanning, solid lines can also be drawn between adjacent columns. With lines, spacing between columns need not be as great.

Vertical Spacing

- Leave at least one space line between columnized "groups" of related information.

```
Driver Name:       ┌─────────────────────────┐
License Number:    ├─────────────────────────┘
Restrictions:      ├──────────────┘
Expires:           └──────────────┘

Make:              ┌──────────────┐
Model:             ├──────────────┘
Year:              ├───────┘
Color:             └───────────┘
```

- For long columns of related elements, leave a space line after every fifth row. (If space permits, leave a space line after every third row.) Never exceed seven rows without a space line.

```
Policy Number:     ┌──────────────┐
Account Number:    ├───────────┘
Effective Date:    ├───────────┤
Expiration Date:   ├───────────┘
Policy Status:     └──┘

Policy Form:       ┌──┐
Property:          ├──────────┘
Liability:         ├──────────┘
Deductible:        ├───┘
Endorsement:       └──────────┘
```

Status

```
┌──────────────┐
├──────────────┤
├──────────────┤
├──────────────┤
└──────────────┘

┌──────────────┐
├──────────────┤
├──────────────┤
├──────────────┤
├──────────────┤
└──────────────┘
```

Occasional space lines on screens will improve the screen's readability and reduce the screen's density.

Dependent Fields

- Position a conditional field or fields to the right of the field to which it relates, or below the field to which it relates.
- Either:
  — Do not display these conditional fields until the selection to which it relates is chosen.
  — Display these conditional fields but in a subdued or grayed manner. When it is relevant, return it to a normal intensity.
- Inscribe a filled-in arrow between the selected choice and its dependent fields to visually relate them to each other.
  — Leave two (2) spaces between the choice description and the arrow for horizontally arrayed dependent fields.
  — Leave two (2) spaces between the arrow and the caption of the dependent field.

Number of Children: [ ] ▶ Names: [   ]

Number of Children: [ ]
        ▶ Names: [   ]

In some circumstances, a field may be conditionally active. Only when a particular response is made is this additional information needed. For example, a question such as "Do you have any children?" might necessitate knowing their names. If this question is answered affirmatively, a field requesting their names can be displayed at that point on the screen. A "No" response will cause the cursor to move to the next field, and the children name field will not appear.

Locate dependent or conditional fields to the right or below the field or choice that necessitates it. The displayed arrow serves to tie the dependent field to the triggering field. The field may either be shown in a grayed or subdued manner, or not displayed at all until it is needed.

Displaying an area as grayed or subdued allows the user to be aware of its existence but reduces the visual competition between it and other needed information on the screen. Not displaying dependent fields until they are triggered reduces screen clutter. Hiding their existence, however, does not give the screen user a full picture of all the possible needed data and the relationships that may exist. By hiding them, then, there may be a slight learning price to pay, depending upon the complexity of the needed data.

SELECTION FIELDS

A selection field is a field that displays on the screen all the possible alternatives, conditions, or choices that may exist for a data element or action. From those displayed the relevant choice, or choices, are selected.

Two kinds of selection fields exist. One kind allows the user to choose only one alternative, all the presented choices being mutually exclusive. These kinds of exclusive selection fields are now most commonly called radio buttons, although they may take several different forms on screens. The other kind of selection field presents multiple choices from which the user may choose one, two, or all alternatives. These kinds of nonexclusive selection fields are most often called check boxes, although, again, they make take different forms. To make each kind immediately obvious to the viewer, the types are displayed on a screen in a different manner.

Selection fields most often contain field captions and textual descriptions of the alternatives. A selection field, however, may consist of representations of the values themselves. These kind are referred to as value sets or palettes. Another special kind of selection field is the spin button where the choices are displayed successively within a single field resembling an entry field.

Radio Buttons and Other Methods For Presenting Exclusive Choices

Fields presenting mutually exclusive choices are sometimes called different names and can be seen in a variety of forms. One common display method used is the radio button, which, like its namesake, consists of a circle associated with each choice description. When an alternative is selected, the center of the circle is partially filled in to provide a visual indication that it is the active choice. Macintosh, OS/2 Presentation Manager, Microsoft Windows, DECwindows, and IBM's SAA CUA follow this approach. Other styles of radio buttons may also be seen. NeXTStep uses small circular buttons that look recessed when not selected and are raised when selected. OSF/Motif uses small diamond-shaped buttons that look raised when not selected and depressed when selected. These various radio button styles are illustrated in Figure 10.22.

Figure 10.22   Representative radio button style exclusive choice fields.

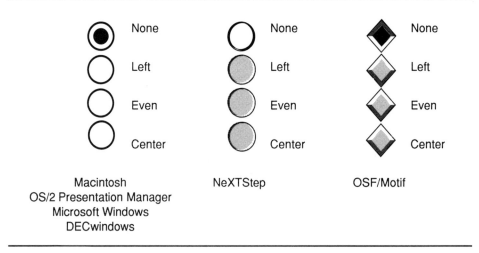

A different method for presenting exclusive choices is the butted box or button where the alternatives are inscribed in adjoining rectangles horizontally arrayed, and the selected alternative is highlighted in some way. Xerox's Star, OPEN LOOK (which calls them "two state exclusive settings"), and Silicon Graphics's SGI use this approach. Butted boxes or buttons are illustrated in Figure 10.23.

Figure 10.23   Examples of butted box or button exclusive selection fields.

None	Left	Even	Center

Deciding on which style to use seems to be more a matter of preference than performance. No published comparison studies are available for guidance. There does, however, seem to be a few definite advantages and disadvantages for the different methods. These will be discussed in the guidelines that follow.

Selection Descriptions

- Provide meaningful, fully spelled-out choice descriptions.
- Display using mixed-case letters.
- Locate descriptions associated with a radio button, or similar small button-type indicator, to the right of the button. Separation by one (1) space is usually sufficient.
- Locate descriptions for rectangular-shaped boxes within the box.

Choice descriptions must be clear, meaningful, fully spelled out, and displayed in a mixed-case text. For multiword descriptions, capitalize the first letter of each significant word. Small button-type indicators should be located to the left of the choice description; rectangular-shaped boxes will find the description within the box. Small buttons associated with text are advantageous when the choice description must be lengthy. Descriptions in boxes impose restrictions on the number of words that can be inscribed within them.

Size

- Restrict the number of choices displayed in the field to eight or less.

Selection fields of this style should not present more than eight choices. Displaying more than eight is usually not efficient, being wasteful of screen space. If the number of field choices exceeds this maximum, consider using a list box or a drop-down list box.

Structure

- a columnar orientation is the preferred manner.
  — If radio buttons are used, left-align the buttons and choice descriptions.

○ None
○ Left
○ Even
○ Center

  — If rectangular boxes are used
    — create boxes of equal height.
    — position the boxes adjacent to, or butted up against, one another.

None
Left
Even
Center

- If vertical space on the screen is limited, orient the choices horizontally.
  — If small buttons are used, provide adequate separation between choices so that the buttons are associated with the proper description. A distance equal to three (3) spaces is usually sufficient.

○ Nonexxx○ Left   ○ Even   ○ Center

  — If rectangular boxes are used
    — create boxes of equal width.
    — position the boxes adjacent to, or butted up against, one another.

None	Left	Even	Center

The preferred orientation of selection fields is columnar. Fields with small button indicators usually fit best in this manner because choice descriptions are not restricted in size. Fields designated with rectangular boxes are most often arrayed horizontally because of their smaller choice descriptions. Rectangular boxes should be of equal height and/or width and be butted up against one another. This will distinguish them from nonexclusive choice fields that will be separated from one another.

Organization

- Arrange selections in expected orders or follow other patterns such as frequency of occurrence, sequence of use, or importance.
  - For selections arrayed top-to-bottom, begin ordering at the top.
  - For selections arrayed left-to-right, begin ordering at the left.
- If, under certain conditions, a choice is not available, do not display the non-selectable choice, or display it subdued or less brightly than the available choices.

Selection choices should be organized logically. If the alternatives have an expected order, follow it. Other ordering schemes such as frequency of use, sequence of use, or importance may also be considered. Always begin ordering at the top or left. If, under certain conditions, a choice is not available, it is recommended that the choice not be displayed in the selection listing and the list be closed up (no blank spaces left in it). If this is not feasible, display the nonselectable choice subdued or less brightly than the available choices.

Captions

- Provide a caption for each selection field.
  - In screens containing only one selection field, the screen title may serve as the caption.
- Display the caption fully spelled out using mixed-case letters. A slightly larger type size may also be used.

Columnar Orientation

- The preferred location of the field caption is right-justified above the selection descriptions.
  - If small buttons are used to designate the choices, separate the caption from the choice descriptions by a space line.

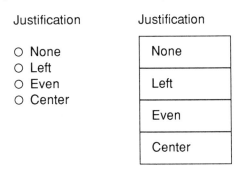

- Alternatively, the caption may be located to the left of the topmost choice description.

Justification: ○ None   Justification:

○ Left

○ Even

○ Center

None
Left
Even
Center

Horizontal Orientation

- The preferred location of the field caption is to the left of the selection descriptions.

  Justification: ○ None   ○ Left   ○ Even   ○ Center

Justification:	None	Left	Even	Center

- Alternatively, the caption may be located above the topmost choice description.
  - If small buttons are used to designate the choices, separate the caption from the choice descriptions by a space line.

  Justification

  ○ None   ○ Left   ○ Even   ○ Center

  Justification

None	Left	Even	Center

- Be consistent in caption style and orientation within an application.

Display the caption fully spelled out using mixed-case letters. Some occasional common abbreviations may be used, however, to achieve the alignment goals to be specified. A slightly larger type size may also be used for captions, if available. The preferred location of a field caption is above columns and to the left of horizontal selection descriptions. This will help achieve screen efficiency, minimize viewer eye movements, and provide caption and choice distinctiveness. If the screen contains only one field, the screen title may serve as the field caption. Be consistent in caption style and orientation within an application.

Selection Method and Indication

Pointing

- The selection target area should be as large as possible.
  — If a small button is the selection indication method used, the target area should include the button and the choice description text.
- Highlight the selection choice in some visually distinctive way when the pointer is resting on it and the choice is available for selection.
  — If a small button is the selection indication method used, a reverse video, reverse color, or dotted or dashed box selection cursor or bar may be used to surround the selected choice description.
  — This cursor should be as long as the longest description plus one (1) space at each end. Do not place the cursor over the small button.

○ Left

⊙ │ Even │

○ Center

- Alternatively, change the shape of the pointer to signal that a selection can be performed.

Activation

- When a choice is selected, distinguish it visually from the nonselected choices.
  — A radio button should be filled in with a solid dark dot.
  — A small button should be made to look depressed, or higher, through use of drop shadows.
  — A rectangular box can be highlighted in a manner different from when it is pointed at, or a bolder border can be drawn around it.
- When a choice is selected, any other selected choice must be deselected.

Defaults

- If a selection field is displayed with a choice previously selected or a default choice, display the currently active choice in the manner used when it is selected.

Pointing.   The selection target area should be as large as possible in order to make it easy to move to. If a small button is the selection indication method used, the target area should include the button and the choice description text. If the rectangular box selection method is used, the entire box should be the target.

Highlight the selection choice in some visually distinctive way when the pointer is resting on it and the choice is available for selection. If a small button is the selection indication method used, a distinctive reverse video, reverse color, or dotted or dashed box selection cursor or bar may be used to surround the selected choice description. This cursor should be as long as the longest description plus one (1) space at each end. The cursor should not cover the small button. An alternative method to indicate that the selection can be performed is to change the shape of the pointer when it is positioned correctly over a selection.

Activation. When a choice is selected, distinguish it visually from the nonselected choices. A radio button should be filled in with a solid dark dot. Other methods include making the button look depressed or higher than the others through the use of drop shadows. A rectangular box can be highlighted in a manner different from when it is pointed at, or a bolder border can be drawn around it. When a choice is selected, any other selected choice must be deselected or made inactive.

Defaults. If a selection field is displayed with a choice previously selected or a default choice, display the currently active choice in the same manner shown when it is selected.

Check Boxes and Other Methods for Presenting Nonexclusive Choices

Fields with multiple choices from which one or more alternatives can be selected are called by a variety of different names. The most common term is "check boxes," used, for example, by Macintosh, OS/2 Presentation Manager, Microsoft Windows, and IBM's SAA CUA. Others include "toggle buttons" (OSF/Motif and DECwindows), "switches" (NexTStep), and "two state nonexclusive settings" (OPEN LOOK). As their names differ, differences also exist in the way these fields are presented on screens. One very common display method is the check box, which, resembling its namesake, consists of a square placed adjacent to each alternative. When the choice is selected, some systems place an "X" in the square to provide a visual indication that it is active. Macintosh, OS/2 Presentation Manager, Microsoft Windows, and IBM's SAA CUA follow this approach. Others place a check mark (✓) in the square (NexTStep), fill in the selected square (DECwindows), or make it look depressed when selected (OSF/Motif). Examples of these styles are illustrated in Figure 10.24.

Another style for this type of field is a button or box with the choice description inscribed inside. When selected, the alternative is highlighted in some way. To visually distinguish these fields from similarly constructed fields presenting mutually exclusive choices, the buttons are not adjacent to, or butted up against, one another. OPEN LOOK also uses this approach. Examples of rectangular boxes or buttons are illustrated in Figure 10.25.

Again, deciding on which style to use seems to be more a matter of

Figure 10.24   Representative check box style nonexclusive choice fields.

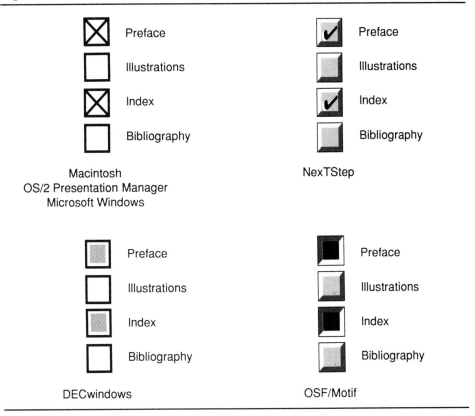

preference than performance. No published comparison studies are available for guidance. There does seem to be, however, a few possible advantages and disadvantages for the different methods, which we will look at in the following guidelines.

Selection Descriptions

- Provide meaningful, fully spelled-out choice descriptions.
- Display using mixed-case letters.
- Locate descriptions associated with a check box, or similar small box-type indicator, to the right of the box. Separation by one (1) space is usually sufficient.
- Locate descriptions for rectangular-shaped boxes within the box.

Choice descriptions must be clear, meaningful, fully spelled out, and displayed in a mixed-case text. For multiword descriptions, capitalize the first letter of each significant word. Small box-type indicators should be located to

Figure 10.25   Examples of box or button nonexclusive selection fields.

| Preface | Illustrations | Index | Bibliography |

the left of the choice description, rectangular-shaped boxes will find the description within the box. Small boxes associated with text are advantageous when the choice description must be lengthy. Descriptions in boxes impose restrictions on the number of words that can be inscribed within them.

Size

- Restrict the number of choices displayed in the field to eight or less.

Selection fields of this style should not offer more than eight choices. Displaying more than eight is usually not efficient as it wastes screen space.

Structure

- A columnar orientation is the preferred style.
  — If check boxes are used, left-align the check boxes and choice descriptions.

☐ Preface
☐ Illustrations
☐ Index
☐ Bibliography

— If rectangular boxes are used:
  — Create boxes of equal width.
  — Separate the boxes from one another by small equidistant spaces.

| Preface |

| Illustrations |

| Index |

| Bibliography |

- If vertical space on the screen is limited, orient the choices horizontally.
  - If check boxes are used, provide adequate separation between choices so that the boxes are associated with the proper description. A distance equal to three (3) spaces is usually sufficient.

☐ Prefacexxx☐ Illustrations   ☐ Index   ☐ Bibliography

  - If rectangular boxes are used:
    - Create boxes of equal height.
    - Separate the boxes from one another by small equidistant spaces.

| Preface | Illustrations | Index | Bibliography |

The preferred orientation of selection fields is columnar. Fields with check-box indicators usually fit best in this manner because choice descriptions are not restricted in size. Fields designated with rectangular boxes are most often arrayed horizontally because of their smaller choice descriptions. Rectangular boxes should be of equal width and separated from one another by small and equidistant spaces. This will distinguish them from mutually exclusive choices that will be butted up against one another.

Organization

- Arrange selections in logical order or follow other patterns such as frequency of occurrence, sequence of use, or importance.
  - For selections arrayed top-to-bottom, begin ordering at the top.
  - For selections arrayed left-to-right, begin ordering at the left.
- If, under certain conditions, a choice is not available, do not display the unavailable choice, or display it subdued or less brightly than the available choices.

Selection choices should be organized logically. If the alternatives have an expected order, follow it. Other ordering schemes such as frequency of use sequence of use, or importance may also be considered. Always begin ordering at the top or left. If, under certain conditions, a choice is not available, it is recommended that the choice not be displayed in the selection listing and the list be closed up (no blank spaces left in it). If this is not feasible, display the unavailable choice subdued or less brightly than the available choices.

Captions

- Provide a caption for each selection field.
  - In screens containing only one selection field, the screen title may serve as the caption.

- Display the caption fully spelled out using mixed-case letters. A slightly larger type size may also be used.

Columnar Orientation

- The preferred location of the field caption is above the selection descriptions.
  - If check boxes are used to designate the choices, separate the caption from the choice descriptions by a space line.

Contents   Contents

   ☐ Preface   ┌─────────────┐
   ☐ Illustrations   │ Preface   │
   ☐ Index   └─────────────┘
   ☐ Bibliography   ┌─────────────┐
                              │ Illustrations │
                              └─────────────┘
                              ┌─────────────┐
                              │ Index   │
                              └─────────────┘
                              ┌─────────────┐
                              │ Bibliography │
                              └─────────────┘

- Alternatively, the caption may be located to the left of the topmost choice description.

Contents: ☐ Preface
          ☐ Illustrations
          ☐ Index
          ☐ Bibliography

Contents: ┌─────────────┐
          │ Preface   │
          └─────────────┘
          ┌─────────────┐
          │ Illustrations │
          └─────────────┘
          ┌─────────────┐
          │ Index   │
          └─────────────┘
          ┌─────────────┐
          │ Bibliography │
          └─────────────┘

Horizontal Orientation

- The preferred location of the field caption is to the left of the selection descriptions.

Contents: ☐ Preface   ☐ Illustrations   ☐ Index   ☐ Bibliography

Contents: | Preface | | Illustrations | | Index | | Bibliography |

- Alternatively, the caption may be located above the topmost choice description.
    - If small buttons are used to designate the choices, separate the caption from the choice descriptions by a space line.

Contents

☐ Preface   ☐ Illustrations   ☐ Index   ☐ Bibliography

Contents

| Preface | | Illustrations | | Index | | Bibliography |

- Be consistent in caption style and orientation within an application.

Display the caption fully spelled out using mixed-case letters. Some common abbreviations may be used, however, to achieve the alignment goals to be specified. A slightly larger type size may also be used for captions, if available. The preferred location of a field caption is above columns and to the left of horizontal selection descriptions. This will help achieve screen efficiency, minimize viewer eye movements, and provide caption and choice distinctiveness. If the screen contains only one field, the screen title may serve as the field caption. Be consistent in caption style and orientation within an application.

Selection Method and Indication

Pointing

- The selection target area should be as large as possible.
    - If a check box is the selection indication method used, the target area should include the button and the choice description text.
- Highlight the selection choice in some visually distinctive way when the pointer is resting on it and the choice is available for selection.
    - If a check box is the selection indication method used, a reverse video, reverse color, or dotted or dashed box selection cursor or bar may be used to surround the selected choice description.
    - This cursor should be as long as the longest description plus one (1) space at each end. Do not place the cursor over the check box.

☐   Preface

☐ | Illustrations |

☐   Index

• Alternatively, change the shape of the pointer to signal that a selection can be performed.

Activation

• When a choice is selected, distinguish it visually from the nonselected choices.
  — A check box should be marked with an "X" or check mark (✓) or filled in.
  — A small button should be made to look depressed, or higher, through use of drop shadows.
  — A rectangular box can be highlighted in a manner different from when it is pointed at, or a bolder border can be drawn around it.
  — The style chosen should be consistently applied throughout an application or system.

Defaults

• If a selection field is displayed with a choice previously selected or a default choice, display the currently active choice in the manner used when it is selected.

Pointing.   The selection target area should be as large as possible in order to make it easy to move to. If a check box is the selection indication method used, the target area should include the box and the choice description text. If the rectangular box selection method is used, the entire box should be the target. Highlight the selection choice in some visually distinctive way when the pointer is resting on it and the choice is available for selection. If a check box is the selection indication method used, a distinctive reverse video, reverse color, or dotted or dashed box selection cursor or bar may be used to surround the selected choice description. This cursor should be as long as the longest description plus one (1) space at each end. The cursor should not cover the check box. An alternative method to indicate that the selection can be performed is to change the shape of the pointer when it is positioned correctly over a selection.

Activation.   When a choice is selected, distinguish it visually from the nonselected choices. A check box may be marked with an "X" or check or filled in. Other methods include making the button look depressed or raised through appropriate use of drop shadows. A rectangular box can be highlighted in a manner different from when it is pointed at, or a bolder border can be drawn around it. The style chosen must be consistently applied throughout an application or system.

Defaults.   If a selection field is displayed with a choice previously selected or a default choice, display the currently active choice in the same manner shown when it is selected.

VALUE SETS

Like radio buttons, value sets, or palettes, can also be used to present two or more mutually exclusive alternatives. The choices presented, however, are visually descriptive within themselves. No choice descriptions are needed to identify them. Examples of value sets might be fill-in colors, patterns, or different shades of colors.

When the choice is selected, the choice itself is emphasized. Value sets are preferable to radio buttons in that they take up less space and allow the viewer to focus on the visual characteristics of the choice itself, instead of having to read the choice text and cross-referencing it to a radio button. Value sets may also be used when the rectangular-shaped butted box or button-style technique is employed, the value set replacing the choice description within the box. A value set is illustrated in Figure 10.26.

Consider using a value set when the choices have qualities that can be best described by actual illustration. Also, value sets are more effective because one can directly compare the various choices with one another.

Selection Descriptions

• Provide meaningful, accurate, and clear illustrations or representations of alternative choices.

Value set choices must be meaningful, accurate, and clear illustrations of the available alternatives. Do not use value sets when the choices cannot be faithfully reproduced on the screen. While most value sets will not possess textual choice descriptions, under certain circumstances textual descriptions may be needed. For example, a choice might require selection of a style of font. The value set may contain the names of the available styles (like Roman) with the text displayed as the font style would actually appear.

Figure 10.26   A value set.

Size

• Present all available alternatives, if possible.

Since value sets will consume less screen space, more are capable of being displayed in the same area of a screen than can be displayed using textual choice descriptions. In general, all available alternatives should be presented. Human limitations in ability to differentiate various kinds of codes may limit the number of choices that can effectively be displayed, however. See Figure 11.1 for more information on human code differentiation limitations.

Structure

- Create boxes large enough to
  - effectively illustrate the available alternatives.
  - permit ease in pointing and selecting.
- Create boxes of equal size.
- Position the boxes adjacent to, or butted up against, one another.
- A columnar orientation is the preferred manner.

- If vertical space on the screen is limited, orient the choices horizontally.

Value set boxes must be large enough to effectively illustrate the available alternatives and to maximize ease in selecting. Created boxes should be of equal size and positioned adjacent to, or butted up against, one another, since they are mutually exclusive choices. Columns are preferred, but horizontal rows can be used if space constraints exist on the screen.

Organization

- Arrange value sets in expected or normal orders.
  - For value sets arrayed top-to-bottom, begin ordering at the top.
  - For value sets arrayed left-to-right, begin ordering at the left.
- If an expected or normal order does not exist, arrange choices by frequency of occurrence, sequence of use, importance, or alphabetically (if textual).
- If, under certain conditions, a choice is not available, do not display the unavailable choice, or display it subdued or less brightly than the other choices.

Value sets should be organized logically. If the alternatives have an expected order, follow it. Colors, for example, should be ordered from the right or top by their spectral position: red, orange, yellow, green, blue, indigo, and violet. If an expected or normal order does not exist, arrange choices by frequency of occurrence, sequence of use, or importance. Value sets with text may be arranged alphabetically. If, under certain conditions, a choice is not available, it is recommended it not be displayed. If this is not feasible, display the unavailable choice subdued or less brightly than the available choices.

Captions

- Provide a caption for each value set.
  — In screens containing only one value set, the screen title may serve as the caption.
- Display the caption fully spelled out using mixed-case letters.

Columnar Orientation

- The field caption may be located above the value set.

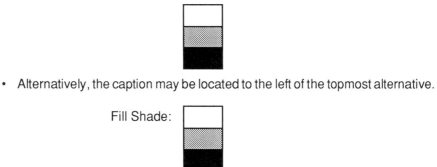

- Alternatively, the caption may be located to the left of the topmost alternative.

Horizontal Orientation

- The field caption may be located above the value set.

- Alternatively, the caption may be located to the left of the alternatives.

Fill Shade:

Provide a caption for each value set. In screens containing only one value set, the screen title may serve as the caption. Display the caption fully spelled out using mixed-case letters, although some abbreviations may be used to achieve the alignment goals to be specified. Field captions may be located above, or to the left of, the value set.

Selection Method and Indicator

Pointing

- Highlight the choice in some visually distinctive way when the pointer or cursor is resting on it and the choice is available for selection.
- Also, change the shape of the pointer to indicate that a selection can be performed.

Activation

- When a choice is selected, distinguish it visually from the nonselected choices by highlighting it in a manner different from when it is pointed at, or by placing a bold border around it.

Defaults

- If a value set is displayed with a choice previously selected or a default choice, display the currently active choice in the manner used when selected.

Pointing.   The selection target should be as large as possible in order to make it easy to move to. Highlight the selection choice in some visually distinctive way when the pointer or cursor is resting on it and the choice is available for selection. Also, change the shape of the pointer to indicate that a selection can be performed.

Activation.   When a choice is selected, distinguish it visually from the nonselected choices by highlighting it in a manner different from when it is pointed at, or by placing a bolder border around it.

Defaults.   If a value set is displayed with a choice previously selected or a default choice, display the currently active choice in the manner used when selected.

LIST BOXES AND OTHER METHODS FOR PRESENTING EXTENDED LISTS OF MUTUALLY EXCLUSIVE CHOICES

Variable-length lists as well as large fixed-length lists can be displayed in what are commonly called list boxes. List boxes are most useful when screen

Figure 10.27   List boxes. "Location" is not scrollable; "destination" is scrollable vertically.

Location

| Amphitheater |
| Chicago Stadium |
| Comiskey Park |
| Dyche Stadium |
| Melbourne Cricket Ground |
| Soldier Field |
| Stagg Field |
| Wrigley Field |

Destination

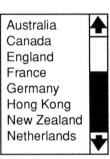

space constraints are not critical. They are usually rectangular in shape and may be scrollable horizontally as well as vertically. List boxes may stand alone or be associated with a field where the selected choice is displayed. IBM's SAA CUA uses the term "list box" for these kinds of fields. OSF/Motif refers to them as simply "lists." Examples of list boxes are illustrated in Figure 10.27.

Selection Descriptions

- Selection descriptions will reflect the choices available. They should be meaningful and spelled out as fully as possible.
- Organize the descriptions left-aligned in columns.
- Order the descriptions in a meaningful way or in alphabetical order.
- Display the descriptions using mixed-case letters.
- If associated with a display field, display the descriptions in the same color as the display field text.

Selection descriptions will reflect the selection alternatives available. They should be meaningful, fully spelled out, and organized in columns. Meaningful ordering schemes include logical order, frequency of use, sequence of use, or importance. If no such pattern exists, arrange the list alphabetically. Display the list of choices using mixed-case letters. If the list is associated with a display field and the screen uses color, the color scheme of the display field and the list box should be consistent.

Size

- Restrict the number of choices visible at one time to eight or less.
  - If more than eight choices are available, provide vertical scrolling to display all choices.

— If vertical scrolling is necessary, provide a scroll bar on the right side of
the fixed box.
• The box should be wide enough to display most selections without horizontal scrolling.
— If horizontal scrolling is necessary, provide a scroll bar at the bottom of
the list box.

The exact size of a list box will depend on the application and screen
space constraints. Generally, list boxes should be restricted to no more than
eight choices at one time. Slightly larger boxes that eliminate the need for
scrolling, however, are preferable to list boxes that require a little scrolling. If
scrolling is necessary, include a scroll bar on the right side of the box. The list
box should be wide enough to fully display most, if not all, of the selection
choices. When horizontal scrolling is necessary, provide a scroll bar at the
bottom of the list box.

Layout and Separation

• Enclose the choices in a box with a solid border.
— The border should be the same color as the choice descriptions.
• Leave one (1) blank character position between the choice descriptions
and the left border.
• Leave one (1) blank character position between the longest choice descrip-
tion in the list and the right border, if possible.
• If associated with a display field, use the same background color for the
box as is used in the display field.

```
┌─────────────────┐
│ Australia       │
│ Canada          │
│ England         │
│ France          │
│ Germany         │
│ Hong Kong       │
│ New Zealand     │
│ Netherlands     │
│                 │
└─────────────────┘
```

Enclose the box in a solid border in the color of the choice descriptions. To
provide adequate legibility, leave one space between the choice descriptions
and the left border, and one space between the longest choice description and
the right border. If the box is associated with a display field, visually relate the
box the entry field by using the same background color for the box as is used in
the display field box. Also incorporate a solid line border around the list box in
the same color as the choice descriptions.

Caption

- Display using mixed-case letters.
- The preferred location of the field caption is above the upper left corner of the list box.

Location

```
Amphitheater
Chicago Stadium
Comiskey Park
Dyche Stadium
Melbourne Cricket Ground
Soldier Field
Stagg Field
Wrigley Field
```

- Alternatively, the caption may be located to the left of the topmost choice description.

Location:
```
Amphitheater
Chicago Stadium
Comiskey Park
Dyche Stadium
Melbourne Cricket Ground
Soldier Field
Stagg Field
Wrigley Field
```

- If used with a display field, the list box field caption should be worded similarly to the display field caption.

Location: [   ]

Location

```
Amphitheater
Chicago Stadium
Comiskey Park
Dyche Stadium
Melbourne Cricket Ground
Soldier Field
Stagg Field
Wrigley Field
```

- Be consistent in caption style and orientation within an application.

To identify the list box, a field caption in mixed-case letters with each significant word capitalized is necessary. Place this caption either above the upper left corner of the box or to the left of the first choice description. If the list box is associated with a display field, this caption must be worded similarly to the display field caption. The caption style chosen, above or left, should be consistent within an application.

Selection Method and Indication

Pointing

- Highlight the selection choice in some visually distinctive way when the pointer or cursor is resting on it and the choice is available for selection.

Activation

- Use a reverse video or reverse color bar to surround the choice description when it is selected.
- The cursor should be as wide as the box itself.

Destination

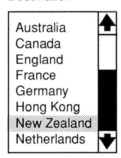

Defaults

- When the list box is first displayed,
  - if a choice has been previously selected, display the currently active choice in the same manner used when it was selected.
  - if a choice has not been previously selected, provide a default choice and display it in the same manner that is used in selecting it.

Pointing. Highlight the selection choice in some visually distinctive way when the pointer or cursor is resting on it and the choice is available for selection. One method for this is a bold border around the choice.

Activation. Indicate the selected choice through use of a reverse video or reverse color bar, as wide as the box itself.

Defaults.   When the list box is first displayed, the active selection will depend upon previous activities. If a choice has been previously selected, display the currently active choice in the same manner used when it was selected. If a choice has not been previously selected, provide a default choice and display it in the same manner that is used in selecting it. If properly organized, the default choice will be the first alternative in the list.

Location

- If a standalone field, position the list box in its logical sequence within the elements on the screen.
- If associated with a display field, locate the list box below, and as close as possible to, the display field to which it applies.
  - If multiple list boxes are included on the screen, they should be in the same order (top-to-bottom or left-to-right) as the display fields appear.

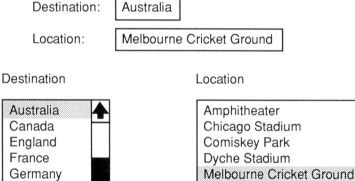

Position the list box or boxes in the logical sequence of elements found within the screen. If the box is associated with an entry field, locate the floating list box below and as close as possible to the entry field to which it relates. For screens containing multiple boxes, arrange the boxes in the same order as the entry fields appear on the screen. If the entry fields are in a top-to-bottom orientation, leave them that way. If this cannot be accomplished, orient them left-to-right.

POP-UP OR DROP-DOWN LIST BOXES

A pop-up or drop-down list box is associated with a single selection field where a choice is presented. The box, which is hidden, appears on request adjacent to this selection field and lists the choices available. An alternative must always be selected from the presented list for display in the selection field. This single selection field must always contain information.

Fields of this nature go by many different names. IBM's SAA CUA refers to them as "drop-down lists" because they appear to drop-down from the single selection field. Xerox's Viewpoint calls them "pull-down lists." Other list boxes of this type seem to pop-up on the screen, either next to or over the selection field. OSF/Motif calls list boxes of the style "option menus," and DECwindows uses the term "list boxes." NexTStep refers to them as "pop-up lists."

This type of field can be used in place of a list box when space on the screen is limited and the value within it does not often change. The availability of a pop-up or drop-down list box is often indicated by an icon placed near to the selection field. A selection field with a drop-down list, similar to those described in SAA CUA, is illustrated in Figure 10.28. Figure 10.29 shows a pop-up list.

Figure 10.28   Drop-down List Box. A drop-down iconic indicator is associated with the "Sport" field in the left grouping of fields. The right grouping shows the drop-down list box.

Sport:	[ ] ▼	Sport:	[Golf] ▼

Baseball
Basketball
Boxing
Cricket
Football
Golf
Ice Hockey
Ice Skating

Date:
Date:
Location:
Location:
Time:
Time:

Selection Field Prompt Box

- Provide a visual cue that a list box is hidden by including a downward-pointing arrow, or other meaningful icon, to the right of the selection field.

Sport: [   ] ▼

—When the arrow or icon is selected by the user and the list appears, reverse its polarity, using either reverse video or reverse color.

Many systems indicate the presence of a drop-down or pop-up list by associating a meaningful icon with the applicable field. This icon can be seen positioned to the left of the selection field (OPEN LOOK), within the selection field (NeXTStep), or to the right of the selection field (IBM's SAA CUA). Others

Figure 10.29   Pop-up list box illustrated in the right grouping.

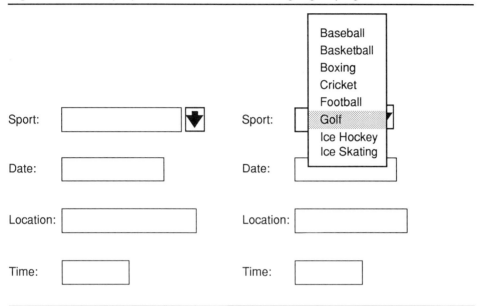

do not provide any visual indication that a hidden list is available (OSF/Motif and DECwindows).

An indication to the user that a drop-down or pop-up list is available should be indicated on the screen. This is especially critical if not all fields have associated hidden lists. The best location is to the right of the selection field where it is out of the way until needed. The indicator should be large enough to provide a good pointing target. When the list is selected, reverse the polarity of the indicator using either reverse video or reverse color.

Selection Descriptions

- Selection descriptions will reflect the choices available. They should be meaningful and spelled out as fully as possible.
- Organize the descriptions left-aligned in columns.
- Order the descriptions in a meaningful way or in alphabetical order.
- Display the descriptions using mixed-case letters.
- Display the descriptions in the same color as the selection field text.

Selection descriptions will reflect what may be placed in the selection field. They should be meaningful, fully spelled out, and organized in columns. Meaningful ordering schemes include logical order, frequency of use, sequence of use, or importance. If no such pattern exists, arrange the list alphabetically. Display the list of choices using mixed-case letters. Descriptions should be displayed in the same color as the selection field text.

Size

- Restrict the number of choices visible at one time to eight or less.
  - — If more than eight choices are available, provide scrolling to display all choices.
  - — If scrolling is necessary, provide a scroll bar on the right side of the box.

Pop-up or drop-down list boxes should be restricted to eight or less choices. If more must be displayed, permit scrolling and include a scroll bar on the right side of the box.

Location

- Locate:
  - — A drop-down list box beneath the selection field to which it applies.

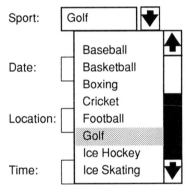

  - — A pop-up list box:
    - — adjacent to the selection field to which it applies, or
    - — over the selection field to which it applies.

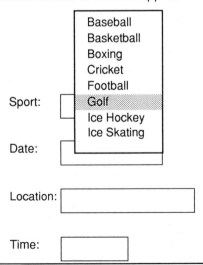

Locate a drop-down list box directly beneath the selection field to which it applies. Pop-up lists should be positioned adjacent to, or over, the selection field. If the list is located over the selection fields, position the selected or default choice in the list directly over the selection field, as illustrated above. This means the box will slightly change position as selection field entries change. Never reorder the list.

Layout and Separation

- Enclose the choices in a box composed of a solid line border.
  - — The border should be the same color as the choice descriptions.
- Left-align the choices in the list.
- Leave one (1) blank character position to the left of the column of choices.
- Leave one (1) blank character position to the right of the longest choice description in the list.
- Use the same background color for the box as is displayed in the selection field.

To provide adequate legibility, leave one space between the choice descriptions and the left border, and one space between the longest choice description and the right border. To set off the box from the screen body background, use the same color background for the box as is used in the entry field. Also incorporate a solid line border around the box in the same color as the choice descriptions.

Selection Method and Indication

Pointing

- Highlight the selection choice in some visually distinctive way when the pointer or cursor is resting on it and the choice is available for selection.

Activation

- Display the choice in the selection field and remove the list box from the screen.

Defaults

- When the list box is first displayed,
  - — if a choice has been previously selected, display the currently active choice in the same manner used when it was selected.
  - — if a choice has not been previously selected, provide a default choice and display it in the same manner that is used in selecting it.

Pointing. Highlight the selection choice in some visually distinctive way when the pointer or cursor is resting on it and the choice is available for selection.

Activation. Display the choice in the selection field and remove the list box from the screen.

Defaults. When the list box is first displayed, the active selection will depend upon previous activities. If a choice has been previously selected, display the currently active choice in the same manner used when it was selected. If a choice has not been previously selected, provide a default choice and display it in the same manner that is used in selecting it.

COMBINATION ENTRY/SELECTION FIELDS

It is possible for one field to possess the characteristics of an entry field and a selection field. In this type of field, information may either be typed into the field or selected and placed within it. The following varieties of combination entry/selection fields exist.

Spin Button

A spin button contains a list of the choices that may be selected. The list is searched by scrolling or "spinning" though a ring or circle of alternatives. Spin buttons are most effective when the values they contain have a customary or consecutive order that is predictable (such as days of the week). IBM's SAA CUA describes a spin button as illustrated in Figure 10.30.

Button Display

- When the field is first displayed, it should contain a default choice.
- Order the list in the customary or expected order of the information contained within it.

The field should always contain a default value when first displayed. Information can be letters or numbers with a customary or expected order. Examples would be days of the week, months of the year, shoe sizes, and so on. The user must always be able to anticipate the next choice before it is displayed.

Figure 10.30 Spin button.

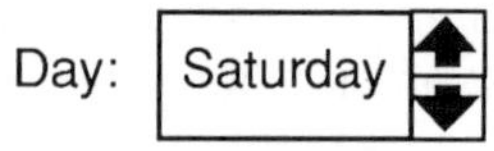

Day: | Saturday ▲▼

Button Indicator

- Provide an indication that a spin button is available by placing up and down arrows immediately to the right of the entry field.

Day: | Saturday ◆

The clue to the user that the field is a spin button is the up and down arrows adjacent to the field. Locate the arrows to the right of the field.

Entry and Selection Methods

- Permit field completion by doing the following:
  — Type directly into the entry field.
  — Scroll and select with a mouse.
  — Scroll and select with the up arrow or down arrow keyboard keys.

Field completion should be possible by directly typing into the field or by scrolling and selecting with a mouse or keyboard keys.

Drop-down Combination Boxes

A drop-down combination box looks and acts exactly like the drop-down list box recently described. The only difference is that in addition to information being selected from the box and then displayed in the field, the information can also be typed directly into the field as well.

This technique is advantageous when the information to be placed in a field is well known, and only occasional reminders of available alternatives are needed. The drop-down approach permits more efficient use of screen space. IBM's SAA CUA also uses the term "drop-down combination box" to describe this kind of field. One is illustrated in Figure 10.31. See the section describing drop-down list boxes for design details.

Attached Combination Boxes

An attached combination box looks and acts exactly like a drop-down list box or drop-down combination box. It is, however, permanently attached to its associated entry field. A choice may be typed directly into the entry field or selected from the list itself for display in the field.

This technique is advantageous when the information to be placed in a field is usually not well known and reminders of available alternatives are needed. It is more wasteful of screen space. IBM's SAA CUA simply uses the

Figure 10.31 Drop-down combination box.

Sport: ▼   Sport: | Golf | ▼

Baseball
Basketball
Date: ▲   Date: Boxing
Cricket
Football
Location: Location: Golf
Ice Hockey
Time: Time: Ice Skating

term "combination box" to describe this kind of field. An attached combination box is illustrated in Figure 10.32. See the section describing drop-down list boxes for design details.

ENTRY FIELDS VERSUS SELECTION FIELDS—A COMPARISON

Experimental determinations of the advantages and disadvantages for using either entry fields or selection fields for data collection on a screen have rarely been attempted. Two studies (Gould et al., 1988; Greene et al., 1988) have performed such a comparison.

Figure 10.32 Attached combination box.

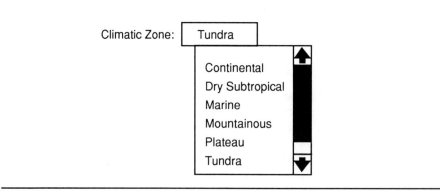

Climatic Zone: | Tundra |

Continental
Dry Subtropical
Marine
Mountainous
Plateau
Tundra

Choosing a Type of Field

- For familiar, meaningful data, choose the technique that, in theory, requires the fewest number of keystrokes to complete.
- If the data is unfamiliar, or prone to typing errors, choose a selection technique.

Both studies found that if the data to be entered was familiar, the technique that required the minimum theoretical number of keystrokes to complete the task was the fastest. Theoretical keystrokes are the minimum number possible, excluding miskeys and erroneous cursor or selection movements. However, as the data became less familiar or became subject to spelling or typing errors, the minimum keystroke principle broke down. Selection techniques, and the reminders and structure they provide, become advantageous. The point at which the changeover occurs is not known, and it would be influenced by the nature of the task and the nature of the user.

These studies point out the advantages of the techniques that permit both typed entry and selection to enter the data (spin list, drop-down combination box, and attached combination box).

Tables 10-6 and 10-7 provide some guidance in choosing entry and selection fields.

Aided Versus Unaided Entry

Greene et al. (1988) also compared unaided typed entry (the entire field had to be keyed) with aided entry (the system automatically and immediately completed the field when enough characters were keyed to make the desired data known). They found that autocompletion was preferred over unaided entry methods, and it was also the fastest. Autocompletion was also preferable to, and faster than, some selection methods.

The result is that, where possible, autocompletion of entry fields should be provided. Autocompletion will minimize the user's effort by reducing input time and keystrokes. It should also enhance the user's opinion of the system.

PROMPTING MESSAGES

- Incorporate prompting on a screen, as necessary
  - in a position just preceding the part, or parts, of a screen to which they apply.
  - in a manner that visually distinguishes them, such as
    - displaying them in a unique type style.
    - displaying them in a unique color.
  - in a position that visually distinguishes them by
    - left-justifying the prompt and indenting the related field captions (or headings) a minimum of three (3) spaces to the right.

Table 10.6 Choosing a selection field or an entry field.

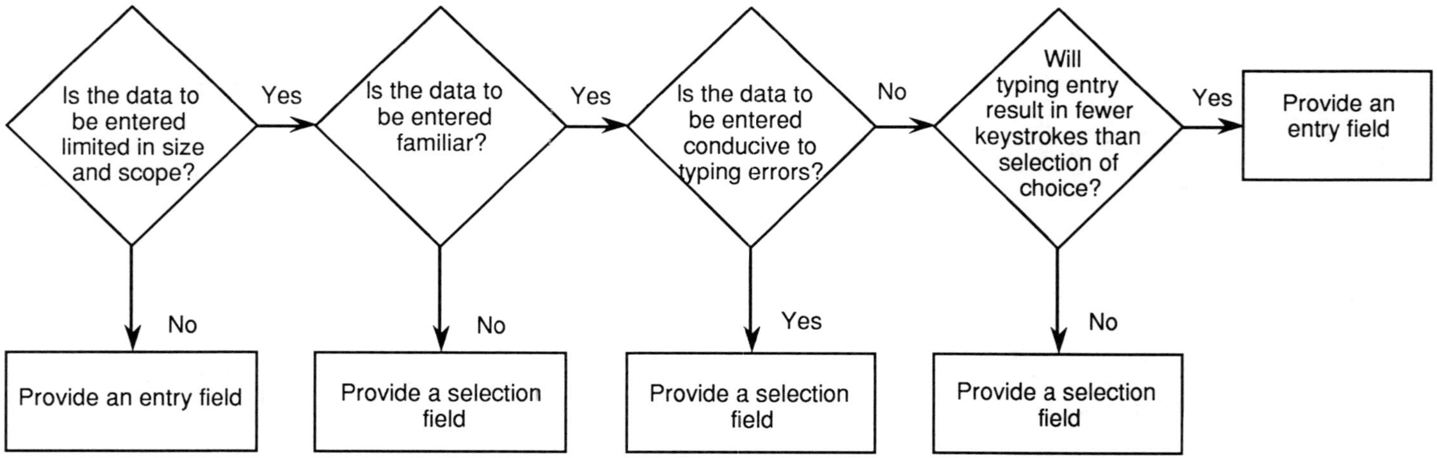

Table 10.7 Choosing a selection field.

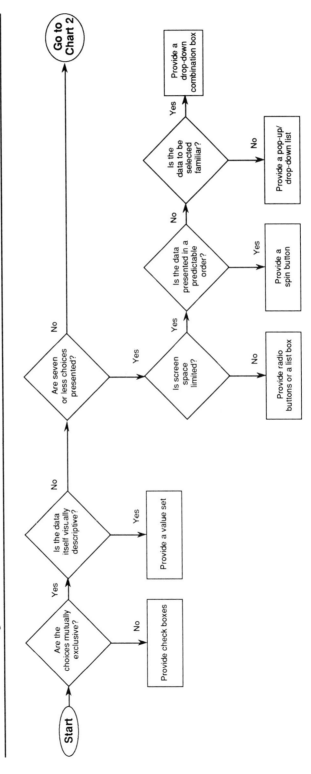

Table 10.7 (cont'd). Choosing a selection field—Chart 2.

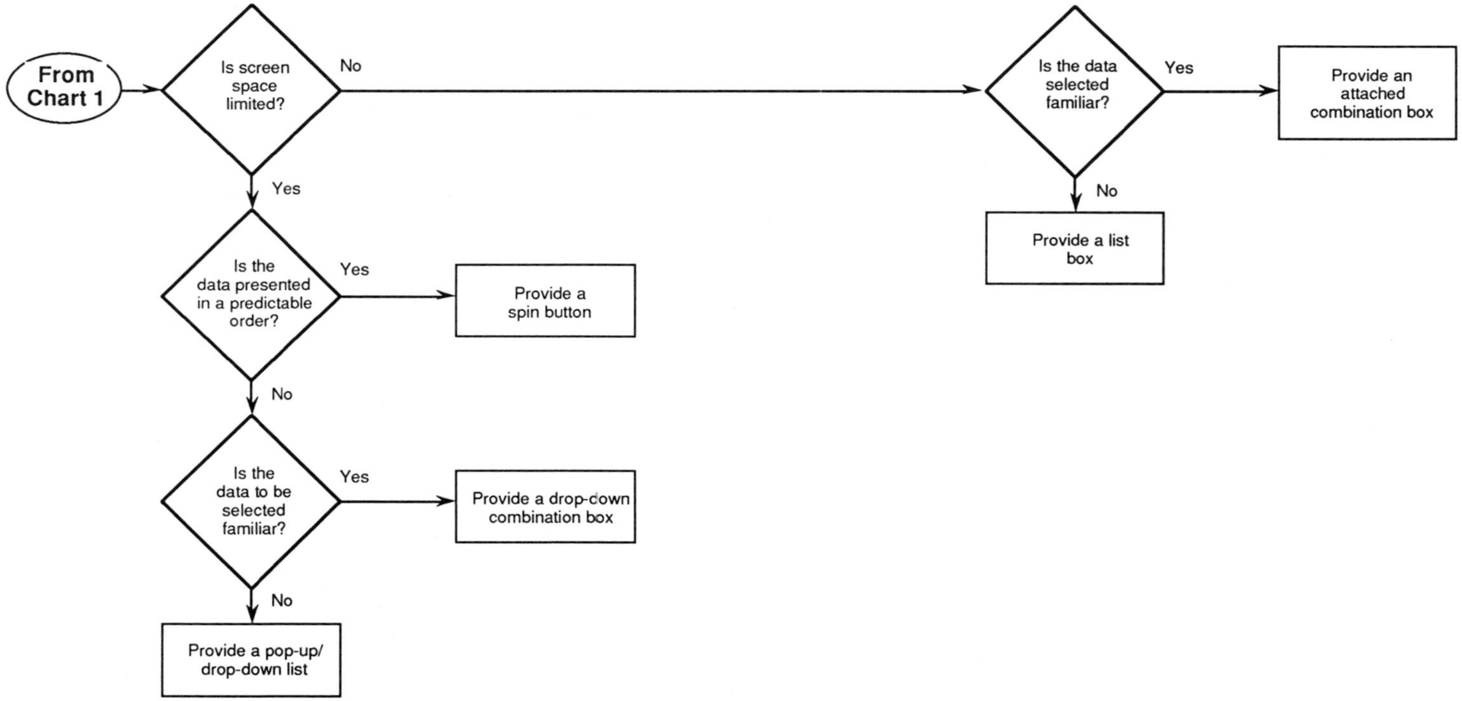

— leaving a space line between the prompt and the fields to which they refer, if possible.
— using a mixed-case font.

Type the following for changes only.

Kind:

Amount:

Effective Date:

Prompting messages are instructions to the screen user on what to do with, or how to work with, the screen being presented. They are analogous to instructions for filling out a paper form.

When it is necessary to place them on a screen, they must be identified as prompts. This will permit them to be easily ignored when they are not needed. Therefore, some visual aspect of the prompt must indicate that it *is* a prompt.

Displaying them in a unique color or in a unique font on all screens is one way to do this. If one of these methods is used, the cautions concerning the excessive use of color and different font styles must be heeded. Another method is to identify the prompt simply by its location. Begin the prompt to the left of the field captions (or headings) to which it applies. This left-justification will identify it as a prompt.

Try to leave a space line between the prompting message and the fields to which it relates, whenever possible. Screen space constraints may not always permit the space line, however. The prompt should be displayed in normal sentence-style capitalization.

MULTIPLE FIELD ALIGNMENT

On screens containing multiple fields, it is important to provide the viewer an obvious and efficient scanning and handling sequence. Eye and pointer movements must be minimized, eye movement direction must be obvious, and a consistent and predictable pattern must be followed. This is best achieved when the fields are arrayed in columns.

Columns

Selection Fields

- Align both choice descriptions and selection indicators.
- Field captions may be left- or right-aligned.

Justification: ○   None
                 ○   Left
                 ○   Even
                 ○   Center

Contents: ☐   Preface
            ☐   Illustrations
            ☐   Index
            ☐   Bibliography

Entry Fields

- Left-align the entry fields.
  — If the screen will be used for inquiry or display purposes, numeric fields should be right-aligned.
- Field captions may be left- or right-aligned.

Number of Chapters: ▢

Number of Pages: ▢

Cost: ▢

Mixed Entry and Selection Fields

- Align the entry fields and the buttons and/or check boxes.
- Field captions may be left- or right-aligned.
- Leave one (1) space between the longest columnized caption and the column of buttons, check boxes, and/or entry fields.

Left-Aligned Captions

Justification: ○   None
                     ○   Left
                     ○   Even
                     ○   Center

Contents: ☐   Preface
                     ☐   Illustrations
                     ☐   Index
                     ☐   Bibliography

Number of Chapters: ▢

Number of Pages: ▢

Cost: ▢

Right-Aligned Captions

Justification: ○ None
○ Left
○ Even
○ Center

Contents: ☐ Preface
☐ Illustrations
☐ Index
☐ Bibliography

Number of Chapters: [   ]

Number of Pages: [   ]

Cost: [   ]

A columnar list of fields is always the preferred manner of screen structuring. Two, or sometimes three, columns of data may be created. When multicolumns are created, column separation may be emphasized through borders, to be described shortly.

In some cases, screen space constraints may dictate a horizontal orientation of fields. The scanning and entry pattern created must again be consistent and predictable.

Horizontal Alignment

Selection Fields

- Align leftmost radio buttons and/or check boxes.
- Field captions may be left- or right-aligned.

Left-Aligned Captions

Justification: ○ None   ○ Left   ○ Even   ○ Center

Contents: ☐ Preface   ☐ Illustrations   ☐ Index   ☐ Bibliography

Right-Aligned Captions

Justification: ○ None   ○ Left   ○ Even   ○ Center

Contents: ☐ Preface   ☐ Illustrations   ☐ Index   ☐ Bibliography

Entry Fields

- Left-align entry fields into columns.
- Captions may be left- or right-aligned.

Left-Aligned Captions

Author: [   ]   Organization: [   ]

Location: [   ]   Building: [   ]

Right-Aligned Captions

Author: [   ]   Organization: [   ]

Location: [   ]   Building: [   ]

— Numeric data fields should be right-aligned.

Length: [   ]   Width: [   ]

Thickness: [   ]   Weight: [   ]

Mixed Entry and Selection Fields

- Align leftmost radio buttons and/or check boxes.
- Align leftmost entry field under leftmost choice description button or box.
- Captions may be left- or right-aligned.

Left-Aligned Captions

Justification: ○ None   ○ Left   ○ Even   ○ Center

Contents: □ Preface   □ Illustrations   □ Index   □ Bibliography

Author: [   ]   Organization: [   ]

Location: [   ]   Building: [   ]

Right-Aligned Captions

Justification: ○ None   ○ Left   ○ Even   ○ Center

Contents: ☐ Preface   ☐ Illustrations   ☐ Index   ☐ Bibliography

Author: [   ]   Organization: [   ]

Location: [   ]   Building: [   ]

For horizontally oriented fields, the objective is to create as few alignment points as possible. Since the information will be read left-to-right, care must be exercised, however, not to excessively separate related information. Final positioning will be a tradeoff between minimizing column alignments and keeping related information together. Although the above example illustrates the entry fields structured left-to-right, every attempt should be made to maintain a top-to-bottom orientation of entry fields. The information in the above example will be more effectively structured as follows:

Justification: ○ None   ○ Left   ○ Even   ○ Center

Contents: ☐ Preface   ☐ Illustrations   ☐ Index   ☐ Bibliography

Author: [   ]

Location: [   ]

Organization: [   ]

Building: [   ]

HEADINGS

Headings are used to give related fields a common identity. In addition to providing meaning, they foster the concept of grouping. As studies have shown (see Grouping in Chapter 4), groupings aid learning. Three kinds of headings may be incorporated on graphic screens: section, subsection or row, and field group.

Section Headings

- Locate section headings above their related screen fields, separated by one (1) space line.

- Indent the field captions a minimum of five spaces to the right of the start of the heading.
- Fully spell out in an upper-case font.
  — If a larger or bolder typeface is available, they may be displayed larger or bolder in mixed case.
- Display in normal intensity.
- Section headings may be left- or right-aligned.

DOCUMENT
x x x x x Justification: ○ None
                          ○ Left
                          ○ Even
                          ○ Center

Contents: ☐ Preface
           ☐ Illustrations
           ☐ Index
           ☐ Bibliography

Sections headings should be visually distinguishable through a combination of location and font style. They should not be overly emphasized, however. Displaying in upper case and positioning to the left will provide the moderate emphasis needed. Use of a slightly larger or slightly bolder typeface in mixed case is also acceptable, if available. IBM's SAA CUA gives visual emphasis to section headings through higher intensity in a mixed-case font. Higher intensity should be reserved for the more important screen data. Mixed case should only be used if it can be made slightly larger or bolder than the field captions.

If right-aligned or justified captions are used, an indention greater than five spaces may be necessary to properly set off the heading from the captions. Other techniques than positional cues may be used to set off section headings. Choices may include different style characters, underlining, etc. The method chosen should always permit easy, but subtle, discrimination of the section headings from other components of the screen. It should also be visually compatible with other screen components. Whatever methods are chosen, they should be consistently followed throughout a family of screens or a system.

Subsection or Row Headings

- Locate to the left of the
  — row of associated fields.
  — topmost row of a group of associated fields.
- Fully spell out in an upper-case font.
- Separate from the adjacent caption through the use of a unique symbol, such as two "greater than" signs or a filled-in arrow.

- Separate the symbol from the heading by one (1) space and from the caption by a minimum of three (3) spaces.
- Display in normal intensity.
- Subsection or row headings may be left- or right-aligned.

AUTO ▶   Make: [   ]   Model: [   ]

                Year: [   ]   Color: [   ]

REGISTRATIONx▶xxxNumber: [   ]   Expires: [   ]

A meaningful convention to designate subsection or row headings is a filled-in arrow or "greater than" sign. It directs the viewers attention to the right and indicates that everything that follows refers to this category. Subsections should be broken by space lines. They may also be right-aligned instead of left-aligned as follows:

AUTO ▶
REGISTRATION ▶

Field Group Headings

- Center field group headings above the captions to which they apply.
- Relate to those captions by a solid line.
- Spell out fully in an upper-case font.
- Display in normal intensity.

————————— AUTOMOBILE —————————

Driver   License Number

[   ]   [   ]

[   ]   [   ]

[   ]   [   ]

Occasionally a group heading above a series of multiple-occurring captions may be needed. It should be centered above the captions to which it applies and related to them through a solid line extending to each end of the grouping. This will provide closure to the grouping.

BORDERS

Borders can be used to provide a stronger visual grouping of the elements on a screen. They also enhance a screen's structure. Borders may be placed around fields or sections.

Field Borders

- Incorporate a thin single-line border around the elements of a selection field.
- For spacing:
    - Vertically, leave one (1) space line above and below the field elements.
    - Horizontally:
        - Leave at least two (2) character positions between the border and the left side of the field elements.
        - Leave at least two (2) character positions between the border and the right side of the longest field element.
    - Locate the field caption in the top border, indented one (1) character position from the left border.

```
 ┌ Contents ───────────┐
 │                      │
 │xx ☐ Preface          │
 │   ☐ Illustrationsxx  │
 │   ☐ Index            │
 │   ☐ Bibliography     │
 │                      │
 └──────────────────────┘
```

- If the field caption exceeds the length of the choice descriptions, extend the border two (2) character positions to the right of the caption.

```
 ┌Justification┐
 │          xx │
 │   ○ None     │
 │   ○ Left     │
 │   ○ Center   │
 │   ○ Right    │
 └──────────────┘
```

- If more than one field with borders is incorporated within a column on a screen,
    - align the field elements following the guidelines for multiple-field alignment.
    - align the left and right borders of all groups.
    - establish the left and right border positions by the spacing required for the widest element within the groups.

┌─ Contents ─────────────────┐
│   │
│   ☐ Preface   │
│   ☐ Illustrations   │
│   ☐ Index   │
│   ☐ Bibliography   │
│   │
└────────────────────────────┘

┌─ Justification ────────────┐
│   │
│   ○ None   │
│   ○ Left   │
│   ○ Center   │
│   ○ Right   │
│   │
└────────────────────────────┘

With multigroupings and multicolumns, create a balanced screen by
— maintaining equal column widths as much as practical.
— maintaining equal column heights as much as practical.

With boxed-in fields, the caption may be placed within the border itself. Screen balance, equal alignments, and group sizes should be attained as much as possible. Do not sacrifice screen functionality to achieve balance, however. Never rearrange fields to simply make the screen "look nice." A meaningful order of elements is most important. The "look" will be the best that can be achieved within the limits imposed by functionality.

Section Borders

- Incorporate a thin single-line border around groups of related entry or selection fields.
- For spacing:
  — Vertically, leave one (1) space line between the top and bottom row of the entry or selection field elements.

—Horizontally, leave at least four (4) character positions to the left and right of the longest caption and/or entry field.
- Locate the section heading in the top border, indented two (2) character positions from the left border.

```
┌─ DOCUMENT ─────────────────────┐
│                                │
│ xxxxJustification:  ○ None     │
│                     ○ Left     │
│                     ○ Center   │
│                     ○ Right    │
│                                │
│                                │
│         Contents:  ☐ Preface   │
│                    ☐ Illustrationsxxxx│
│                    ☐ Index     │
│                    ☐ Bibliography│
│                                │
└────────────────────────────────┘
```

- If more than one section with borders is incorporated within a column on a screen:
    —Align the left and right borders of all groups.
    —Establish the left and right border positions by the spacing required by the widest element within the groups.

```
┌─ DOCUMENT ─────────────────────────┐
│                                    │
│ xxxxJustification:    ○ None       │
│                       ○ Left       │
│                       ○ Center     │
│                       ○ Right      │
│                                    │
│                                    │
│           Contents:   ☐ Preface    │
│                       ☐ Illustrations│
│                       ☐ Index      │
│                       ☐ Bibliography│
│                                    │
└────────────────────────────────────┘
┌─ AUTHOR ───────────────────────────┐
│                                    │
│         Name:  [                ]xxxx│
│                                    │
│    Telephone:  [            ]      │
│                                    │
└────────────────────────────────────┘
```

—With multigroupings and multicolumns, create a balanced screen by
    — maintaining equal column widths as much as practical.

— maintaining equal column heights as much as practical.

With boxed-in groupings, the section heading may be placed within the border itself. With a group border, the indention of the caption under the section heading is less (only two characters) because the border helps visually set off the heading.

Screen balance, equal alignments, and group sizes should be attained as much as possible. Again, do not sacrifice screen functionality to achieve balance. Never rearrange elements for appearance only. Also, do not overuse line borders. If field borders are incorporated on the screen, section borders are probably not necessary. Too many lines leads to a cluttered look.

OTHER WINDOW COMPONENTS

Windows will contain many of the same elements found on full screens plus some additional elements. In some cases they may look like a full screen as they consume the full screen display area. Most windows, however, are smaller than full-screen size, being just large enough to clearly display what they must present. Windows may contain the following additional components.

Window Title

- All windows must have a title located in a centered position at the top.
  — Exception: Window containing messages.
- Clearly and concisely describe the purpose of the window.
- Spell out fully using an upper-case font.
- If title truncation is necessary, truncate from right to left.
- If presented above an action/menu bar, display with a background that contrasts with the bar.

The window title should be positioned at the top center and fully spelled out using upper-case or capital letters. Using an upper-case font will give it the needed moderate emphasis, aiding setting it off from the screen body (IBM's SAA CUA displays the title, like all screen components, in mixed-case letters). Windows containing messages, however, need not have a title. The title should clearly and concisely describe the screen's purpose. If the window appears as a result of a previous selection, the title should clearly reflect the wording of the selection made to retrieve it. For small windows where title truncation is necessary, truncate from right to left.

If the title appears above an action/menu bar, the title's background should contrast with that of the bar. A recommendation is to use the same background color, and caption color, as the screen body. A title can always be identified by its topmost location on the screen, so using a color different from other screen components may add to visual confusion.

Special Fields

- Display any special fields
  - —in the right corner of the title line if there is only one such field.
  - —in the left and right corners of the title line if there are two fields.
- Use a mixed-case font.
- Maintain a consistent positioning of the same field on all screens.

Display special fields, such as file names, in a consistent location on all screens. Display in a mixed-case font, or the font style in which the information is normally found. If multiple special fields are needed, provide screen balance by displaying them in the left and right corners of the title line.

Command/Action Techniques

- Each window should have its own commands and functions, either an action/menu bar, pull-downs, buttons, or function key listing.

Action/Menu Bars

- Follow the action/menu bar guidelines in this chapter.

Pull-Downs

- Follow the pull-down guidelines in this chapter.

Buttons

- Follow the button guidelines in this chapter.

Function Keys

- Follow the function key guidelines in Chapter 4.

Each window should have its own commands and functions. See the relevant guidelines for these components in this text.

Messages

- Display all messages in windows.
- Use a mixed-case font.
- Fully spell out using clear, concise words.
- Precede each type of message with a unique icon, if possible:
  — For informational or status messages, use a lower-case "i" within a circle.

  — For warning messages, use an exclamation point within a circle.

  — For critical, error, or action messages, use a stop sign.

- Use contrasting background and foreground colors for each type of message.

Precede each message with the icons described above. They will make each message type instantly recognizable. More information on message style and structure will be found in the section on Messages in Chapter 4. Additional information concerning color in messages will be found in Chapter 13.

Window Borders and Separation

- A window must be crisply, clearly, and pleasingly demarcated from the background of the screen on which it appears.
  — Provide a surrounding solid-line border for the window.
  — Provide a window background that sets off well against the overall screen background.
  — Incorporate a drop shadow beneath the window.
- To identify different kinds of windows, different kinds of borders or different color backgrounds may be used.
  — Limit variations to no more than three of each kind.
- If the window is the active window, display it brighter or lighter than the remainder of the screen.

Clearly demarcate windows from screen background. All windows must be clearly set off from the underlying screen or windows. The demarcation must be crisp and visually pleasing. A solid single-line border is recommended for this purpose. Also provide a window background that sets off well against the overall screen background. If color is used, exercise caution and choose compatible colors. (See Chapter 13, Color in Screen Design.) Another alternative is to use for the window a lighter shade of the color used for the screen background. Changes in the density of shades are often more visually pleasing. To emphasize the three-dimensional aspects of graphic windows, incorporate a drop shadow beneath each window.

Identifying different kinds of windows. To designate different kinds of windows, different kinds of borders or different color backgrounds may be used. Care must be exercised if this is done, however. Too many variations will only lead to confusion. No more than three different line widths or styles, or three background colors, should ever be used. (Also see Figure 11.1 in Chapter 11.)

Identifying the active window. If the window is the active window, display it brighter or lighter than other windows and the screen background.

Example 1. The "personal automobile" data elements illustrated in Chapters 5 and 6 are illustrated using windows in a graphical environment.

Screens 1-1 and 1-2. Supplemental insurance for automobiles is selected from the action/menu bar and related pull-down.

```
               QUALITY PERSONAL INSURANCE
┌──────────────┬────────────┬─────────────────────────────────────────┐
│ Application  │ Supplement │ Change  Renew  Quote  Cancel   Help  Exit │
└──────────────┴────────────┴─────────────────────────────────────────┘
```

```
               QUALITY PERSONAL INSURANCE
┌──────────────┬────────────┬─────────────────────────────────────────┐
│ Application  │ Supplement │ Change  Renew  Quote  Cancel   Help  Exit │
└──────────────┼────────────┴──────────────┐──────────────────────────┘
               │ Automobile...              │
               │ Fire...                    │
               │ Health...                  │
               │ Homeowners...              │
               │ Life...                    │
               └────────────────────────────┘
```

Screen 1-3. The applicant's name and policy number is requested in the first window displayed. The fields are aligned and columnized. An "OK" action triggers display of the next window.

```
               QUALITY PERSONAL INSURANCE
┌──────────────┬────────────┬─────────────────────────────────────────┐
│ Application  │ Supplement │ Change  Renew  Quote  Cancel   Help  Exit │
└──────────────┴────────────┴─────────────────────────────────────────┘
┌────────────────────────────────────────────────────────┐
│         AUTOMOBILE SUPPLEMENT - APPLICANT                │
│                                                          │
│                                                          │
│   Name:              ┌─────────────────────────────┐     │
│                      └─────────────────────────────┘     │
│   Policy Number:     ┌───────────────────────┐           │
│                      └───────────────────────┘           │
│                                                          │
│         ┌──────────┐  ┌──────────┐  ┌──────────┐         │
│         │    OK    │  │  Cancel  │  │   Help   │         │
│         └──────────┘  └──────────┘  └──────────┘         │
│                                                          │
└────────────────────────────────────────────────────────┘
```

Screen 1-4. Driver 1 personal data is requested. Captions and data fields are left-aligned (with the exception of the "If student" field which only appears if the occupation is answered as "student." This window, and following windows, cascade below-right one another. Title is left visible on lower windows and the hidden windows are displayed less brighterly (or subdued).

```
                      QUALITY PERSONAL INSURANCE
┌──────────────────────────────────────────────────────────────────────┐
│ Application  Supplement  Change  Renew  Quote  Cancel    Help  Exit    │
└──────────────────────────────────────────────────────────────────────┘

        ┌──────────────────────────────────────────────────┐
        │    AUTOMOBILE SUPPLEMENT - APPLICANT               │
     ┌──┴──────────────────────────────────────────────┐   │
     │             DRIVER 1 - PERSONAL DATA              │   │
     │                                                   │──┘
     │                                                   │
     │   Name:            ┌──────────────────────────┐   │
     │                    └──────────────────────────┘   │
     │   Birth Date:      ┌──────────────────┐           │
     │                    └──────────────────┘           │
     │   Sex:             O Male      O Female           │
     │   Marital Status:  O Single    O Married          │
     │   Occupation:      ┌──────────────────────────┐   │
     │                    └──────────────────────────┘   │
     │        If Student, Miles from Home:  ┌────────┐   │
     │                                      └────────┘   │
     │                                                   │
     │     ┌──────────┐  ┌──────────┐  ┌──────────┐     │
     │     │    OK    │  │  Cancel  │  │   Help   │     │
     │     └──────────┘  └──────────┘  └──────────┘     │
     └───────────────────────────────────────────────────┘
```

Screen 1-5.   Driver 1 license, discount, and restriction information is requested. If additional drivers exist, the "More Drivers" button can be selected and a pair of Driver 2 windows will be displayed next. If "OK" is selected, a Vehicle 1 Description window will be displayed.

QUALITY PERSONAL INSURANCE

| Application | Supplement | Change Renew Quote Cancel   Help Exit |

AUTOMOBILE SUPPLEMENT - APPLICANT

DRIVER 1 - PERSONAL DATA

DRIVER 1 - LICENSE / DISCOUNTS / RESTRICTIONS

License Number: [   ]

State: [   ]

Years Licensed: [   ]

Good Student: O Yes   O No

Driver Training: O Yes   O No

Impaired Driver: O Yes   O No

| More Drivers... | | OK | | Cancel | | Help |

Screens 1-6 and 1-7. These screens request information regarding vehicle description and usage. If additional vehicles exist, a "More Vehicles" button can be selected.

```
                    QUALITY PERSONAL INSURANCE
 ┌─────────────────────────────────────────────────────────────┐
 │ Application │Supplement│ Change  Renew  Quote  Cancel   Help  Exit │
 └─────────────────────────────────────────────────────────────┘

        ┌──────────────────────────────────────────────┐
        │        AUTOMOBILE SUPPLEMENT - APPLICANT      │
      ┌─┴──────────────────────────────────────────────┴─┐
      │            DRIVER 1 - PERSONAL DATA               │
    ┌─┴───────────────────────────────────────────────────┴─┐
    │    DRIVER 1 - LICENSE / DISCOUNTS / RESTRICTIONS       │
  ┌─┴───────────────────────────────────────────────────────┴─┐
  │               VEHICLE 1 - DESCRIPTION                      │
  │                                                            │
  │                                                            │
  │     Vehicle Year:         ┌─────┐                          │
  │                           └─────┘                          │
  │     New/Used:             O New        O Used              │
  │                                                            │
  │     Make/Model/Style:     ┌──────────────────────┐         │
  │                           └──────────────────────┘         │
  │     Identification #:     ┌──────────────────┐             │
  │                           └──────────────────┘             │
  │     Horsepower:           ┌────┐                           │
  │                           └────┘                           │
  │     Symbol:               ┌─────┐                          │
  │                           └─────┘                          │
  │     Modified:             O Yes        O No                │
  │                                                            │
  │     Damaged:              O Yes        O No                │
  │                                                            │
  │            ┌────────┐  ┌────────┐  ┌────────┐              │
  │            │   OK   │  │ Cancel │  │  Help  │              │
  │            └────────┘  └────────┘  └────────┘              │
  └────────────────────────────────────────────────────────────┘
```

QUALITY PERSONAL INSURANCE

| <u>A</u>pplication | <u>S</u>upplement | <u>C</u>hange | <u>R</u>enew | <u>Q</u>uote | Ca<u>n</u>cel | <u>H</u>elp | <u>E</u>xit |

AUTOMOBILE SUPPLEMENT - APPLICANT

DRIVER 1 - PERSONAL DATA

DRIVER 1 - LICENSE / DISCOUNTS / RESTRICTIONS

VEHICLE 1 - DESCRIPTION

VEHICLE 1 - USAGE

Class: [   ]

Territory: [   ]

Use: ○ Pleasure ○ Work

  Miles to Work: [   ]

Annual Miles: [   ]

[More Vehicles...]   [OK]   [Cancel]   [Help]

Screens 1-8 and 1-9. Lienholder and payor information is requested. Captions and data are columnized and aligned. Both windows are repeatable, if necessary.

QUALITY PERSONAL INSURANCE

| Application | Supplement | Change Renew Quote Cancel | Help Exit |

AUTOMOBILE SUPPLEMENT - APPLICANT

DRIVER 1 - PERSONAL DATA

DRIVER 1 - LICENSE / DISCOUNTS / RESTRICTIONS

VEHICLE 1 - DESCRIPTION

VEHICLE 1 - USAGE

LIENHOLDER 1

Vehicle #: [   ]

Name 1: [   ]

Name 2: [   ]

Street: [   ]

City/St/Zip: [   ] [   ] [   ]

| More Lienhldr... | OK | Cancel | Help |

QUALITY PERSONAL INSURANCE

| Application | Supplement | Change | Renew | Quote | Cancel | Help | Exit |

AUTOMOBILE SUPPLEMENT - APPLICANT

DRIVER 1 - PERSONAL DATA

DRIVER 1 - LICENSE / DISCOUNTS / RESTRICTIONS

VEHICLE 1 - DESCRIPTION

VEHICLE 1 - USAGE

LIENHOLDER 1

PAYOR 1

Complete only if payor is other than insured.

Name 1:

Name 2:

Street:

City/St/Zip:

Account #:

Telephone #:

| More Payors... | OK | Cancel | Help |

Example 2. A series of screens containing the same entry fields, selection fields (check boxes and radio buttons), and buttons. An evolution in design, from poor to good, is illustrated.

Screen 2-1.   A poor screen. Problems include poor alignment of entry and selection fields and poor visual differentiation of section headings from field captions. Equal spacing between selection field choice descriptions and check boxes/radio buttons makes association with correct description difficult. The variable widths of the buttons located to the right of the screen create a visually ragged edge, create inconsistent size selection targets, and in one case, creates a very small selection target (OK button). The most desirable location of buttons is at the bottom of the screen.

Screen 2-2. A better screen. The screen title and section headings are set off from the field captions through use of capital letters. The amount of indention of the captions under the section headings is also increased. The entry fields and selection fields are aligned. The check boxes/radio buttons are properly associated with their choice descriptions through increased spacing between alternatives. The buttons are made equal in size, creating a more pleasing visual array and larger-size targets.

```
                          PROPERTY

  LOCATION
                                                        ┌─────────┐
        Address:  ┌──────────────────────────────┐      │   OK    │
                  └──────────────────────────────┘      └─────────┘
                                                        ┌─────────┐
        Township: ┌────────────────────────────┐        │  Reset  │
                  └────────────────────────────┘        └─────────┘
  DESCRIPTION                                           ┌─────────┐
                                                        │ Cancel  │
        Acres:    ┌────────┐                            └─────────┘
                  └────────┘                            ┌─────────┐
        Frontage: ┌──────────┐                          │  Help   │
                  └──────────┘                          └─────────┘

        Terrain:   □ Open  □ Wooded  □ Level  □ Rolling  □ Water

        Dwellings: □ House  □ Garage  □ Barn  □ Store  □ Other

        Zoning:    ○ Agricultural  ○ Commercial  ○ Residential
```

Screen 2-3.   A still better screen. Borders are included around groups of related information. Buttons are moved to the bottom of the screen.

```
                            PROPERTY
   ┌─ LOCATION ──────────────────────────────────────────┐
   │                                                      │
   │    Address:   ┌──────────────────────────────┐       │
   │               └──────────────────────────────┘       │
   │    Township:  ┌─────────────────────────┐            │
   │               └─────────────────────────┘            │
   └──────────────────────────────────────────────────────┘
   ┌─ DESCRIPTION ────────────────────────────────────────┐
   │                                                      │
   │    Acres:     ┌──────┐                                │
   │               └──────┘                                │
   │    Frontage:  ┌──────────┐                            │
   │               └──────────┘                            │
   │    Terrain:    □ Open  □ Wooded  □ Level  □ Rolling  □ Water │
   │    Dwellings: □ House  □ Garage  □ Barn  □ Store  □ Other │
   │    Zoning:     ○ Agricultural  ○ Commercial  ○ Residential │
   └──────────────────────────────────────────────────────┘

        ┌────────┐   ┌────────┐   ┌────────┐   ┌────────┐
        │   OK   │   │ Reset  │   │ Cancel │   │ Help   │
        └────────┘   └────────┘   └────────┘   └────────┘
```

Screen 2-4.   The best alternative. The entire screen, including the DESCRIP-
TION section is oriented for consistent top-to-bottom entry. The selection fields
and alternatives are set off from one another much better and more efficiently
and easily scanned.

```
                              PROPERTY
    ┌ LOCATION ─────────────────────────────────────────────┐
    │     Address:  [                                   ]     │
    │    Township:  [                             ]           │
    └────────────────────────────────────────────────────────┘
    ┌ DESCRIPTION ──────────────────────────────────────────┐
    │      Acres:    [              ]  │ Dwellings:  ☐ House  │
    │                                  │             ☐ Garage │
    │   Frontage:    [        ]        │             ☐ Barn   │
    │                                  │             ☐ Store  │
    │    Terrain:  ☐ Open              │             ☐ Other  │
    │              ☐ Wooded            │                      │
    │              ☐ Level             │   Zoning:   ○ Agricultural │
    │              ☐ Rolling           │             ○ Commercial   │
    │              ☐ Water             │             ○ Residential  │
    └────────────────────────────────────────────────────────┘
         [   OK   ]   [  Reset  ]   [  Cancel  ]   [  Help  ]
```

Example 3. A series of screens containing the same entry fields, selection fields, and buttons as shown in Example 2. The selection field technique is rectangular boxes, however, not radio buttons or check boxes. An evolution in design, from poor to good, is again illustrated.

Screen 3-1. A poor screen. Problems include poor alignment of entry and selection fields and poor visual differentiation of section headings from field captions. The nonexclusive choice fields (Terrain and Dwellings) are not visually discernible from the exclusive choice field (Zoning). The variable widths of the buttons located to the right of the screen create a visually ragged edge, create inconsistent-size selection targets, and in one case, creates a very small selection target (OK button). The most desirable location of buttons is at the bottom of the screen.

```
                          Property


      Location                                    ┌──────┐
                                                  │  OK  │
           Address:  ┌──────────────────────┐     └──────┘
                     └──────────────────────┘     ┌──────┐
           Township: ┌──────────────────────┐     │Reset │
                     └──────────────────────┘     └──────┘
      Description                                 ┌──────┐
                                                  │Cancel│
           Acres:    ┌─────────┐                  └──────┘
                     └─────────┘                  ┌──────┐
           Frontage: ┌────┐                       │ Help │
                     └────┘                       └──────┘
           Terrain:  │ Open │ Wooded │ Level │ Rolling │ Water │

           Dwellings: │ House │ Garage │ Barn │ Store │ Other │

           Zoning:   │ Agricultural │ Commercial │ Residential │
```

Screen 3-2. A better screen. The screen title and section headings are set off from the field captions through use of capital letters. The amount of indention of the captions under the section headings is also increased. The entry fields and selection fields are aligned. Nonexclusive and exclusive fields are differentiated through separating the nonexclusive field (Terrain and Dwelling) rectangular boxes.

Screen 3-3.   A still better screen. Borders are included around groups of related information. Buttons are moved to the bottom of the screen.

Screen 3-4.   The best alternative. The entire screen, including the DESCRIP-
TION section is oriented for consistent top-to-bottom entry. The selection fields
and alternatives are set off from one another much better and more efficiently
and easily scanned.

```
┌────────────────────────────────────────────────────────────────────┐
│                          PROPERTY                                   │
│   ┌─ LOCATION ──────────────────────────────────────────────────┐  │
│   │                                                              │  │
│   │      Address:  ┌─────────────────────────────┐              │  │
│   │                └─────────────────────────────┘              │  │
│   │      Township: ┌─────────────────────────────┐              │  │
│   │                └─────────────────────────────┘              │  │
│   └──────────────────────────────────────────────────────────────┘ │
│                                                                     │
│   ┌─ DESCRIPTION ────────────────────────────────────────────────┐ │
│   │                                                              │  │
│   │      Acres:    ┌─────────┐      Dwellings: ┌─House────────┐  │  │
│   │                └─────────┘                 ├─Garage───────┤  │  │
│   │                                            ├─Barn─────────┤  │  │
│   │      Frontage: ┌────┐                      ├─Store────────┤  │  │
│   │                └────┘                      └─Other────────┘  │  │
│   │                                                              │  │
│   │      Terrain:  ┌─Open─────┐                                  │  │
│   │                ├─Wooded───┤                                  │  │
│   │                ├─Level────┤     Zoning:    ┌─Agricultural─┐  │  │
│   │                ├─Rolling──┤                ├─Commercial───┤  │  │
│   │                └─Water────┘                └─Residential──┘  │  │
│   └──────────────────────────────────────────────────────────────┘ │
│                                                                     │
│     ┌─────────┐   ┌─────────┐    ┌─────────┐    ┌─────────┐         │
│     │   OK    │   │  Reset  │    │ Cancel  │    │  Help   │         │
│     └─────────┘   └─────────┘    └─────────┘    └─────────┘         │
└────────────────────────────────────────────────────────────────────┘
```

Example 4. A series of screens containing the same entry fields, selection fields, and buttons as shown in Examples 2 and 3. The selection fields, however, are radio buttons and check boxes with field borders incorporated around them. An evolution in design, from poor to good, is again illustrated.

Screen 4-1. A poor screen. Problems again include poor alignment of entry and selection fields. Required eye movement through the screen is inconsistent, flowing left to right through the first four fields, then switching down at Terrain, then back and to the right to Zoning, then across Zoning and then down and across Dwelling. Section headings are not included within the screen. The screen's overall appearance is irregular and disjointed. The buttons located at the bottom of the screen are not centered and inconsistent in size, in one case, creating a very small selection target (OK button).

```
                         Property

  Address: [                    ]  Township: [              ]

  Acres: [      ]  Frontage: [      ]

   ┌─Terrain ─┐ ┌─Zoning ──────────────────────────────┐
   │          │ │                                       │
   │ ☐ Open   │ │ ○ Agricultural ○ Commercial ○ Residential │
   │ ☐ Wooded │ │    ┌─Dwellings ─────────────────────┐ │
   │ ☐ Level  │ │    │                                │ │
   │ ☐ Rolling│ │    │ ☐ House     ☐ Garage   ☐ Barn │ │
   │ ☐ Water  │ │    │ ☐ Store     ☐ Other           │ │
   └──────────┘ │    └────────────────────────────────┘ │
                └───────────────────────────────────────┘

   [ OK ]  [ Reset ]  [ Cancel ]  [ Help ]
```

Screen 4-2. A better screen. Section headings have been added and they, and the title, are set off from the field captions through use of capital letters. The entry fields and selection fields are aligned, space constraints dictating that the DE-SCRIPTION section maintain a left-to-right ordering. The buttons are made equal in size and centered, creating a more pleasing visual array and larger size targets.

PROPERTY

LOCATION

      Address: [   ]

    Township: [   ]

DESCRIPTION

       Acres: [   ]   Frontage: [   ]

┌─ Terrain ──┐ ┌─ Dwellings ─┐ ┌─ Zoning ─────────┐
│ ☐ Open   │ │ ☐ House   │ │ ○ Agricultural   │
│ ☐ Wooded   │ │ ☐ Garage   │ │ ○ Commercial   │
│ ☐ Level   │ │ ☐ Barn   │ │ ○ Residential   │
│ ☐ Rolling │ │ ☐ Store   │ │   │
│ ☐ Water   │ │ ☐ Other   │ │   │
└────────────┘ └─────────────┘ └──────────────────┘

[OK   ]   [Reset   ]   [Cancel   ]   [Help   ]

Screen 4-3. The best alternative. Thick line borders are incorporated around the two sections. The selection fields (Terrain, Dwelling, and Zoning) are made equal size for balance and symmetry.

```
                            PROPERTY
   ┌ LOCATION ──────────────────────────────────────────
   │
   │   Address:  ┌─────────────────────────────────────┐
   │             └─────────────────────────────────────┘
   │   Township: ┌──────────────────────────────┐
   │             └──────────────────────────────┘
   └───────────────────────────────────────────────────

   ┌ DESCRIPTION ───────────────────────────────────────
   │
   │   Acres:     ┌──────┐   Frontage: ┌──────┐
   │             └──────┘             └──────┘
   │
   │   ┌ Terrain ──────┐ ┌ Dwellings ────┐ ┌ Zoning ──────┐
   │   │ ☐ Open        │ │ ☐ House       │ │ ○ Agricultural│
   │   │ ☐ Wooded      │ │ ☐ Garage      │ │ ○ Commercial  │
   │   │ ☐ Level       │ │ ☐ Barn        │ │ ○ Residential │
   │   │ ☐ Rolling     │ │ ☐ Store       │ │               │
   │   │ ☐ Water       │ │ ☐ Other       │ │               │
   │   └───────────────┘ └───────────────┘ └──────────────┘
   └───────────────────────────────────────────────────

        ┌────────┐   ┌────────┐   ┌────────┐   ┌────────┐
        │   OK   │   │ Reset  │   │ Cancel │   │ Help   │
        └────────┘   └────────┘   └────────┘   └────────┘
```

Example 5.   A series of pull-down menu screens containing the same choices. An evolution in design, from poor to good, is illustrated.

Screens 5-1 and 5-2.   Poor screens. Groupings of related alternatives do not exist. The keyboard accelerators are too visually dominant, competing with the choice descriptions for the viewer's attention. Screen 5-1 has no line separators, screen 5-2 has too many line separators. Too many lines serve to visually disassociate all the choices.

File	Edit	View		Help	Exit
	Undo	Alt+Backspace			
	Cut	Shift+Del			
	Copy	Ctrl+Ins			
	Paste	Shift+Ins			
	Clear				
	Delete				

File	Edit	View		Help	Exit
	Undo	Alt+Backspace			
	Cut	Shift+Del			
	Copy	Ctrl+Ins			
	Paste	Shift+Ins			
	Clear				
	Delete				

Screen 5-3.   A better screen. Line separators have been drawn only between related groupings. These lines, extending from menu border to border, are too long however. These border-to-border lines create a visual break between menu elements that is too strong. A more subtle break is desirable. The keyboard accelerators have been reduced in emphasis by enclosing them within parentheses.

```
┌────────┬──────┬──────────────────────────────┬───────────────┐
│  File  │ Edit │ View                         │ Help    Exit  │
└────────┼──────┴─────────────────────────────────┬────────────┘
         │ Undo      (Alt+Backspace)              │
         ├────────────────────────────────────────┤
         │ Cut       (Shift+Del)                  │
         │                                        │
         │ Copy      (Ctrl+Ins)                   │
         │                                        │
         │ Paste     (Shift+Ins)                  │
         ├────────────────────────────────────────┤
         │ Clear                                  │
         │                                        │
         │ Delete                                 │
         └────────────────────────────────────────┘
```

Screen 5-4. The best alternative. The line separators have been reduced to extend the width of the menu alternative descriptions (including accelerators). The strong break between groupings is softened. The keyboard accelerators are right-aligned to create less visual competition with the descriptions.

File	Edit	View		Help	Exit

```
         Undo    (Alt+Backspace)
         ──────────────────────
         Cut          (Shift+Del)

         Copy          (Ctrl+Ins)

         Paste        (Shift+Ins)
         ──────────────────────
         Clear

         Delete
```

Iconic Screens   11

The symbolic representation of objects, such as office tools or storage locations, and optional actions on a screen began with Xerox's Star, continued with Apple's Lisa and Macintosh, and has been building ever since. Indeed, the faces of many 1990s screens scarcely resemble their older siblings of the early 1980s.

Direct-manipulation iconic systems burst upon the office with great promise. The symbols reflecting various familiar office objects and actions are presented on the screen and the user selects and manipulates them with a cursor typically controlled by a device such as the mouse. This simplification of the interface is thought to reduce the memory requirements imposed on the user, make more effective use of one's information-processing capabilities, and dramatically reduce system learning requirements. For many users it has done all these things.

However, as direct-manipulation iconic systems become increasingly sophisticated and continue to expand, interfaces have become increasingly more complex, sometimes arcane, and even bizarre (Baecker, et al., 1991). Many are neither easy to learn nor easy to use. It has become clear that the design of an interface and not its style is the best determinant of ease of use.

Characteristics of a Direct-Manipulation System

- Portrayal of the system as an extension of the real world.
- Continuous visibility of objects and actions of interest.
- Rapid incremental actions with immediate visible display of results.
- Easily reversible incremental actions.

An iconic system is a direct-manipulation system. This term was first used by Shneiderman (1982) to describe systems using this style of human-computer interaction. Direct-manipulation systems, more fully described in Chapter 10, have the following characteristics.

An extension of the real world.   It is assumed that the system user is already familiar with the objects and actions in the environment of interest. The system replicates and portrays them in a different medium, the screen. The user is allowed to work in a familiar environment and in a familiar way, focusing on the data, not the application and tools. The physical organization of the system, which may be unfamiliar, is hidden and not a distraction.

Continuous visibility of objects and actions.   Like one's desktop and office, objects are continuously visible. Reminders of actions to be performed are also obvious, labelled buttons replacing complex syntax and command names (Shneiderman, 1982). Cursor action and motion occurs in physically obvious and intuitively natural ways. Nelson (1980) described this as "virtual reality," a representation of reality that can be manipulated. Hatfield (1981) is credited with calling it "WYSIWYG" (what you see is what you get). Rutkowski (1982) described it as "transparency," where one's intellect is applied to the task, not the tool. Hutchins et al. (1986) consider it direct involvement with the world of objects rather than communicating with an intermediary.

Rapid incremental actions and visible display of results.   The results of actions are immediately displayed in their current form. The impact of a previous action is quickly seen. Evolution of tasks is graceful.

Easily reversible incremental actions.   Actions, if incorrect or unacceptable, can be easily undone.

Kinds of Icons

- Icon   — Something that looks like what it means.
- Index   — A sign that was caused by the thing to which it refers.
- Symbol   — A sign that may be completely arbitrary in appearance.

Objects and actions are depicted on screens through pictograms or symbols called icons. Marcus (1984) observes that what are commonly referred to as icons may really be indexes or symbols.

A true icon is something that looks like what it means. It is representational and easy to understand. A picture of a telephone or a clock on a screen is a true icon. An index is a sign caused by the thing to which it refers. An open door with a broken window indicates the possible presence of a burglar. The meaning of an index may or may not be clear, depending upon one's past experiences. A symbol is a sign that may be completely arbitrary in appearance and whose meaning must be learned. The menu and sizing icons on screens are examples of symbols. Strictly speaking, so-called icons on screens are probably a mixture of true icons, signs, and indexes.

Actually, icons to reflect objects, ideas, and actions are not new to mankind. We've been there before. Early humans (100,000 years or so ago) used pictographs and then ideographs to communicate. Some of these early communications can be found on rock walls and in caves around the world. Until recently this was also a way to communicate in some cultures (North American Indians, Australian Aborigines, for example). Again, traces can still be seen.

Word writing is traced back to Egyptian hieroglyphics from about 3000 B.C. This was followed by cuneiform (Babylonia and Assyria) from about 1900 B.C. and Chinese word signs (numbering about 50,000) around 1300 B.C. In 1000 B.C. the Phoenicians developed a 22-sign alphabet that the Greeks adopted about 800–600 B.C. The Greeks passed this alphabet on to the Romans about 400 B.C., who then developed a 23-character alphabet. It has been modified and embellished but has remained essentially the same for the last 2000 years.

Pictorial representations, then, have played a prominent role in mankind's history. Word writing, however, unleashed much more flexibility and richness in communication. This has caused some skeptics, such as Bigelow (1985), to wonder why, after taking 2500 years to get rid of iconic shapes, we are now reviving it on screens.

Characteristics of Icons

- Syntactics—   Their physical appearance.
- Semantics—   Their meaning.
- Pragmatics—   How they are produced or depicted.

An icon possesses the technical qualities of syntactics, semantics, and pragmatics (Marcus, 1984).

Syntactics refers to an icon's physical structure. Is it square, round, red, green, big, small? Are the similarities and differences obvious? Similar shapes and colors can classify a group of related icons, communicating a common relationship.

Semantics is the icon's meaning. To what does it refer—a file, a wastebasket, some other object? Is this clear?

Pragmatics are how the icons are physically produced and depicted. Is the screen resolution sufficient to clearly illustrate the icon?

Syntactics, semantics, and pragmatics determine an icon's effectiveness and useability.

Advantages of an Iconic System

- Faster recognition.
- Faster learning.
- Faster use and problem solving.
- Easier remembering.
- More natural.

- Exploits human use of visual/spatial cues.
- Fosters more concrete thinking.
- Provides context.
- Fewer errors.
- Increased feelings of control.
- Immediate feedback.
- Predictable system responses.
- Easily reversible actions.
- Less anxiety concerning use.
- More attractive.
- May consume less space.
- Replaces "national" languages.
- Easily augmented with alphanumeric displays.
- Low typing requirements.
- Smooth transition from a command language system.

The success of direct manipulation systems have been attributed to a host of factors. The following are commonly referenced in literature and endorsed by their advocates as advantages of these systems.

Faster recognition.   Symbols have been found to be recognized faster and more accurately than text (Ellis and Dewar, 1979). The graphical attributes of icons such as shape and color are very useful for quickly classifying objects, elements, or text by some common property (Gittens, 1986). An example of a good classification scheme that speeds up recognition are icons developed for indicating the kind of message presented to the viewer by the system. The text of an informational message is preceded by a small letter *i* in a circle, the text for action messages by a stop sign.

Faster learning.   A graphical, pictorial representation has been found to aid learning (Polya, 1957). Symbols can also be easily learned (Walker et al., 1965).

Faster use and problem solving.   Visual or spatial representation of information has been found to be easier to retain and manipulate (Wertheimer, 1959) and leads to faster and more successful problem solving (Carroll et al., 1980). Symbols have also been found to be effective in conveying simple instructions (Dickey and Schneider, 1971).

Easier remembering.   Because of greater simplicity, it is easier for casual users to retain operational concepts.

More natural.   Graphic representations of objects are thought to be more "natural" and closer to innate human capabilities. In humans, actions and visual skills emerge before languages. Lodding (1983) suggests symbolic displays are more natural and advantageous because the human mind has a powerful image memory.

Exploits visual/spatial cues.   Spatial relationships are usually found to be understood more quickly than verbal representations. Heckel (1984) suggests that thinking visually is better than thinking logically.

Fosters more concrete thinking.   Displayed objects are directly in the high-level task domain. There is no need to mentally decompose tasks into multiple commands with complex syntactic form (Shneiderman, 1982). Abstract thinking is therefore minimized.

Provides context.   Displayed objects are visible providing current context.

Fewer errors.   More concrete thinking affords fewer opportunities for errors. Reversibility of actions reduces error rates because it is always possible to undo the last step. Error messages are rarely needed.

Increased feeling of control.   The user initiates actions and feels in control. This increases user confidence and hastens system mastery.

Immediate feedback.   The results of actions furthering user goals can be seen immediately. Learning is quickened. If response is not in the desired direction, the direction can be quickly changed.

Predictable system responses.   Predictable system responses also speed learning.

Easily reversible actions.   The user has more control. This ability to reverse unwanted actions also increases user confidence and hastens system mastery.

Less anxiety concerning use.   Hesitant or new users feel less anxiety when using the system because it is so easily comprehended, easy to control, has predictable responses, and can reverse actions.

More attractive.   Direct-manipulation systems are more entertaining, more clever, and more appealing. This is especially important for the cautious or skeptical user.

May consume less space.   Icons may take up less space than the equivalent in words. More information can be packed in a given area of the screen.

Replaces "national" languages.   Language-based systems are seldom universally applicable. Language translations frequently cause problems in a text-based system. Icons possess much more universality than text and are much more easily comprehended worldwide.

Easily augmented with text displays.   Where iconic design limitations exist, direct-manipulation systems can easily be augmented with text displays. The reverse is not true.

Low typing requirements.   Pointing and selection controls such as the mouse or trackball eliminate the need for typing skills.

Smooth transition from command language system.   Moving from a command language to direct-manipulation has been found to be easy. The reverse is not true (Tombaugh, et al., 1989).

Disadvantages of an Iconic System

- Limited power, difficult to design for more complex applications.
- Working domain is the "present."
- Not always familiar.
- Learning still necessary.
- Human comprehension limitations restrict the number of different icons that can be introduced.
- Design limitations restrict the number of different icons that can be introduced.
- Few "tested" icons exist in necessary sizes, weights, and styles.
- Inefficient for touch typists.
- Inefficient for expert users.
- Not always preferred style of interaction.
- Not always fastest style of interaction.
- Increased chances of clutter and confusion.
- May consume more screen space.

The body of positive research, hypotheses, and comment concerning direct-manipulation systems is now being challenged by some studies, findings, and opinions that symbolic representation may not necessarily always be better, and in some cases may be worse than textual or alphanumeric displays. The disadvantages put forth are these.

Limited power.   Direct manipulation systems are more difficult to design. For more complex applications this can be a severe restriction. Poor design can undermine acceptance.

Working domain is the present.   Direct-manipulation systems, while providing context, also require the user to work in the "present." Hulteen (1989), in a parody of "WYSIWYG," suggests, "What you see is all you get." Walker (1989) argues that language takes you out of the here and now and the visually present. Language, she continues, makes it easier to find things.

Not always familiar.   Icons may not be as familiar as words or numbers. We have been exposed to words and numbers for a long time. Remington and Williams (1986) found that numeric symbols elicited faster responses than graphic symbols in a visual search task. Carney and Sless (1982) and Zwaga and Boersema (1983) found some current or proposed symbols were not very effective. Hair (1991) had to modify a new system during testing by replacing iconic representations with a textual outline format. The users, lawyers, were unfamiliar with icons and preferred a more familiar format.

Learning still necessary.   While many icons are instantly recognizable, many others are not, especially the more arbitrary "symbols." It is not often possible to guess the meaning of an icon. Some systems may still impose a substantial learning, and remembering, requirement on some users.

Human comprehension limitations.   The number of different icons that can be introduced is restricted due to human comprehension limitations. Studies continually find that the number of different symbols a person can differentiate and deal with is much more limited than text. (See Figure 11.1.) Gittens (1986) argues it will be difficult to find or develop and use icons dealing with the large number of computer system concepts and command parameters that exist. Kolers (1969) notes that claims for the easy understanding of pictograms are exaggerated, and that recognizing icons requires much perceptual learning, abstracting ability, and intelligence.

Design limitations.   The number of symbols that can be clearly produced using today's technology is limited. A body of recognizable symbols must be produced that are equally legible and equally recognizable using differing technologies. This is extremely difficult today.

Few "tested" icons exist.   Icons, as with typefaces, must appear in different sizes, weights, and styles. As with text, an entire "font" of clearly recognizable symbols must be developed. It is not simply a question of developing an icon and simply enlarging or reducing it. Changed size can differentially affect symbol line widths, open areas, and so forth, dramatically affecting its recognizability. Typeface design for words and text is literally the product of 300 years of experimentation and studies. Icons must be researched, designed, tested, and then introduced into the marketplace. Marcus (1984) says the consequences of poor, or improper, design will be confusion and lower productivity for users.

Inefficient for touch typists.   For an experienced touch typist, the keyboard is a very fast and powerful device. Moving a mouse or some other pointing mechanism may be slower.

Inefficient for expert users.   Inefficiencies develop when there are more objects and actions than can fit on the screen. Concatenation for a command language is impossible.

Not always preferred style of interaction.   Not all users prefer an iconic interface. Brems and Whitten (1987), in comparing commands illustrated by icons, icons with text, or text-only, found that users preferred alternatives with textual captions.

Figure 11.1   Maximum number of codes for effective human differentiation.

Encoding Method	Recommended Maximum	Comments
Alphanumerics	Unlimited	Highly versatile. Meaning usually self-evident. Location time may be longer than for graphic coding.
Geometric Shapes	10–20	High mnemonic value. Very effective if shape relates to object or operation being represented.
Size	3–5	Fair. Considerable space required. Location time longer than for colors and shapes.
Line Length	3–4	Will clutter the display if many are used.
Line Width	2–3	Good.
Line Style	5–9	Good.
Line Angle	8–11	Good in special cases (such as wind direction).
Solid and Broken Lines	3–4	Good.
Number of Dots or Marks	5	Minimize number for quick assimilation.
Brightness	2–3	Creates problems on screens with poor contrast.
Flashing/Blinking	2–3	Confusing for general encoding but the best way to attract attention. Interacts poorly with other codes. Annoying if overused. Limit to small fields.
Underlining	No data	Useful but can reduce text legibility.
Reverse Video	No data	Effective for making data stand out. Flicker easily perceived in large areas, however.
Orientation (location on display surface)	4–8	—
Color	6–8	Attractive and efficient. Short location time. Excessive use confusing. Poor for color blind.
Combinations of Codes	Unlimited	Can reinforce coding but complex combinations can be confusing.

Data derived from Martin, 1973; Barmack and Sinaiko, 1966; Mallory et al., 1980; Damodaran et al., 1980; and Maguire, 1985.

Not always fastest style of interaction.   Stern (1984) found that graphic instructions on an automated bank teller machine were inferior to textual instructions.

Increased chances of clutter and confusion.   An iconic system does not guarantee elimination of clutter on a screen. The converse is true, the chance for clutter is increased, thereby increasing the chance of possibility of confusion. How much screen clutter one can deal with is open to speculation.

May consume more screen space.   Not all applications will consume less screen space. A listing of names and telephone numbers in a textual format will be more efficient than a card file.

Some Studies and a Conclusion

Walker (1989) points out that most of the benefits of one interaction style versus another are anecdotal. This has made the debate between advocates of direct-manipulation and other styles of interaction more religious than scientific. This is certainly true for many of the arguments. In the last several years, however, there have been a handful of studies comparing alternative interaction styles. It is useful to summarize what they have found.

One of the first studies was undertaken by Whiteside et al. (1985). They compared the useability characteristics of seven systems, including direct-manipulation, menu, and command language styles of interaction. They found that user performance did not depend on the type of system. There were large differences in learnability and useability between all. How well the system was designed was the best indicator of success, not the style of interaction.

Brems and Whitten (1987) evaluated a family of seven commands for user preferences. The alternative design styles were commands described by icons only, icons with textual captions, and textual captions only. While the meanings of the icons were easily learned, textual captions were preferred to uncaptioned icons. Learning, they concluded, was not a good indicator of preference.

Frese, et al. (1987) compared learning and performance for direct-manipulation and command-based word processing systems. While no differences existed after the first experimental session, the direct-manipulation system user's performance became increasingly superior as the study progressed (and task complexity increased). It appeared that the direct-manipulation system facilitated the learning process as task complexity increased.

Shneiderman and Margono (1987) compared some simple file manipulation tasks using a direct-manipulation system (Macintosh) and a command language system (DOS). The direct-manipulation system was found best in learnability, performance time, and subjective ratings. Two other studies have found also graphical systems superior to command language styles for some kinds of tasks (Karat, 1987; Guastello, et al., 1989).

The conclusion, based upon what research and experience have shown, is that the different interface styles have different strengths and weaknesses. Some concepts and tasks are very hard to convey symbolically and do not seem to be suited for a direct-manipulation system. Other concepts and tasks, however, may be well suited. Which tasks are best suited for which styles still needs much study. It is also clear that user preferences must be considered, and that the success of a symbolic system depends upon the skills of its designers in following established principles of useability.

Usability Influences

- Familiarity.
- Clarity.
- Simplicity.
- Consistency.
- Directness of "link."
- Context in which used.
- Complexity of task.
- Expectancies of users.
- Efficiency.
- Discriminability.

The usability of an icon, or icons, is dependent on the following factors.

Familiarity.   How familiar is the object being depicted? Familiarity will reduce learning time (Carroll and White, 1973; Wingfield, 1968). How familiar are the commonly seen icons in Figure 11.2? Lack of familiarity requires learning the icon's meaning. Many unfamiliar icons require a great deal of learning.

Experience makes words and numbers often more familiar to a person than symbols. Confusion matrices have been developed through extensive research for alphanumeric data (0 versus O, 1 versus I). Graphic symbols may be more visually similar.

Clarity.   Is the icon legible? Does the shape, structure, and formation technique on the screen permit a clear and unambiguous depiction of what it is. Screen resolution should be sufficiently fine to establish clear differences of form at the normal working distance. The resolution and pixel shapes for CGA, EGA, and VGA screens differ from one another. Icons must appear correctly and consistently no matter what kind of screen. If color is used, it should contrast well with the background. Poor clarity will lead to identification errors and slower performance.

Simplicity.   Is the icon simple? Is the shape clean and devoid of unnecessary embellishments. Too many parts will only confuse the screen viewer.

Consistency.   Are families of icons consistent in structure and shape? Are the same icons displayed in different sizes also consistent in structure and shape? Marcus (1984) says consistency is achieved through limiting the variations of angles, line thicknesses, shapes, and amount of empty space.

Directness of link.   How "sign-like" is the icon; how well does it convey its intended meaning? For concrete objects and actions direct links are more easily established. Adjectives, adverbs, conjunctions, and prepositions can cause problems, however. Also, how does one easily convey concepts like bigger, smaller, wider, or narrower?

Context.   The context of a symbol may change its meaning. Does the "rabbit" symbol illustrated in Figure 11.2, if seen on a road sign in a national park, mean "go faster"?

Complexity of task.   The more abstract or complex the symbol, the more difficult it is to extract or interpret its intended meaning. In the 1984 Stern study the more concrete graphic messages were easier to comprehend than the more abstract. Icons, therefore, cannot completely replace words in some more complex situations.

Expectancies.   The symbol may be comprehended, but a false conclusion may be reached about the desired action because of an incorrect expectancy. Bailey (1984) reported that a study of international road signs found that 8 percent of all drivers never saw the "slash" through the symbol on a road sign, which indicates "do not" do the pictured action. Their expectancy was that they could do it.

Efficiency.   In some situations, a graphics screen may be less efficient, consuming more screen display space than a word or requiring more physical actions by the user. A telephone directory of 50 names and numbers listed on an alphanumeric screen may consume the same screen space required for 15 file

Figure 11.2 Some common icons. What do they stand for? (From Micro Switch, 1984) See page 401 for the answers.

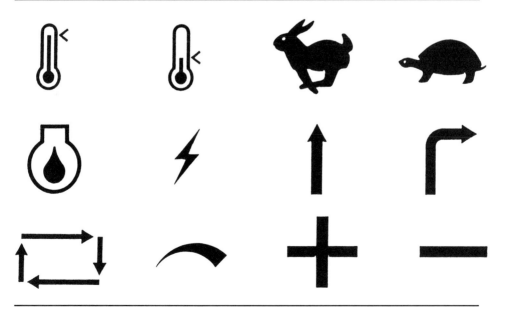

cards. Raising an arm or moving a "mouse" may be slower than simply typing. In other situations icons can be more effective than words in communicating concepts in a smaller area of space. Their strength lies in situations where this occurs.

Discriminability.   Symbols chosen must be visually distinguishable from other symbols. A person's powers of differentiation for shapes and other forms of codes have been experimentally determined over the years. The maximum number of codes for effective human differentiation, including geometric shapes, are summarized in Figure 11.1. A person's ability to discriminate alphabetic or alphanumeric information is much more potent.

The impact on the user of a poorly designed iconic screen is similar to that of a poorly designed alphanumeric screen: excessive learning, confusion, information overload, and possible rejection. New techniques may still result in old problems. Research, and experience, leads to the following design guidelines.

Icon Design Guidelines

- Use for familiar objects and actions.
- Create meaningful, recognizable, and discriminable shapes.
- Create shapes of the proper emotional tone.
- Clearly and simply reflect objects represented.
- Create consistent shapes.
- Conform to standards, if existing.
- Test for:
  - Expectations.
  - Recognition.
  - Learning.
- Attach a caption to assure intended meaning.
- Consider animating the icons.

In creating icons, keep in mind the following:

Use for familiar objects and actions.   Shneiderman (1987) suggests that simple metaphors, analogies, or models with a minimal set of concepts are the best places to start in developing icons. He also suggests that mixing metaphors from two or more sources should be avoided.

Create meaningful, recognizable, and discriminable shapes.   Ideally, an icon's meaning should be self-evident. It should be intuitive or obvious based upon a person's preexisting knowledge. If the icon is new and more abstract, it must be capable of being learned quickly and easily recalled. All icons must also be discriminable or visually distinct from one another to assure recognition.

Create shapes of the proper emotional tone.   The icon should appropriately reflect the environment in which it is used. A sewage disposal system would be an inappropriate metaphor for an electronic mail system wastebasket.

Clearly and simply reflect objects represented.   The characteristics of the display itself should permit drawings of adequate quality. Poorly formed or fuzzy shapes will inhibit recognition. Construct icons with as few graphical components as necessary, using no more than two or three, if possible. Also, use simple, clean lines, avoiding ornamentation. Too much detail inhibits rather than facilitates perception.

Create consistent shapes.   Create consistency in shapes of families of icons and in identical icons of differing sizing. Marcus (1984) says consistency is achieved through limiting the variations of angles, line thicknesses, shapes, and amount of empty space.

Conform to standards, if existing.   Many symbols have already been established by the International Standards Organization (ISO) and other organizations. Consult all relevant reference books before inventing new symbols or modifying existing ones.

Test for expectation, recognition, and learning.   Choosing the objects and actions, and the icons to represent them, will not be easy. So, as in any screen design activity, adequate testing and possible refinement of developed symbols must be built into the design process. Icon recognition and learning should both be measured.

Attach a caption to assure intended meaning.   The ability to comprehend, and learn, icons can be greatly improved by attaching textual captions or labels to the symbols. The preferred location is directly beneath the icon. Labels should always be positionally related to icons in a consistent way.

Consider animation.   Recent research (Baecker et al., 1991) has explored the use of bringing to life on screens the icons representing the objects and actions. An animated icon appears to move instead of maintaining a static position on the screen. Existing examples of animated icons may be seen in the Sapphire windowing environment (Myers, 1984), and in the common "percent done progress indicators" (Myers, 1985).

Baecker et al., created a set of animated versions of the painting icons that appear in the HyperCard tool palette. Study participants found the animated icons useful and helpful in clarifying the purpose and functionality of the icons. These researchers caution, however, that there are many outstanding issues. Among them are that few animation creation rules exist, prototyping is difficult, a scheme for how they fit into a larger system is lacking, and whether they can be made useful for more complex and abstract concepts is not known. The reader interested in more information is referred to Baecker and Small (1990).

Screen Design Guidelines

- Keep the number of symbols under 20.
- Arrange icons in a meaningful way.
- Organize icons to facilitate visual scanning.
- Object and action icons should be placed in different groups.
- Permit arrangement of icons by the user.
- The cursor should
  - — indicate the pointing location through display of a unique symbol.
  - — be modifiable by the user.
- Facilitate the pointing process by
  - — providing a pointing mechanism suitable for the task.
  - — minimizing shifting from one control mechanism to another.
  - — permitting "zooming" for fine positioning.
- Facilitate the selecting process by
  - — requiring separate actions for positioning and selecting.
  - — highlighting the selected element.
  - — permitting deletion of selected elements.
  - — permitting "undo" of the deletion.
- Provide an alternative interface for expert users.

In designing iconic screens, consider the following:

Keep the number of symbols under 20.   A person's ability to identify shapes is limited (see Figure 11.2). Brems and Whitten (1987), based upon a literature review, suggest using no more than eight or so functions that require icons at one time. If labels are attached to icons, however, the meaning of the icon is greatly clarified. Too many icons on a screen, however, will greatly increase screen clutter and create confusion. In general, fewer is better.

Arrange icons in a meaningful way.   Organize icons in a way that reflects the real-world organization of the user. Place object icons and action icons in different groups.

Arrange icons to facilitate visual scanning.   Visual scanning studies, in a non-iconic world, universally find that a top-to-bottom scan of columnar-oriented information is fastest. Generalization of these findings to an icon screen may not necessarily be warranted if icons have attached labels. Columnar orientation of icons (with labels below the icon) will separate the labels from one another by the icons themselves. The labels will be farther apart and fewer icons will fit in a column than in a horizontal, or row, orientation. A row orientation would seem to be more efficient in many cases, as adjacent icons will be in closer physical proximity. Until research evidence is established to the contrary, organizing icons either in a column or a row seems appropriate. In either case, a consistently straight eye movement must be maintained through the icons.

Permit arrangement of icons by the user.   Allow the user to arrange the icons in a manner that is meaningful for the task. A default arrangement should be provided, however.

The cursor should indicate the pointing location and be modifiable.   When the cursor is positioned over a selectable point on the screen, it should change its shape in some recognizable way. The characters of the cursor (color, shape, etc.) should also be modifiable by the user (with a default provided).

Facilitate the pointing process.   A pointing mechanism suitable to the task should be provided. Mack and Lang (1989), in evaluating pointing using the keyboard cursor and alphanumeric keys, a mouse, a stylus, and one's finger, found that the fastest in order were 1) stylus, 2) mouse, and 3) keyboard. Most errors were made by the finger. Most preferred were stylus and mouse equally. The task will, of course, greatly affect the chosen mechanism. The requirement for continuous shifting between different selection mechanisms (such as the mouse and keyboard) should be avoided. Also, permit enlarging or "zooming" of the screen image to make fine positioning easier.

Facilitate the selecting process.   Require separate actions for positioning the cursor and then selecting the screen element of interest. Indicate the element has been selected by highlighting it, outlining it, changing its shape, or providing some other form of visual feedback. Permit the deletion, or "unselection," of a selected element. Also, permit "undo" of the deletion.

Provide an alternate interface for expert users.   An efficient alternate interface, such as a command language, should be provided for expert users (Koved and Shneiderman, 1986).

The icons depicted in Figure 11.2 have the following meanings (reading from left to right):

Hot
Cold
Fast
Slow
Engine Oil
Ammeter/Generator
Straight
Turn
Automatic
Variable Regulation (Increase/decrease)
Plus/Positive
Minus/Negative

Statistical Graphics **12**

A well-designed statistical graphic display consists of complex ideas communicated with clarity, precision, and efficiency. It gives its viewer the greatest number of ideas, in the shortest time, in the smallest space, and with the least clutter possible. It will also induce the viewer to think of substance, not techniques or methodology. It will provide coherence to large amounts of information by tying them together in a meaningful way, and it will encourage data comparisons of its different pieces by the eye. A well-designed graphic display also avoids data distortions by telling the truth about the data.

Much of this material on statistical graphics is based upon Tufte (1983) and Smith and Mosier (1986).

Utilization

- Reserve for material that is rich, complex, or difficult.

Graphics should be reserved for large data sets with real variability. The power of graphics should not be wasted on simple linear changes or situations where one or two numbers would summarize the result better. Tufte (1983) says that tables usually outperform graphics on small data sets of 20 or fewer numbers, or when data sets are noncomparative or highly labeled.

Data Presentation

- Emphasize the data.
- Minimize the nondata.
- Minimize redundant data.

- Show data variation, not design variation.
- Provide proper context for data interpretation.
- Restrict the number of information-carrying dimensions depicted to the number of data dimensions being illustrated.
- Employ data in multiple ways, whenever possible.
- Maximize data density.
- Employ simple data coding schemes.
- Avoid unnecessary embellishment:
  — grids,
  — vibration,
  — ornamentation.

The most important part of a graphics display, as with an alphanumeric display, is the data itself.

Emphasize the data, minimize the nondata.   A user's attention should be drawn to the measured quantities. The largest share of the graphic's "ink" should present data. Nondata such as elaborate grid lines, gratuitous decoration, and extensive, detailed, and wordy labels draw attention to themselves and hide the data. So, nondata should be minimized or, if possible, eliminated completely.

Minimize redundant data.   Redundant data—information that depicts the same number over and over—should also be minimized or eliminated. The height illustrated in Figure 12.1, one inch, can be unambiguously established in at least five ways, says Tufte. They are

1. height of left line,
2. height of shading,
3. height of right line,
4. position of top horizontal line, and
5. number itself.

Any four of the five ways can be erased and the height still established. These are four more ways than are needed.

Redundancy, on occasion, will be useful, however. It may aid in providing context and order, facilitating comparisons, and creating an aesthetic balance. Use redundancy only if necessary.

Show data variation, not design variation.   Each part of a graphic generates visual expectations about its other parts. The expectancies created in one part of a graphic should be fulfilled in other parts so that the viewer does not confuse changes in design with changes in data. Scales should move in regular intervals; proportions should be consistent for all design elements. If the viewer does confuse changes in design with changes in data, ambiguity and deception result.

Figure 12.1 One inch. (From Tufte, 1983)

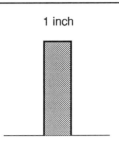

1 inch

Provide the proper context for data interpretation. Graphics often lie by omission. Data for making comparisons or establishing trends must always be included to provide a proper point of reference. "Thin" data must be viewed with suspicion. The graphic in Figure 12.2, for example, might have a number of possible interpretations, as illustrated in Figure 12.3. All important, possible questions must be foreseen and answered by the graphic.

Restrict the number of information-carrying dimensions depicted to the number of data dimensions being illustrated. Displaying one-dimensional data in a multidimensional format is perceptually ambiguous. With multidimensional data, changes in the physical area on the surface of the graphic do not produce an appropriate proportional change in the perceived area. Examples of multidimensional formats to display one-dimensional data would be different-sized human bodies to connote populations or different-sized automobiles to connote numbers of cars. Often the impression on the viewer is that the change is actually much greater than it really is. This problem can be

Figure 12.2 A change between 1982 and 1983 without proper context for interpretation.

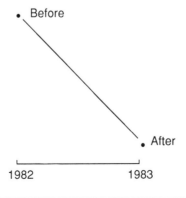

Figure 12.3 Changes between 1982 and 1983 with proper contexts for interpretation.

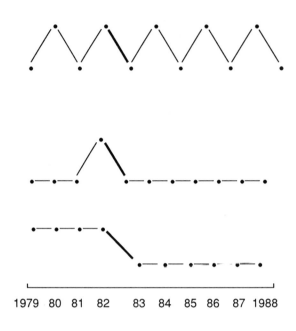

1979 80 81 82   83 84 85 86 87 1988

avoided if the number of information-carrying dimensions on the graphic are restricted to the number of data dimensions being illustrated.

Employ data in multiple ways, whenever possible.   Parts of a graph can be designed to serve more than one graphical purpose. A piece of data may at the same time convey information and perform a design function usually left to nondata. A grid to aid readability of a bar chart, instead of being inscribed on the graphic background, may be constructed within the bar itself, as illustrated in Figure 12.4.

One part of a graph might show several pieces of data. The size of what is being measured can be conveyed through element size, and the intensity of the measured element can be conveyed through color or level of shading. Population maps, for example, can indicate community size through dot size and population density through intensity of dot shading.

The data itself may also serve as the graph. Figure 12.5, from Ayres (1919) (as described in Tufte, 1983), uses data (a U.S. Army Division numerical designation) to create a graphic that tells: 1) the number of divisions serving in France each month for the period shown, 2) what divisions were in France each month, and 3) how long each division stayed in France each month.

Figure 12.4   Piece of data performing a nondata function. (From Tufte, 1983)

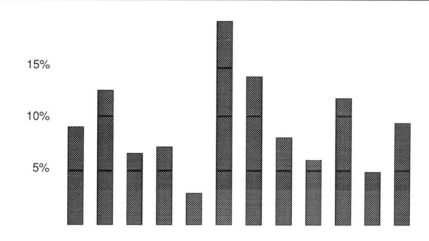

Graphics can be designed to have multiple viewing depths. The top level is what is seen from a distance—the overall structure. A population density map of the United States viewed from this level shows patterns of habitation with heavy concentration in some areas and sparse concentration in others. The second level is what is seen up close and in detail. City names may be associated with areas of high population concentration, and population corridors connecting major urban complexes may be identified. The third level is what is seen implicitly, underlying the graphic. Here, the map reveals the effect of land-form—mountains, valleys, lakes, and rivers—on population distribution.

Finally, graphics may be designed to have different viewing angles or lines of sight. The Ayres graphic (Figure 12.5) can be viewed from three visual angles. The upward-moving horizon conveys the ever-increasing number of American divisions in France in World War I; the vertical identifies which divisions were in France in each month; and the horizontal identifies the length of each division's stay.

The danger in employing data in multiple ways is that it can thus generate graphical puzzles. A sign of a puzzle is that the graphic, instead of being interpreted visually, must be interpreted verbally. Symptoms of a puzzle are frequent references to a legend to interpret what is presented and extensive memorization of design rules before one can comprehend what is presented. By contrast, a well-designed, multiple-function graphic permits a quickly learned, implicit translation of the visual to verbal.

Maximize data density.   In graphics more information is better than less information—the greater the amount of information displayed on a screen, the larger number of visual comparisons can be made, improving comprehension.

Figure 12.5 U.S. Army Divisions in France in World War I. (Ayres, 1919 in Tufte, 1983)

Jun	Jul	Aug	Sep	Oct	Nov	Dec	Jan	Feb	Mar	Apr	May	Jun	Jul	Aug	Sep	Oct
																8
																38
																31
															34	34
															86	86
															84	84
															87	87
														40	40	40
														39	39	39
														88	88	88
														81	81	81
														7	7	7
														85	85	85
													36	36	36	36
													91	91	91	91
													79	79	79	79
													76	76	76	76
												29	29	29	29	29
												37	37	37	37	37
												90	90	90	90	90
												92	92	92	92	92
												89	89	89	89	89
												83	83	83	83	83
												78	78	78	78	78
											80	80	80	80	80	80
											30	30	30	30	30	30
											33	33	33	33	33	33
											6	6	6	6	6	6
											27	27	27	27	27	27
											4	4	4	4	4	4
											28	28	28	28	28	28
											35	35	35	35	35	35
											82	82	82	82	82	82
										77	77	77	77	77	77	77
									3	3	3	3	3	3	3	3
									5	5	5	5	5	5	5	5
								32	32	32	32	32	32	32	32	32
							41	41	41	41	41	41	41	41	41	41
						42	42	42	42	42	42	42	42	42	42	42
					26	26	26	26	26	26	26	26	26	26	26	26
	2	2	2	2	2	2	2	2	2	2	2	2	2	2	2	2
1	1	1	1	1	1	1	1	1	1	1	1	1	1	1	1	1
Jun	Jul	Aug	Sep	Oct	Nov	Dec	Jan	Feb	Mar	Apr	May	Jun	Jul	Aug	Sep	Oct
1917							1918									

This is so because the eye can detect large amounts of information in a small space. As mentioned earlier, simple things belong in a table or in the text.

Data density of a screen can be maximized in two ways: enlarging the data matrix or shrinking the graphic. Enlarging the data matrix involves displaying as much information as possible. If the graphic becomes overcrowded, techniques such as averaging, clustering, smoothing, or providing summaries can reduce the numbers to be displayed. Shrinking the graphic means reducing it in size, but screen resolution may impose limitations on how much shrinking can be performed.

Employ simple data coding schemes.   If visual differentiation in the types of data being displayed is necessary, use simple coding methods in the areas being depicted. Elaborate schemes or patterns can be eye straining (as will be illustrated shortly) and can actually impede the flow of information. Some possible acceptable coding alternatives include:

- Varying densities or shades of gray,
- Labeling with words instead, and
- Varying colors.

In using color, the considerations discussed in Chapter 10 should be kept in mind.

Avoid unnecessary embellishments.   The pieces of a graphic display must tell the viewer something new. An unnecessary embellishment is information or "chartjunk" that does not add anything new to the meaning of the graphic. It is decoration, or noise, that hinders assimilation of the message the graphic is trying to communicate. Nondata and redundant data are forms of chartjunk. Three other common kinds are vibration, heavy grids, and ornamentation.

Grids.   A grid on a graphic display carries no information, contributes noise, and focuses attention away from the data. An excessively heavy grid can even mask the data.

Grids should be suppressed or eliminated so they do not compete with data. When a grid serves as an aid in reading or extrapolating, it should, of course, be included. Its tendency to overwhelm can be reduced by constructing it with delicate lines or muted colors.

Vibration.   The eye is never absolutely still; it produces continuous, slight tremors that aid visual acuity. The result, when small patterns of lines, boxes, or dots are viewed, is the distracting sensation of vibration or shimmer, a kind of optical art. Examples of this effect can be seen in the patterns in Figures 12.6 and 12.7. While eye-catching, vibrations also strain the eye. The data-coding schemes described above can serve as alternatives to vibration producing symbols.

Figure 12.6   Examples of patterns creating vibrations. (From Tufte, 1983)

Ornamentation.   When the quantitative information on a graphic is over-whelmed by decoration, the result is a designer's self-tribute—more effective as a piece of art hung on the wall than as an effective conveyer of information. Ornamentation can take many forms: extensive use of color when it is not necessary; creating multidimensional graphics when single-dimensional will do; pointless use of different of vibrating patterns; or forcing data into a graphic when a table would work much better. Ornamentation is really a symptom of

Figure 12.7 Examples of patterns creating vibrations. From professional journals.

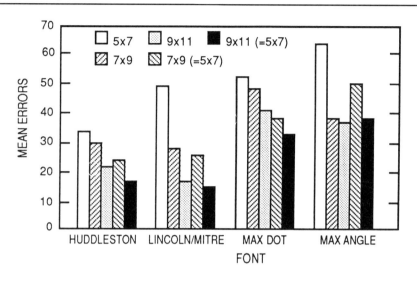

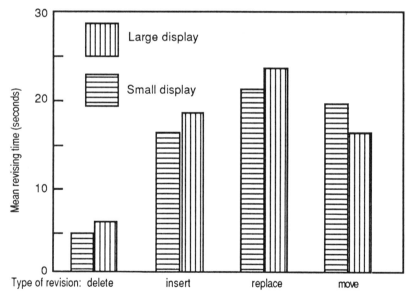

Figure 12.7 Continued

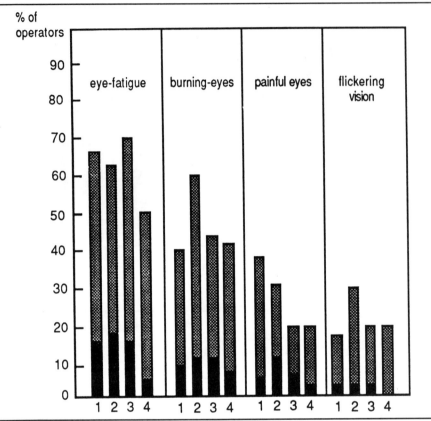

"See what I can do with my computer" rather than an effort to provide the system user with the proper data in the most comprehensible way possible. The best graphic display is the simplest graphic display.

Scaling

- Values on an axis should increase as they move away from the origin.
- Use the horizontal axis (X) to show time or cause of an event (the independent variable).
- Use the vertical axis (Y) to show a caused effect (the dependent variable).
- Employ a linear scale for displayed data.
- Mark scales at standard or customary intervals.
- Start numeric scales at zero (0).
- Keep the number of digits in the scales to a minimum.
- Display only a single scale on each axis.
- For large data matrices, consider displaying duplicate axes.

- Provide aids for scale interpolation.
- Provide scaling consistency across two or more related displays.
- Clearly label each axis in a left-to-right reading orientation.

Scaling is the positioning of data in relation to the measurement points or markers. Standard scaling practices are those below.

Increase axis values as they move away from the origin.   If the numeric values displayed are positive, the origin point will be the lower left point of the graph. If the data includes negative values and the axes must extend in both directions from the zero point, position the origin in the center of the graph.

Use the horizontal or X-axis to show time or cause of an event (the independent variable); use the vertical or Y-axis to show a caused effect (the dependent variable).   When the X-axis plots time intervals, the labeled points should represent the end of each time interval.

Employ a linear scale for displayed data.   Most people are more familiar with linear scales than with logarithmic or other nonlinear scales and will interpret them more accurately.

Mark scales at standard or customary intervals.   Standard or customary intervals on scales aid comprehension. Familiar standard intervals are 1, 2, 5, 10, and multiples of 10; familiar customary intervals include days of the week and months of the year. Construct scales with tick marks at these intervals.

To aid visual interpretation, it may be necessary to provide intermediate tick marks as well. These intermediate tick marks should be consistent with the scale interval shown.

Start numeric scales at zero.   Using zero as the starting point on scales aids comparisons. If a zero point is omitted, this omission should be clearly indicated on the display.

Keep the number of digits to a minimum.   Smaller numbers aid understanding. Round off all numbers to two digits or less.

Display only a single scale on each axis.   Avoid multiple scales associated with a single axis. For all but the most experienced users, multiple scales can be confusing and can lead to interpretation errors. Meanings can also be greatly distorted.

If multiple-scale graphs must be used, permit the user to select any data curve individually and have the computer highlight its corresponding scale.

Display duplicate axes for large data matrices.   The readability of large data matrices is improved if the X-axis scale appears at the top as well as the bottom of the graph, and the Y-axis scale at the right as well as the left side.

Provide aids for scale interpretation.   Where reading accuracy is extremely critical, provide computer aids for interpretation, such as the following:

- Displaying a fine grid upon request,
- Vertical and horizontal rules that the user can move to the intersection point.
- Letting the user "point" at a data item and the computer then provide the exact values.

When grid lines are displayed, ensure that they are not confused with data by making them thinner. Also ensure that grid lines do not obscure data elements by positioning them behind depicted data (and thus invisible).

Provide scaling consistency.   If comparisons must be made between multiple graphs or charts, use the same scale for each. Data sets that are scaled differently will lead to interpretation errors.

Clearly label each axis.   Each scale axis should be clearly labeled in conventional left-to-right reading orientation. A complete description with measurement units should be provided.

Proportion

- Provide accurate proportion of displayed surfaces to data they represent.
- Provide proper proportion by
  - conforming to data shape,
  - making the width greater than the height.

Provide accurate proportion of displayed surfaces to data they represent.   The displayed surfaces on graphics should be directly proportional to the numerical quantities they represent. Failure to do this can create false impressions of magnitudes of differences in sizes or changes. Violations of this principle can be measured by the "lie factor," which is calculated as follows:

$$\text{Lie Factor} = \frac{\text{Size of effect shown in graphic}}{\text{Size of effect in data}}$$

Lie factors equal to 1 accurately represent the underlying numbers. Lie factors more than 1.05 or less than .95 indicate distortion. Most lie factors involve overstating an effect in the graphic, with factors of 2 to 5 being very common. Graphics with lie factors of 50 or more are occasionally seen.

This kind of graphical distortion can be eliminated through clear, detailed, and thorough labeling, to be addressed shortly.

Provide proper proportion.   When the relative proportions of a graphic are in balance, it looks better. Graphics should tend toward the horizontal, assuming a greater length than height. There are a number of reasons for this recommendation. First, the eye has greater practice in detecting deviations from a horizon. Second, it is easier to read words arranged left to right rather than stacked one above the other, and a wider horizontal plane aids left-to-right word positioning. Third, many graphics plot cause and effect relationships, with effect on the vertical axis and cause on the horizontal. An elongated horizontal axis helps describe the causal variable in more detail. Fourth, mathematical aesthetic properties exist more for wide than high shapes (see Chapter 4). Fifth, visual preferences appear to exist for these same shapes. However, if the data being displayed suggests a graphic shape square or higher than wide, conform to the shape suggested by the data.

Lines

- Data lines should be the heaviest.
- Axes lines should be a medium weight.
    - Extend the axes lines entirely around the graphic.
- Grid lines should be very thin or absent.

The most important part of a graphic is the data. Emphasize the data by making the data lines the heaviest. Of secondary importance are the axes lines. Display them in a medium thickness. Axes lines should be extended entirely around the graphic to create a rectangle (or box). This will define the graphic area and help focus attention on the data itself. Grid lines, when necessary, should be very thin. Grid lines should not be used, unless absolutely needed for accurate data interpretation.

Labeling

- Employ clear, detailed, and thorough labeling.
- Maintain a left-to-right reading orientation.
- Integrate labeling with drawing.

The labeling principles for graphic screens should follow the principles outlined for alphanumeric screens.

Employ clear, detailed, and thorough labeling.   Words should be fully spelled out. Both upper- and lowercase should be used, with lowercase for textual information. Use the simplest and shortest forms of words possible.

Maintain a left-to-right reading orientation.   Display all labels horizontally. Avoid words that are organized vertically or words that run in different directions. Whereas nonhorizontal words on hard copy graphics can be read by turning the paper, this is impossible on a screen.

Integrate words and numbers with drawing. Explanations on graphics help the viewer and should be incorporated as much as possible. Words are data, and they can occupy space freed up by eliminating nondata or redundant data. Integrating words and captions with the graphic eliminates the need for a legend and the eye movements back and forth required to read it. Also, incorporate messages to explain the data, and label interesting or important data points. Pictures and words used together aid comprehension.

Using the same type style for graphics and text aids the visual integration of the two. Do not use ruled lines to separate them.

Title

- Create a short, simple, clear, and distinctive title describing the purpose of the graphic.
- Locate the title above, centered, or left-aligned to the rectangle formed by the extended axes.
- Spell out fully using a mixed-case or upper-case font.

Titles should be brief and descriptive of the graphic. Titles may be centered or flush left to the rectangle formed by the extended axes. Marcus (1985) feels aligned-left yields a stronger composition. With the availability of differing character sizes and boldnesses, titles may be displayed larger, bolder, and in mixed case. If different character sizes and weights are not available, the use of upper case is recommended.

Curves and Line Graphs

- Display data curves or lines that must be compared in a single graph.
- Display no more than four to five curves or lines in a single graph.
- Identify each curve or line with an adjacent label whenever possible.
- If a legend must be included, order the legend to match the spatial ordering of the curves or lines.
- For tightly packed curves or lines, provide data differentiation through a line coding technique such as different colors or line types.
- Highlight curves or lines representing important or critical data.
- When comparing actual to projected data,
  — use solid curves or lines for actual data,
  — use broken curves or lines for projected data.
- Display a reference index if displayed data must be compared to a standard or critical value.
- Display differences between two data sets as a curve or line itself.

Curves and line graphs can be used to show relations between sets of data defined by two continuous variables. They are especially useful for showing data changes over time, being superior to other graphic methods for speed and accuracy in interpreting data trends. With a "curve" the data relations are summarized by a smoothed line. With a "line" the data plots are connected by straight line segments. This kind of graph implies a continuous function. If the data point elements are discrete, it is better to use a bar graph.

Display data to be compared in one graph. If several curves must be compared, display them in one combined graph to facilitate the comparisons.

Display no more than four to five curves or lines in one graph. As more curves or lines are added to a graph, visual discrimination among them becomes more difficult. The maximum number of lines should be limited. If one particular line or curve must be compared with several others, consider multiple graphs where the line of interest is compared separately with each other line.

Identify each curve or line with an adjacent label. A label associated with each curve or line is preferable to a separate legend. If direct labeling is impossible due to the "tightness" of the lines, a legend may be the only alternative. If a legend is used, visually differentiate the lines (colors, line types, etc.) and include the coding scheme in the legend.

Order legends to match the spatial ordering of the curves or lines. If the legends are to be used with a series of graphs, however, maintain one consistent order for the legends on all the graphs.

For tightly packed curves or lines, use a coding technique for line differentiation. Common coding techniques include different colors and line types. Do not exceed the maximum number of alternatives for the coding technique selected, as shown in Figure 11.1. If color coding is used, choose colors on the basis of the considerations described in Chapter 10. Line width and dot size coding should be avoided because of their similarity to grids and scatterplot data points. If a series of related graphs are line coded, be consistent in the selection of techniques for corresponding data.

Highlight important or critical data. If one curve or line in a multiple-line graph is of particular significance, highlight that curve (high intensity, different color, etc.) to call attention to it. The coding scheme selected should be different from that selected for spatial differentiation.

Actual vs. projected data. Use solid curves or lines for actual data; use broken curves or lines for projected data.

Display reference indexes if necessary. When a curve or line must be compared to some standard or critical value, display a reference curve or line reflecting that value.

Directly display differences.   If the difference between two sets of data must be determined, display the difference itself as a separate curve or line. This is preferable to requiring the user to visually compare the two values and calculate the difference between them.

If the difference between the related curves is of interest, consider a band chart where both lines or curves are displayed and the area between them coded through texture, shading, or color.

Surface Charts

- Order the data categories so that
  - —the least variable is at the bottom,
  - —the most variable is at the top.
- Use different texture or shading coding schemes to differentiate the areas below each curve or line.
- Incorporate labels within the bands of data, if possible.

If the data being depicted by a curve or line represents all the parts of a whole, consider developing a surface chart. In this kind of graph the curves or lines arc stacked above one another to indicate aggregated amounts, and the area between each curve or line is differentially coded, usually by textures or shadings. A surface chart is similar to a segmented bar chart.

Order data categories to show least variable at bottom and most variable at top.   Irregularities in the bottom curve or line will affect those above it. This can make it difficult for a user to determine whether the irregularity in the upper curves reflects "real" data differences or is the result of this style of graph. Displaying least variable data at the bottom will minimize this effect. If the data itself implies that some logical organization must be followed, and the resulting organization creates confusing distortions in the curves, this method should not be used.

Use different texture or shading coding schemes.   Ensure that the coding scheme chosen for each area is visually distinguishable from all others.

Incorporate labels within the bands of data.   Labels with left-to-right reading orientation should be included within the textured or shaded bands, if possible. Legends should only be incorporated where space constraints exist within the bands.

Scatterplots

- Limit use to two-dimensional displays of data.
- Visually distinguish points of particular significance through a highlighting technique.

Scatterplots can be used to show relationships among individual data points in a two-dimensional array. Three-dimensional scatterplots, while possible, do not yield clear, unambiguous displays. Points of particular significance on scatterplots can be made distinctive through highlighting techniques such as high intensity, different colors, or different shapes. Correlations and trends on scatterplots can be indicated by the superimposition of curves (thus combining with the scatterplot another kind of graphic display).

Bar Graphs

- Orient bars consistently, either horizontally or vertically.
- Make the spacing between bars half of the width of the bars, or less.
- If different bars must be easily distinguished, provide differentiation through a coding technique.
- Highlight bars representing important or critical data.
- Provide a consistent ordering to related groups of bars.
- Display a reference index if displayed data must be compared to a standard or critical value.
- Identify each bar with an adjacent label.
- When a great many pieces of data must be compared, consider using histograms or step charts.

Bar graphs can be used to show differences between separate entities or to show differences in a variable at discrete intervals. Bar graphs may extend from a common origin or baseline, or they may extend between separately plotted high and low points.

Orient bars consistently.   Bars may be oriented either horizontally or vertically. A consistent orientation should be maintained for bars displaying similar information. In general, frequency counts are displayed in vertical bars, and time durations in horizontal bars.

Space bars for ease of visual comparison.   Comparison of bars should be accomplishable without eye movement. Generally, the spacing between bars should be one-half or less of the bar width. If many bars are to be displayed, the alternating pattern of bright and dark bands that results can be visually disturbing to some viewers. In this case it is better to completely eliminate the spacing between bars. (The graph is then called a histogram.)

Visually distinguish different groups of bars.   If different groups of bars must be easily distinguished, provide differentiation through a coding technique such as color, texture, or shading.

Highlight important or critical data.   If one bar represents data of unusual significance, call attention to that bar through a different coding technique.

Consistently order related groups of bars.   Related groups of bars should be ordered in a consistent manner.

Display reference indexes if necessary.   When bars must be compared to some standard or critical value, display a reference line to aid that comparison.

Identify each bar with an adjacent label.   A label associated with each bar, in left-to-right reading orientation, is preferable to a separate legend. If groups of bars are repeated, it is only necessary to label one group rather than all bars in all groups.

Consider histograms or step charts when a great many pieces of data must be compared.   Histograms or step charts are bar graphs without spaces between the bars.

Segmented or Stacked Bars

- Order the data categories in the same sequence.
- Order the data categories so that
  - the least variable is at the bottom,
  - the most variable is at the top.
- Use different texture or shading coding schemes to differentiate the areas within each bar.
- Clearly associate labels with bars and segments.

   If both the total measures and the portions represented by segments are of interest, consider segmented or stacked bars. This kind of graph is similar to a surface chart.

Order the data categories in the same sequence.   To provide consistency, order the data categories in the same sequence.

Order data categories to show least variable at bottom and most variable at top.   Irregularities in the bottom segment will affect those above it. This can make it difficult for a user to determine whether the irregularity in the upper segments reflects "real" data differences or is the result of this style of graph. Displaying least variable data at the bottom will minimize this effect. If the data itself implies that some logical organization must be followed, this logical organization should be followed.

Use different texture or shading coding schemes.   Ensure that the coding scheme chosen for each segment is visually distinguishable from all others.

Associate labels with bars and segments.   Labels, with a left-to-right reading orientation, are preferable to legends. Legends should only be used if space does not allow labels.

Pie Charts

- Pie charts should be used with caution.
- If pie charts are used,
  — use five segments or less;
  — each segment should take up at least 5 percent (18 degrees) of the circle;
  — directly label each segment in the normal orientation for reading;
    — If leader lines for labels in small segments are necessary, orient them in as few angles as possible.
  — include numbers with the segment labels to indicate percentages or absolute values;
  — textures or colors selected for segments should not emphasize one segment over another (unless it is intended);
  — highlight segments requiring particular emphasis through a contrasting display technique or by "exploding" it.

Pie charts can be used to show an apportionment of a total into its component parts. Bar graphs, however, usually permit more accurate estimates of proportions.

Use pie charts with caution.   Experts caution against the use of pie charts because

- they provide no means of absolute measurement,
- they cannot represent totals greater than 100 percent,
- they can only represent a fixed point in time, and
- human estimation of relationships is more accurate with linear than with angular representations.

If pie charts are used, the guidelines below should be followed.

Use five segments or less.   To minimize confusion, provide adequate differentiation of pieces and permit accurate labeling.

Avoid very small segments.   Segments should take up at least 5 percent (18 degrees) of the circle.

Directly label each segment in the normal reading orientation.   To provide maximum association of label with data and for reading clarity, use a left-to-right reading orientation.

If it is impossible to include the label within the segment, it may be placed outside and tied to the segment with a leader line. If multiple outside labels and leader lines are necessary, orient the lines in as few angles as possible.

Include numbers with the segment labels to indicate percentages or absolute values. Only by including numbers with segment labels can numeric values be accurately established.

Do not overemphasize one segment. The kinds of textures or colors selected for segments should not emphasize one segment over another, unless emphasis is intended.

Highlight segments requiring emphasis. Use a contrasting display technique or "explode" segments requiring emphasis by displacing them slightly from the remainder of the pie.

Flowcharts

- Displayed steps should be designed to
  - — follow some logical order, or
  - — minimize path length.
- Orient following common reading conventions such as left to right or top to bottom.
- Follow common flowchart coding conventions to distinguish elements.
- Use arrows in conventional ways to indicate directional relationships.
- Highlight elements requiring particular attention through a contrasting display technique.
- Require only one decision at each step.
- Display options to be considered in a logical order.
- Be consistent in all option ordering and wording.

If the data to be displayed flows in a complex, yet sequential, process, consider using a flowchart to schematically represent it. Flowcharts can also be used to aid problem solving in which a solution can be reached by answering a series of questions. They are not useful when tradeoffs must be made.

Order steps logically or to minimize path length. One logical ordering scheme is to follow a sequence of operations or processes from start to finish. Other potential ordering schemes include placing the most important decisions first or the decisions that can be made with the most certainty. If no logical order is apparent, order the flowchart to minimize the length of the path through it. If some decision paths are more likely to occur than others, minimize the length of the most likely path.

Orient for conventional reading. Follow a left-to-right and top-to-bottom orientation.

Follow common coding conventions to distinguish elements. Follow existing shape coding conventions for the kinds of "boxes" being displayed. Adhere to standards and user expectations.

Use arrows in conventional ways. Use arrows to indicate directional relations and sequential links.

Highlight elements requiring particular attention. Contrasting display techniques, such as high intensity or color, should be used to call attention to relevant paths or elements. Color is particularly effective in this regard.

Require only one decision at each step. Multiple decisions reduce flowchart size. But requiring multiple decisions such as "Is A true and B false?" can be confusing. Require that only single decisions be made.

Display options to be considered in a logical order. Use orders that are natural, sequenced numerically, or meaningful.

Consistently order and word all choices. Consistency always aids learning.

Color in Screen Design

13

The addition of color can add a new dimension to screen usability. Color draws attention because it attracts the user's eye. If used properly, it can emphasize the logical organization of a screen, facilitate the discrimination of screen components, accentuate differences, and make displays more interesting. If used improperly, color can be distracting and visually fatiguing, impairing the system's usability.

The discussion to follow begins by defining color. Next is a review of how color may be used in screen design and some critical cautions in its use. Then, the human visual system and the implications for color are discussed. Finally, guidelines are presented for choosing and using colors.

COLOR—WHAT IS IT?

Wavelengths of light themselves are not colored. What is perceived as actual color results from the stimulation by a received light wave of the proper receptor in the eye. The "name" that a color is given is a learned phenomenon, based on previous experiences and associations of specific visual sensations with color names. Therefore, a color can only be described in terms of a person's report of his or her perceptions.

The visual spectrum of wavelengths to which the eye is sensitive ranges from about 400 to 700 millimicrons. Objects in the visual environment often emit or reflect light waves in a limited area of this visual spectrum, absorbing light waves in other areas of the spectrum. The dominant wavelength being "seen" is the one that we come to associate with a specific color name. The visible color spectrum and the names commonly associated with the various light wavelengths are shown in Figure 13.1.

To describe a color, it is useful to refer to the three properties it possesses: hue, chroma or saturation, and value or intensity, as illustrated in Figure 13.2.

Figure 13.1 The visible spectrum.

Color	Approximate Wavelengths in Millimicrons
Red	700
Orange	600
Yellow	570
Yellow-green	535
Green	500
Blue-green	493
Blue	470
Violet	400

Figure 13.2 The Relationship of hue, chroma, and value.

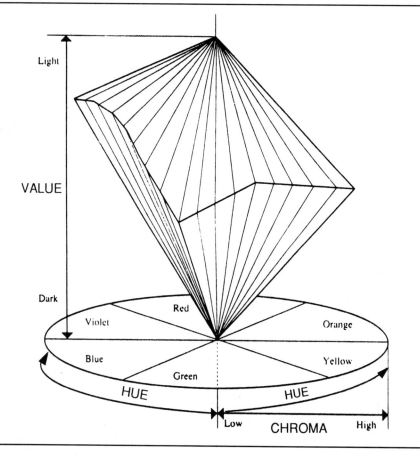

Hue is the spectral wavelength composition of a color. It is to this we attach a meaning such as green or red. Chroma or saturation is the purity of a color in a scale from gray to the most vivid version of the color. Value or intensity is the relative lightness or darkness of a color in a range from black to white. Lightness differences are usually described by two-word descriptors such as light red or dark blue.

Primary colors of illuminated light are red, green, and blue, whose wavelengths additively combine in pairs to produce magenta, cyan, and yellow. The three primary colors additively combine to produce white. The long-wavelength colors (red) are commonly referred to as "warm," and short-wavelength colors (blue) as "cool."

Color Uses

- Use color as a formatting aid to
  - relate or tie fields into groupings.
  - differentiate groupings of information.
  - associate information that is spatially separated.
  - highlight or call attention to important information.
- Use color as a visual code to identify
  - screen components.
  - the logical structure of ideas, processes, or sequences.
  - sources of information.
  - status of information.
- Other color uses
  - realistically portray natural objects.
  - increase screen appeal.

Color Uses

Color may be used as a formatting aid in structuring a screen, or it may be used as a visual code to categorize information or data.

As a formatting aid.   As a formatting aid, color can provide better structure and meaning to a screen. It is especially useful when large amounts of data must be included on a screen and spacing to differentiate components is difficult to employ.

For example, differentiation of logical groupings of fields can be enhanced by displaying them in different colors. Spatially separated but related fields can also be tied together through a color scheme.

Color can also replace highlighting as a means of calling attention to a field or fields. Color is much more flexible than other techniques because of the number of colors that are available. Color as an attention-getting mechanism must, however, be chosen in light of the psychological and physiological considerations, to be described shortly.

As a visual code.   A color code shows what category the data being displayed falls into. It has meaning to the screen's user. A properly selected color coding scheme permits a user to identify a relevant category quickly without having to first read its contents. This permits focusing concentration on this category while the remaining data is excluded from attention.

One common color-coding scheme to differentiate screen components is to display captions and data fields in different colors. Another is to identify data from different sources—data added to a transaction from different locations, or text added to a message from different departments, may be colored differently. Color coding to convey status might involve displaying, in a different color, data that passed or failed system edits. Color can also be used as a prompt, guiding a person through a complex transaction.

Color as a visual code must be relevant and known. Relevance is achieved when the code enables a user to attend only to the data that is needed. A relevant code, however, will be useless unless it is also understood by the persons who must use it. Not knowing a code's meaning will only distract and degrade performance.

Other color uses.   Color can also be used to more realistically portray objects in the world around us that must be displayed on a screen. It is also thought that the addition of color increases a screen's appeal and makes display work more pleasant.

Possible Problems with Color

- Color's high attention-getting quality may be distracting if it causes a person to
  - notice differences in color, regardless of whether the differences have any real meaning.
  - visually group items of the same color together, regardless of whether these grouped items are related.
- Indiscriminate or poor use of color on one screen may interfere with color's attention-getting capacity on another screen.
- The sensitivity of the eye to different colors and color combinations varies, some being visually fatiguing.
- Some people have color-viewing deficiencies.
- Some colors may exhibit confusing cross-disciplinary and cross-cultural connotations.

The simple addition of color to a screen will not guarantee improved performance. What may have been a poorly designed product will simply become a colorful poorly defined product. When used improperly, color may even impair performance by distracting the viewer and interfering with the handling of information. Possible problems may be caused by the perceptual system itself and/or the physiological characteristics of the human eye.

High attention-getting capacity.   Color has an extremely high attention-getting capacity, which causes the screen viewer to associate or "tie together" screen elements of the same color, whether or not such an association should be made. The user thus might search for relationships and differences that do not exist or that are not valid. The result is often bewilderment, confusion, and slower reading. The effect achieved is often described as a "Christmas tree."

Interference with use of other screens.   Indiscriminate or poor use of color on some screens will diminish the effectiveness of color on other screens. The rationale for color will be difficult to understand and its attention-getting capacity severely restricted.

Varying sensitivity of the eye to different colors.   All colors, in the eye of the viewer, are not equal. The eye is more sensitive to those in the middle of the visual spectrum (yellow and green), which appear brighter than the extremes (blue and red). Thus, text comprised of colors at the extremes is thought to be more difficult to read. Research evidence on this topic is mixed. Watanabe et al. (1968), Pinkus (1982), Post (1985), and Matthews and Mertins (1987, 1988) found that acuity, contrast sensitivity, target recognition, legibility, or performance were not influenced by color. On the other hand, Haines et al. (1975), Pokorny et al. (1968), and Radl (1980, 1984) found advantages for spectral center colors in reaction times, resolution, and error rates.

Also, it is thought that some combinations of screen colors can strain the eyes accommodation mechanism. The wavelengths of light producing blue are normally focused in front of the eye's retina, the red wavelengths behind it. Simultaneous or sequential viewing of red and blue cause the eye to continually refocus to bring the image directly onto the retina, thereby increasing the potential for eye fatigue. Those expressing this view include Ostberg (1982), Sivak and Woo (1983), Murch (1984), and the Human Factors Society (1988). Again the research evidence is mixed. Donohoo and Snyder (1984) found refocusing problems with a relatively saturated blue phospher. No refocusing problems were reported in studies addressing short-term display viewing by Matthews and Mertins (1987), Walraven (1984), and Matthews et al. (1989). Matthews does say that his test materials included relatively simple screens, and "Failure to find a large influence of display color on visual performance might be attributed to the moderate density of screen information." Thus the accommodation mechanism was not severely tested, and generalization to more dense screen is not warranted.

What does one conclude after looking at the research addressing the above problems? The reasonable assumption is that they have neither been proved nor disproved. We have not properly defined all the terminal-based tasks being performed, the studies have used only a few of the many terminals in existence, and a firm definition of "visual fatigue" remains elusive. Finally, none of the studies have addressed extended terminal viewing. The prudent course is to be cautious and avoid using colors, and combinations, which color theory claims could create problems. As shall be seen, the color palette to be used in screen design will be small, so avoiding potential problem areas will not be terribly restrictive.

The perceived appearance of a color is also affected by a variety of other factors, including the size of the area of color, the ambient illumination level, and other colors in the viewing area. Failure to consider the eye and how it handles color, then, can also lead to mistakes in color identification, misinterpretations, slower reading, and, perhaps, visual fatigue.

Color viewing deficiencies.   Another disadvantage of color is that about 8 percent of males and 0.4 percent of females have some form of color-perception deficiency—colorblindness. The most common form of colorblindness is red-green, which affects about 2.5 percent of the population. Red and orange is confused with green and yellow. The visual color spectrum in this form of colorblindness ranges from blue to white to yellow. Another common color-blindness exists for blue and yellow. For an individual with color-perception deficiency, all the normal colors may not be discernible, but often differences in lightness or intensity can be seen. A person experiencing any form of colorblindness must not be prohibited from effectively using a screen.

Cross-disciplinary and cross-cultural differences.   Colors can have different meanings in different situations to different people. A color used in an unexpected way can cause confusion. An error signaled in green would contradict the expected association of red with stop or danger. The same color may also have a different connotation, depending upon its viewer. Marcus (1986b) provides the following quite different meanings for the color blue:

> For American movie audiences—tenderness or pornography.
> For financial managers—corporate qualities or reliability.
> For health care professionals—death.
> For nuclear reactor monitors—coolness or water.

The proper use of color requires an analysis of the expectations and experiences of the screen viewer.

The use of color in screen design must always keep these possible problems clearly in focus. The designer must work to minimize their disruptive and destructive effects. Always keep in mind that poor use of color is worse than not using it at all.

COLOR AND SCREEN DESIGN—WHAT THE RESEARCH SHOWS

The effectiveness of color in improving the usability of a display has yielded mixed research results. On a positive note, color has been shown to improve performance (Kopala, 1981; Sidorsky, 1982), to improve visual search (Christ, 1975; Carter, 1982), to be useful for organizing information (Engel, 1980), to aid memory (Marcus, 1986b), and to demarcate a portion of a screen (as opposed to lines or type font, Wopking et al., 1985). Color has also created positive user reactions (Tullis, 1981), was preferred to monochromatic screens for being less monotonous and reducing eye strain and fatigue (Christ, 1975), and is more enjoyable (Marcus, 1986b).

On the other hand, it has also been shown that color does not improve performance (Tullis, 1981), may impair performance (Christ and Teichner, 1973; Christ, 1975), and is less important than display spacing (Haubner and Benz, 1983). It has also been demonstrated that poor character—background color combinations lead to poorer performance (McTyre and Frommer, 1985). Finally, no evidence was produced that color, as compared to black and white, can significantly improve aesthetics or legibility or reduce eye strain (Pastoor, 1990).

Research has found, moreover, that as the number of colors on a display increases, the time to respond to a single color increases, and the probability of color confusions increases (Luria et al., 1986). Many studies have found that the maximum number of colors that a person can handle is in the range of 4 to 10, with emphasis on the lower numbers (for example, Brooks, 1965; Halsey and Chapanis, 1951; Luria et al., 1986).

The conclusion to be derived from these studies is that for simple displays, color may have no dramatic impact. Indeed, a monochromatic display may serve the purpose just as well. As display complexity increases, however, so does the value of color. A second conclusion is that people like using color and think it has a positive influence on their productivity, even though it may not.

To be effective color must be properly used. Poor use of color will actually impair performance, not help it.

When using color, keep in mind its value will be dependent upon the task being performed, the colors selected, how many are used, and the viewing environment.

COLOR AND HUMAN VISION

To understand how color should be used on a screen, it is helpful to know something of the physiology of the human eye. The reader requiring a detailed discussion of this subject is referred to Murch (1983, 1984a).

The lens.   The lens of the eye, controlled by muscles, focuses wavelengths of light on the retina. The lens itself is not color corrected. The wavelengths of light creating different colors are focused at different distances behind the lens, the longer wavelengths (red) being focused further back than the shorter wavelengths (blue). The result is that colors of a different wavelength than the color actually being focused by the lens appear out of focus. To create a sharp image of the out-of-focus colors requires a refocusing of the eye. Excessive refocusing (such as between red and blue) can lead to eye fatigue.

The effect of this focusing for most people is that reds appear more distant and blues appear closer. It can give a three-dimensional appearance to what is being viewed. A critical problem is that the wavelength of light creating blue can never be brought into focus on the retina but is always focused in front of it. A sharp blue image is impossible to obtain.

Very pure colors require more refocusing than less pure colors. Therefore, a color with a large "white" component will require less refocusing.

The lens does not transmit all light wavelengths equally. It absorbs more wavelengths in the blue region of the spectrum than those in the other regions. Additionally, as the lens ages, it tends to yellow, filtering out the shorter blue wavelengths. Thus, as people get older, their sensitivity to blue decreases.

The retina.   The retina is the light-sensitive surface of the eye. It comprises two kinds of receptors, rods and cones, that translate the incoming light into nervous impulses. Rods are sensitive to lower light levels and function primarily at night. Cones are stimulated by higher light levels and react to color. The sensitivity of cones to colors varies, different cones possessing maximum sensitivity to different light wavelengths. About two-thirds (64 percent) of the cones are maximally sensitive to longer light wavelengths, showing a peak response at about 575 millimicrons. These cones have traditionally been referred to as "red" sensitive cones. In actuality, however, the peak sensitivity is in the yellow portion of the visual spectrum (see Figure 13.1). About one-third (32 percent) of the cones achieve maximum sensitivity at about 535 millimicrons and are commonly referred to as "green" sensitive cones. The remainder (2 percent) primarily react to short light wavelengths, achieving maximum sensitivity at about 445 millimicrons. These are known as "blue" sensitive cones. Any lightwave impinging on the retina evokes a response, to a greater or less degree, from most or all these cones. A perceived "color" results from the proportion of "stimulation" of the various kinds.

Rods and cones vary in distribution across the retina. The center is tightly packed with cones and has no rods. Toward the periphery of the retina, rods increase and cones decrease. Thus, color sensitivity does not exist at the retina's outer edges, although yellows and blues can be detected further into the periphery than reds and greens. The very center of the retina is devoid of "blue" cones, creating a "blue-blindness" for small objects fixated upon.

The receptors in the eye also adjust, or adapt, their level of sensitivity to the overall light level and the color being viewed. Adaptation to increases in brightness improves color sensitivity. Color adaptation "softens" colors.

The brightness sensitivity of the eye to different colors also varies. It is governed by output from the "red" and "green" cones. The greater the output, the higher the brightness, which results in the eye being most sensitive to colors in the middle of the visual spectrum and less sensitive to colors at the extremes. A blue or red must be of a much greater intensity than a green or yellow to even be perceived.

The ability of the eye to detect a form is accomplished by focusing the viewed image on the body of receptors to establish "edges." Distinct edges yield distinct images. Edges formed by color differences alone cannot be accurately focused and thus create fuzzy and nondistinct images. A clear, sharp image requires a difference in brightness between adjacent objects, as well as differences in color.

The components of the eye—the lens and retina—govern the choices, and combinations, of colors to be displayed on a screen. The proper colors will enhance performance; improper colors will have the opposite effect, as well as greatly increase the probability of visual fatigue.

COLORS IN CONTEXT

Colors are subject to contextual effects. The size of a colored image, the color of images adjacent to it, and the ambient illumination all exert an influence on what is actually perceived. At the normal viewing distance for a screen, maximal color sensitivity is not reached until the size of a colored area exceeds about a three-inch square. Smaller size images become desaturated (having a greater white component) and change slightly in color. Also, small differences in actual color may not be discernible. Blues and yellows are particularly susceptible to difficulties in detecting slight changes. Finally, small adjacent colored images may appear to the eye to merge or mix. Red and green, for example, might appear as yellow.

Adjacent images can influence the perceived color. A color on a dark background, for example, will look lighter and brighter than the same color on a light background. A color can be *induced* into a neutral foreground area (gray) by the presence of a colored background. A red background can change a gray into a green. Induced colors are the complementary of the inducing color. Complementary afterimages can also be induced by looking at a saturated color for a period of time.

Colors change as light levels change. Higher levels of ambient light tend to desaturate colors. Saturated colors will also appear larger than desaturated colors.

CHOOSING CATEGORIES OF INFORMATION FOR COLOR

- Choosing categories of information for color requires a clear understanding of how the information will be used.
- Some examples:
  - if different parts of the screen are attended to separately, color code the different parts to focus selective attention on each in turn;
  - if decisions are made based on the status of certain types of information on the screen, color code the types of status the information may possess;
  - if screen searching is performed to locate information of a particular kind or quality, color code these kinds or qualities for contrast;
  - if the sequence of information use is constrained or ordered, use color to identify the sequence;
  - if the information displayed on a screen is packed or crowded, use color to provide visual groupings.

Color chosen to classify data on a screen must aid the transfer of information from the display to the user. This requires a clear understanding of how the information is selected and used. The examples above describe some common ways of classifying information for color coding purposes.

It is important to remember, however, that data on one screen may be used in more than one way. What is useful in one context may not be in another and may only cause interference. Therefore, when developing a color strategy, consider how spatial formatting, highlighting, and messages may also be useful.

CHOOSING COLORS TO DISPLAY

General Considerations

Colors chosen for display on a screen must consider these factors: the human visual system, the possible problems that its use may cause, the contextual effects that may occur, the viewing environment in which the display is used, and the task of the user. The primary objective in using color is communication, to aid the transfer of information from the screen to the user.

Usage

- Design for monochrome first.
- Use colors conservatively.
  - Do not use color where other identification techniques such as location are available.

Design for monochrome first. A screen should be capable of being effectively used as if it were in a monochrome environment. Spatial formatting, consistent locations, and display techniques such as highlighting, mixed- and upper-case characters should all be utilized to give it a structure independent of the color. This will permit the screen to be effectively used

- by colorblind people.
- on monochrome displays.
- in conditions where ambient lighting distorts the perceived color.
- if the color ever fails.

Use colors conservatively. Only enough colors to achieve the design objective should be used. More colors increase response times, increase the chance of errors due to colors confusions, and increase the chance of the "Christmas tree" effect. If two colors serve the need, use two colors. If three colors are needed, by all means use three. A way to minimize the need for too many different colors is to not use it in situations where other identification methods are available. An action bar, for example, will always be located at the top of the screen. Its position and structure will identify it as an action bar. To also color code it would be redundant.

Discrimination and Harmony

- For best absolute discrimination, select no more than four or five colors widely spaced on the color spectrum.
  - Good colors: red, yellow, green, blue, brown.
- For best comparative discrimination, select no more than six or seven colors widely spaced on the color spectrum.
  - Other acceptable colors: orange, yellow-green, cyan, violet, or magenta.
- Choose harmonious colors.
  - One color plus two colors on either side of its complement.
  - Three colors in equidistant points around the color circle.
- For older viewers or extended viewing, use brighter colors.

For best absolute discrimination, use four to five colors.   The population of measurable colors is about 7.5 million (Geldard, 1953). From this vast number, the eye cannot effectively distinguish many more than a handful. If color memorization and absolute discrimination is necessary (a color must be correctly identified while no other color is in the field of vision), select no more than four to five colors widely spaced along the color spectrum (Smith, 1988; Marcus, 1986b). Selecting widely spaced colors will maximize the probability of their being correctly identified. Good choices are red, yellow, green, blue, and brown (Marcus, 1986b).

Two good color opponent pairs are red/green and yellow/blue. All of these colors except blue are easy to resolve visually. Again, be cautious in using blue for data, text, or small symbols on screens because it may not always be legible. If the meaning for more than five colors is absolutely necessary, a legend should be provided illustrating the colors and describing their associated meanings.

For best comparative discrimination, use six to seven colors.   If comparative discrimination will be performed (a color must be correctly identified while other colors are in the field of vision), select no more than six or seven colors widely spaced along the visual spectrum. In addition to those above, other colors could be chosen from orange, yellow-green, cyan, and violet or magenta. Again, be cautious of using blue for data, text, or small symbols.

If the intent is to realistically portray natural objects, the use of more colors might be necessary.

Choose harmonious colors.   Harmonious colors are those that work well together or meet without sharp contrast. Harmony is most easily achieved with a monochromatic palette. For each background color, different lightnesses or values are established through mixing it with black and white. Marcus (1986a) suggests a minimum of three values should be obtained.

Harmonious combinations in a multicolor environment are more difficult to obtain. Marcus recommends avoiding complementary colors—those at opposite sides of the circle of hues in the Munsell color system, a standard commercial color system. He suggests using split complements, one color plus two colors on either side of its complement, or choosing three colors at equidistant points around the color circle.

For older viewers or extended viewing, use bright colors.   As eye capacity diminishes with age, data, text, and symbols in the less bright colors may be harder to read. Distinguishing colors may also be more difficult. For any viewer, long viewing periods result in the eye adapting to the brightness level. Brighter colors will be needed if either of these conditions exist.

Emphasis

- To draw attention or to emphasize, use bright or highlighted colors. To deemphasize, use less bright colors.
  - The perceived brightness of colors from most to least is white, yellow, green, blue, red.
- To emphasize separation, use contrasting colors.
  - Red and green, blue and yellow.
- To convey similarity, use similar colors.
  - Orange and yellow, blue and violet.

To draw attention or emphasize, use bright colors.   The eye is drawn to brighter or highlighted colors, so use them for the more important screen components. The data or text is the most important component on most screens, so it is a good candidate for highlighting or the brightest color. Danger signals should also be brighter or highlighted. The perceived brightness of colors, from most to least, is white, yellow, green, blue, and red.

Keep in mind, however, that under levels of high ambient illumination, colors frequently appear washed out or unsaturated. If some means of light attenuation is not possible, or if colors chosen are not bright enough to counter the illumination, color should be used with caution.

Use contrasting colors to emphasize separation.   To emphasize the separation of screen components, use contrasting colors. Possible pairs would be red/green and blue/yellow.

Use similar colors to convey similarity.   Similar colors convey a similar meaning. Related elements can be brought together by displaying them in a similar color. Blue and green, for example, are more closely related than red and green.

Common Meanings

- To indicate that actions are necessary, use warm colors.
  - Red, orange, yellow.
- To provide status or background information, use cool colors.
  - Green, blue, violet, purple.

- Conform to human expectancies
  — in the job.
  — in the world at large.

To indicate that actions are necessary, use warm colors.   The warm colors, red, yellow, and orange, imply active situations or that actions are necessary. Warm colors advance, forcing attention.

To provide background or status, use cool colors.   The cool colors, green, blue, violet, and purple, imply background or status information. Cool colors recede or draw away.

Conform to human expectancies.   Use color meanings that already exist in a person's job or the world at large. They are ingrained in behavior and difficult to unlearn. Some common color associations, as described by Marcus (1986b) are the following:

- Red   — Stop, fire, hot, danger.
- Yellow   — Caution, slow, test.
- Green   — Go, OK, clear, vegetation, safety.
- Blue   — Cold, water, calm, sky, neutrality.
- Gray   — Neutrality
- White   — Neutrality
- Warm colors — Action, response required, spatial closeness.
- Cool colors — Status, background information, spatial remoteness.

Some typical implications of color with dramatic portrayal, also by Marcus, are the following:

- High illumination — Hot, active, comic situations.
- Low illumination   — Emotional, tense, tragic, melodramatic, romantic situations.
- High saturation   — Emotional, tense, hot, melodramatic, comic situations.
- Warm colors   — Active, leisure, recreation, comic situations.
- Cool colors   — Efficiency, work, tragic and romantic situations.

Proper use of color also requires consideration of the experiences and expectations of the screen viewers.

Location

- In the center of the visual field, use red and green.
- For peripheral viewing, use blue, yellow, black, and white.
- Use adjacent colors that differ by hue and value or lightness.

In the center of the visual field, use red and green.   The eye is most
sensitive to red and green in the center of the visual field. The edges of the
retina are not sensitive to these colors. If used in the viewing periphery, some
other attention-getting method such as blinking must also be used.

For peripheral viewing, use blue, yellow, black, or white.   The retina is
most sensitive to these colors at its periphery.

Use adjacent colors that differ by hue and value.   Colors appearing
adjacent to one another should differ in hue and lightness for a sharp "edge"
and maximum differentiation. Also, adjacent colors differing only in their blue
component should not be used so that differentiation is possible. The eye is
poorly suited for dealing with blue.

Ordering

- Order colors by their spectral position.
  — Red, orange, yellow, green, blue, indigo, violet.

If an ordering of colors is needed, such as high to low, levels of depth, and
so on, arrange colors by their spectral position. There is evidence that people
see the spectral order as a natural one (Fromme, 1983). The spectral order is
red, orange, yellow, green, blue, indigo, and violet, most easily remembered as
"ROY G BIV."

Foregrounds and Backgrounds

Foregrounds

- Use colors as different as possible from background colors.
- Use warmer, more active colors.
- Use colors that possess the same saturation and lightness.
- For text or data, use desaturated or spectrum center colors.
  — White, yellow, green.
- To emphasize, highlight in a light value of the foreground color, pure white,
  or yellow.
- To deemphasize, lowlight in a dark value of the foreground color.

Backgrounds

- Use a background color to organize a group of elements into a unified
  whole.
- Use colors that do not compete with the foreground.
- Use cool, dark colors.
  — Blue, black.
- Use colors at the extreme end of the color spectrum.
  — Red, magenta.

Foregrounds

Use colors as different as possible from background colors.   Widely different foreground will maximize legibility.

Use warmer, more active colors.   Warmer colors advance, forcing attention.

Use colors that possess the same saturation and lightness.   Exercise caution in using more fully saturated red and orange, however, as they may be difficult to distinguish from one another.

For text or data, use desaturated or spectrum center colors.   Desaturated or spectrum center colors do not excessively stimulate the eye and appear brighter to the eye. Saturated colors excessively stimulate the eye. Marcus (1986a) recommends avoiding the use of pure white in text (except for some highlighting) because of the harsh contrast between the text and background. He suggests text should be off-white in a multicolor palette. The ISO Color Standard (Smith, 1988) suggests that for continuous reading tasks desaturated, spectrally close colors (yellow, cyan, green) should be used to minimize disruptive eye problems.

Highlight in a light value of the foreground color, pure white, or yellow.
Lowlight in a dark value of the foreground color.   Marcus (1986a) suggests that to call attention to a screen element, it may be highlighted in a light value of the foreground color. If off-white is the foreground color, highlight in pure white. Yellow can also be used to highlight. To deemphasize an element, lowlight in a darker value of the foreground color. In lowlighting, a strong enough contrast with both the background and the non-lowlighted element must be maintained so that legibility and visual differentiation is possible.

The simultaneous use of highlighting and lowlighting should be avoided. Used together they may create confusion for the viewer. Also, as with other display techniques, be conservative in using highlighting and lowlighting so that simplicity and clarity are maintained.

Backgrounds

Use a background color to organize a group of elements into a unified whole.   A background color should organize a group of element into a unified whole, isolating them from the remainder of the screen.

Use colors that do not compete with the foreground.   A background must be subtle and subservient to the data, text, or symbols on top of it.

Use cool, dark colors.   Cool, dark colors visually recede, providing good contrast to the advancing lighter, foreground colors. Blue is especially good because of the eye's lack of sensitivity to it in the retina's central area and increased sensitivity to it in the periphery. Lalomia and Happ (1987) in a study addressing foreground and background color combinations, found the best background colors to be black and blue. In a similar study, Pastoor (1990) found that cool colors, blue and bluish cyan, were preferred for dark background screens.

Use colors at the extreme end of the color spectrum. Other spectrally extreme colors, such as red and magenta, also make better background colors. Marcus (1986a) recommends, in order of priority, the following background colors: blue, black, gray, brown, red, green, purple.

Color Palette and Default

- Provide a default set of colors for all screen components.
- Provide a palette of six or seven foreground colors.
  - —Provide two to five values or lightness shades for each foreground color.
- Provide a palette of six or seven background colors.

Provide a default set of colors. Most people do not know how to apply color to create a clear and appealing screen. Others may have the talent and skills but not the time to select a proper combination. For these users, a preselected set of colors should be developed for all screen elements.

Provide a palette of six or seven foreground and background colors. To provide some flexibility, and to permit users the opportunity to change colors if they so desire, a palette of colors should be available. Marcus (1986a) suggests a maximum of six or seven foreground and background colors will provide the necessary variety. He also recommends that two to five values or lightnesses for each foreground color be developed.

With these palettes, however, some sort of guidance concerning maximum number of colors to use and what are good and poor combinations should be provided. This will make the color selection process more efficient and reduce the likelihood of visually straining conditions developing.

Gray Scale

- For fine discriminations use a black-gray-white scale.
  - —Recommended values are white, light gray, medium gray, dark gray, black.

The perception of fine detail is poor with color. The eye resolves fine detail much better on a black-white scale. Marcus (1986b) recommends five tonal values for a black and white, higher resolution screens: black, dark gray, medium gray, light gray, and white. He suggests the following general uses:

- White   — Screen background
                   Text located in any black area.

- Light Gray   — Pushbutton background area

- Medium Gray   — Icon background area
                   Menu dropshadow
                   Window dropshadow
                   Inside area of system icons
                   Filename bar

- Dark gray   — Window border

- Black   — Text
                   Window title bar
                   Icon border
                   Icon elements
                   Ruled lines

Consistency

- Be consistent in color use.

Consistency in color usage should exist within a screen, a set of screens, and a system. A person can sense the relatedness of color in space and over time, thereby linking elements not immediately together. An identical background color in windows on different screens, for example, will be seen as related. Changing color meanings must be avoided. It will lead to difficulties in interpretation, confusion, and errors. In general, broadly defined meanings (such as red indicating a problem) permit more scope for variations without inconsistency.

ALPHANUMERIC AND GRAPHIC SCREENS

For displaying data, text, and symbols, colors selected should have adequate visibility, contrast, and harmony.

- Use effective foreground/background combinations.
- Use effective character combinations.
- Display no more than four colors at one time.
- Choose the background color first.

Use Effective Foreground/Background Combinations

Lalomia and Happ (1987) established effective foreground/background color combinations for the IBM 5153 Color Display. From a color set of 16 different foregrounds and 8 different backgrounds, 120 color combinations were evaluated for 1) response time to identify characters, and 2) subjective preferences of users. The results from each measure were ranked and combined to derive an overall measure of color combination effectiveness. The best and poorest color combinations are summarized in Table 13.1. In this table "Best" means the specified combination was in the top 20 percent for overall effectiveness; "Poor" means it was in the bottom 20 percent. Those combinations comprising the "middle" 60 percent are indicated by a dash (–).

The results yield some interesting conclusions.

- The majority of good combinations possess a bright or high-intensity color as the foreground color.
- The majority of poor combinations are those with low contrast.
- The best overall color is black.
- The poorest overall color is brown.
- Maximum flexibility and variety in choosing a foreground color exists with black or blue backgrounds (these backgrounds account for almost one-half of the good combinations).
- Brown and green are the poorest background choices.

Bailey and Bailey (1989) in their screen creation utility Protoscreens have a table summarizing research-derived good foreground/background combinations. This table, which uses the results of the Lalomia and Happ study plus some others, is shown in modified form in Table 13.2.

The studies referenced above did not control character-background luminance-contrast ratios. Because of the characteristics of the eye, some colors appear brighter to the eye than others. A conclusion of the Lalomia and Happ study was that good combinations usually possessed a bright or high-intensity foreground color.

Pastoor (1990) equalized luminance-contrast ratios at preoptimized levels for about 800 foreground/background color combinations. For foregrounds brighter than backgrounds, the ratio was 10:1; for brighter backgrounds, 1:6.5. He then had the combinations rated with the following results:

- For dark on light polarity:
  — Any foreground color is acceptable if the background color is chosen properly.
  — Increased saturation of the foreground only marginally affected ratings, implying that any dark, saturated, foreground color is satisfactory.
  — Saturated backgrounds yield unsatisfactory ratings.
  — Less saturated backgrounds generally receive high ratings with any foreground color.
- For light on dark polarity:
  — Combinations involving saturated colors tend to be unsatisfactory.
  — As foreground color saturation increases; the number of background colors yielding high ratings diminishes.

Table 13.1 Effective foreground/background combinations. (From Lalomia and Happ, 1987)

Foreground	Background							
	Black	Blue	Green	Cyan	Red	Magenta	Brown	White
BLACK	x	–	–	Good	–	Good	–	Good
BLUE	–	x	–	–	Poor	–	–	Good
H.I. BLUE	–	–	Poor	Poor	–	–	Poor	Poor
CYAN	Good	–	Poor	x	–	–	Poor	–
H.I. CYAN	Good	Good	–	Good	Good	Good	–	–
GREEN	Good	Good	x	Poor	Good	–	Poor	Poor
H.I. GREEN	–	Good	–	–	–	–	–	–
YELLOW	Good	Good	–	Good	–	Good	–	–
RED	–	–	Poor	–	x	Poor	Poor	–
H.I. RED	–	–	Poor	–	–	–	–	–
MAGENTA	–	–	Poor	–	Poor	x	Poor	–
H.I. MAGENTA	Good	–	Good	–	–	Poor	–	–
BROWN	–	–	Poor	–	–	Poor	x	–
GRAY	–	Poor	–	–	Poor	–	Poor	–
WHITE	–	Good	–	Poor	–	–	–	x
H.I. WHITE	Good	–	Good	Good	–	–	–	–

(H.I. = High Intensity)

Table 13.2 Preferred foreground/background combinations from Protoscreens.

Backgrounds	Acceptable Foregrounds	
Black	Dark Cyan	Light Green
	Dark Yellow	Light Cyan
	Dark White	Light Magenta
		Light Yellow
		Light White
Blue	Dark Green	Light Green
	Dark Yellow	Light Cyan
	Dark White	Light Yellow
		Light White
Green	Black	Light Yellow
	Dark Blue	Light White
Cyan	Black	Light Yellow
	Dark Blue	Light White
Red	—	Light Green
		Light Cyan
		Light Yellow
		Light White
Magenta	Black	Light Cyan
		Light Yellow
		Light White
Yellow	Black	—
	Dark Blue	
	Dark Red	
White	Black	—
	Dark Blue	

— Generally, desaturated foreground/background color combinations yielded the best ratings.
— Short wavelength, cool colors were preferred for backgrounds (blue, bluish cyan, cyan).

In general, Pastoor concluded that 1) there was no evidence suggesting a differential effect of color on subjective ratings or performance (except that for light on dark polarity, blue, bluish cyan, or cyan were preferred as backgrounds), and 2) overall, desaturated color combinations yielded the best results.

Use effective character combinations.   Smith (1986) has recommended the two- and three-color combinations summarized at the left of Table 13.3 as being

Table 13.3   Effective two- and three-color combinations for dark background screens from Smith (1986).

Two-Color Combinations

Good	*Poor*
White / Green	Red / Blue
Gold / Cyan	Red / Green
Gold / Green	Red / Purple
Green / Magenta	Red / Yellow
Green / Lavender	Red / Magenta
Cyan / Red	White / Cyan
	White / Yellow
	Blue / Green
	Blue / Purple
	Green / Cyan
	Cyan / Lavender

Three-Color Combinations

Good	*Poor*
White / Gold / Green	Red / Yellow / Green
White / Gold / Blue	Red / Blue / Green
White / Gold / Magenta	Red / Magenta / Blue
White / Red / Cyan	White / Cyan / Yellow
Red / Cyan/ Gold	Green / Cyan / Blue
Cyan / Yellow / Lavender	
Gold / Magenta / Blue	
Gold / Magenta / Green	
Gold / Lavender / Green	

effective for dark background screens. She cautions against using the combinations described on the table's right side. She also suggests that light background screens should contain pastel colors with dark characters.

Display no more than four colors at one time.   While not experimentally verified, experience indicates that more than four colors displayed at one time on a screen gives rise to a feeling of overkill. Marcus (1986a) suggests an even more conservative approach, a maximum of three foreground colors and, even better, only two. An application of good use of color can often be viewed in one's living room. Note the use of color by the television networks when textual or tabular information is presented (for example, sport scores, news highlights, and so on). The use of only two, or sometimes three, colors is most commonly seen.

So, while more than four colors may be displayed over a period of time or a series of screens, do not display more than four colors at one time on a single screen. For most cases, restrict the number of colors to two or three.

Choose the background color first.   When choosing colors to display, it is best to select the background color first. Then choose acceptable foreground colors.

Statistical Graphics Screens

The visual, spatial, or physical representation of information—as opposed to numeric, alphanumeric, textual, or symbol representation—is known as statistical or data graphics. Common kinds of statistical graphics include bar graphs, line graphs, scatterplots, and pie charts. Color can also be used to render a statistical graphic screen more legible and meaningful.

Emphasis

- Emphasize the data display area.

The main emphasis of color in a statistical graphics screen should be in the data area. Brighter colors and highlighting should attract the eye to the presented data so that trends and conclusions can be quickly perceived. Supporting text, numbers, and legends should receive slightly less emphasis. Aids in data interpretation such as grids should receive the least emphasis.

Number of Colors

- Use no more than
  - six colors at one time.
  - five values or lightnesses of one color.

Experience indicates that displaying more than six colors at one time on statistical graphics screens is "too much." Even five or six colors, however, may be distracting or confusing if they are not properly chosen or are not harmonious. Marcus (1986a) suggests a more pleasing arrangement can often be achieved for graphics with five or less segments by using one color and displaying each segment in a different value or lightness. (Five, as described earlier, is the maximum number for easy human differentiation.)

Backgrounds

- Surround images
  - — in a neutral color.
  - — in a color complementary to the main image.

A neutral background will help set off a full color. A background in the complementary color of the main image will minimize visual afterimages.

Size

- Provide images of an adequate size for the task.
- If the image changes in size, use colors exhibiting a minimum shift in hue or lightness.
  - — White, yellow, and red on dark backgrounds.

As color areas decrease in size, they appear to change in lightness and saturation. Similar colors may look different and different colors may look similar. Interactions with the background color also increase. Thin gray images (lines or borders, for example) appear as a desaturated color complement of their background.

Provide adequate-size images. Where color identification is important, an image should be large enough to eliminate these distortions.

For images changing in size, use colors exhibiting minimum hue or lightness shifts. Marcus (1986b) recommends that white, yellow, and red be used for light text, thin lines, and small shapes on dark backgrounds (blue, green, red, light gray).

Status

- To indicate a status, use the following colors:
  - — Proper, normal, or OK   — Green, white, or blue
  - — Caution   — Yellow or gold
  - — Emergency or abnormal   — Red

The use of red, yellow, and green are well-learned color conventions.

Measurements and Area-Fill Patterns

- Display measurements in the following colors:
  - Grids   — Gray
  - Data points   — Yellow
  - Variance or error bars   — Blue
  - Out of specified range data   — Red
  - Captions and labels   — Lavender, lime green, or cyan

- Display area-fill patterns in the following colors:
  - Widely spaced dots   — Red
  - Closely spaced dots   — Green
  - Wide dashed lines   — Magenta
  - Narrow dashed lines   — Cyan
  - Wide crosshatch   — Blue
  - Narrow crosshatch   — Yellow

Measurements.   For measurements, Smith (1986) recommends the above. They balance emphasis considerations (gray for grids, yellow for data points, lavender, lime green, or cyan for labels) and human expectancies (red for out-of-specified range). Marcus (1986a) recommends that all text and the horizontal and vertical axis lines of a statistical graphic should be off-white. This will aid focusing main attention on the colored data.

Fill-in area patterns.   To ensure that fill-in area patterns are identifiable, discriminable, and free from unintended brightness effects, the ISO Draft Color Standard (Smith, 1988) recommends the above.

Physical Impressions

Size

- To convey an impression of
  - Larger   — Use bright or saturated colors.
  - Smaller   — Use dark or desaturated colors.
  - Similar   — Use colors of equal lightness.

Weight

- To convey an impression of
  - Heavy   — Use dark, saturated colors.
  - Light   — Use light, desaturated colors.

Distance

- To convey an impression of
  - Close   — Use saturated, bright, long-wavelength (red) colors.
  - Far   — Use saturated, dark, short-wavelength (blue) colors.

Height

- To convey an impression of height, use desaturated, light colors.

Depth

- To convey an impression of depth, use saturated, dark colors.

Concentration Level

- To convey an impression of concentration level use
  - High — Saturated colors.
  - Low — Desaturated colors.

Magnitude of Change

- To convey an impression of magnitude of change use
  - Lowest — Short-wavelength (blue) colors.
  - Highest — Long-wavelength (red) colors.

Actions

- To convey an impression of action use
  - Required — Long-wavelength (red) colors.
  - Not required — Short-wavelength (blue) colors.

Order

- To convey an impression of order with color use
  - Low end of a continuum — Short-wavelength (blue) colors.
  - High end of a continuum — Long-wavelength (red) colors.
- When displaying an array of ordered colors, position
  - Short-wavelength colors to the left side or at the bottom.
  - Long-wavelength colors to the right side or at the top.
- To convey an impression of order with value or lightness, use lightness order of a color (darkest to lightest or vice versa).

Neutrality

- To convey an impression of neutrality use black, gray, and white.

Colors yield different physical impressions (Tedford, et al. 1977; Smith, 1986; ISO Draft Color Standard; Smith, 1988). Bright, saturated colors convey a feeling of large and close. Dark, saturated colors mean heavy, far, and impression of depth. Desaturated, light colors indicate a light weight and height. Desaturated dark colors mean smaller. Long-wavelength (red) colors are associated with high rate of change, action required, and the high end of a continuum. Short-wavelength (blue) colors are associated with low rate of change, no actions required, and the low end of a continuum. Neutrality is best indicated by black, gray, or white.

Avoid

- Relying exclusively on color.
- Too many colors at one time.
- Highly saturated, spectrally extreme colors together:
  — Red and blue, yellow and purple.
- Low-brightness colors for extended viewing or older viewers.
- Colors of equal brightness.
- Colors lacking contrast:
  — For example, yellow and white, black and brown, reds, blues, and browns against a light background.
- Using colors in unexpected ways.
- Fully saturated colors for text or other frequently read screen components.
- Pure blue for text, thin lines, and small shapes.
- Colors in small areas.
- Color for fine details.
- Red and green in the periphery of large-scale displays.
- Adjacent colors only differing in the amount of blue they possess.
- Color to improve legibility of densely packed text.
- Too many colors at one time (again).

The proper use of color in screen design also suggests some things to avoid.

Relying exclusively on color. Consider the needs of colorblind viewers and the effects of ambient lighting on color perception. Do not underestimate the value and role of other techniques such as spatial formatting and component locations in good screen design.

Too many colors at one time. Using too many colors can increase response times, cause erroneous associations, interfere with the handling of information, and create confusion. The objective is a screen that communicates; a colorful screen is not the objective. Use just enough colors to create an effective communication. Again, consider the value of other techniques like spatial formatting and consistent component locations in good design.

Highly saturated, spectrally extreme colors together. Spectrally extreme combinations can create eye focus problems, vibrations, illusions of shadows, and afterimages. In addition to red/blue and yellow/purple, other combinations that might cause problems are yellow/blue, green/blue, and red/green (Marcus, 1985a).

Low-brightness colors for extended viewing or older viewers. The eye adapts to color during extended viewing. The eye's capacity also diminishes with age as the amount of light passing through the lens decreases. All colors will look less bright, and colors that are dim to begin with may not be legible. Brighter colors are needed to prevent reading problems.

Colors of equal brightness.   Colors of equal brightness cannot be easily distinguished. A brightness difference must exist between adjacent colors.

Colors lacking contrast.   Colors lacking contrast also cannot be easily distinguished.

Using colors in unexpected ways.   Colors have become associated with certain meanings. Red, for example, is always associated with stop or danger. To display a critical or error message in green would violate an ingrained association and cause confusion.

Fully saturated colors for text and other frequently read screen components.   Fully saturated colors excessively stimulate the eye, again possibly causing visual confusion.

Pure blue for text, thin lines, and small shapes.   Due to its physical make-up, the eye has difficulty creating a clear and legible image for small blue shapes. They will look fuzzy.

Colors in small areas.   Distortions in color, lightness, and saturation may occur.

Colors for fine details.   Black, gray, and white will provide much better resolution.

Red and green in the periphery of large-scale displays.   The edges of the retina are not particularly sensitive to red and green.

Adjacent colors only differing in the amount of blue they possess.   Because of the eye's difficulty in dealing with blue, differences in color based upon varying amounts of blue in the color's mixture will not be noticed.

Color to improve legibility of densely packed text.   Space lines between paragraphs of text or after about every five lines of data will work much better.

Too many colors at one time (again).   Never overuse color (again). Too many colors at one time may make a screen confusing or unpleasant to look at. Use only enough color to fulfill the system's objectives.

Source Documents

14

A well-designed source document will

- reduce manual subsystem processing times.
- permit the user to perform rapid
  - coding,
  - use of coded data, and
  - data entry.
- reduce errors
  - made in coding,
  - made in data interpretation, and
  - stored in the system database.

Ideally, the development of data entry screens is accomplished in conjunction with that of the source documents from which data is keyed. The system development effort that permits joint screen and document development usually yields the most effective human-machine data entry interface.

The screen designer should also, ideally, be the person who develops the source documents, since occasional design tradeoffs affecting both documents and screens must be performed. A designer who fully understands both components is in the best position to make the necessary judgments.

In this chapter a series of design guidelines is presented to enable a screen designer to develop a source document of sufficient detail for presentation to an organization's Form Design department. The focus is on document organization and style, and the desired product is a hand-printed draft from which a Form Design department can create the final printed version.

GENERAL DESIGN CRITERIA

- A well-designed source document meets the following criteria:
  - It reflects the needs and idiosyncrasies of its human users.
  - It allows hand, typed, or hand/typed completion.
  - It permits development of associated screen formats in its image.
  - It is economical regarding composition, paper, and printing within utilization ease limits.
  - It is consistent within itself, within related forms, within an application, and within an organization.

A well-designed source document, like a well-designed screen format, must meet certain broad criteria, as outlined above. In the pages that follow, guidelines for achieving these criteria are described. One important caution, however: Document economy is a desirable design goal but only within human ease of use limits. Too often documents and forms are developed with composition economy as the dominant design factor. Since various analyses show that form handling costs are about 100 times their composition and printing costs, this is a false economy. The most important design objective must be utilization ease.

SOURCE DOCUMENT DESIGN CONSIDERATIONS

The guidelines begin with a brief discussion of the philosophy that data should be collected at its source. Following a reiteration of the importance of design consistency is a general review of the alternative document design concepts available. Then an extensive series of document design guidelines are presented.

Source Data Collection

- Collect data at its source.
- Use the data-collection vehicle as the source document for data entry.
- Never require transcription of data from one document to another.

Data transcription is an error-prone process. Any time a data transcription occurs the chance of errors being introduced into a database is increased.

Galitz (1973) surveyed a sample of insurance agents regarding their attitude toward a source document (an application form) that, while imposing completion constraints, became the vehicle from which data entry keying was performed. A large majority (85 percent) said they would complete the document. More than one-half (53 percent) said they would complete the document even if it took half again as long to complete as the existing form. These agents realized the personal advantages to be gained by improving the quality of data reaching the system database.

Design Consistency

---

* Incorporate and use documents developed following a single design philosophy.

The larger the number of different documents that must be processed, the slower will be the overall data entry rate. Each dissimilar document to be keyed necessitates a certain amount of operator learning. The more similar the documents, the faster the learning. Significant differences between documents can impair data entry rates on all documents, as rules, formats, and handling requirements negatively impact one another.

This effect is minimized if a wide variety of source documents are developed according to the same standards. Processing in batches also has a positive effect on overall data entry rate, but this is usually not under control of the designer and is not usually a design consideration.

Alternative Source Document Design Concepts

---

* Caption preceding fill-in area.
* Caption within fill-in area.
* Caption above fill-in area (floating box).

The most common source document design concepts, illustrated in Figure 14.1, find the caption preceding, within, or above the fill-in area. Most currently available forms utilize one of these techniques. For source document design purposes, the first alternative, caption preceding fill-in area, can be readily eliminated as a viable method. Among its deficiencies are inefficient use of screens in matching a source document and poor visibility of fill-in fields.

The acceptable alternatives are the latter two: captions within and above fill-in areas. Table 14.1 provides a general comparison of these design alternatives by a number of factors. The recommended approach to source document design is the caption-above or floating box approach. Among its advantages are that it minimizes the visibility of irrelevant information, provides the best visibility of fill-in data (white boxes are generally imposed on a light-colored background), and fosters ease in keeping one's place in a document through built-in perceived visual rulers. This method also provides the best "perceptual match" between document and screen. The floating boxes are easily identifiable as separate entities and can be most easily associated with fields on a screen.

Sless (1987), in evaluating the floating box form, found that it helps both those coding the form and those processing the information contained on the form. The areas where answers go are obvious, how much work is involved in filling out the form can be ascertained by a glance, and checking for verification that all fields are completed is made easier. Information can also be retrieved easier with this style form.

Figure 14.1 A, B, and C Alternative source document design concepts.

A—Caption Preceding Fill-In Area:

Description and No. of messengers _____

Average amount each: Money $ _____ Securities $ _____ Checks $ _____

Merchandise $ _____

Type of conveyances used _____ No. guards _____

Average daily receipts plus bank: Money $ _____ Securities $ _____

Checks $ _____ How often are bank deposits made? _____

Payroll Money $ _____ Checks $ _____ How often? _____

No. of employees on duty in premises _____ Guards _____

Holdup alarm _____ Hours of business _____

Are checks cashed? _____ How much extra cash is brought in? $ _____

Are all checks listed? _____

Public sale of: Travelers Checks $ _____ Money Orders $ _____ Securities $ _____ Others $ _____

Exposures within the Banking Premises: Amount of Money $ _____ Securities $ _____ contained within

a leased safe deposit box or boxes or Securities $ _____ held by a bank for safekeeping in any Banking Premises

or similar recognized places of safe deposit, at _____

(NAME OF BANK)

_____ _____ _____ _____
(STREET AND NUMBER)   (CITY OR TOWN)   (COUNTY)   (STATE)

B Caption Within Fill-In Area:

INSURED INFORMATION

Insured

Business of Insured

Insured is:
☐ Individual ☐ Corporation ☐ Joint Venture ☐ Partnership
☐ Other:

Name and Telephone Number of Person to Contact for Loss Control Survey

Address		
City	State	Zip Code

Previous Carrier(s) & Policy Number(s)

Mortgagee		Item No.(s)

Address		
City	State	Zip Code

C Caption Above Fill-In Area (Floating Box):

3. RESIDENCE AND INSURED INFORMATION ▼

INSURED NAME (last, first, middle initial)

RESIDENCE TELEPHONE NUMBER (Area)

INSURED BIRTH DATE
MO   DAY   YEAR

MARITAL STATUS
Married Single
M☐   S☐
If ▲ Married

SPOUSE EMPLOYED
Yes   No
Y☐   N☐

INSURED OCCUPATION

SPOUSE OCCUPATION

PREMISES ADDRESS (If other than mailing)

STREET ADDRESS (MAILING)

CITY	STATE	ZIP CODE

CITY	STATE	ZIP CODE

COUNTY IN WHICH INSURED PREMISES LOCATED

PROPERTY LEGAL DESCRIPTION ATTACHED (If Required)
Yes
Y☐

INSURED PREMISES OTHER THAN MAILING ADDRESS
Yes
Y☐
▲ If yes, be sure to complete Premise Address

457

Table 14.1   The most common document design concepts.

Caption Within Fill-In Area	Floating Box Design
Coding Factors	
• Sufficient writing space	• Sufficient writing space
• Permits hand or typed entry	• Permits hand or typed data
• Permits clearly stated captions	• Permits clearly stated captions
• Clear Association—captions to fill-in data	• Clear Association—captions to fill-in data
	• Easy to achieve consistent size writing space
	• Best visibility of fill-in area
	• Easy to incorporate coding aids
	• Easy to minimize visibility of irrelevant information
Processing Factors	
• Fill-in data readable	• Fill-in data readable
	• Best visibility of fill-in area
Data Entry Factors	
• Fill-in data readable	• Fill-in data readable
• Screen fields easily associated with form captions	• Screen fields easily associated with form captions
	• Form/screen relationship easily maintained
	• Best visibility of fill-in data
	• Easy to minimize irrelevant information
	• Perceptual ease in keeping place on form
Composition and Economy Factors	
• Sometimes more efficient use of form space	• Usually more efficient use of screens
	• Easiest to conform to screen design guidelines

Sless also uncovered a particular problem with the Caption Within Fill-In Area forms. In many cases people filling out this style form began to write the required data after the captions instead of at the beginning of the boxes. As a result, the space available for writing wasn't used.

The primary disadvantages of this approach are its newness and its frequent association with computers. Some resistance to forms like this has been caused by these factors. Form users, however, have shown a willingness to use self-coding source documents when they perceive the benefits (Galitz, 1973). These kinds of documents have been successfully used in some information systems for 15 to 20 years.

In the guidelines that follow, both the caption-above and floating box concepts will be addressed. The document designers should "test the water" in their own organizations to ascertain what document design standards do exist and what potential feelings toward the floating box approach might be. Where no severe roadblocks are encountered (or where confrontation of existing roadblocks may be desired), the floating box method is suggested.

SOURCE DOCUMENT PHYSICAL CHARACTERISTICS

Most of a source document's physical characteristics are specified by an organization's Form Design department. The following concepts are presented to familiarize the source document designer with the variables that must be considered, and to provide background for discussions with that department. The designer will find that greater care exercised in the specification of all document requirements will usually yield the desired product much more quickly.

Source Document Physical Characteristics

Size

- 8½" × 11".
- 8½" × 7".
- 8½" × 5½".

Margins

- At least ⅓" on all sides.

Type Style

- Clear, simple styles such as Univers or Helvetica.

Type Size

- A minimum of 5 points for captions and check box codes. Section headings and form title should be larger, possibly 10 to 14 points.

Line Rules

- Utilize line rules of varying widths to identify major document components. For example,
  - section divisions—heavy lines,
  - subsection divisions—medium lines,
  - fill-in fields—light lines.

Turns

- Utilize the book-turn method for documents printed on both sides.

Colors

- Paper:
  - white or yellow.
- Titles, headings, captions, and codes:
  - black ink.
- Rules:
  - basic color or black ink.
- Background (floating box approach):
  - basic colors screened at about 30 percent.

Source document design can be accomplished simply by choosing a standard form size (such as 8½" × 11") and laying out fields and information within a ⅓-inch margin on all sides. Depending on printing requirements, exact margin requirements may vary slightly from this recommendation, but this approximation will permit Form Design to easily make any necessary adjustments.

Type style and size and line rules will ultimately be selected by the Form Design department in light of organization standards and legibility requirements. The document designer should feel free to make recommendations, however.

Turns refer to the method by which documents printed on both sides are turned over. "Book turn" means printing the front and back side of source documents head to head (with the top of each side back to back on the page). The paper is then turned, as the page of a book is turned. This is contrasted to the "tumble turn," where the top of the backside of a document is opposite and bottom of the front side. Turning requires grasping the bottom of the page and flipping it to the top as the page is turned. The most important point is not whether a document requires book- or tumble-turning, but that one consistent method is chosen. Confusion and frustration can result if a mix of documents requires turning by the different methods.

Color is a vital ingredient of forms developed with the floating box method. Best legibility is usually obtained if all alphanumerics (title, headings, captions, and codes) are printed in black ink and the document background is a basic color screened at about 30 percent. Some colors, if used for alphanumerics, may provide adequate contrast with the background, but these should be carefully selected.

DOCUMENT ORGANIZATION

- Provide clear design and clean reproduction by using perceptual groupings.
- Arrange information according to an acceptable combination of
  — sequence of use,
  — frequency of use,
  — function, and
  — importance.
- Use orderly and logical data sequence (top to bottom, left to right).
- Permit development of a screen format that is an exact image of the form.
- Minimize irrelevant information.

People's reactions to a form, like a screen, will be influenced by their first perceptions. The form may be perceived as cluttered, busy, and confusing, or conversely, meaningful and with evident purpose. The former is most often the result of trying to jam too much within its boundaries. The latter can only occur through plentiful use of "white space" and segmentation into logical pieces.

It is very important that source document design occur within constraints imposed by the physical limitations of the screens to which they are related. The design of the source document must permit development of a screen, or screens, in its exact image. The design of the source document must be the controlling factor, as this data collection vehicle must make sense to the person who is filling it out. Experience has shown that the standard 8½-inch form width is usually the primary constraining factor in developing a source document and related screen. That is, one usually runs out of space on the form before one runs out of space on a typical 80-column-wide screen (while using the methods described in this book).

Information arrangement on source documents should be based on sequence and frequency of use, function, and importance—principles described earlier.

To reiterate:

Sequence of use grouping involves arranging information items in the order in which they are commonly received or transmitted, or in natural groups. A person's address, for example, is normally given by street, city, state, and zip code. Another example of natural grouping is the league standings of football teams, which appear in order of best to worst records.

Frequency of use is a design technique based on the principle that information items used most frequently should be grouped at the beginning of the form. The second-most frequently used items are grouped next, and so forth.

Function involves grouping information items according to their purpose. All items pertaining to insurance coverage, for example, may be placed in one location. Such grouping also allows convenient group identification for both preparer and user.

Importance grouping is based on the information's importance to the task being performed. Important items are placed in the most prominent positions.

Source document design normally reflects a combination of these techniques. Information may be organized functionally, but within each function individual items may be arranged by sequence or importance. Numerous permutations are possible.

SOURCE DOCUMENT CONTENT

Captions

- Provide intelligent and clearly stated captions.
- Spell out fully, using words meaningful to the form coder.
- Clearly associate captions with fill-in areas.

Floating Box

- Center caption above fill-in area.

Caption

- If fill-in area is excessively long, position caption above upper left corner.

Caption

- For columnar-oriented, multiple fields, center caption above topmost fill-in area.

Caption

Caption Within Fill-In Area

- Position caption in upper left-hand corner.

Caption

- For columnar-oriented, multiple fill-in areas center caption above topmost fill-in area separated by a line.

Caption

- Do not mix methods on one document or family of documents.

Captions must clearly communicate to the form coder what data or information must be placed in a fill-in field. Which fill-in field should receive the data or information must also be obvious. These simple rules are often violated in the design of forms. How often have you found yourself encoding the wrong information, or putting it in the wrong place? The rules described above, for the alternative design methods, are intended to eliminate the chances of these errors occurring.

Fill-In Areas

- Maximize visibility of fill-in areas.
- Provide sufficient writing space.
- Develop for completion by handwriting, typewriter, or both, as necessary.

FLOATING BOX

Hand Only Composition

— Vertical spacing:
   Multiples of $\frac{1}{6}$";
— Fill-in area height:
   Optimally—$\frac{1}{3}$";
   Minimally—$\frac{1}{5}$";
— Fill-in area width:
   Optimally—$\frac{1}{4}$" per expected character;
   Minimally—$\frac{1}{6}$" per expected character.

Typewriter Only Completion

— Vertical spacing:
   Multiples of $\frac{1}{6}$";
— Fill-in area height:
   Optimum and minimum—$\frac{1}{5}$";

— Fill-in area width:
Minimally—$\frac{1}{10}$" per expected character (plus an additional $\frac{1}{10}$" per field).

Hand or Typewriter Completion

— Vertical spacing:
Multiples of $\frac{1}{6}$";
— Fill-in area height:
Optimum and minimum—$\frac{1}{5}$";
— Fill-in area width:
Optimally—$\frac{1}{5}$" per expected character;
Minimally—$\frac{1}{6}$" per expected character.

CAPTION WITHIN FILL-IN AREA

Hand Only Completion

— Vertical spacing:
Multiples of $\frac{1}{6}$";
— Fill-in area height:
Optimally—$\frac{1}{2}$";
Minimally—$\frac{1}{3}$";
— Fill-in area width:
Optimally—at least $\frac{1}{4}$" per expected character;
Minimally—at least $\frac{1}{6}$" per expected character.

Typewriter Only Completion

— Vertical spacing:
Multiples of $\frac{1}{6}$";
— Fill-in area height:
Optimum and minimum——$\frac{1}{3}$";
— Fill-in area width:
Minimally—$\frac{1}{10}$" per expected character (plus an additional $\frac{1}{10}$" per field).

Hand or Typewriter Completion

— vertical spacing:
multiples of $\frac{1}{6}$";
— fill-in area height:
optimum and minimum—$\frac{1}{3}$";
— fill-in area width:
optimally—at least $\frac{1}{5}$" per expected character;
minimally—at least $\frac{1}{6}$" per expected character.

Some source documents are always completed by hand, others by hand or typewriter. Some are always completed by typewriter. The method of completion is the driving factor in establishing field sizes and spacing. The guidelines summarized above provide optimums and minimums for the various alternatives. The optimums are always recommended, the minimums only if absolutely necessary. The requirements described can be illustrated as follows:

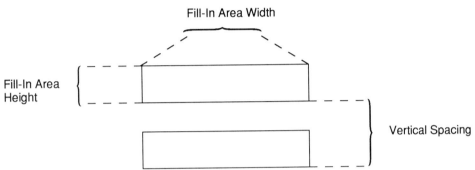

Many forms lack sufficient writing space for encoding information. Information legibility can be severely impaired if the size of fill-in areas is reduced to squeeze too many elements onto one piece of paper. In a study by a large insurance company (Galitz, 1973), adequate spacing for form completion or encoding was ranked by insurance agents as the most important factor in simplifying forms.

Coding Techniques—Alternatives

Ballot Box Checking

- Should be used when the required responses can be segmented into clearly identifiable categories.
- May be used for hand or typewriter completed documents.
- Do not exceed six or seven alternatives for a field.

Circling

- Should be used when the required responses can be segmented into clearly identifiable categories.
- Use only for hand completed documents.
- Do not exceed six or seven alternatives per field.

Character Inscription

- Should be used when the variety of information to be coded is too great to be categorized.
- May be used for hand or typewriter completed documents.

Coding is the process by which data is manually written or typed into a fill-in field. It is most commonly accomplished through ballot box checking, alternative circling, and character inscription.

Ballot box checking is a method commonly used when alternative responses can be segmented into clearly identifiable categories. The selected alternative can then be "x"ed or checked by the form coder. This method may be used for documents completed either by hand or typewriter.

Circling is another method that may be used when alternative responses can be segmented into clearly identifiable categories. The selected alternative can then be circled by the form coder. For this reason, circling is most often used when a document is usually completed by hand. It is possible to typewriter-complete documents using this method by instructing the document coder to enclose the relevant alternative within parentheses ( ).

Character inscription involves the hand printing or coding of data into an open fill-in field. Character inscription is normally used when the variety of information to be coded is too great to be categorized. Names and addresses are good examples of data requiring this kind of coding technique.

The advantages of the ballot box checking and circling approaches are that they rely upon the coder's more effective powers of recognition rather than recall, and legibility is guaranteed because the codes are printed. (Hand-inscribed characters may occasionally suffer in legibility.) The chief disadvantage of these methods is the amount of space that may be consumed to develop one field. Therefore, six or seven is about the maximum number of alternatives that should be included within this type of field. A larger number of alternatives usually requires reverting to the character inscription method. One reasonable compromise which may be implemented for fields with more than six or seven alternatives, and some alternatives infrequently occur, is to use ballot box checking or circling for the frequent alternatives and character inscription for the infrequent ones.

Coding Techniques—Design

Ballot Box Checking

- Place the alternative caption above the box.
- Center the check box below the alternative caption.
- Position the code to the right of the check box.
- Leave space equal to at least one-half of the combined length of an alternative ballot box, caption, and code between each alternative in the field.

Circling

- Place the alternative caption above the code.
- Center the code below the alternative caption.
- Leave space equal to the least one-half of the length of an alternative caption between each alternative in a field.

LOCATION			APPROVED	
Los Angeles	New York	Chicago	Yes	No
LA	NY	CH	Y	N

LOCATION			APPROVED	
Los Angeles	New York	Chicago	Yes	No
LA	NY	CH	Y	N

Character Inscription

- The code is inscribed in a free-form manner.

CITY

While either the ballot box or circling technique may be used, the circling technique is recommended because it results in a less cluttered-looking fill-in field. When a two-part document can be developed (part one, or the top page, is coded and part two, or the back page, becomes the document from which key entry is performed), data irrelevant to the user of each document part may be left off that document part. For example, using the ballot box technique illustrated above, part one would look like:

CITY

and part two:

LOCATION			APPROVED	
Los Angeles ☐	New York ☐	Chicago ☐	Yes ☐	No ☐

LOCATION			APPROVED	
☐ LA	☐ NY	☐ CH	☐ Y	☐ N

Coding Aids

FIELD SIZE INDICATORS

- For fill-in fields requiring a fixed number of characters in field:
  — fields may be partitioned using $\frac{1}{12}$" high thin (000 rule) tick marks.

PRODUCER CODE

PRODUCER CODE

  — fields may be segmented into logical pieces using $\frac{1}{12}$" high thicker (two point) tick marks.

DATE

DATE

- For fill-in fields in which a variable number of characters may be coded in field:

Floating Box

  — inscribe the maximum number of characters permitted in upper leftmost corner of fill-in field;
  — Increase field width by one character space.

LOAN NUMBER

12

Caption Within Fill-In Field

  — locate the maximum number of characters permitted immediately to the right of caption.

LOAN NUMBER (12)

To expedite completion, various coding aids may be built into a document. Included are field size indicators, assumed value indicators, dollar signs, decimal points, and required field completion indicators.

Field size indicators are optional in document design. They may take the form of either tick marks to identify the individual character positions in a field, or a numeric value to simply indicate the maximum number of characters that may be encoded within its boundaries. Tick marks, when used, should only be incorporated within fields requiring a fixed number of characters. Incorporating tick marks within variable length fields constrains the coder for the worst case condition, which is seldom achieved. Two studies (Wright and Barnard, 1975; and Barnard et al., 1978) found that field spacing constraints, including tick marks, actually impair performance in terms of speed of information entry and legibility of the final product. These investigators concluded that spatial constraints are deleterious to the perception of individual letters. Possible causes are that they contribute noise to the visual field or that they may modify the way characters are written so that they become less legible. Since the reading process is holistic (using a word's general features such as its overall shape and letter sequence probabilities), spatial arrangements that distort perceptual features may disrupt the reading process.

In light of these findings, use tick marks only for fixed-length fields that generally contain less meaningful data (rates, factors, etc.) with less established perceptual features. The tick marks will also remind the document coder that all character positions must be filled. For variable-length fields generally containing more meaningful data, restrict field size indicators, if used at all, to a simple value that indicates maximum field size. The probability of exceeding field size is low, and if it happens it will be immediately detected at data entry, where remedial action can be taken. Excessive restrictions to the coding process itself do not seem worth the effort involved for the small gains to be made.

Coding Aids (Continued)

ASSUMED VALUE INDICATORS

Floating Box

- Place value to right and outside of fill-in field.

DEDUCTIBLE

LIMIT

00

000

Caption Within Fill-In Field

- Place value within fill-in field.
- Increase field size to compensate for assumed value indicator inclusion.

DEDUCTIBLE

00

LIMIT

000

DOLLAR SIGNS

Floating Box

- Place dollar sign to left and outside of fill-in field.

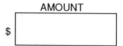

Caption Within Fill-In Field

- Place dollar sign within fill-in field.
- Increase field size to compensate for dollar sign inclusion.

Assumed value indicators and dollar signs, while of value to the document coder, are irrelevant to data entry. The general design philosophy, then, is to sublimate their appearance on the document. This can be accomplished, at least, when using the floating box approach, by positioning them outside the fill-in field. They are visible to the document coder but are not "noise" to data entry. For documents using captions within the fill-in field, this sublimation cannot be accomplished because adjacent fields share common borders.

Coding Aids (Continued)

Decimal Points

- Inscribe the decimal point at its proper location within the fill-in field.

Required Completion Field Indicators (for coding)

- Incorporate a heavier rule around the fill-in field.

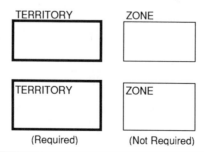

To indicate that a document fill-in field must always be completed, incorporate a heavier rule around the fill-in field. This convention is for the ease of the document coder, not data entry. Computer edits will normally provide the necessary feedback at data entry.

Care must be exercised in using bold borders on fields with captions within the box, since fields share common borders. For these kinds of documents this convention cannot always be applied.

OTHER CONSIDERATIONS

Title

- Locate at the document's top.
- Clearly describe document's intent or use.
- Spell out fully all words.
- Do not include redundant words (such as document or form).

A document must be identified by a title that describes its intent or use. An organization's conventions may dictate its exact placement. Normal positioning will be centered. Some organizations may require inclusion of a corporate logo on documents completed externally. Care must be exercised to allow for its inclusion as well.

Completion Instructions

- Describe instructions in the sequence in which they must be performed.
- Be brief and use clear and concise words.
- Locate instructions on the document cover, top, or before the section or item to which they apply.
- Instructions pertaining to an action to be taken with a completed document may appear at the document end or bottom.

Although it should be obvious how to complete a well-designed document, it may occasionally be necessary to provide brief instructions or clarification information. These instructions should always precede that part of the document to which it applies. Brevity of completion instructions is a virtue.

Section Headings

- Identify logical groupings of related fill-in fields through section headings.
- Provide short, clear, fully spelled-out descriptions of the section's content.
- Locate section headings above the associated fill-in fields and justify to left margin.

Documents will normally be segmented into groupings or sections of related information. These groupings or sections may be preceded by a section heading. If so, the section heading will be left-justified above its grouping of related data fields. Section headings are recommended because they aid in developing perceptual groupings of document elements.

Fill-In Area Alignment

- Align fill-in areas in rows.

- Align (left-justified) the starting points on fill-in areas.

- Align, where possible (right-justified), the end points of fill-in areas in each row.

- On forms completed by typewriter, the starting points of fields should be aligned under one another, where possible, to facilitate the setting of typewriter tab stops.

Fill-in area alignment must follow a left-to-right, top-to-bottom orientation. Always align the starting points of fill-in areas in each row. Attempt to align the end points of the last field in each row. Do not, however, leave large gaps between fields in a row to achieve this right-justified alignment. Where these large gaps do occur, close the fill-in fields to the left and omit the right-justification for that particular row.

Fill-in area spacing should always be accomplished with the idea of facilitating tab stop setting for typewriter completion. It is usually easier to accomplish this with the caption within the fill-in box approach rather than with the floating box approach, since the former provides more leeway in establishing field widths. Bear in mind, however, that more documents generally are completed by hand than by typewriter, so compromises for ease of typing at the expense of ease of hand completion can be self-defeating.

Screen Design Steps

15

NECESSARY DESIGN STEPS

I. Review screen design documentation and services.
II. Identify system inputs and outputs.
III. Identify unique user requirements.
IV. Describe data elements.
V. Develop transactions.
VI. Develop final paper screens.
VII. Define computer screens.
VIII. Test screens.
IX. Implement screens.
X. Evaluate screens.

In this chapter the design steps necessary to develop and implement screens are reviewed and illustrated. Some guidelines and design aids are also presented.

Screen design is an orderly process, flowing through the requirements, design, testing, and implementation phases of a system development cycle. Screen design will normally move through those design steps summarized above. Most of these steps are common to all parts of a system development effort. Since this handbook is focusing only on screen design, the emphasis is on steps 4, 5, and 6. The remaining steps are reviewed only to the detail necessary to provide continuity of thought.

The subject matter to illustrate the design steps is a data entry screen developed for use with a dedicated source document. This kind of screen has been chosen because it is the most complex design activity and is subject to the most design tradeoffs. Design of other kinds of screens is normally less complex.

I. Review screen design documentation and services.
   A. Standards
      1. Screens
      2. Source documents/forms
      3. System development
   B. Handbooks
      1. Screen design
   C. Manuals
      1. Display terminal
      2. Data entry utility/system
      3. Screen definition
      4. Data element
   D. Consulting services
      1. Internal
      2. External

Before beginning any screen design activity, the designer must be aware of the services and documentation available for referral and assistance. Included are various standards, handbooks, manuals, and consulting services.

The design *standards* contain all the rules that must be adhered to in the screen design process. They may describe the specific methods, timing, and products for an organization's system development cycle.

Handbooks   normally contain guidelines to aid the design process (such as are found in this document).

Important *manuals* are those that describe the characters of the terminal for which the screens will be designed, the characteristics of the system or utility with which the screens will be used, the characteristics of screen creation utilities on which screens may be created, and manuals that provide guidance in the specification of system data elements.

Consulting services   are those available both within and outside the organization that can provide guidance concerning all aspects of the screen design process, including technical assistance and standard interpretations.

I. Review screen design documentation and services.
II. Identify system inputs and outputs.

Data entry screen formats are developed for the purpose of providing inputs to a system. System outputs affect the content of inquiry screens. The product of the phase that identifies a system's inputs and output—the data elements—will be the building blocks used in the screen design process.

I. Review screen design documentation and services.
II. Identify system inputs and outputs.
III. Identify unique user requirements.

User requirements of importance to the screen designer are those of the people performing the data entry, inquiry, or interactive function. The screen design guidelines described in previous chapters have been developed for optimum ease of use by a wide range of users. They assume the following:

- Job level may be clerical or managerial.
- Touch-typing skills may or may not exist.
- Turnover rate may be high or low.
- Business knowledge may be minimal or extensive.
- The potential for using more than one system exists.
- System usage may be frequent or infrequent.

Since the screen standards have been developed at a fairly "low" common denominator, users exceeding these requirements will still find the screens very usable.

This phase, then, will ascertain where the screen users fall within this broad spectrum. This knowledge may then be applied as design tradeoffs are performed throughout the design process. For example, in-depth business knowledge and low turnover rates may allow incorporation of more cryptic screen captions as an occasional design tradeoff. The designer is cautioned, however, not to let user characteristics wield too much influence, as these characteristics can change in time.

In this requirements step, the necessity for developing associated source documents for data entry must also be determined. This decision will direct data entry screen design to the proper design guidelines.

I. Review screen design documentation and services.
II. Identify system inputs and outputs.
III. Identify unique user requirements.
IV. Describe data elements.
    A. Title/name.
    B. Screen caption.
    C. Size.
    D. Required or optional status.
    E. Logical relationship with other data elements.

Data elements, the building blocks of screens, were defined in step 2. The screen design process itself begins with the specification of some important data element characteristics. Most of this information can probably be captured from worksheets that are normally prepared during the input/output design process.

The *title* will be the name of the data element. This name must be a clear description of the data element for the screen user (and document coder). Titles on system worksheets may have to be clarified because they often include extraneous information (to the user), such as system descriptors.

Screen captions must be developed from the data element title. Rules for developing screen captions are included in the chapters on guidelines for the kind of screens being created.

Size is the length of the field in character positions. It is a numeric value ranging from 1 to n.

Required or optional status will define the frequency of occurrence of a data element. A required field is one into which data is always keyed or always displayed every time a screen is used.

Logical relationship with other data elements is the rule for cross-field validation checking and customary associations between data elements.

This data element descriptive information must be recorded in some meaningful and easily used format. A computer printout of data elements may be available, but its size, information content, and format normally make a printout difficult to use. A manual solution is to prepare a simple listing of all relevant data elements, as illustrated in Figure 15.1. Throughout the remainder of this chapter many of the design steps will be illustrated with figures and examples. The information shown is based upon an actual design, but it has, however, been extensively edited and shortened for illustrative simplicity, and should not be construed as a technically valid transaction.)

I. Review screen design documentation and services.
II. Identify system inputs and outputs.
III. Identify unique user requirements.
IV. Describe data elements.
V. **Develop transactions.**
   A. **Summarize design requirements affecting screen design.**
   B. **Specify data elements that will comprise a transaction.**
   C. **Organize transaction data elements into sections.**
   D. **Identify and lay out screens.**

A *transaction*, sometimes called a function, is a screen or series of screens comprising an activity whose conclusion results in an output or action fulfilling a system requirement. Transaction design, like most design, is a deductive process,

Figure 15.1   Example data element list.

Title	Screen Caption	Size	Req/ Opt.	Logical Relationships
Street Address (Mailing)	MAIL-ADD:	30	R	With Mail City, St, Zip
City (Mailing)	CITY:	13	R	With Mail Add, St, Zip
State (Mailing)	ST:	2	R	With Mail Add, City, Zip
Zip Code (Mailing)	ZIP:	5	R	With Mail Add, City, St
Company	CO:	2	R	With Branch Code
Branch Code	BR-CD:	3	R	With Company
Marital Status	MAR-STS:	1	O	With Spouse Emp.
Spouse Employed	SP-EMP:	1	O	With Marital Status
Effective Date	EFF-DT:	6	R	With Expiration Date
Expiration Date	EXP-DT:	6	R	With Effective Date
HO Policy Form Number	POL-FORM:	1	R	With Coverages
Producer Code	PROD-CD:	6	R	With Sub-Prod Code
Sub-Producer Code	SUB-PROD:	4	O	With Producer Code
Account Number	ACCT#:	9	R	
Primary Policy Number	PRI-POL#:	8	O	With Sec. Res. Policy
Insured Premises Other Than Mailing Address	PRMS-OTH:	8	O	With Premises Address
Premises Address	PRMS-ADD	30	O	With Prms City, St, Zip
Premises City	CITY:	13	O	With Prms Add, St, Zip
Premises State	ST:	2	O	With Prms Add, City, Zip
Premises Zip Code	ZIP:	5	O	With Prms Add, City, St
A. Building Limits	A-BLDGS:	7	O	Coverage Type I
B. Other Structures Limits	B-OTH-STR:	5	O	Coverage Type I
C. Unsched. Personal Property Limits	C-UNS-PR:	7	R	Coverage Type I
D. Add'l Living Expenses Limits	D-ADD-LIV:	5	R	Coverage Type I
E. Pers. Liab.-Each Occur. Limits	E-PER-LI:	7	R	Coverage Type II
F. Med. Payment-Each Pers. Limits	F-MED-PAY:	5	R	Coverage Type II
Deductible Amount	DED-AMT:	5	R	Coverage with Ded Form #
Deductible Form Number	DED-FORM#:	3	O	Coverage with Ded Amt.
Producer Issued Dec	PROD-ISS:	1	R	
Secondary Residence Policy	SEC-RES	1	O	With Primary Policy No
Property Legal Descript. Attach.	LEG-DESC:	1	O	
250 Theft Deductible	250-DED:	1	O	Coverage with Ded Amt.
Policy Type	POL-TYPE:	1	R	
New York Coinsurance	NY-CINS:	1	O	
County In Which Insured Premises Located	PRMS-CNY:	5	R	With Prms City, St, Zip
Policy Number	POL#:	13	R	
Insured Name–1	NM-1:	30	R	With Insured Name-2
Insured Name–2	NM-2:	30	O	With Insured Name-1

proceeding from a general set of requirements to a specific solution—one screen format or a series of screen formats. It is also an iterative process, with frequent starts, stops, and steps backward. The steps summarized above reflect the normal sequential flow of transaction design. The loops in design may cause many steps to be performed several times. This is normal and to be expected. (This fact, however, should not discourage the designer from trying to achieve minimal iterations. This is a goal toward which one should strive.)

I. Review screen design documentation and services.
II. Identify system inputs and outputs.
III. Identify unique user requirements.
IV. Describe data elements.
V. Develop transactions.
   A. Summarize design requirements affecting screen design.
      1. Important design requirements
         a. Human
         b. Hardware
         c. Software
         d. Source document (if applicable)
         e. Application
      2. Considerations and requirements are reflected in
         a. Standards
         b. System requirements documents
         c. Handbooks
         d. Manuals
         e. Manually prepared data element listing

The design considerations impacting screen design have been a topic of discussion in this handbook. Before beginning design, the handbook along with all relevant standards should be reviewed.

System requirements must be abstracted from the design documents prepared during the system development phases. All design must be accomplished within the standards, limits, and guidelines described. The manually prepared data element list will be an important reference source throughout the design.

If the application transactions being developed are to include as their data source an especially designed source document, then source document considerations are important. One important factor affecting screen design is the non-data-entry data elements, which must be included only on the source document.

To aid in application transaction development, these non-data-entry data elements should also be summarized on the data element list. This has been done for the example and is illustrated in Figure 15.2.

The non-data-entry data elements can usually be obtained from the application requirements document. Screen captions are, of course, not necessary.

I. Review screen design documentation and services.
II. Identify system inputs and outputs.
III. Identify unique user requirements.
IV. Describe data elements.
V. Develop transactions.
   A. Summarize design requirements affecting screen design.
   B. **Specify data elements that will comprise a transaction.**
      1. **Considerations in transaction development**
         a. **Application requirements**
         b. **Computer transaction requirements**
         c. **User requirements**

Application transaction development is a major facet of all the system design activity that has occurred to this point. It will reflect the requirements of the application, the unique requirements of the structure of computer transactions, and the requirements of people generating and using the data. Throughout development activities, application transaction development has been a primary objective.

The screen designer's role in this activity is to ensure that the application transactions adequately reflect user requirements and that application transactions "make sense" to all systems users; that is, that they reflect the environment as it is commonly perceived.

The product of this activity is one or more application transactions, each consisting of a series of defined data elements. Completion of this step initiates what has commonly been called screen design.

In our example, let us assume that all the specified data elements will comprise one transaction called "Homeowner's New Business." This transaction with its data element list is illustrated in Figure 15.3. (Had it been required to develop two application transactions for all the data elements, these data elements would have had to be split into two separate application transactions data element listings.)

I. Review screen design documentation and services.
II. Identify system inputs and outputs.
III. Identify unique user requirements.
IV. Describe data elements.
V. Develop transactions.
   A. Summarize design requirements affecting screen design.
   B. Specify data elements that will comprise a transaction.
   C. **Organize transaction data elements into sections.**
      1. **Calculate data element lengths**
         a. **Data element length is the sum of**
            1) **The number of characters in the screen caption**
            2) **The number of characters in the field**
            3) **The data element attribute characters (always 2)**
         b. **Add length to each data element in the data element listing**

Figure 15.2   Example data element list with non-data-entry data elements.

Title	Screen Caption	Size	Req/ Opt.	Logical Relationships
Street Address (Mailing)	MAIL-ADD:	30	R	With Mail City, St, Zip
City (Mailing)	CITY:	13	R	With Mail Add, St, Zip
State (Mailing)	ST:	2	R	With Mail Add, City, Zip
Zip Code (Mailing)	ZIP:	5	R	With Mail Add, City, St
Company	CO:	2	R	With Branch Code
Branch Code	BR-CD:	3	R	With Company
Marital Status	MAR-STS:	1	O	With Spouse Emp.
Spouse Employed	SP-EMP:	1	O	With Marital Status
Effective Date	EFF-DT:	6	R	With Expiration Date
Expiration Date	EXP-DT:	6	R	With Effective Date
HO Policy Form Number	POL-FORM:	1	R	With Coverages
Producer Code	PROD-CD:	6	R	With Sub-Prod Code
Sub-Producer Code	SUB-PROD:	4	O	With Producer Code
Account Number	ACCT#:	9	R	
Primary Policy Number	PRI-POL#:	8	O	With Sec. Res. Policy
Insured Premises Other Than Mailing Address	PRMS-OTH:	8	O	With Premises Address
Premises Address	PRMS-ADD	30	O	With Prms City, St, Zip
Premises City	CITY:	13	O	With Prms Add, St, Zip
Premises State	ST:	2	O	With Prms Add, City, Zip
Premises Zip Code	ZIP:	5	O	With Prms Add, City, St
A. Building Limits	A-BLDGS:	7	O	Coverage Type I
B. Other Structures Limits	B-OTH-STR:	5	O	Coverage Type I
C. Unsched. Personal Property Limits	C-UNS-PR:	7	R	Coverage Type I
D. Add'l Living Expenses Limits	D-ADD-LIV:	5	R	Coverage Type I
E. Pers. Liab.-Each Occur. Limits	E-PER-LI:	7	R	Coverage Type II
F. Med. Payment-Each Pers. Limits	F-MED-PAY:	5	R	Coverage Type II
Deductible Amount	DED-AMT:	5	R	Coverage with Ded Form #
Deductible Form Number	DED-FORM#:	3	O	Coverage with Ded Amt.
Producer Issued Dec	PROD-ISS:	1	R	
Secondary Residence Policy	SEC-RES	1	O	With Primary Policy No
Property Legal Descript. Attach.	LEG-DESC:	1	O	
250 Theft Deductible	250-DED:	1	O	Coverage with Ded Amt.
Policy Type	POL-TYPE:	1	R	
New York Coinsurance	NY-CINS:	1	O	
County In Which Insured Premises Located	PRMS-CNY:	5	R	With Prms City, St, Zip
Policy Number	POL#:	13	R	
Insured Name–1	NM-1:	30	R	With Insured Name-2
Insured Name–2	NM-2:	30	O	With Insured Name-1
Non-Data Entry				
Residence Telephone Number		10		
Insured Occupation		15		
Spouse Occupation		15		
Birth Date of Insured		6		
Existing Account		1		
Med. Payment— Each Accid. Limits		7		

Figure 15.3 Example "Homeowner's New Business" application transaction data element list.

Title	Screen Caption	Size	Req/ Opt.	Logical Relationships
Street Address (Mailing)	MAIL-ADD:	30	R	With Mail City, St, Zip
City (Mailing)	CITY:	13	R	With Mail Add, St, Zip
State (Mailing)	ST:	2	R	With Mail Add, City, Zip
Zip Code (Mailing)	ZIP:	5	R	With Mail Add, City, St
Company	CO:	2	R	With Branch Code
Branch Code	BR-CD:	3	R	With Company
Marital Status	MAR-STS:	1	O	With Spouse Emp.
Spouse Employed	SP-EMP:	1	O	With Marital Status
Effective Date	EFF-DT:	6	R	With Expiration Date
Expiration Date	EXP-DT:	6	R	With Effective Date
HO Policy Form Number	POL-FORM:	1	R	With Coverages
Producer Code	PROD-CD:	6	R	With Sub-Prod Code
Sub-Producer Code	SUB-PROD:	4	O	With Producer Code
Account Number	ACCT#:	9	R	
Primary Policy Number	PRI-POL#:	8	O	With Sec. Res. Policy
Insured Premises Other Than Mailing Address	PRMS-OTH:	8	O	With Premises Address
Premises Address	PRMS-ADD	30	O	With Prms City, St, Zip
Premises City	CITY:	13	O	With Prms Add, St, Zip
Premises State	ST:	2	O	With Prms Add, City, Zip
Premises Zip Code	ZIP:	5	O	With Prms Add, City, St
A. Building Limits	A-BLDGS:	7	O	Coverage Type I
B. Other Structures Limits	B-OTH-STR:	5	O	Coverage Type I
C. Unsched. Personal Property Limits	C-UNS-PR:	7	R	Coverage Type I
D. Add'l Living Expenses Limits	D-ADD-LIV:	5	R	Coverage Type I
E. Pers. Liab.-Each Occur. Limits	E-PER-LI:	7	R	Coverage Type II
F. Med. Payment-Each Pers. Limits	F-MED-PAY:	5	R	Coverage Type II
Deductible Amount	DED-AMT:	5	R	Coverage with Ded Form #
Deductible Form Number	DED-FORM#:	3	O	Coverage with Ded Amt.
Producer Issued Dec	PROD-ISS:	1	R	
Secondary Residence Policy	SEC-RES	1	O	With Primary Policy No
Property Legal Descript. Attach.	LEG-DESC:	1	O	
250 Theft Deductible	250-DED:	1	O	Coverage with Ded Amt.
Policy Type	POL-TYPE:	1	R	
New York Coinsurance	NY-CINS:	1	O	
County In Which Insured Premises Located	PRMS-CNY:	5	R	With Prms City, St, Zip
Policy Number	POL#:	13	R	
Insured Name–1	NM-1:	30	R	With Insured Name-2
Insured Name–2	NM-2:	30	O	With Insured Name-1
Non-Data Entry				
Residence Telephone Number		10		
Insured Occupation		15		
Spouse Occupation		15		
Birth Date of Insured		6		
Existing Account		1		
Med. Payment— Each Accid. Limits		7		

The development and organization of screens can be facilitated by adding to the prepared DATA ELEMENT LISTING a descriptive field called DATA ELEMENT LENGTH. Data element length will be the sum of

- the number of characters in the screen caption,
- the number of characters in the field,
- the attribute characters.

Screen caption—The number of characters in the screen caption is figured by counting the total number of characters in the caption, including dashes, special characters, and the separator (:). For example,

- EFF-DT: is 7 characters;
- PROD-CD: is 8 characters;
- CO: is 3 characters.

Field—The number of characters in the field is the expected number of entry characters as described in the size field. For example,

- EFFECTIVE DATE is a 6-character entry field;
- PRODUCER CODE is a 6-character entry field;
- COMPANY is a 2-character entry field.

Attributes—Each part of the data element—the screen caption and the entry field—will be preceded by an attribute character.

- Allow 2 characters for attribute positions.

Lengths for the illustrated data element will be:

- EFFECTIVE DATE—15(7 + 6 + 2),
- PRODUCER CODE—16(8 + 6 + 2),
- COMPANY—7(3 + 2 + 2).

Data element lengths have been calculated for the example and are illustrated in Figure 15.4.

V. Develop transactions.
   C. Organize transaction data elements into sections. (Cont'd)
      1. Calculate data element lengths.
      2. **Apply grouping techniques and design considerations.**
         a. **Information grouping techniques**
            1) **Sequence of use**
            2) **Frequency of use**
            3) **Function**
            4) **Importance**

b. Screen design considerations
1) Human
2) Hardware
3) Software
4) Source document
5) Application

The objective of this design step is to segment the transaction's data elements into logical groupings and then to place the groupings into a logical order. No attempt is made to organize the data elements within a section or grouping.

Information grouping techniques were summarized in section 1 of Chapter 5. Screen format design considerations are the subject of this entire handbook. The *most important factor* in grouping and ordering is the *natural working habits* of the people who generate, record, and use the source data.

If the application transaction is going to reflect the structure of an associated source document, attention must be directed to source document design as well as screen format layout.

Any one design will normally reflect a combination of these grouping techniques. Information may be organized functionally, and within each function individual items may be arranged by sequence or importance. Numerous permutations are possible.

It is important to recognize that many of the design considerations may be partially incompatible with one another. Computer editing needs may not be fully achieved in light of the grouping requirements, or processing and edit requirements may be inconsistent. In these cases, the final organization of items within the transaction will be a compromise between all the considerations. The designer must weigh the alternatives and use judgment based upon transaction accuracy, time, cost, and ease requirements. It is important to remember, however, that *human requirements take precedence over machine processing requirements*, and that the avenue chosen, regardless of direction, must be consistent within itself.

V. Develop transactions.
   C. Organize transaction data elements into sections. (Cont'd)
      1. Calculate data element lengths.
      2. Apply grouping techniques and design considerations.
         c. Design product:
            1) Data elements are segmented into logical groupings
            2) The groupings are ordered in the manner in which they will occur in the transaction

---

The order and groupings of data elements for this example are summarized in Figure 15.5.

Figure 15.4 Example data element list with data element lengths.

Title	Screen Caption	Size	Req/ Opt.	Logical Relationships	DE Length
Street Address (Mailing)	MAIL-ADD:	30	R	With Mail City, St, Zip	41
City (Mailing)	CITY:	13	R	With Mail Add, St, Zip	20
State (Mailing)	ST:	2	R	With Mail Add, City, Zip	7
Zip Code (Mailing)	ZIP:	5	R	With Mail Add, City, St	13
Company	CO:	2	R	With Branch Code	7
Branch Code	BR-CD:	3	R	With Company	11
Marital Status	MAR-STS:	1	O	With Spouse Emp.	11
Spouse Employed	SP-EMP:	1	O	With Marital Status	10
Effective Date	EFF-DT:	6	R	With Expiration Date	15
Expiration Date	EXP-DT:	6	R	With Effective Date	15
HO Policy Form Number	POL-FORM:	1	R	With Coverages	12
Producer Code	PROD-CD:	6	R	With Sub-Prod Code	16
Sub-Producer Code	SUB-PROD:	4	O	With Producer Code	15
Account Number	ACCT#:	9	R		17
Primary Policy Number	PRI-POL#:	8	O	With Sec. Res. Policy	19
Insured Premises Other Than Mailing Address	PRMS-OTH:	8	O	With Premises Address	19
Premises Address	PRMS-ADD	30	O	With Prms City, St, Zip	41
Premises City	CITY:	13	O	With Prms Add, St, Zip	20
Premises State	ST:	2	O	With Prms Add, City, Zip	7
Premises Zip Code	ZIP:	5	O	With Prms Add, City, St	11
A. Building Limits	A-BLDGS:	7	O	Coverage Type I	17
B. Other Structures Limits	B-OTH-STR:	5	O	Coverage Type I	17
C. Unsched. Personal Property Limits	C-UNS-PR:	7	R	Coverage Type I	18
D. Add'l Living Expenses Limits	D-ADD-LIV:	5	R	Coverage Type I	17
E. Pers. Liab.-Each Occur. Limits	E-PER-LI:	7	R	Coverage Type II	18
F. Med. Payment-Each Pers. Limits	F-MED-PAY:	5	R	Coverage Type II	17
Deductible Amount	DED-AMT:	5	R	Coverage with Ded Form #	15
Deductible Form Number	DED-FORM#:	3	O	Coverage with Ded Amt.	15
Producer Issued Dec	PROD-ISS:	1	R		12
Secondary Residence Policy	SEC-RES	1	O	With Primary Policy No	11
Property Legal Descript. Attach.	LEG-DESC:	1	O		10
250 Theft Deductible	250-DED:	1	O	Coverage with Ded Amt.	11
Policy Type	POL-TYPE:	1	R		11
New York Coinsurance	NY-CINS:	1	O		11
County In Which Insured Premises Located	PRMS-CNY:	5	R	With Prms City, St, Zip	36
Policy Number	POL#:	13	R		20
Insured Name–1	NM-1:	30	R	With Insured Name-2	37
Insured Name–2	NM-2:	30	O	With Insured Name-1	37
Non-Data Entry					
Residence Telephone Number		10			
Insured Occupation		15			
Spouse Occupation		15			
Birth Date of Insured		6			
Existing Account		1			
Med. Payment— Each Accid. Limits		7			

V. Develop transactions
    C. Organize transaction data elements into sections. (Cont'd)
        1. Calculate data element lengths
        2. Apply grouping techniques and design considerations
        3. Specify necessary supplemental information
            a. Title
            b. Screen/page number
            c. Section headings
            d. Messages and instructional information
            e. Space lines

The *title* will be the source document title or a meaningful abbreviation of that title. For multiscreen transactions the title should only appear on the first screen.

The *screen or page number* may also be used to give identity to a screen by incorporating within it a mnemonic descriptive of the name of the transaction. Screen/page numbers will be located in a consistent position in the upper right-hand corner of the screen.

Data entry screen formats should not be packed with data. Inclusion of *section headings* serves to provide visual breaks in the screen formats and gives the user an additional reference "point" in visually moving from the source document to the screen. Section headings should be those found on the source document.

Space lines   or blank lines also serve to provide visual breaks in the screen and give the user another reference "point" in visually moving from the source document to the screen. They may be substituted for section headings at section boundaries, or they may be used where a wider than normal visual break exists between lines of the source document data entry field. (These breaks may occur when the source document contains rows of non-data-entry data elements or other supplementary information not used in the data entry process.)

Messages and instructional information   are usually not necessary and are not recommended for inclusion on this kind of screen format.

At the conclusion of this activity, there will have been specified:

- the content of the screen title,
- the structure and content of page numbers,
- whether section headings will be included (and their content),
- whether instructions and messages will be included (and their content),
- whether space lines will be included.

Supplemental information requirements for this example are illustrated in Figure 15.6. Included are screen title, page numbers, section headings, and space lines. There will be no instructions and messages. The screen number is

Figure 15.5 Example order and general grouping of data elements in an application transaction.

1. *Policy-Related Data Elements*
   Expiration Date
   Effective Date
   Account Number
   Primary Policy Number
   Producer Issued Dec
   Policy Type
   Policy Number
   Existing Account (NON-DE)
   Secondary Residence Policy

2. *Producer- and Company-Related Data Elements*
   Producer Code
   Branch Code
   Sub-Producer Code
   Company

3. *Residence- and Insured-Related Data Elements*
   Street Address (mailing)
   City (mailing)
   State (mailing)
   Zip Code (mailing)
   Marital Status
   Spouse Employed
   Insured Premises other than mailing address
   Premises Address
   Premises City
   Premises State
   Premises Zip Code
   County in which Premises located
   Property Legal Description Attached
   Residence Telephone Number (NON-DE)
   Insured Occupation (NON-DE)
   Spouse Occupation (NON-DE)
   Insured Birth Date (NON-DE)
   Insured Name 1
   Insured Name–2

4. *Coverage-Related Data Elements*
   HO Policy Form Number
   Deductible Amount
   Deductible Form Number
   Building Limits
   Other Structure Limits
   Unscheduled Personal Property Limits
   Additional Living Expenses Limits
   Personal Liability—Each Occurrence Limits
   Medical Payments—Each Person Limits
   $250 Theft Deductible
   New York Coinsurance
   Medical Payments—Each Accident Limits (NON-DE)

Figure 15.6   Example supplemental information requirements.

Title:	Homeowners Application
Page/Screen Number:	HMAP nn
Section Headings:	Will Be Included
Instructions/Messages:	None
Space Lines:	Will Be Included

a contraction of the transaction name (HMAP) with specific pages designated by a numeric value beginning with 01.

    I. Review screen design documentation and services.
   II. Identify system inputs and outputs.
  III. Identify unique user requirement.
  IV. Describe data elements.
   V. Develop transactions.
      A. Summarize design requirements affecting screen design.
      B. Specify data elements that will comprise a transaction.
      C. Organize transaction data elements into sections.
      D. Identify and lay out screens.
         1. Apply to each grouping (section) of data elements
            a. Information grouping techniques
            b. Screen design considerations

The information grouping techniques summarized in the previous step (V. C. 2.) are now applied to each specific section of the transaction. This grouping is carried out within the described hardware limitations, according to the described field specification rules, and in conjunction with all the reviewed design considerations. The guidelines following are also helpful.

---

      2. Conform to the following guidelines:
         a. Confine screen line usage to data elements consuming about three-fourths of its available width (60–65 characters in an 80-character-wide line)
            1) The data element lengths calculated in step V. C. 1. are used to determine line space consumed.
         b. For multiscreen transactions, break screens at natural points.
            1) Between sections on a source document
            2) At the end of a source document page
            3) Never break a screen such that its parts are contained on two sides of a source document.
         c. If the guidelines result in the final transaction screen containing only a few lines (2–3), consider the following tradeoffs (in recommended order of implementation):
            1) Omit a space line or lines.
            2) Combine section headings.

Limiting each screen line to fields containing 60 to 65 characters leaves space for 1) developing perceptual groupings, and 2) transforming the completed screen into an image of its source document. For a source document-oriented data entry system with an 8-character caption limitation, source document space limits are usually reached before screen limits are reached. The screen limit can be quickly exceeded, however, if a line contains a large number of small fields. In screen format (or source document) design, therefore, try to avoid including a large number of small fields on one line.

Again, design tradeoffs may have to be performed. The discussion in step V. C. 2. is again appropriate, as are the above tradeoff guidelines.

The ordering of data elements within screen formats may be performed on a standard printed layout sheet. Because of the general nature of the product, these kinds of screen format drafts can, however, be completed on a plain piece of paper. This is the recommended methodology.

Figure 15.7 illustrates the first screen draft of the first screen prepared for the example data elements. This draft was developed in conjunction with a related source document that is illustrated in Figure 15.8.

Figure 15.7   Example preliminary screen format draft.

	Line Information and Data Elements	Total Character Count
1.	*** HMAP01 ***	14
2.	HOMEOWNERS APPLICATION (TITLE)	23
3.	1. POLICY INFORMATION (SECTION HEADING)	21
4.	EFF-DT(15)EXP-DT(15)ACCT#(17)POL#(20)	67
5.	PROD-ISS(12)SEC-RES(11)PRI-POL#(19)POL-TYP(11)	53
6.	2. PRODUCER AND COMPANY INFORMATION (SECTION HEADING)	35
7.	CO(7)BR-CD(11)PROD-CD(16)SUB-PROD(15)	49
8.	3. RESIDENCE AND INSURED INFORMATION (SECTION HEADING)	36
9.	NM-1(37)	37
10.	NM-2(37)MAR-STS(11)SP-EMP(10)	58
11.	(BLANK)	0
12.	MAIL-ADD(41)PRMS-ADD(41)	82
13.	CITY(20)ST(7)ZIP(13)CCITY(20)ST(7)ZIP(13)	80
14.	PRMS-OTH(19)PRMS-CNY(36)LEG-DESC(10)	65
15.	4. COVERAGES(SECTION HEADING)	12
16.	POL-FORM(12)A-BLDGS(17)B-OTH-STR(17)C-UNS-PR(18) D-ADD-LIV(17)	81
17.	E-PER-LI(18)F-MED-PAY(17)NY-CINS(11)	46
18.	DED-AMT(15)250-DED(11)DED-FORM#(15)	41

Figure 15.8 Source document example.

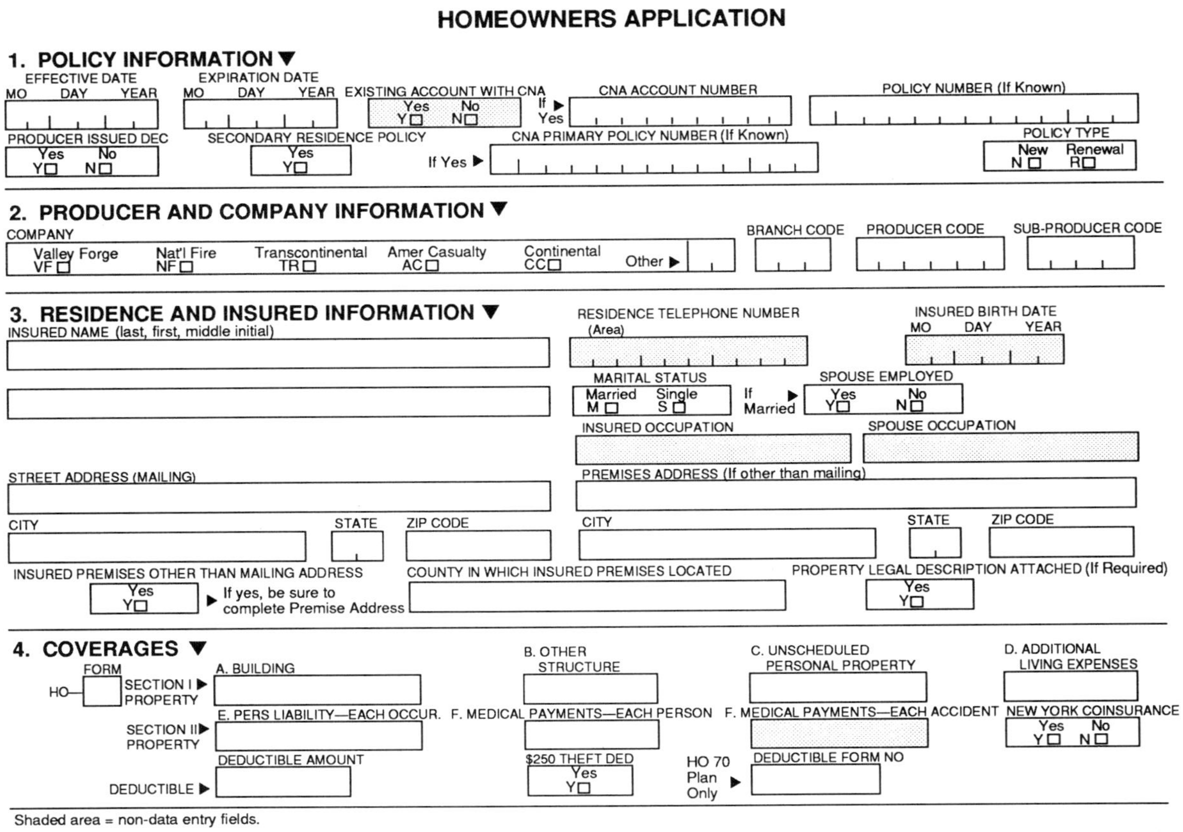

HOMEOWNERS APPLICATION

1. POLICY INFORMATION ▶

EFFECTIVE DATE
MO   DAY   YEAR

EXPIRATION DATE
MO   DAY   YEAR

EXISTING ACCOUNT WITH CNA
Yes   No   If
Y☐   N☐   Yes ▶

CNA ACCOUNT NUMBER

POLICY NUMBER (If Known)

PRODUCER ISSUED DEC
Yes   No
Y☐   N☐

SECONDARY RESIDENCE POLICY
Yes
Y☐

CNA PRIMARY POLICY NUMBER (If Known)
If Yes ▶

POLICY TYPE
New   Renewal
N☐   R☐

2. PRODUCER AND COMPANY INFORMATION ▶

COMPANY

| Valley Forge | Nat'l Fire | Transcontinental | Amer Casualty | Continental | Other ▶ |
| VF☐ | NF☐ | TR☐ | AC☐ | CC☐ | |

BRANCH CODE

PRODUCER CODE

SUB-PRODUCER CODE

3. RESIDENCE AND INSURED INFORMATION ▶

INSURED NAME (last, first, middle initial)

RESIDENCE TELEPHONE NUMBER
(Area)

INSURED BIRTH DATE
MO   DAY   YEAR

MARITAL STATUS
Married   Single
M☐   S☐

If
Married ▶

SPOUSE EMPLOYED
Yes   No
Y☐   N☐

INSURED OCCUPATION

SPOUSE OCCUPATION

STREET ADDRESS (MAILING)

PREMISES ADDRESS (If other than mailing)

CITY

STATE

ZIP CODE

CITY

STATE

ZIP CODE

INSURED PREMISES OTHER THAN MAILING ADDRESS
Yes
Y☐
▶ If yes, be sure to complete Premise Address

COUNTY IN WHICH INSURED PREMISES LOCATED

PROPERTY LEGAL DESCRIPTION ATTACHED (If Required)
Yes
Y☐

4. COVERAGES ▶

FORM

HO ☐

SECTION I ▶
PROPERTY

A. BUILDING

B. OTHER STRUCTURE

C. UNSCHEDULED PERSONAL PROPERTY

D. ADDITIONAL LIVING EXPENSES

NEW YORK COINSURANCE
Yes   No
Y☐   N☐

SECTION III ▶
PROPERTY

E. PERS LIABILITY—EACH OCCUR.

F. MEDICAL PAYMENTS—EACH PERSON

F. MEDICAL PAYMENTS—EACH ACCIDENT

DEDUCTIBLE ▶

DEDUCTIBLE AMOUNT

$250 THEFT DED
Yes
Y☐

HO 70
Plan
Only ▶

DEDUCTIBLE FORM NO

Shaded area = non-data entry fields.

491

SOME TRADEOFFS

This first draft fits well with the designed source document. However, some problems are immediately obvious: lines 12, 13, and 16 exceed the recommended 60- to 65-character maximum. In fact, two exceed the 80-character absolute and final maximum.

Lines 12 and 13. This situation frequently occurs when two sets of addresses are placed next to one another. The form provides a nice fit; the screen gets tight. The solution is to reduce the size of the screen captions. Since the fields on the document use up the entire line, creating a source document image will be fairly easy once the screen field data is compressed to within 80 characters.

So, to achieve an image relationship and effectively use the document, reduce MAIL-ADD to ML-AD, PRMS-ADD to P-AD, CITY to CT and ZIP to ZP. The result is illustrated in Figure 15.9. Line 12 now contains 75 characters and line 13 contains 74. Identifiable contractions of the source document caption still exist. (Remember, the document will always be available to aid in interpretation.)

Figure 15.9   Example preliminary screen format draft (revision).

	Line Information and Data Elements	Total Character Count
1.	*** HMAP01 ***	14
2.	HOMEOWNERS APPLICATION (TITLE)	23
3.	1. POLICY INFORMATION (SECTION HEADING)	21
4.	EFF-DT(15)EXP-DT(15)ACCT#(17)POL#(20)	67
5.	PROD-ISS(12)SEC-RES(11)PRI-POL#(19)POL-TYP(11)	53
6.	2. PRODUCER AND COMPANY INFORMATION (SECTION HEADING)	35
7.	CO(7)BR-CD(11)PROD-CD(16)SUB-PROD(15)	49
8.	3. RESIDENCE AND INSURED INFORMATION (SECTION HEADING)	36
9.	NM-1(37)	37
10.	NM-2(37)MAR-STS(11)SP-EMP(10)	58
11.	(BLANK)	0
	ML-AD(38) P-AD(37)	75
12.	~~MAIL-ADD(41)PRMS-ADD(41)~~	~~82~~
	CT(18) ZP(12)CT(18) ZP(12)	74
13.	~~CITY(20)ST(7)ZIP(13)CCITY(20)ST(7)ZIP(13)~~	~~80~~
14.	PRMS-OTH(19)PRMS-CNY(36)LEG-DESC(10)	65
15.	4. COVERAGES(SECTION HEADING)	12
	FORM(8) B-OTH(13)	
16.	~~POL-FORM(12)~~A-BLDGS(17)~~B-OTH-STR(17)~~	73
	C-UNS-PR(18)D-ADD-LIV(17)	~~81~~
17.	E-PER-LI(18)F-MED-PAY(17)NY-CINS(11)	46
18.	DED-AMT(15)250-DED(11)DED-FORM#(15)	41

Line 16. The exceeded capacity problem in line 16 is different—fields on the source document do not fill up the document line. Screen caption reduction in this case will primarily be directed toward creating a screen document image relationship. To reduce the size, change POL-FORM to FORM and B-OTH-STR to B-OTH. The result is also illustrated in Figure 15.9. Line 16 now contains 73 characters. This is still high but should be workable. Identifiable contractions of the source document captions still exist.

V. Develop transactions.
   D. Identify and lay out screens. (Cont'd)
      1. Group data elements.
      2. Conform to guidelines.
      3. Design step conclusion:
         a. Properly organize screen drafts including all data elements, title, screen number, section headings, and space lines

---

All the components of each screen have now been defined. These components have been properly sequenced and positioned on the proper lines. The final step is to develop paper screens in the exact image of the designed document.

   I. Review screen design documentation and services.
   II. Identify system inputs and outputs.
   III. Identify unique user requirements.
   IV. Describe data elements.
   V. Develop transactions.
 VI. Define final paper screen.
   A. Using the spacing guidelines summarized in section 5-2 of this handbook, transfer the fields and information from the draft layout worksheet to a standard printed screen layout form.
      1. Some important reminders
         a. Allow a cursor rest position at the end of each line (in this 80-character-wide example, an entry field cannot extend beyond column 78)
         b. In maintaining an image relationship between document and screen, align entry fields (not captions)
   B. Use the attribute definition conventions of the system for which the screens are being defined.

The information on the draft layout worksheet is now transferred to a standard printout screen layout form available from many vendors. The spacing and clarity guidelines described in the previous chapters must be implemented in this transfer process. The experienced designer who has an on-line screen generation facility may find it easier to perform this design on-line, using a terminal.

The attribute definition conventions of the system for which the screens are being designed must also be implemented at this time. This involves following rules for specifically identifying protected fields, unprotected fields, highlighted fields, and so forth. Since the specific methods may vary, they are not addressed here. Screen designers must see that they are properly specified for their own environment at this point.

The following pages describe a paper screen developed for the example problem, and review some final design tradeoffs. For clarity, no specification of attributes is included in the layout. Entry (or unprotected) fields are designated by periods (.). The remaining fields (captions, titles, etc.) may be assumed to be protected.

   I. Review screen design documentation and services.
  II. Identify system inputs and outputs.
 III. Identify unique user requirements.
 IV. Describe data elements.
  V. Develop transactions.
 VI. Develop final paper screens.
VII. Define computer screens.

Completed paper screens are next defined within the system. Screen generation facilities are frequently used for this purpose. Figure 15.17 is a printout of the screen created through a screen generation facility.

   I. Review screen design documentation and services.
  II. Identify system inputs and outputs.
 III. Identify unique user requirements.
 IV. Describe data elements.
  V. Develop transactions.
 VI. Develop final paper screens.
 VII. Define computer screens.
VIII. Test screens.
 IX. Implement screens.
  X. Evaluate screens.

Screen testing occurs as part of the normal course of unit, subsystem, and system testing. Modifications are made as necessary. Care must be exercised to assure that any changes implemented conform to the design philosophy and guidelines being followed.

Screens like any part of a system, must be evaluated to ensure that they are achieving their design objectives—including clarity and ease of use. Any system evaluation plans should address them as part of the evaluation process.

Figure 15.10 Development of paper screens (screen number and title).

```
                                                              HMAP01
❶ ─────────────────────────────────────────────────────
❷ ─────────── HOMEOWNERS APPLICATION ──────────────────

1.  POLICY INFORMATION
      EFF-DT: --/--/--     EXP-DT: --/--/--   ACCT#: ---------   POL#: ---------
      PROD-ISS: --------    SEC-RES: -    PRI-POL#: ---------      POL-TYP: -
2.  PRODUCER AND COMPANY INFORMATION
      CO: --               BR-CD: --    PROD-CD: ------   SUB-PROD: -----
3.  RESIDENCE AND INSURED INFORMATION
      NM-1: ------------------------    MAR-STS: -    SP-EMP: -
      NM-2: ------------------------

    ML-AD: -----------------------   P-AD: -------------------------
      CTY: ---------------   ST: --  ZP: -----       CTY: ---------------  ST: --  ZP: -----
    PRMS-OTH: -           PRMS-CNY: ---------------            LEG-DISC: -
4.  COVERAGES
    FORM: -    A-BLDG: --------   B-OTH: -------   C-UNS-PR: --------   D-ADD-LIV: -------
               E-PER-L: --------   F-MED: ------                        NY-CINS: -
               DED-AMT: ------   250-DED: -   DED-FORM#: ---

──────────────────────────────────────────────────────
```

1. The screen number is placed in the upper right-hand corner.
2. The title is placed in centered position below the screen number and above the body of the screen.

495

Figure 15.11 Development of paper screens (section headings and data elements).

```
                                    HMAP01

                      HOMEOWNERS APPLICATION

1. POLICY INFORMATION
   EFF-DT: ------    EXP-DT: ------    ACCT#: ---------    POL#: ---------
   PROD-ISS: -    SEC-RES: -    PRI-POL#: ----------    POL-TYP: -
2. PRODUCER AND COMPANY INFORMATION
   CO: --    BR-CD: --    PROD-CD: ------    SUB-PROD: ----
3. RESIDENCE AND INSURED INFORMATION
   NM-1: -------------    MAR-STS: -    SP-EMP: -
   NM-2: -------------

   ML-AD: -------------    P-AD: -------------
   CTY: -------- ST: -- ZP: -----    CTY: -------- ST: -- ZP: -----
   PRMS-OTH: -    PRMS-CNY: ------    LEG-DISC: -
4. COVERAGES
   FORM: -    A-BLDG: ------    B-OTH: -----    C-UNS-PR: ------    D-ADD-LIV: -----
              E-PER-L: -----    F-MED: -----    NY-CINS: -
              DED-AMT: -----    250-DED: -    DED-FORM#: ---
```

3. Section headings begin in column 2. Column 1 will be reserved for an attribute (or a blank).
4. The longest field caption (PROD-ISS) is indented three spaces from the section heading.
5. The other data element beginning a line (EFF-DT) is aligned by entry fields.
6. The end point for entry fields is Column 78.

496

Figure 15.12 Development of paper screens (section headings and data elements).

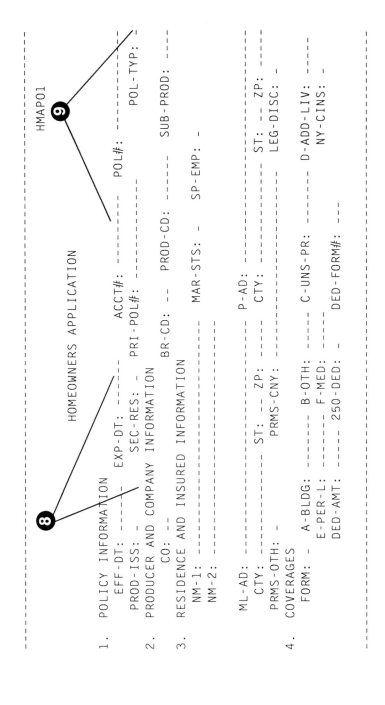

```
                                                       HMAP01

                     HOMEOWNERS APPLICATION                8           9

1.  POLICY INFORMATION
    EFF-DT: ----    EXP-DT: ----      ACCT#: -----    POL#: -----
    PROD-ISS: -     SEC-RES: -    PRI-POL#: -----             POL-TYP: ----
2.  PRODUCER AND COMPANY INFORMATION
    CO: --          BR-CD: --    PROD-CD: -----   SUB-PROD: ----
3.  RESIDENCE AND INSURED INFORMATION
    NM-1: ----------------         MAR-STS: -    SP-EMP: -
    NM-2: ----------------

    ML-AD: ----------------        P-AD: ----------------
      CTY: ----------  ST: -- ZP: -----    CTY: ----------  ST: -- ZP: -----
    PRMS-OTH: -     PRMS-CNY: -                       LEG-DISC: -
4.  COVERAGES
    FORM: -    A-BLDG: ------    B-OTH: -----    C-UNS-PR: ------    D-ADD-LIV: -----
               E-PER-L: ------   F-MED: -----                        NY-CINS: -
    DED-AMT: ----- 250-DED: -    DED-FORM#: ---
```

7. Fields are located in the same relative position that they occupy on the source document.
8. Larger gaps are left where larger spaces exist on the source document.
9. Entry fields under one another in a line are relatively positioned as best as possible. Due to varying caption and entry fields sizes, exact representation cannot always be achieved. Tradeoffs must be performed and the best overall representation achieved.

497

Figure 15.13 Development of paper screens (section headings and data elements).

```
                                                                          HMAP01

                        HOMEOWNERS APPLICATION

     1.  POLICY INFORMATION
         EFF-DT: ------     EXP-DT: ------     ACCT#: --------     POL#: ----------
         PROD-ISS: -        SEC-RES: -     PRI-POL#: ----------                POL-TYP: -
     2.  PRODUCER AND COMPANY INFORMATION
             CO: -         BR-CD: --     PROD-CD: -----     SUB-PROD: ----
     3.  RESIDENCE AND INSURED INFORMATION
         NM-1: ----------------------     MAR-STS: -     SP-EMP: -
         NM-2: ----------------------
         ML-AD: --------------------     P-AD: ------------------
         CTY: -----------     ST: -- ZP: -----     CTY: -----------     ST: -- ZP: -----
         PRMS-OTH: -     PRMS-CNY: ------     LEG-DISC: -
     4.  COVERAGES
         FORM: -     A-BLDG: ------     B-OTH: ------     C-UNS-PR: ------     D-ADD-LIV: -----
         DED-AMT: -----     E-PER-L: ------     F-MED: -----                  NY-CINS: -
                 250-DED: -     DED-FORM#: ---
```

10. Since there are no data entry data elements in this line on the document, a space line is left on the screen.
11. The city-state-zip line size requires the beginning position of the entry field for the first data element (CT) be moved back to column 12. It cannot be aligned under the above entry field (EFF-DT, PROD-ISS and CO.)
12. For consistency, the remaining data element entry fields beginning lines within that section are moved back to align with CT (NM-1, NM-2, and ML-AD). It is desirable to align all entry fields beginning a line with each other. It is not a requirement. However, it is necessary to align those within a section. Do try, however, to keep misalignments between sections to a minimum.
13. PRMS-OTH is not aligned because it is indented on the document.

Figure 15.14 Development of paper screens (section headings and data elements).

```
                                                    HMAP01


                        HOMEOWNERS  APPLICATION


        1.  POLICY INFORMATION
            EFF-DT: -----    EXP-DT: -----    ACCT#: --------    POL#: --------
            PROD-ISS: -      SEC-RES: -    PRI-POL#: --------            POL-TYP: -
        2.  PRODUCER AND COMPANY INFORMATION
                CO: --            BR-CD: --    PROD-CD: -----    SUB-PROD: ----
        3.  RESIDENCE AND INSURED INFORMATION
            NM-1: --------------------    MAR-STS: -    SP-EMP: -
            NM-2: --------------------

            ML-AD: --------------------    P-AD: --------------------
            CTY: ----------    ST: -- ZP: -----    CTY: ----------    ST: -- ZP: -----
            PRMS-OTH: -        PRMS-CNY: ----------           LEG-DISC: -
        4.  COVERAGES
            FORM: -        A-BLDG: ------    B-OTH: ------    C-UNS-PR: ------    D-ADD-LIV: ------
                           E-PER-L: ------    F-MED: ------                       NY-CINS: -
            DED-AMT: ------    250-DED: ------    DED-FORM#: ---
```

14. Because of the earlier reduction in caption sizes, line 16 now fits. The first data element (FORM) entry field is aligned under the previous section.

15. It is desirable to align the entry fields in line 17 under those in line 16 since they appear "aligned" on the document. To do this requires reducing the captions E-PER-LIAB and F-MED-PAY to E-PER-L and F-MED. This is done. (In changing captions, always make sure that if the same data elements are used on other screens, these captions are also changed).

499

Figure 15.15 Development of paper screens (section headings and data elements).

```
                                        HOMEOWNERS APPLICATION                    HMAP01

1.  POLICY INFORMATION
       EFF-DT: ------    EXP-DT: ------              ACCT#: ---------    POL#: ---------
       PROD-ISS: -       SEC-RES: -        PRI-POL#: ---------                       POL-TYP: -
2.  PRODUCER AND COMPANY INFORMATION
       CO: --                                  BR-CD: --    PROD-CD: ------    SUB-PROD: ---
3.  RESIDENCE AND INSURED INFORMATION
       NM-1: ---------                          MAR-STS: -    SP-EMP: -
       NM-2: ---------

    ML-AD: ---------                            P-AD: ---------
       CTY: ---------    ST: --  ZP: -----      CTY: ---------    ST: --  ZP: -----
       PRMS-OTH: -       PRMS-CNY: ---------                      LEG-DISC: -
4.  COVERAGES
       FORM: -    A-BLDG: ---------    B-OTH: ------    C-UNS-PR: ------    D-ADD-LIV: ------
                  E-PER-L: ------      F-MED: ------                       NY-CINS: -
       DED-AMT: ------    250-DED: -    DED-FORM#: --
```

16.

16. Line 18 easily aligns under the above two lines in the section. The screen is finished.

Figure 15.16 Source document for designed screen.

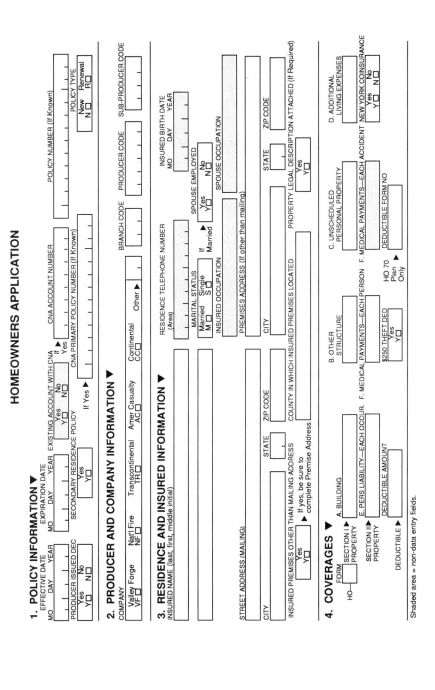

Figure 15.17 Screen printout.

```
                                                         HMAP01

                   HOMEOWNERS APPLICATION

1.  POLICY INFORMATION
      EFF-DT: ------  EXP-DT: ------  ACCT#: --------  POL#: ----------
      PROD-ISS: -  SEC-RES: -  PRI-POL#: -----------       POL-TYP: -
2.  PRODUCER AND COMPANY INFORMATION
      CO: --          BR-CD: --  PROD-CD: ------  SUB-PROD: ----
3.  RESIDENCE AND INSURED INFORMATION
      NM-1: ------------------------  MAR-STS: -  SP-EMP: -
      NM-2: ------------------------

      ML-AD: -------------------------  P-AC: -----------
      CTY: ------------  ST: -- ZP: ----------  CTY: -----------  ST: -- ZP: -----------
      PRMS-OTH: -  PRMS-CNY: -----------         LEG-DISC: -
4.  COVERAGES
      FORM: -  A-BLDG: -------  B-OTH: ------  C-LNS-PR: -------  D-ADD-LIV: -------
               E-PER-L: ------  F-MED: ------                    NY-CINS: -
               DED-AMT: ------ 250-DED: -  DED-FORM#: ---
```

References

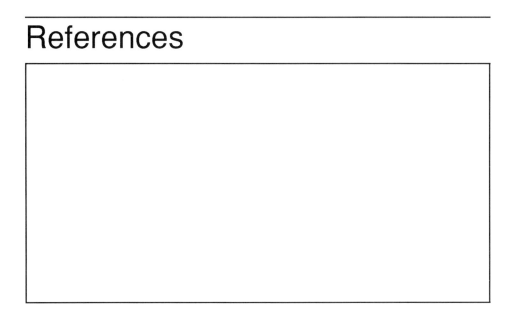

Apple Computer, *Human Interface Guidelines: The Apple Desktop Interface*, Addison-Wesley Publishing Company, Inc., Reading, MA, 1987.

Ayres, Leonard P., *The War with Germany*, Washington, DC, 1919, p. 102.

Backs, Richard W., Walrath, Larry C., and Hancock, Glenn A., Comparison of Horizontal and Vertical Menu Formats. *Proceedings of the Human Factors Society—31st Annual Meeting*, 1987, Santa Monica, CA.

Baecker, R., and Small, I., Animation at the Interface, Laurel, B. (Ed.). *The Art of Human-Computer Interface Design*, Addison-Wesley, 1990, pp. 251–267.

Baecker, Ronald; Small, Ian; and Mander, Richard, Bringing Icons to Life. In *Proceedings Human Factors in Computing Systems*, CHI '91, pp. 1–6.

Bailey, R.W., Ph.D., Is Ergonomics Worth the Investment? *Proceedings: World Conference on Ergonomics in Computer Systems*, pp. 37–108, Los Angeles, CA.; Chicago, IL.; New York, NY; Amsterdam, The Netherlands; Dusseldorf, West Germany; Helsinki, Finland. Sept. 24–Oct. 4, 1984.

Bailey and Bailey Software Corporation, Protoscreens, Ogden, Utah, 1989.

Baker, J.D., and Goldstein, I., Batch vs. Sequential Displays: Effects on Human Problem Solving. *Human Factors*, 1966, 8: pp. 225–235.

Barber, Raymond E., *Response Time, Operator Productivity and Job Satisfaction*. Ph.D. dissertation, NYU Graduate School of Business Administration, 1979.

Barber, Raymond E., and Lucas, H.C., System Response Time, Operator Productivity and Job Satisfaction. *Communications of the ACM 26*, Nov. 1983, 11: pp. 972–986.

Barmack, J.E., and Sinaiko, H.W., *Human Factors Problems in Computer-Generated Graphic Displays*. Inst. for Defense Analysis. AD-636170, 1966.

Barnard, P., *Presuppositions in Active and Passive Questions*. Paper read to the Experimental Psychology Society, 1974.

Barnard, P.; Wright, P.; and Wilcox, P., The effects of spatial constraints on the legibility of handwritten alphanumeric codes. *Ergonomics*, 1978, 21: pp. 73–78.

Barnard, P.; Hammond, N.; Morton, J.; Long, J.; and Clark, I., Consistency and Compatibility in Human-Computer Dialogue. *International Journal of Man-Machine Studies*, 1981, 15: pp. 87–134.

Barnard, P.; Hammond, N.; MacLean, A.; and Morton, J., Learning and Remembering Interactive Commands. In *Proceedings: Human Factors in Computer Systems*, pp. 2–7. Gaithersburg, MD., March 15–17, 1982.

Bayerl, Jeanne P.; Millen, David R.; and Lewis, Steven H., Consistent Layout of Function Keys and Screen Labels Speeds User Responses. In *Proceedings of the Human Factors Society—32nd Annual Meeting*, 1988, pp. 344–346.

Benest, I.D., and Dukic, D., High-Level User-Interface Objects. *Designing and Using Human-Computer Interfaces and Knowledge Based Systems*, G. Salvendy and M.J. Smith (eds.). Elsevier Science Publishers B.V., Amsterdam, 1989, pp. 597–604.

Bennett, J.L., The commercial impact of usability in interactive systems, B. Shackel (ed.). *Man-Computer Communication, Infotech State-of-the Art*, Vol. 2, Maidenhead: Infotech International, 1979, pp. 1–17.

Bennett, J.L., Managing to meet usability requirements, J.L. Bennett, D. Case, J. Sandelin, and M. Smith (eds.). *Visual Display Terminals: Usability Issues and Health Concerns*, Englewood Cliffs, NJ: Prentice-Hall, 1984, pp. 161–184.

Bergman, Hans; Brinkman, Albert; and Loelega, Harry S., System Response Time and Problem Solving Behavior. *Proceedings of the Human Factors Society–25th Annual Meeting–1981*, pp. 749–753, Santa Monica, CA.

Bigelow, C., Proceedings of the Typography Interest Group ACM CHI '85. *SIGCHI Bulletin*, 17(1), 1985, pp. 10–11.

Billingsley, Patricia A., Navigation Through Hierarchical Menu Structures: Does It Help to Have a Map? In *Proceedings of the Human Factors Society–26th Annual Meeting*, 1982, pp. 103–107. Santa Monica, CA., 1982.

Billingsley, Patricia A., The Standards Factor: Catching Up With Committees. *SIGCHI Bulletin*, Volume 23, Number 1, January 1991, pp. 6–10.

Billingsley, Patricia A., Taking Panes: Issues in the Design of Windowing Systems. *Handbook of Human-Computer Interaction*, M. Helander (ed.). Elsevier Science Publishers B.V. (North-Holland), 1988, pp. 413–436.

Black, J.B., and Moran, T.P., Learning and Remembering Command Names. In *Proceedings: Human Factors in Computer Systems*, pp. 8–11. Gaithersburg, MD., March 15–17, 1982.

Black, J.B.; Carroll, J.M.; and McGuigan, S.M., What kind of minimal instruction manual is most effective? *Proceedings of CHI+GI 1987*, New York: ACM, pp. 159–162.

Bly, Sara A., and Rosenberg, Jarrett K., A Comparison of Tiled and Overlapping Windows. *Proceedings CHI '86 Human Factors in Computing Systems*, pp. 101–105.

Boies, S.J., User Behavior on an Interactive Computer System. *IBM Systems Journal* 13, 1, 1974, pp. 1–18.

Bonsiepe, G., A Method of Quantifying Order in Typographic Design. *Journal of typographic research*, 1968, 2, pp. 203–220.

Borenstein, N.S., The design and evaluation of on-line help systems. Unpublished doctoral dissertation, Department of Computer Science, Carnegie-Mellon University, Pittsburgh, PA (1985).

Bouma, H., Interaction Effects in Parafoveal Letter Recognition. *Nature, 226*, 1970, pp. 177–178.

Bower, G.H.; Clark, M.C.; Lesgold, A.M.; and Winenz, D., Hierarchical Retrieval Schemes in Recall of Categorical Word Lists. *Journal of Verbal Learning and Verbal Behavior*, 1969, 8: pp. 323–343.

Brems, Douglas J., and Whitten, William B., II, Learning and Preference for Icon-Based Interface. In *Proceedings of the Human Factors Society–31st Annual Meeting*, 1987, pp. 125–129.

Brod, Craig, *Technostress: The Human Cost of the Computer Revolution*. Addison-Wesley Publishing Company, Reading, MA, 1984.

Brooke, J.; Bevan, N.; Brigham, F.; Harker, S.; and Youmans, D., Usability assurance and standardization—work in progress in ISO. *Proceedings IFIP Interact '90*, Cambridge, U.K., August 17–31, 1990, pp. 357–361.

Brooks, R., Search Time and Color Coding. *Psychonomic Science*, 1965, 2:281–282.

Burns, Michael J., and Warren, Dianne L., Formatting Space-Related Displays to Optimize Expert and Nonexpert User Performance. *Proceedings CHI '86 Human Factors in Computing Systems*, April 1986, pp. 274–280.

Bury, K.F.; Boyle, J.M.; Evey, R.J.; and Neal, A.S., Windowing Versus Scrolling on a Visual Display Terminal. *Human Factors, 24*, pp. 385–394 (1982).

Butler, T.W., Computer Response Time and User Performance. *ACM SIGCHI '83 Proceedings: Human Factors in Computer Systems*, Dec. 1983, pp. 56–62.

Cairney, P. & Sless, D., Communication Effectiveness of Symbolic Safety Signs with Different User Groups. *Applied Ergonomics*, 13, 1982:91–97.

Callan, J.R., Curran, L.E.; and Lane, J.L., Visual Search Times for Navy Tactical Information Displays (Report # NPRDC-TR-77-32). San Diego, CA: Navy Personnel Research and Development Center, 1977. (NTIS No. AD A040543)

Carbonell, J.R.; Elkind, J.I.; and Nickerson, R.S., On the Psychological Importance of Time in a Time-Sharing System. *Human Factors* 10, 1969: pp. 135–142.

Card, S.K., User Perceptual Mechanisms in the Search of Computer Command Menus. In *Proceedings: Human Factors in Computer Systems*, pp. 190–196. Gaithersburg, MD., March 15–17, 1982.

Card, S.K.; Moran, T.P.; and Newell, A., *The Psychology of Human-Computer Interaction*, Hillsdale, NJ: Lawrence Erlbaum, 1983.

Card, S.K.; Pavel, M.; and Farrell, J.E., Window-Based Computer Dialogues. *Human Computer Interaction—INTERACT '84*/B. Shackel (ed.). Elsevier Science Publishers B.V. North Holland IFIP, 1985, pp. 239–243.

Card, Stuart; Moran, Thomas P.; and Newell, Allen, The Keystroke-Level Model for User Performance with Interactive Systems. *Communications of the ACM 23*, 1980, pp. 396–410.

Carroll, J.B., and White, M.N., Word Frequency and Age of Acquisition as Determiners of Picture Naming Latency. *Quarterly Journal of Experimental Psychology, 25*, 1973, pp. 85–95.

Carroll, J.M., *Learning, Using and Designing Command Paradigms*. IBM Research Report RC 8141. 1980.

Carroll, J.M.; Thomas, J.C.; and Malhotra, A., Presentation and representation in design problem-solving. *British Journal of Psychology*, 71, 1980, pp. 143–153.

Carroll, J.M.; Smith-Kerker, P.L.; Ford, J.R.; and Mazur, S.A., *The Minimal Manual* (Research Report RC 11637), Yorktown Heights, NY: IBM T.J. Watson Research Center (1986).

Carroll, John M., Minimalist Design for Active Users. *Human-Computer Interaction–INTERACT '84*/B. Shackel (ed.) Elsevier Science Publishers B.V. (North Holland) IFIP, 1985, pp. 39–44.

Carroll, John M., and Carrithers, Caroline, Blocking Learner Error States in a Training-Wheels Systems. *Human Factors*, 26(4), 1984, pp. 377–389.

Carter, R.L., Visual search with color. *Journal of Experimental Psychology: Human Perception and Performance*, 8, 1982, pp. 127–136.

Chafin, R., and Martin, T. *DSN Human Factors Project Final Report*. Los Angeles, Calif.: University of Southern California, 1980. Contract No. 955013mRD—142.

Chapanis, A.; Parrish, R.N.; Ochsman, R.B.; and Weeks, G.D., Studies in Interactive Communication: II. The Effects of Four Communication Modes on the Linguistic Performance of Teams During Cooperative Problem Solving. *Human Factors 19*, No. 2 (1977): pp. 101–126.

Charney, D.H., and Reder, L.M., Designing interactive tutorials for computer users. *Human-Computer Interaction*, 2, 1986, pp. 297–317.

Christ, R.E., Review and Analysis of Color Coding Research for Visual Displays. *Human Factors 17*, No. 6 (1975): pp. 542–570.

Christ, R.E., and Teichner, W.H., Color Research for Visual Displays. *JANAIR Report No. 730703*, Department of Psychology, New Mexico State University, 1973.

Citibank, reported in *USA Today*, Arlington, VA 1989.

Clark, H.H., and Clark, E.V., Semantic distinctions and memory for complex sentences. *Quarterly Journal of Experimental Psychology*, 20, 1968, pp. 56–72.

Clark, H.H., and Card, S.K., Role of semantics in remembering complex sentences. *Journal of Experimental Psychology*, 82, 1969, pp. 545–553.

Cohill, Andrew M., and Williges, Robert C., Retrieval of HELP Information for Novice Users of Interactive Computer Systems. *Human Factors 27(3)*, 1985, pp. 335–343.

Cooper, A., Remark: Window viper. *PC World*, August 1985, pp. 25–37.

Cotton, Ira W., Measurement of Interactive Computing: Methodology and Application. National Bureau of Standards Special Publication 500–548, 1978, 101 pages.

Cuff, R.N., On Casual Users. *International Journal of Man-Machine Studies 12*, (1980), pp. 163–187.

Cushman, William H., Reading for Microfiche, a VDT, and the Printed Page: Subjective Fatigue and Performance. *Human Factors, 28(1)*, (1986), pp. 63–73.

Czaja, S.J.; Hammond, K.; Blascovich, J.J.; and Swede, H., Learning to use a word-processing system as a function of training strategy. *Behavior and Information Technology*, 5, 1986, pp. 203–216.

Dainoff, M.J.; Happ, A.; and Crane, P., Visual fatigue and occupational stress in VDU operators. *Human Factors*, 23, 1986, pp. 421–438.

Damodaran, L.; Simpson, A.; and Wilson, P., Designing Systems for People. *NCC*, Manchester and Loughborough University of Technology, 1980.

Danchak, M.M., CRT Displays for Power Plants *Instrumentation Technology 23*, No. 10, (1976), pp. 29–36.

Davies, Susan E.; Bury, Kevin F.; and Darnell, Michael J., An Experimental Comparison of a Windowed vs. a Non-Windowed Operating System Environment. *Proceedings of the Human Factors Society—29th Annual Meeting*—1985, pp. 250–254, Santa Monica, CA.

Dede, C., A review and synthesis of recent research in intelligent computer-assisted instruction. *International Journal of Man-Machine Studies*, 24, 1986, pp. 329–353.

Desaulniers, David R., and Gillan, Douglas J., The Effects of Format in Computer-Based Procedure Displays. *Proceedings of the Human Factors Society—32nd Annual Meeting—1988*, 1988, pp. 291–295.

de Souza, F., and Bevan, N., The use of guidelines in menu interface design. In *Proceedings IFIP Interact '90* (Cambridge, U.K., August 27–31, 1990) pp. 435–440.

Dickey, G.L., and Schneider, M.H., Multichannel Communication of an Industrial Task. *International Journal of Production Research, 9*, 1971, pp. 487–499.

Dodson, D.W., and Shields, N.J., Jr., Development of User Guidelines for ECAS Display Design. (Vol. 1) (Report No. NASA-CR-150877). Huntsville, AL: Essex Corp., 1978.

Doherty, W.J., The Commercial Significance of Man-Computer Interaction. In *Man/Computer Communication*. Vol. 2, pp. 81–94. Maidenhead, Berkshire, England: Infotech International, 1979.

Dondis, Donis A., *A Primer of Visual Literacy*, The MIT Press, Cambridge, MA (1973).

Donohoo, D.T., and Snyder, H.L., Accommodation during color contrast. In *Society for Information Display Digest of Technical Papers*, New York Palisades Institute for Research Sciences, 1985, pp. 200–203.

Draper, Stephen W., The Nature of Expertise in Unix. *Human-Computer Interaction–INTERACT '84*/B. Shackel (ed.) Elsevier Science Publishers B.V. (North Holland) IFIP, 1985, pp. 465–471.

Dray, S.M.; Ogden, W.G.; and Vestewig, R.E., Measuring Performance with a Menu Selection Human-Computer Interface. In *Proceedings of the Human Factors Society–25th Annual Meeting, 1981*, pp. 746–748. Santa Monica, CA., 1981.

Dunsmore, H.E., Using Formal Grammars to Predict the Most Useful Characteristics of Interactive Systems. In *Office Automation Conference Digest*, pp. 53–56. San Francisco, April 5–7, 1982.

Dunsmore, H.E., Designing an Interactive Facility for Non-Programmers, *Proceedings ACM National Conference*, (1980), pp. 475–483.

Durding, B.M.; Becker, C.A.; and Gould, J.D., Data Organization. *Human Factors 19*, No. 1 (1977): pp. 1–14.

Eason, K., *Man-Computer Communication in Public and Private Computing*. HUSAT Memo 173. Loughborough, Leicester, England, 1979.

Ehrenreich, S.L., Computer Abbreviations: Evidence and Synthesis. *Human Factors 27(2)*, (1985), pp. 143–155.

Elam, P.G., Considering Human Needs Can Boost Network Efficiency. *Data Communications*, October 1978, pp. 50–60.

Elkerton, J., and Willeges, R.C., The effectiveness of a performance-based assistant in an information retrieval environment. In *Proceedings of the Human Factors Society 28th Annual Meeting*, Santa Monica, CA: Human Factors Society, 1984, pp. 634–638.

Elkerton, Jay, Online Aiding for Human-Computer Interfaces. *Handbook of Human-Computer Interaction*, M. Helander (ed.). Elsevier Science Publishers B.V. (North-Holland), 1988m, pp. 345–364.

Elkerton, Jay, and Palmiter, Susan L., Designing Help Using a GOMS Model: An Information Retrieval Evaluation. *Human Factors*, 33(2), 1991, pp. 185–204.

Ells, J.G., and Dewar, R.E., Rapid Comprehension of Verbal and Symbolic Traffic Sign Messages. *Human Factors*, 21, 1979, pp. 161–168.

Engel, F.L., Information Selection From Visual Displays. In *Ergonomic Aspects of Visual Display Terminals*, E. Grandjean and E. Vigliani (Eds.). London: Taylor and Francis Ltd, 1980.

Engel, S.E., and Granda, R.E., *Guidelines for Man/Display Interfaces*. IBM Technical Report, 19 December 1975. TR 00.2720.

Foley, J., and Wallace, V., The Art of Natural Graphic Man-Machine Conversation. *Proceedings of the IEEE* 62, No. 4 (April 1974).

Francik, E.P., and Kane, R.M., Optimizing visual search and cursor movement in pull-down menus. In *Proceedings of the Human Factors Society 31st Annual Meeting*. Santa Monica, CA: Human Factors Society, 1987, pp. 722–726.

Francik, Ellen P., and Kane, Richard M., Optimizing Visual Search and Cursor Movement in Pull-Down Menus. *Proceedings of the Human Factors Society–31st Annual Meeting*, 1987, Santa Monica, CA.

Frankenhaeuser, M., Psychoneuroendocrine Approaches to the Study of Emotion as Related to Stress and Coping. In *Nebraska Symposium on Motivation* (1978), edited by H.E. Howe and R.A. Dienstabier, pp. 123–161. Lincoln: University of Nebraska Press, 1979.

Frese, M.; Schulte-Gocking, H.; and Altmann, A., Lernprozesse in Abhangigkeit von der Trainingsmethode, von Personenmerkmalen und von der Benutzeroberflache (Direkte Manipulation vs. konventionelle interaktion). In W. Schonpflu/M. Wittstock (eds.), *Software-Ergonomie '87*, Tagung 11/1987 des German Chapter of the ACM, Berlin: Teubner.

Fromme, F., Incorporating the Human Factor in Color CAD Systems. *IEEE Proceedings of the 20th Design Automation Conference*, 1983, pp. 189–195.

Furnas, G.W.; Gomez, L.M.; Landauer, T.K.; and Dumais, S.T., Statistical Semantics: How Can a Computer Use What People Name Things to Guess What Things People Mean When They Name Things? In *Proceedings: Human Factors in Computer Systems*. Gaithersburg, MD., March 15–17, 1982.

Galitz, W.O., IBM 3270 On-Line Evaluation. *INA Technical Report*, E5320-A02/M72-0001, January 20, 1972.

Galitz, W.O., *Summary Report of the Personal Lines Form Questionnaire and Agency Visits*. INA Technical Report, 20 September 1973. E5710-A05/N73-0001.

Galitz, W.O., *An Evaluation of the Impact of Mnemonic CRT Labels on the Design and Use of EIS Forms and Screens* INA Technical Report, March 1975.

Galitz, W.O., DEBUT II—The CNA Data Entry Utility. *Proceedings of the Human Factors Society-23rd Annual Meeting (1979)*, pp. 50–54. Santa Monica, Calif., 1979.

Galitz, Wilbert O., CRT Viewing and Visual Aftereffects. *UNIVAC Internal Report*. Roseville, MN, 1 August 1968.

Gardell, B., Tjanstemannens Arbetsmiljoer (Work Environment of White-collar Workers). Preliminary report. The research group for social psychology work. Department of Psychology, University of Stockholm, Report No. 24, 1979.

Gaylin, Kenneth B., How are Windows Used? Some Notes on Creating an Empirically-Based Windowing Benchmark Task. *Proceedings CHI '86 Human Factors in Computing Systems*, pp. 96–100.

Geldard, F.A., *The Human Senses*. New York: John Wiley, 1953.

Gilfoil, D.M., Warming Up to Computers: A Study of Cognitive and Affective Interactions Over Time. In *Proceedings: Human Factors in Computer Systems*, Gaithersburg, MD., March 15–17, 1982, pp. 245–250.

Gittens, D., Icon-Based Human-Computer Interaction. *International Journal of Man-Machine Studies*, 24, 1986, pp. 519–543.

Good, Michael, Developing the XUI Style. *Coordinating User Interfaces for Consistency*, Jakob Nielsen (ed.). Academic Press, Inc., San Diego, CA, 1989, pp. 75–88.

Goodwin, N.C., Effect of Interface Design on Usability of Message Handling Systems. In *Proceedings of the Human Factors Society–26th Annual Meeting*—1982, Santa Monica, CA, 1982, pp. 69–73.

Goodwin, N.C., Designing a Multipurpose Menu Driven User Interface to Computer Based Tools. In *Proceedings of the Human Factors Society–27th Annual Meeting*, Santa Monica, CA, 1983, pp. 816–820.

Gould, J.D.; Lewis, C.; and Becker, A., *Writing and Following Procedural, Descriptive and Restricted Syntax Language Instructions*. Yorktown Heights, NY: IBM, 1976.

Gould, John D. and Grischkowsky, Nancy, Doing the Same Work with Hard Copy and with Cathode-Ray Tube (CRT) Computer Terminals. *Human Factors, 26(3)*, 1984, pp. 323–337.

Gould, John D., How to Design Usable Systems. *Handbook of Human-Computer Interaction*, M. Helander (ed.). Elsevier Science Publishers B.V. (North-Holland) 1988, pp. 757–789.

Gould, John D.; Boies, Stephen J.; Meluson, Mia; Rasamny, Marwan; and Vosburgh, Ann Marie, Empirical Evaluation of Entry and Selection Methods for Specifying Dates. In *Proceedings of the Human Factors Society—32nd Annual Meeting—1988*, pp. 279–283.

Granda, R.E.; Teitelbaum, R.C.; and Dunlap, G.L., The Effect of VDT Command Line Location on Data Entry Behavior. In *Proceedings of the Human Factors Society–26th Annual Meeting, 1982*, Santa Monica, CA. (1982), pp. 621–624.

Greene, J.M., *Psycholinguistics: Chomsky and Psychology*. Harmondsworth, Middlesex, U.K.: Penguin, 1972.

Greene, Sharon L.; Gould, John D.; Boies, Stephen J.; Meluson, Antonia; and Rasamny, Marwan, Entry-Based Versus Selection-Based Interaction Methods. In *Proceedings of the Human Factors Society—32nd Annual Meeting—1988*, pp. 284–287.

Greenstein, Joel S., and Arnaut, Lynn Y., Input Devices. *Handbook of Human-Computer Interaction*, M. Helander (ed.). Elsevier Science Publishers B.V. (North-Holland), 1988, pp. 495–519.

Grudin, Jonathan, and Barnard, Phil, When Does an Abbreviation Become a Word? and Related Questions. *CHI '85 Proceedings*, pp. 121–.

Guastello, S.J.; Traut, M.; and Korienek, G., Verbal versus pictorial representation of objects in a human-computer interface. *International Journal of Man-Machine Studies*, 31, 1989, pp. 99–120.

Haines, R.M.; Dawson, L.M.; Galvan, T.; and Reid, L.M., Response time to colored stimuli in the full visual field (NASA TN D-7927). Moffett Field, CA: NASA. 1975.

Hair, D. Charles, Legalese: A Legal Argumentation Tool. *SIGCHI Bulletin*, Vol. 23, No. 1, January 1991, pp. 71–74.

Halsey, R.M., and Chapanis, A., On the Number Absolutely Identifiable Spectral Hues. *Journal of Optical Society of America*, 41, 1951, pp. 1057–1058.

Hammond, N.; Barnard, P.; Clark, I.; Morton, J.; and Long, J., *Structure and Content in Interactive Dialogue*. Paper presented at American Psychological Association Annual Meeting, Montreal, September 1980, and IBM Human Factors Report HFO 34. October 1980.

Hammond, N.; Long, J.; Clark, I.; Barnard, P.; and Morton, J., Documenting Human-Computer Mismatch in Interactive Systems. In *Proceedings of the Ninth Annual Symposium on Human Factors in Telecommunications*. 1980B.

Hansen, J., Man-Machine Communication. *IEEE Transactions on Man, Systems and Cybernetics*. Vol. SMC-6, No. 11, November 1976.

Harpster, Jeffrey L.; Freivalds, Andris; Shulman, Gordon L.; and Leibowitz, Herschel W., Visual Performance on CRT Screens and Hard-Copy Displays. *Human Factors*, 31(3), 1989, pp. 247–257.

Hatfield, Don, Lecture at Conference on Easier and More Productive Use of Computer Systems, Ann Arbor, MI, 1981. (In Shneiderman 1986)

Haubner, P., and Benz, C., Information Display on Monochrome and Colour Screens.

Abstracts: International Scientific Conference on Ergonomic and Health Aspects in Modern Offices, Turin, Italy, November 7–9, 1983, p. 72.

Haubner, Peter, and Neumann, Frank, Structuring Alphanumerically Coded Information on Visual Display Units. *Proceedings: International Scientific Conference: Work With Display Units*, Stockholm, Sweden, May 12–15, 1986, pp. 606–609.

Heckel, Paul, The Elements of Friendly Software Design. Warner Books, New York, NY, 1984, 205 pages.

Hendrickson, Jeffrey J., Performance, Preference, and Visual Scan Patterns on a Menu-Based System: Implications for Interface Design. In *Proceedings Human Factors in Computing Systems*, CHI '89, May 1989, pp. 217–222.

Herriot, P., *An Introduction to the Psychology of Language*. London: Methuen, 1970.

Hiltz, S.R., *Online Communities: A Case Study of the Office of the Future*. Ablex Publishers, Norwood, NJ, 1984.

Hiltz, Starr Roxanne, and Kerr, Elaine B., Learning Modes and Subsequent Use of Computer-Mediated Communication Systems. *Proceedings CHI '86 Human Factors in Computing Systems*, pp. 149–155.

Human Factors Society, American national standard for human factors engineering of visual display terminal workstations. Santa Monica, CA: Author, 1988.

Hutchins, Edwin L.; Hollan, James D., and Norman, Don A., Direct manipulation interfaces. In Norman, Don A., and Draper, Stephen W. (eds.), *User Centered System Design: New Perspectives on Human-Computer Interaction*, Lawrence Erlbaum Associates, Hillsdale, NJ, 1986.

International Business Machines, Software Design Principles. *Proceedings: Software Ease of Use Workshop*, Boca Raton, FL, Oct. 22, 1984.

International Business Machines, Systems Application Architecture. *Common User Access, Panel Design and User Interaction*, SC26-4351-0, IBM, Boca Raton, FL 1987.

International Business Machines, System Application Architecture. *Common User Access, Advanced Interface Design Guide*, SC26-4582, IBM, Cary, NC, 1989b.

International Business Machines, Systems Application Architecture. *Common User Access, Basic Interface Design Guide*, SC26-4583, IBM, Cary, NC, 1989b.

Johansson, G.; Aronsson, G.; and Lindstrom, B., Social, Psychological and Neuroendocrine Stress Reactions in Highly Mechanized Work. *Ergonomics*. 21 (1978): pp. 583–599.

Johnson-Laird, A., They look good in demos, but windows are a real pain. *Software News*, 42, April 1985, pp. 36–37.

Jones, P.F., Four Principles of Man-Computer Dialogue. *Computer Aided Design* 10 (1978): pp. 197–202.

Kaplow, R., and Molnar, M., A Computer Terminal Hardware/Software System With Enhanced User Input Capabilities. In *Computer Graphics*. New York: ACM, 1976.

Karasek, R.A., Job Demands, Decision Latitude, and Mental Strain: Implications for Job Redesign. *Administrative Science Quarterly* 24, 1979, pp. 285–311.

Karasek, R.A.; Baker, D.; Marxer, F.; Ahlbom, A.; and Theorell, T., Job Design Latitude, Job Demands, and Cardiovascular Disease: A Prospective Study of Swedish Men. *American Journal of Public Health* 71, 1981: pp. 694–705.

Karat, John, Transfer Between Word Processing Systems. *Proceedings: International Scientific Conference: Work With Display Units*, pp. 745–748. Stockholm, Sweden, May 12–15, 1986.

Karat, John, Evaluating user interface complexity. *Proceedings of the Human Factors Society—31st Annual Meeting*, 1987, pp. 566–570.

Kaster, Jürgen, and Widdel, Heino, The Effect of Visual Presentation of Different Dialogue Structures on Ease of Human-Computer Interaction. *Proceedings: International Scientific Conference: Work With Display Units*, Stockholm, Sweden, May 12–15, 1986, pp. 772–776.

Kearsley, G., *On-Line Help: Design and Implementation*, Addison-Wesley, Menlo Park, CA, 1988.

Keister, R.S., and Gallaway, G.R., Making Software User Friendly: An Assessment of Data Entry Performance. In *Proceedings of the Human Factors Society—27th Annual Meeting—1983*, Santa Monica, CA., 1983, pp. 1031–1034.

Kelly, M.J., and Chapanis, A., Limited Vocabulary Natural Language Dialogue. *International Journal of Man-Machine Studies*. 9, 1977: pp. 479–501.

Kiger, J.I., The Depth/Breadth Tradeoff in the Design of Menu Driven User Interfaces. *International Journal of Man-Machine Studies*, 1984, 20, pp. 201–213.

Kintish, W., Comprehension and Memory of Text. In *Handbook of Learning and Cognitive Processes*, edited by W.K. Estes, vol. 6. Hillsdale, NJ: Lawrence Erlbaum Associates, 1978.

Kolers, P., Some Formal Characteristics of Pictograms. *American Scientist*, 57(3), 1969, pp. 348–363.

Kopala, C.J., The Use of Color Coded Symbols in a Highly Dense Situation Display. *Proceedings of the Human Factors Society—23rd Annual Meeting—1981*, Santa Monica, CA, pp. 736–740.

Koved, Lawrence, and Shneiderman, Ben, Embedded menus: Menu selection in context. *Communications of the ACM 29*, 1986, pp. 312–318.

Kruk, Richard S., and Muter, Paul, Reading of Continuous Text on Video Screens. *Human Factors, 26(3)*, 1984, pp. 339–345.

Kühne, Andreas; Krueger, Helmut; Graf, Werner; and Merz, Loretta, Positive Versus Negative Image Polarity. *Proceedings: International Scientific Conference: Work With Display Units*, Stockholm, Sweden, May 12–15, 1986, pp. 208–211.

Lalomia, Mary J., and Happ, Alan J., The Effective Use of Color for Text on the IBM 5153 Color Display. *Proceedings of the Human Factors Society—31st Annual Meeting—1987*, Santa Monica, CA, pp. 1091–1095.

Landauer, T.K., and Nachbar, D.W., Selection from Alphabetic and Numeric Menu Trees Using A Touch Screen: Breadth, Depth, and Width. *Proceedings CHI '85 Human Factors in Computing Systems*, pp. 73–78.

Ledgard, H.; Whiteside, J.A.; Singer, A.; and Seymour, W., The Natural Language of Interactive Systems. *Communications of the ACM 23*, No. 10, Oct. 1980, pp. 556–563.

Lee, Eric, and MacGregor, James, Minimizing User Search Time in Menu Retrieval Systems. *Human Factors, 27(2)* (1985), pp. 157–162.

Lichty, Tom, *Design Principles for Desktop Publishers*, Scott, Foresman and Company, Glenview, IL, 1989, 201 p.

Liebelt, L.S.; McDonald, J.E.; Stone, J.D.; and Karat, J., The Effect of Organization on Learning Menu Access. In *Proceedings of the Human Factors Society—26th Annual Meeting*, 1982, Santa Monica, CA, 1982, pp. 546–550.

Lodding, K., Iconic Interfacing. *IEEE Computer Graphics and Applications*, 3(2), March/April 1983, pp. 11–20.

Loftus, E. F.; Freedman, J.L.; and Loftus, G.R., Retrieval of Words from Subordinate and Supraordinate Categories in Semantic Hierarchies. *Psychonomic Science*, 1970, pp. 235–236.

Luria, S.M.; Neri, David F.; and Jacobsen, Alan R., The Effects of Set Size on Color

Matching Using CRT Displays. *Proceedings of the Human Factors Society—30th Annual Meeting—1986*, Santa Monica, CA, pp. 49–61.

Mack, Robert, and Lang, Kathy, A Benchmark Comparison of Mouse and Touch Interface Techniques for an Intelligent Workstation Windowing Environment. *CSTG Bulletin*, Vol. 16, Issue 2, 1989, pp. 22–23.

MacKenzie, J. Scott; Sellen, Abigail; and Buxton, William, A Comparison of Input Devices in Elemental Pointing and Dragging Tasks. In *Proceedings Human Factors in Computing Systems, CHI '91*, 1991, pp. 161–166.

Magers, Celeste S., An Experimental Evaluation on On-Line HELP for Non-Programmers. *Proceedings CHI '83 Human Factors in Computing Systems*, pp. 277–281.

Maguire, M.C., A Review of Human Factors Guidelines and Techniques for the Design of Graphical Human-Computer Interfaces. *Comput & Graphics*, Vol. 9, No. 3, 1985, pp. 221–235.

Mallory, K., et al., Human engineering guide to control room evaluation. Essex Corporation. Technical Report NUREG/CR-1580, Alexandria, VA, July 1980.

Mann, T.L., and Schnetzler, L.A., Evaluation of formats for aircraft control/display units. *Applied Ergonomics*, 17.4, 1986, pp. 265–270.

Marcus, Aaron, Icon design requires clarity, consistency. *Computer Graphics Today*, November 1984.

Marcus, Aaron, Proper color, type use improve instruction. *Computer Graphics Today*, 1986A.

Marcus, Aaron, Ten Commandments of Color. *Computer Graphics Today*, 1986B.

Marcus, Aaron, *Graphic Design for Electronic Documents and User Interfaces*, ACM Press, New York, NY, 263 p., 1992.

Martin, J. *Design of Man-Computer Dialogues*. Englewood Cliffs, NJ: Prentice-Hall, 1973.

Matthews, M.L., and Mertins, K., The influence of color on visual search and subjective discomfort using CRT displays. In *Proceedings of the Human Factors Society 31st Annual Meeting*, Santa Monica, CA: Human Factors Society, 1987, pp. 1271–1275.

Matthews, M.L., and Mertins, K., Working with color CRTs: Pink eye, yellow fever, and feeling blue. In *Proceedings of the Ergonomics Society's 1988 Annual Conference*, E.D. Megaw (ed.). London: Taylor & Francis, 1988, pp. 228–233.

Matthews, Michael L.; Lovasik, John V.; and Mertins, Karen, Visual Performance and Subjective Discomfort in Prolonged Viewing of Chromatic Displays. *Human Factors*, 31(3), 1989, pp. 259–271.

Mayer, Richard E., From Novice to Expert. *Handbook of Human-Computer Interaction*, M. Helander (ed.). Elsevier Science Publishers B.V. (North-Holland) 1988, pp. 569–580.

McDonald, J.E.; Stone, J.D.; and Liebelt, L.S., Searching for Items in Menus: The Effects of Organization and Type of Target. In *Proceedings of the Human Factors Society—27th Annual Meeting*, 1983, Santa Monica, CA, pp. 834–837.

McTyre, John H., and Frommer, W. David., Effects of Character/Background Color Combinations on CRT Character Legibility. *Proceedings of the Human Factors Society—29th Annual Meeting*, 1985, Santa Monica, CA, pp. 779–781.

Microswitch (A Honeywell Division), *Applying Manual Controls and Displays: A Practical Guide to Panel Design*, Freeport, IL, 1984.

Miller, D.P., The Depth/Breadth Tradeoff in Hierarchical Computer Menus. In *Proceedings of the Human Factors Society—25th Annual Meeting, 1981*, Santa Monica, CA, 1981.

Miller, G.A., The Magical Number Seven, Plus or Minus Two: Some Limits on our Capability for Processing Information. *Psychological Science 63*, 1956, pp. 81–97.

Miller, L.A., and Thomas, J.C., Behavioral Issues in the Use of Interactive Systems. *International Journal of Man-Machine Studies* 9, No. 5, Sept. 1977, pp. 509–536.

Miller, L.H., A Study in Man-Machine Interaction. *Proceedings of the National Computer Conference*, 46, AFIPS Press, Montvale, NJ, 1977, pp. 409–421.

Miller, R.B., *Human Ease-of-Use Criteria and Their Trade-offs*. TR00.2185. Poughkeepsie, NY: IBM Corp., 12 April 1971.

Mitchell, Jeffrey, and Shneiderman, Ben, Dynamic Versus Static Menus: An Exploratory Comparison. *SIGCHI Bulletin*, Vol. 20, No. 4, April 1989, pp. 33–37.

Mosier, J.N., and Smith, S.L., Application of guidelines for designing user interface software. *Behaviour and Information Technology* 5, 1 (January–March 1986) pp. 39–46.

Moskel, Sonya; Erno, Judy; and Shneiderman, Ben, Proofreading and Comprehension of Text on Screens and Paper. *University of Maryland Computer Science Technical Report*, June 1984.

Murch, G., The Effective Use of Color: Physiological Principles. Tektronix, Inc. 4 p., 1983.

Murch, G., The Effective Use of Color: Perceptual Principles. Tektronix, Inc. 6 p., 1984A.

Murch, G., The Effective Use of Color: Cognitive Principles. Tektronix, Inc., 7 p., 1984B.

Murch, G., Human visual accommodation and convergence to multichromatic information displays. In *Proceedings of NATO Workshop; Color Coded vs. Monochrome Electronic Displays*, C.P. Gibson (ed.). Farnborough, England: Royal Aircraft Establishment, pp. 16.1–16.10. 1984

Muter, Paul; Latremouille, S.A.; Treurniet, W.C.; and Beam, P., Extended Reading of Continuous Text on Television Screens. *Human Factors 24*, 1982, pp. 501–508.

Myers, B., The User Interface for Sapphire. *IEEE Computer Graphics and Applications*, 4(12), 1984, pp. 13–23.

Myers, B., The Importance of Percent-Done Progress Indicators for Computer-Human Interfaces. *Proceedings of CHI '85*, 1985, pp. 11–17.

Nelson, Ted, Interactive systems and the design of virtuality. *Creative Computing*, Vol. 6, No. 11 (November 1980), 56 ff., and Vol. 6, No. 12 (December 1980), 94 ff.

Nemeth, C., *User-Oriented Computer Input Devices*. Master's thesis. Chicago, IL: The Institute of Design, Illinois Institute of Technology, 1982.

Nickerson, R.S., Man-Computer Interaction: A Challenge for Human Factors Research. In *IEEE Transactions of Man-Machine Systems*, MSS-10, No. 4, Dec. 1969.

Nielsen, Jakob; Mack, Robert L.; Bergendorff, Keith H.; and Grischkowsky, Nancy L., Integrated Software Usage in the Professional Work Environment: Evidence from Questionnaires and Interviews. *Proceedings CHI '86 Human Factors in Computing Systems*, pp. 162–167.

Ogden, W.C., and Boyle, J.M., Evaluating Human-Computer Dialogue Styles: Command vs. Form/Fill-in for Report Modification. In *Proceedings of the Human Factors Society—26th Annual Meeting*, 1982, Santa Monica, CA, pp. 542–545.

Open Software Foundation, OSF/Motif Style Guide, Prentice Hall, Englewood Cliffs, New Jersey, 1991.

Ostberg, O., Accommodation and visual fatigue in display work. In *Ergonomics Aspects of Video Display Terminals*, E. Grandjean and E. Vigliana (eds.). London: Taylor & Francis, 1982, pp. 41–52.

Paap, Kenneth R., and Roske-Hofstrand, Renate J., The Optimal Number of Menu Options per Panel. *Human Factors, 28(4)*, 1986, pp. 377–385.

Paap, Kenneth R., and Roske-Hofstrand, Renate J., Design of Menus. In *Handbook of Human-Computer Interaction*, M. Helander (ed.). Elsevier Science Publishers B.V. (North-Holland), 1988, pp. 205–235.

Paradies, Mark, Root Cause Analysis and Human Factors. *Human Factors Bulletin*, 34(8), August 1991, pp. 1–4.

Parton, Diana; Huffman, Keith; Pridgen, Patty; Norman, Kent; and Shneiderman, Ben, Learning a Menu Selection Tree: Training Methods Compared. *Behaviour and Information Technology 4*, 2, 1985, pp. 81–91.

Parkinson, Stanley R.; Sisson, Norwood; and Snowberry, Kathleen, Organization of Broad Computer Menu Displays. *International Journal Man-Machine Studies, 23*, 1985, pp. 689–697.

Pastoor, Siegmund, Legibility and Subjective Preference for Color Combinations in Text. *Human Factors*, 32, (2), 1990, pp. 157–171.

Perlman, Gary, Making the Right Choices with Menus. *Human Computer Interaction—INTERACT '84/B.* Shackel (ed.). Elsevier Science Publishers B.V. (North Holland) IFIP, 1985, pp. 317–321.

Pinkus, A.R., The effects of color and contrast on target recognition performance using monochromatic television displays (Report AFAMRL-TR-82-9). Wright-Patterson AFB, OH: AFAMRL, 1982.

Pokorny, J.; Graham, C.H.; and Lanson, R.N., Effects of wavelength on foveal grating acuity. *Journal of the Optical Society of America*, 58, 1410, 1968.

Polya, G., *How to Solve It*. Doubleday, New York, 1957.

Post, D.I., Effects of color on CRT symbol legibility. *SID Digest*, 16, 1985, pp. 196–199.

Pulat, B.M., and Nwankwo, H.H., Formatting alphanumeric CRT displays. *INT. J. Man-Machine Studies*, 26, 1987, pp. 567–580.

Quinn, Lisa, and Russell, Daniel M., Intelligent Interfaces: User Models and Planners. *Proceedings, CHI '86 Human Factors in Computing Systems*, pp. 314–318.

Quintanar, Leo R.; Crowell, Charles R.; and Pryor, John B., Human-Computer Interaction: A Preliminary Social Psychological Analysis. *Behavior Research Methods & Instrumentation 14,2*, 1982, pp. 210–220.

Radl, G.W., Experimental investigations for optimal presentation mode and colors of symbols on the CRT screen. *Ergonomics Aspects of Video Display Terminals*, E. Grandjean and E. Vigliana (eds.). London: Taylor & Francis, 1980, pp. 127–135.

Radl, G.W., Optimal presentation mode and colors of symbols on VDU's. *Health Hazards of VDT's?*, B.G. Pearce (ed.). Chichester, England: Wiley, 1984, pp. 157–168.

Reed, A.V., Error-Correcting Strategies and Human Interaction with Computer Systems. In *Proceedings: Human Factors in Computer Systems*, Gaithersburg, MD., March 15–17, 1982, pp. 236–238.

Rehe, R.F., *Typography: How to Make It More Legible*. Carmel, IN.: Design Research International, 1974.

Remington, Roger, and Williams, Douglas, On the Selection and Evaluation of Visual Display Symbology: Factors Influencing Search and Identification Times. *Human Factors, 28(4)*, 1986, pp. 407–420.

Robert, Jean-Marc, Some Highlights of Learning by Exploration. *Proceedings: International Scientific Conference: Work With Display Units*, Stockholm, Sweden, May 12–15, 1986, pp. 348–353.

Roemer, J., and Chapanis, A., Learning Performance and Attitudes as a Function of the Reading Grade Level of a Computer-presented Tutorial. In *Proceedings: Human Factors in Computer Systems*, Gaithersburg, MD., March 15–17, 1982, pp. 239–244.

Romano, C., and Sonnino, A., Efficiency of Data Entry by VDUs—A Comparison Between Different Softwares. In *Ergonomics and Health in Modern Offices* (edited by Etienne Grandjean) Taylor & Francis, London and Philadelphia, 1984.

Rosenberg, J., Evaluating the Suggestiveness of Command Names. In *Proceedings: Human Factors in Computer Systems*, Gaithersburg, MD., March 15–17, 1982, pp. 12–16.

Savage, R.E., *A Survey of User Opinions of Various Input Field Designs*. Unpublished study, IBM. Rochester, MN., 1980.

Savage, R.E.; Habinek, J.K.; and Blackstad, N.J., An Experimental Evaluation of Input Field and Cursor Combinations. In *Proceedings of the Human Factors Society—26th Annual Meeting*, 1982, Santa Monica, CA, pp. 629–633.

Scapin, D.L., Computer Commands Labelled by Users versus Imposed Commands and Their Effect of Structuring Rules on Recall. In *Proceedings: Human Factors in Computer Systems*, Gaithersburg, MD., March 15–17, 1982, pp. 17–19.

Schleifer, Lawrence M., Effects of VDT/Computer System Response Delays and Incentive Pay on Mood Disturbances and Somatic Discomfort. *Proceedings: International Scientific Conference: Work With Display Units*, Stockholm, Sweden, May 12–15, 1986, pp. 447–451.

Schoonard, J.W., and Boies, S.J., Short-Type: A Behavioral Analysis of Typing and Text Entry. *Human Factors* 17, No. 2, 1975, pp. 203–214.

Schwarz, Elmar; Beldie, Ian P.; and Pastoor, Siegmund, A Comparison of Paging and Scrolling for Changing Screen Contents by Inexperienced Users. *Human Factors, 25(3)*, 1983, pp. 279–282.

Seppala, Pentti, and Salvendy, Gavriel, Impact of Depth of Menu Hierarchy on Performance Effectiveness in a Supervisory Task: Computerized Flexible Manufacturing System. *Human Factors, 27(6)*, 1985, pp. 713–722.

Shackel, B., The concept of usability. *Proceedings of IBM Software and Information Usability Symposium*, Poughkeepsie, NY, 15–18 September, 1981, pp. 1–30; and in J.L. Bennett, D. Case, J. Sandelin, and M. Smith (eds.). *Visual Display Terminals: Usability Issues and Health Concerns*. Englewood Cliffs, NJ: Prentice-Hall, 1984, pp. 45–88.

Shackel, Brian, Usability—Context, Framework, Definition, Design and Evaluation. *Human Factors for Informatics Usability*, B. Shackel and S.J. Richardson (eds.). Cambridge University Press, 1991, pp. 21–37.

Shinar, David, and Stern, Helman I., Alternative Option Selection Methods in Menu-Driven Computer Programs. *Human Factors, 29(4)*, 1987, pp. 453–459.

Shinar, David; Stern, Helman I.; Bubis, Gad; and Ingram, David, The Relative Effectiveness of Alternative Selection Strategies in Menu Driven Computer Programs. *Proceedings of the Human Factors Society—29th Annual Meeting*, 1985, Santa Monica, CA, pp. 645–647.

Shneiderman, B., *Software Psychology*. Cambridge, MA.: Winthrop Publishers, 1980.

Shneiderman, B., The Future of Interactive Systems and the Emergence of Direct Manipulation. *Behaviour and Information Technology, I*, 1982, pp. 237–256.

Shneiderman, B., Human-computer interaction research at the University of Maryland. *SIGCHI Bulletin*, 17, 1986, pp. 27–32.

Shneiderman, B., and Margono, S., A study of File Manipulation by Novices Using Commands vs. Direct Manipulation. *Proceedings of 26th Annual Technical Symposium of the Washington, DC. Chapter of the ACM*. Gaithersburg, MD: National Bureau of Standards, 1987.

Shneiderman, Ben, Control Flow and Data Structure Documentation: Two Experiments. *Communications of the ACM*, Vol. 25, No. 1, Jan. 1982A, pp. 55–63.

Shneiderman, Ben, System Message Design: Guidelines and Experimental Results, in Badre, A. and Shneiderman, B. (Editors). *Directions in Human / Computer Interaction*, Ablex Publishers, Norwood, NJ, 1982B, pp. 55–78.

Shneiderman, Ben, *Designing the User Interface: Strategies for Effective Human-Computer Interaction*. Addison-Wesley Publishing Co., Reading, MA, 1987, pp. 448.

Shneiderman, Ben; Mayer, R.; McKay, D.; and Heller, P., Experimental Investigations of the Utility of Detailed Flowcharts in Programming. *Communications of the ACM*, Vol. 20, 1977, pp. 373–381.

Sidorsky, R.C., Color Coding in Tactical Displays: Help or Hindrance. *Army Research Institute Research Report*, 1982.

Sivak, J.G., and Woo, G.C., Color of visual display terminals and the eye: Green VDT's provoke the optimal stimulus to accommodation. *American Journal of Optometry and Physiological Optics*, 60, 1983, pp. 640–642.

Sless, David, Name and Address Please . . . A Guide for Form Designers. Prepared for Information Co-ordination Branch, Department of Sport Recreation and Tourism, Canberra, Australia, Feb. 1987, 28 p.

Smith, D., Faster Is Better—A Business Case for Subsecond Response Time. *Computerworld*, 1983.

Smith, Sidney L., and Mosier, Jane N., Guidelines for Designing User Interface Software. Prepared for Deputy Commander for Development Plans and Support Systems, Electronic Systems Division, AFSC, USAF, Hanscom AFB, MA. Mitre ESD-TR-86-278 MTR 10090, Aug. 1986.

Smith, Wanda, Computer Color: Psychophysics, Task Application, and Aesthetics. *Proceedings: International Scientific Conference: Work With Display Units*, Stockholm, Sweden, May 12–15, 1986, pp. 561–564.

Smith, Wanda, Standardizing Colors for Computer Screens. *Proceedings of the Human Factors Society—32nd Annual Meeting—1988*. pp. 1381–1385.

Snowberry, K.; Parkinson, S.R.; and Sisson, N., Computer Display Menus. *Ergonomics*, 26, 1983, pp. 699–712.

Spiliotopoulos, V., and Shackel, B., Towards a Computer Interview Acceptable to the Naive User. *International Journal of Man-Machine Studies 14*, 1981, pp. 77–90.

Springer, Carla J., and Sorce, James F., Accessing Large Data Bases: The Relationship Between Data Entry Time and Output Evaluation Time. *Human Computer Interaction—INTERACT '84*, pp. 263–267.

Stern, Kenneth R., An Evaluation of Written, Graphics, and Voice Messages in Proceduralized Instructions. *Proceedings of the Human Factors Society—28th Annual Meeting*, 1984, pp. 314–318, Santa Monica, CA.

Stewart, T.F.M., Displays and the Software Interface. *Applied Ergonomics*, Sept. 1976.

Streveler, D.J., and Wasserman, A.I. Quantitative measures of the spatial properties of screen designs. In *Proceedings of Interact '84 Conference on Human-Computer Interaction*, England, Sept. 1984.

Sun Microsystems, Inc., *Open Look*™ *Graphical User Interface Application Style Guidelines*, Addison-Wesley, Reading, MA, 1990.

Taylor, I.A., Perception and Design. *Research Principles and Practices in Visual Communication*, J. Ball and F.C. Pyres, Eds. Association for Educational Communication and Technology, 1960, pp. 51–70.

Tedford, W.H.; Berquist, S.L.; and Flynn, W.E., The Size-Color Illusion. *Journal of General Psychology 97*, No. 1, July 1977, pp. 145–149.

Teitelbaum, Richard C., and Granda, Richard, The Effects of Positional Constancy on Searching Menus for Information. *Proceedings CHI '83 Human Factors in Computer Systems.* pp. 150–153.

Tetzlaff, Linda, and Schwartz, David R., The Use of Guidelines in Interface Design. In *Conference Proceedings: Human Factors in Computing Systems*, CHI '91, 1991, pp. 329–334.

Thacker, Pratapray (Paul), Tabular Displays: A Human Factors Study. *CSTG Bulletin,* 14, (1) Human Factors Society, 1987, p. 13.

Thovtrup, Henrik, and Nielsen, Jakob, Assessing the Usability of a User Interface Standard. In *Conference Proceedings: Human Factors in Computing Systems*, CHI '91, 1991, pp. 335–342.

Tinker, M.A., Prolonged Reading Tasks in Visual Research. *Journal of Applied Psychology* 39, 1955, pp. 444–446.

Tombaugh, J.W.; Paynter, B.; Dillon, R.F., Command and Graphic Interfaces: User Performance and Satisfaction. *Designing and Using Human-Computer Interfaces and Knowledge Based Systems* (G. Salvendy and M.J. Smith (eds.). Elsevier Science Publishers B.V., Amsterdam, 1989, pp. 369–375.

Treisman, A., Perceptual Grouping and Attention in Visual Search for Features and for Objects. *Journal of Experimental Psychology: Human Perception and Performance, 8*, 1982, pp. 194–214.

Treu, S., ed., User-Oriented Design of Interactive Graphics Systems. In *Proceedings of the ACM.* SIGGRAPH Workshop, October 14–15, 1976, Pittsburgh, PA. New York: ACM, 1977.

Trollip, Stanley, and Sales, Gregory, Readability of Computer-Generated Fill-Justified Text. *Human Factors 28(2),* 1986, pp. 159–163.

Tufte, Edward R., *The Visual Display of Quantitative Information.* Graphics Press, Cheshire, CT, 1983, 197 pp.

Tullis, T.S., An Evaluation of Alphanumeric, Graphic and Color Information Displays. *Human Factors 23,* 1981, pp. 541–550.

Tullis, Thomas S., Designing a Menu-based Interface to an Operating System. *Proceedings CHI '85 Human Factors in Computing Systems,* pp. 79–84.

Tullis, Thomas S., Screen Design. *Handbook of Human-Computer Interaction*, M. Helander (ed.). Elsevier Science Publishers B.V. (North-Holland), 1988, pp. 377–412.

Tullis, Thomas Stuart, Predicting the Usability of Alphanumeric Displays. Ph.D. dissertation, Rice University, 1983, 172 p.

Turner, Jon A., Computer Mediated Work: The Interplay Between Technology and Structured Jobs. *Communications of the AACM 27,* 12, Dec. 1984, pp. 1210–1217.

Vartabedian, A.G., The Effects of Letter Size, Case and Generation Method on CRT Display Search Time. *Human Factors 13,* No. 4, 1971, pp. 363–368.

Vitz, P.C., Preference for Different Amounts of Visual Complexity. *Behavioral Science 2,* 1966, pp. 105–114.

Walker, Jeff, and Smelcer, John B., A Comparison of Selection Times from Walking and Pull-Down Menus. In *Conference Proceedings: Human Factors in Computing Systems*, CHI '91, 1991, pp. 221–225.

Walker, Marilyn A., Natural Language in a Desktop Environment. In *Designing and Using Human-Computer Interfaces and Knowledge Based Systems*, G. Salvendy and M.J. Smith (eds.). Elsevier Science Publishers B.V., Amsterdam, 1989, pp. 502–509.

Walker, R.E.; Nicolay, R.C.; and Stearns, C.R., Comparative Accuracy of Recognizing

American and International Road Signs. *Journal of Applied Psychology 49*, 1965, pp. 322–325.

Wallace, Daniel, Time Stress Effects on Two Menu Selection Systems. *Proceedings of the Human Factors Society—31st Annual Meeting*, 1987.

Walraven, J., Perceptual artifacts that may interfere with color coding on visual displays. *Proceedings of NATO Workshop: Color Coded vs. Monochrome Electronic Displays*, C.P. Gibson (ed.). Farnborough, England: Royal Aircraft Establishment, 1984, pp. 13.1–13.11.

Wason, P.C., and Johnson-Laird, P.N., *Psychology of Reasoning: Structure and Content*. London: Batsford, 1972.

Watanabe, A.; Mori, T.; Nagata, S.; and Hiwatashi, K., Spatial sine wave response of the human visual system. *Vision Research*, 8, 1968, pp. 1245–1263.

Watley, Charles, and Mulford, Jay, A Comparison of Commands' Documentation: Online vs. Hardcopy. Unpublished student project, University of Maryland, Dec. 8, 1983, In Shneiderman, 1987.

Watson, R.W., User Interface Design Issues for a Large Interactive System. In *AFIPS Conference Proceedings* 45, 1976, pp. 357–364.

Weinberg, G.M., *The Psychology of Computer Programming*. New York: Van Nostrand Reinhold, 1971.

Weiss, Stuart Martin; Boggs, George; Lehto, Mark; Shodja, Sogand; and Martin, David J., Computer System Response Time and Psychophysiological Stress II. *Proceedings of the Human Factors Society—26th Annual Meeting—1982*, pp. 698–702.

Wertheimer, M., *Productive Thinking*, Harper and Row, New York, 1959.

Whiteside, John; Jones, Sandra; Levy, Paula S.; and Wixon, Dennis, User Performance with Command, Menu, and Iconic Interfaces. *Proceedings CHI '85 Human Factors in Computing Systems*, April 1985, pp. 185–191.

Wichansky, Anna M., Legibility and User Acceptance of Monochrome Display Phospher Colors. *Proceedings: International Scientific Conference: Work With Display Units*, Stockholm, Sweden, May 12–15, 1986, pp. 216–219.

Williams, James R., The Effects of Case and Spacing on Menu Option Search Time. In *Proceedings of the Human Factors Society-32nd Annual Meeting—1988*, pp. 341–343.

Wingfield, A., Effects of Frequency on Identification and Naming of Objects. *American Journal of Psychology, 81*, 1968, pp. 226–234.

Wolf, C.E., BNA "HN" command display: Results of user evaluation. Unpublished technical report available from Cynthia Wolf Connally, Unisys Corporation, 19 Morgan, Irvine, CA 92718.

Wright, P., Problems to be solved when creating usable documents. Paper presented at IBM symposium on Software and Information Usability. Available as HF077 from IBM Hursley, Winchester, UK. 1981.

Wright, P., Issues of content and presentation in document design. *Handbook of Human-Computer Interaction*, M. Helander (ed.). Elsevier Science Publishers B.V. (North-Holland), 1988, pp. 629–652.

Wright, P., and Barnard, P., Just Fill in This Form: A Review for Designers. *Applied Ergonomics* 6, 1975, pp. 213–220.

Wright, P., and Lickorish, A., Proof-Reading Texts on Screen and Paper. *Behaviour and Information Technology 2, 3*, 1983, pp. 227–235.

Wright, Patricia, User Documentation. *Proceedings: World Conference on Ergonomics in Computer Systems*, 1984, pp. 110–126, Los Angeles, CA; Chicago, IL; New York, NY; Amsterdam, The Netherlands; Dusseldorf, West Germany; Helsinki, Finland, Sept. 24–Oct. 4, 1984.

Wright, Patricia, Designing and Evaluating Documentation for I.T. Users. *Human Factors for Informatics Usability*, B. Shackel and S.J. Richardson (eds.). Cambridge University Press, 1991, pp. 343–358.

Zahn, C.T., Graph-Theoretical Methods for Detecting and Describing Gestalt Clusters. *IEEE Transactions on Computers, X-20*, 1971, pp. 68–86.

Zwaga, H.J., and Boersema, T., Evaluation of a Set of Graphics Symbols. *Applied Ergonomics, 14*, 1983, pp. 43–54.

Zwahlen, Helmut T., and Kothari, Nimesh, The Effects of Dark and Light Character CRT Displays Upon VDT Operator Performance, Eye Scanning Behavior, Pupil Diameter and Subjective Comfort/Discomfort. *Proceedings: International Scientific Conference: Work With Display Units*, Stockholm, Sweden, May 12–15, 1986, pp. 220–222.

Index